Informed
Individual
Independent

FORTIS

## Investment Management for Generations

With our high quality team of professionals, Fortis Private Investment Management is recognised as a pre-eminent investment services provider in the UK market. Based in London, we provide UK and International clients with investment strategies focused on delivering consistent performance. With the backing of one of the largest financial services organisations in Europe we offer a compelling combination of tradition and progression for the future.

Our forte is always to adapt our investment management services to the requirements of our clients – our approach is as individual as each client. However, our investment strategies are devised to react dynamically to market changes and are based on a clearly structured and disciplined framework.

Please contact us:

**Fortis Private Investment Management**

Telephone +44 (0)20 7369 4800, Fax +44 (0)20 7369 4888

Email fpiminformationuk@fortis.com

**www.fpim.fortis.com**

The value of investments and the income from them varies and you may realise less than the sum invested. Fortis Private Investment Management Ltd is authorised and regulated by the Financial Services Authority. Registered office: 63 St Mary's Axe London EC3A 8LT. Registered in England under company no. 2123174.

**Private Investment Management**

THE HANDBOOK OF

# PERSONAL

# Wealth

## MANAGEMENT

# THE HANDBOOK OF
# PERSONAL
# Wealth
# MANAGEMENT

## How to Ensure Maximum Returns with Security

THIRD EDITION

CONSULTANT EDITOR:
JONATHAN REUVID

INSINGER *de*BEAUFORT

RECOMMENDED BY
INSTITUTE OF DIRECTORS

**KOGAN
PAGE**
London and Philadelphia

This book has been endorsed by the Institute of Directors.

The endorsement is given to selected Kogan Page books which the IoD recognises as being of specific interest to its members and providing them with up-to-date, informative and practical resources for creating business success. Kogan Page books endorsed by the IoD represent the most authoritative guidance available on a wide range of subjects including management, finance, marketing, training and HR.

The views expressed in this book are those of the author and are not necessarily the same as those of the Institute of Directors.

**Publisher's note**
Every possible effort has been made to ensure that the information contained in this book is accurate at the time of going to press, and the publishers and authors cannot accept responsibility for any errors or omissions, however caused. No responsibility for loss or damage occasioned to any person acting, or refraining from action, as a result of the material in this publication can be accepted by the editor, the publisher or any of the authors.

First published in Great Britain and the United States in 2005 by Kogan Page Limited
Second edition 2006
Third edition 2007

120 Pentonville Road
London N1 9JN
United Kingdom
www.kogan-page.co.uk

525 South 4th Street, #241
Philadelphia PA 19147
USA

© Jonathan Reuvid and individual contributors, 2005, 2006, 2007

The right of Jonathan Reuvid and the individual contributors to be identified as the authors of this work has been asserted by them in accordance with the Copyright, Designs and Patents Act 1988.

ISBN-10   0 7494 4952 7
ISBN-13   978 0 7494 4952 0

**British Library Cataloguing-in-Publication Data**

A CIP record for this book is available from the British Library.

**Library of Congress Cataloging-in-Publication Data**

The handbook of personal wealth management : how to ensure maximum returns with security / [edited by] Jonathan Reuvid. – 3rd ed.
       p. cm.
   ISBN-13: 978-0-7494-4952-0
   ISBN-10: 0-7494-4952-7
   1. Finance, Personal. 2. Rich people–Finance, Personal. 3. Investments. I. Reuvid, Jonathan.
   HG179.H2549 2007
   332.024′01–dc22
                                                  2007008565

Typeset by Saxon Graphic Ltd, Derby
Printed and bound in Great Britain by Cambridge University Press

# Contents

## Part 3: Pensions planning and products

## Part 4: Real estate and forestry investments

# We're not afraid to zig when everyone else zags.

RH Asset Management Limited is a privately-owned, wholly independent asset management firm offering comprehensive financial planning and investment management services.

We have absolutely no links to any provider or fund manager. The vast majority of our revenue is fee-based, which means we offer our clients genuinely independent advice.

We invest across all major asset classes, and our independent approach can be seen in our attitude to investment. We are not afraid to offer advice based on our own independent, rigorous economic analysis even if it suggests a route that runs contrary to received wisdom.

Our independent approach and personal service have been successful enough to gain us a faithful following: over 90% of our clients are introduced to us by other clients.

For more information about our financial, tax planning, and investment management service call Tony Marsh on 01689 877725 or visit www.rhasset.co.uk

# Foreword

## A wealth of advice

In introducing the previous edition of this excellent book I commented on how, in today's consumer society, people can spend hours and days looking for 'best buys' for household items, whilst often spending very little time on personal financial planning – and squandering hundreds or thousands of pounds as a result.

The same remains true in 2007. The key point here is that, whatever your lifestyle – and this book is firmly aimed at those with significant income and assets – in order to enjoy spending money while also benefiting from the security that accrues from saving and investing appropriately, it is essential to have some forethought. A careless approach will certainly result in expensive mistakes and, as many a lottery winner can testify, can easily end in financial ruin.

Business people, who should know something about financial matters, are not exempt from criticism here. Indeed, there are business men and women who spend a large part of their professional lives eyeing their companies' profit and loss figures and balance sheets who nevertheless pay woefully inadequate attention to the management of their own finances. Many of them are individuals of 'high net worth' and have more to lose than most.

The aim of *The Handbook of Personal Wealth Management* is to provide wealthy people – whether in business or not – with clear, practical advice on how best to manage their personal financial affairs. It covers a diverse range of subjects: from the first principles of investment to changes in taxation legislation and insurance; from explanations of a wide array of investment products to help on where to seek further information and professional advice. To preserve your own financial health – and your peace of mind – I strongly advise you to give careful consideration to the chapters that follow.

*Miles Templeman, Director General, Institute of Directors*

# Contributors' notes

**Ian Abrey** is Head of Private Clients at business advisers and accountants Mazars and leads the personal tax and trust team in London. He has worked in the field of tax planning for 20 years and is a member of the firm's international high net worth individuals' group.

**Anthony Collinson** is Chairman of Katalyst Ventures Ltd, which is authorized and regulated by the Financial Services Authority. Katalyst is a member of the British Venture Capital Association.

**Carole Cook** is a partner at Mayfair-based solicitors Forsters LLP. Forsters is widely recognized as a leading law firm specializing in tax and trusts. Carole's expertise includes tax and estate planning for both UK and international clients, in particular entrepreneurs, offshore and onshore trust advice and creation, will drafting and advice to charity trustees. She is a member of the Technical Committee of the Society of Trust and Estate Practitioners (STEP).

**Jeff Cornish** is Sales Director of Beringea Ltd. Jeff is responsible for marketing the ProVen range of venture capital trusts (VCTs) to professional intermediaries such as independent financial advisers, fund managers, accountants and solicitors. He has worked in the financial services industry for the last 15 years with some of the UK's major financial institutions. Established for over 20 years, Beringea is a specialized venture capital fund manager that has managed VCTs for over 10 years. It runs the ProVen range of VCTs and also manages venture capital funds on behalf of institutional investors. Total capital funds under management are approximately £105 million.

**Cathy Dixon** joined Cunningham Coates in 1990 and manages a range of institutional and charity clients as well as private clients. Her previous City experience was wide-ranging, and she gained experience as an investment analyst, a derivative products manager and a venture capital executive. She has a degree in economics and is a fellow of the Securities Institute and member of the Chartered Institute of Financial Analysts.

**EFG Private Bank Ltd** is a part of one of Switzerland's largest banks by capitalization, with assets under management of 101 billion Swiss francs as at 31 December 2005. Through EFG, Pathfinder Private Pension holders can gain access to loans to fund larger investments such as property (subject to status), and to a wide range of investment opportunities.

**Spencer Ewen** is a partner in Seymour Management, which provides expert advice for almost every object classification or category in the international art world. Seymour Management was established as a response to the changing art market for those entering it for the first time as well as those who have made art a life-long passion.

**Anna Farrugia** is a sales consultant in Harlon Overseas Property, a division of Harlon Management Services Limited, and a member of the National Association of Estate Agents. Harlon Overseas Property adopts a policy of ongoing research in order to provide clients with a wider choice of property investment. It is now backed by international architects and legal firms, both at home and abroad.

**Simon Gibson** is a director of Atkinson Bolton Consulting Ltd. He has been an independent financial adviser since 1990 and has had experience of the financial services profession since 1984. He specializes in dealing with bespoke client portfolios and especially individual wealth management issues, including SIPPs and investment portfolios, under the brand of Thoroghbred Wealth Management™. Atkinson Bolton Consulting Ltd was established in 2001 with clear objectives of providing the best levels of customer service in the financial services profession and the Directors continue to strive to that end, whilst delivering to clients on their vision of creating and preserving wealth.

**James Goodwin** writes, lectures and consults on art and business. He has written for the *Financial Times*, *The Economist* and several art, antique and finance journals. He is a visiting lecturer at City University, London and Maastricht University, The Netherlands. He is currently writing a guide to the international art market.

**Alan Guy** manages property acquisition services and marketing for the forestry division of fountains plc, an environmental services company operating in the UK and the United States. He worked as a commercial manager and consultant in the project engineering sector for 20 years before moving across to forestry. He is qualified in business, forestry and environmental management.

**Christine Hallett** has been in the financial services industry for over 25 years, spending 18 years at Abbey National. She joined Pointon York SIPP Solutions Limited in 1996 as Operations Director, and became Managing Director in 1998. Christine has been instrumental in developing the business into one of the leading SIPP service companies in the UK, growing the company more than 100 per cent in the last three years. She is passionate about customer service and has structured the business to deliver the best service.

**Peter Hearn** is Director of Business Development at Ashcourt Group. Having spent the first 25 years of his career with institutions focusing upon investment management and product sales, Peter moved into the private and professional adviser area, working initially with a large investment trust company and then stockbroking, before moving to Ashcourt some eight years ago. He is a chartered insurance practitioner. Through its two principal companies, Ashcourt Asset Management and Ashcourt Financial Planning, the Ashcourt Group provides independent investment management services to private and corporate clients, trusts, pension funds and charities, with financial planning advice provided through a coordinated approach designed to develop bespoke relationships and personal service in a professional manner.

**Stephen Hershoff** is Managing Director of Pastor-Genève BVBA. He has over 40 years' of experience in the diamond industry. Beginning in London in the 1960s, he was a dealer in diamonds and other coloured gems. Throughout the late 1960s and 1970s, he concentrated on advising a private client base of international collectors and connoisseurs through his own consulting company. In the early 1980s, he moved to North America to assume responsibility for a company that became one of the four most important gem dealers recommended by the *Dow Jones-Irwin Guide to Fine Gems and Jewelry*. His company, Pastor-Genève, is recognized as one of the most established dealers in the coloured diamond market.

**Allan Holmes** is a partner in the private client practice of Dickinson Dees. The firm currently employs 861 people across three North-East of England bases and is a significant member of the national business community. It was shortlisted for Regional Law Firm of the Year at the Legal Business Awards 2005, and the firm is accredited as a *Sunday Times* best company to work for in the UK.

**Ian Hunter** is Head of Marketing, Business Development and Client Services with Sun Kissed Homes Limited, a national UK-based overseas property and services specialist. Ian is a FOPDAC committee member and writes for a number of publications. He has a broad commercial and marketing background with over 25 years' experience in international marketing, business development, licensing and franchising within the overseas property, travel and leisure sectors, having worked with clients and partners across the world developing and implementing 'go to market' and 'brand development' programmes.

**Trevor James** is the Director of Tax Investigations for Mazars. He joined the firm in September 2005 after 26 years' service with the Inland Revenue (latterly HM Revenue and Customs) where he gained invaluable experience of investigating cases of serious fraud and tackling avoidance for its Special Compliance Office, Special Civil Investigations Office.

**Felix Karthaus** is a forestry graduate of Aberdeen University, born in Holland, with over 30 years of UK forestry experience. His Baltic company was formed in 1997, now manages over 700 woodlands and employs a staff of 10. Felix is a fellow of the Institute of Chartered Foresters. Border Consultants (Forestry) Ltd is a husband-and-wife partnership by Felix and Jane Karthaus, started in 1988. Based in Northumberland, it manages some 12,000 hectares of UK woodlands. Jane Karthaus provides a communication service to the Forestry and Timber Association and edits their magazine.

**Nicholas Lambert** is a divisional director in the private clients team of Sarasin Chiswell where he has responsibility for managing private and charity portfolios. Nicholas was previously a partner at Cazenove where he gained 18 years' experience and was primarily responsible for managing portfolios for private clients and charities. He also had senior management roles for both the UK and the international private client businesses.

**Ian Lane** is a partner and head of KSB Law's tax, trust and probate team. He has over 35 years' experience in all aspects of onshore and offshore tax planning, wills, probate, trust formation and administration and charities.

**Clare McCulloch** is a solicitor at Mayfair-based firm Forsters LLP. Forsters is widely recognized as a leading law firm specializing in tax and trusts. Clare's expertise includes estate planning and tax and offshore trust advice (enhanced by a period working offshore) and relates to the often complex tax issues arising from significant offshore structures for families with a mix of UK-domiciled and non-UK-domiciled beneficiaries.

**Alan McIntosh** is Chief Investment Officer at Cheviot Asset Management. He started as a fund manager at Scottish Life in 1982 and was UK Market Strategist at Credit Suisse Asset Management before joining Laing & Cruickshank in 1999. Following the acquisition of Laing & Cruickshank by UBS he was appointed Executive Director. Cheviot Asset Management is a partnership that has been formed recently with the aim of becoming Britain's leading independent investment manager for private clients. The group is led by former Chief Executive of Laing & Cruickshank, Michael Kerr-Dineen, and former Chairman of the Royal Bank of Scotland, Sir George Matthewson.

**Stan Miranda** is the founder and Chief Executive of Partners Capital Investment Group, an international investment adviser to sophisticated investors. Operating out of London and Boston, Partners Capital was founded by investment professionals who felt that the traditional investment advisory world failed to embrace best practice as a result of built-in conflicts in their businesses. Partners Capital clients are often long-term private asset managers themselves. This demanding client base forces Partners Capital to stay on top of best practice in the industry, but also enables it to gain access to many of the best-of-breed asset managers across all asset classes including fixed income, equities, private equity, hedge funds and real assets.

**John Moret** is Director of Sales and Marketing at Suffolk Life and has worked in the pensions industry for over 35 years. He is a well-known conference speaker and contributes regularly to many magazines and trade papers. He is a passionate believer in the merits of SIPPs, having been involved with their development and growth since their conception in 1989. Based in Ipswich, Suffolk Life is one of the leading providers and administrators of SIPPs and is unusual in being focused entirely on SIPP administration. By March 2007, it had established well over 8,000 SIPPs, with assets in excess of £2 billion including over 1,000 commercial properties.

**Jan Morgan** is Founding Managing Director at Grosvenor International.

**Neil Morris** is a partner in the private client practice of Dawsons Solicitors, which provides expert advice in relation to personal and family affairs. This can involve tax planning advice in respect of the sale of shares, advice on inheritance and wills, and the establishment and administration of a complex estate involving assets in a number of jurisdictions.

**Tony Munson** is an investment director at Fortis Private Investment Management (FPIM). He is responsible for one of FPIM's investment teams and chairs the firm's investment policy group in the UK. He has 20 years' experience in managing international investment portfolios. His career within the forerunner of FPIM began in 1999, with the acquisition of Matheson Investment Management. Prior to that, Tony was a founding member of Binder Hamlyn Investment Management. He is a Fellow of the Securities Institute.

**Amanda Nelson** is a partner in the private client practice of Dawsons Solicitors.

**Chris Powell** had nearly 20 years' investment experience before studying full time for an MBA at Henley Management College. Before joining Arc Fund Management in 2006, he spent several years assisting small businesses to grow and providing consulting services to a variety of organizations in the area of innovation. Arc Fund Management Ltd is an AIM-listed financial services company specializing in sourcing and investing in pre-IPO businesses. Arc manages several funds that concentrate on small enterprises, including five EIS funds and a VCT whose competitive performance speaks volumes for the company's expertise in this highly specialized field.

**Katharine Pulvermacher** is the Managing Director, Investment Research and Marketing at the World Gold Council. She has built up a solid base of research on gold as an investment, catering for the needs of private banking professionals as well as institutional investors and their advisers. In addition to analysis on gold market fundamentals with respect to their impact for investors, Katharine's core research area is the strategic role of gold in investment portfolios.

**Jonathan Reuvid** is Senior Consultant Editor to the business and reference division of Kogan Page and Senior Editor of its GMB Publishing offshoot for its series of international business development titles. Before taking up a second career in publishing, Jonathan held senior management positions in a Fortune 500 multinational and was previously an oil industry economist, investment banker and financial consultant to SMEs.

**Harriet Rochester** was previously Ownership and Bloodstock Marketing Executive at the British Horseracing Board. She now runs her own company, Harriet Rochester Sports Marketing (HRSM). Prior to that, Harriet worked in Australia for William Inglis and Son Ltd, thoroughbred auctioneers, further developing her knowledge of the bloodstock and racing industry on an international level. The British Horseracing Board (BHB) is the governing authority for British racing. Its activities extend from race planning, including the supervision of race programmes and the employment of handicappers, to the collection of the funds required for the administration of racing. The BHB also encourages and promotes racing and fosters the breeding of bloodstock, represents racing in dealing with the government, liaises with the betting industry and represents British racing abroad.

**Nicholas Rundle** is a senior investment manager at Taylor Young Investment Management. He graduated from Oxford University in 1980 and holds an MA in politics, philosophy and economics. He also holds an MSc in business administration from the London Business School, where he was a Sloan Fellow in 1998/99.

**Nick Stephens** developed his appreciation of French wine more than 30 years ago when studying hotel management. Subsequently, he qualified as a chef and an accountant. His philosophy is that wines are like people. You do not build a rapport with everyone you meet, but those you meet and like become friends!

**H John Stollery** is Chairman of DiaMine Explorations, Inc. He began his career in the early 1960s as an engineer after completing a BSc in civil engineering from the University of Alberta in 1961. In 1965 he received a Master's degree in business administration from the University of Western Ontario. From the late 1960s until the early 1980s, Mr Stollery worked as a vice-president and director at Xerox Corporation, specializing in marketing and systems development. After leaving Xerox, he ran two successful transport companies as their CEO, TNT Canada and TST Solutions Inc. Both companies grew significantly and recorded multimillion-dollar sales increases under his tenure. His experience in management and strategic development is an integral component of the direction and guidance of DiaMine Explorations, Inc.

**Stuart Tyler** has been working within fund management at Lincoln Financial Group since 1997 and now manages fixed interest investments worth £725 million. He graduated in 1995 with a BSc in psychology, and is an associate member of the United Kingdom Society of Investment Professionals and a member of the CFA Institute.

**Stefan Velvick** has worked at the Charities Aid Foundation (CAF) for 16 years. He has held the post of Trust Client Manager for four years, administering trusts for high net worth donors. Stefan previously held the position of Investment Officer and has worked in the finance sector at CAF. CAF is a not-for-profit organization that is committed to effective giving, providing a range of specialist services to donors, companies and charities in the UK and internationally. Its aim is to increase both the level and the impact of giving, and it strives to achieve this through all its activities, including working as an advocate for the charitable sector.

**Avril Whitfield** has been a tax partner at Mazars since September 2005, following a period of four years at KPMG as a senior manager, where she headed up the eastern counties property team and was a member of the national property team. Prior to this, Avril held a senior position in Her Majesty's Revenue and Customs where she worked for almost 20 years.

**Paul Willans** is Chief Executive of Mazars Financial Planning Ltd, the fee-based independent financial planning and investment arm of Mazars LLP. Paul has been an independent financial adviser since 1988 and specializes in personal financial planning and investment management. He has spent the majority of his career within professional practices and is a regular commentator in the financial press.

# Foreign Exchange Uncovered

If you are looking at making investments overseas, whether it is in property, antiques, fine wine or even race horses, it is vital that you do not forget about foreign exchange. Unfortunately exposure to exchange rate volatility is an unavoidable aspect of any type of overseas investment and failure to take this into account can have a detrimental affect on your investment.

For example, if you look at the US dollar during 2006 you can see how this movement can affect the cost of your investment. Sterling against the dollar was as high as 1.9846 and as low as 1.7164. So if you had £200,000 to transfer you could have received as much as $396,920 or as little as $343,280 - a difference of over $53,000.

The same affect can be seen if you look at the euro during 2006. Sterling against the euro was as high as 1.4992 and as low as 1.4243. So if you had needed to transfer £100,000 you could have received as much as €149,920 or as little as €142,430 – a difference of over €7,000.

Many people automatically turn to their bank for this foreign exchange not realising that alternatives are available. However, poor exchange rates, high transfer fees and commission charges all eat away at your money and mean that using your bank could cost you dearly. However, by using a foreign exchange specialist such as Currencies Direct you can benefit from tailor-made international payment solutions that help you to manage your foreign exchange exposure and risk.

By using a specialist rather than your bank you can benefit from a proactive service as well as the provision of your own dedicated currency specialist who will monitor the markets on your behalf – advising you of economic factors and currency movements that may impact on the cost of your investment.

In addition foreign exchange specialists are able to offer you extremely competitive exchange rates, no commission charges and free transfers. This can mean considerable savings on your transfer when compared to using a bank.

### Contract Options

A number of buying options are available to you depending on your timing, circumstances and foreign currency needs and your dedicated currency specialist will be able to talk you through the options and help you to decide which is best for you. Buying options include spot deals, forward contracts and limit orders, many of which are not usually available to private individuals through a bank.

**Spot Deal** – If you need to transfer money quickly, this option gives you the best rate available right now and guarantees it. A spot deal is used when an immediate payment is needed, for example, a deposit on an overseas property, a payment for a car, antiques or any other foreign purchase.

**Forward Contract** – This is the buy now, pay later option. It allows you to lock in a rate today for delivery of funds in the future. Whether you're buying or selling currency locking in a rate helps to protect you against changes in the market.

To take advantage of a forward contract you simply need to pay a small deposit up front and then the rest on maturity of the contract. This means that you can keep the rest of your money in a high interest account until it is needed.

This option is ideal if you have payments due on set dates in the future, for example, completion of a property.

**Limit Order** – Limit orders enable you to set a target rate at which you want to buy or sell your currency. Your dedicated currency specialist will help you to determine a rate that is appropriate for existing market conditions and will then monitor the market for you. As soon as the target rate is reached the order is executed.

This option is ideal for when you don't have to make an immediate payment and you have a specific budget avaialble.

### Regular Foreign Currency Transfers

There are a growing number of people who find themselves in the position where they need to make regular foreign currency transfers. Whether to pay an overseas mortgage, transfer a UK company pension abroad or even send money to cover the living expenses of a child at university overseas.

If this is the case using a reputable foreign exchange specialist to do the transfers for you can ensure that you get more of your money each time, even on small amounts. This is because unlike your bank they will offer you competitive exchange rates on these smaller amounts plus they won't charge you commission and transfers are often free.

### Choosing a Foreign Exchange Company

In recent years there has been a huge increase in the number of foreign exchange specialists who want to help you move your money abroad. Deciding which one to go with can be a daunting prospect but there are some simple guidelines that should make the task a little easier, and save you money in the process.

- Select a company that has at least three years of audited accounts and is financially strong.

- Find out more information by doing a quick internet search on the company. Look out for whether they have won any awards or been recommended by a reliable source.

- Do not let a foreign exchange company pressurise you into doing a deal. Make sure you are able to speak directly to a foreign exchange specialist who genuinely wants to understand your needs. The dealer's role is to understand your requirements and to provide you with the information you need, not to hard sell and certainly not to make you trade until you are 100% happy to go ahead.

- Ask what charges apply. If you are unsure, ask them to confirm in writing. You can really save money by using a well established, reputable foreign exchange company; not only through better rates but also as a result of lower transfer charges.
  For example, at Currencies Direct all regular transfers are free and one-off transfers are free over £5,000.

- Find out what foreign exchange buying options they can offer you. Some foreign exchange companies let you specify a rate at which you want to buy your currency (limit order) or fix a rate for up to 2 years (forward contract). These can be great tools to help you stick to your budget.

- If you make regular transfers from the UK overseas find out whether the foreign exchange company has a regular transfer service. This type of service will save you money on transfer fees and commission, and usually get you a much better rate of exchange.

- Be aware that at present in the UK commercial foreign exchange is not an FSA regulated industry because it is not considered 'investment business'. Under the Money Laundering Regulations 2003, commercial foreign exchange companies are treated as "Money Service Businesses" which are covered by regulations administered by HM Customs & Excise. Activities falling within the scope of the Money Service Business include the operations of bureau de change, transmission of money by any means and the cashing of third party cheques.

**Information provided by Currencies Direct**
**Tel: 020 7847 9400**
**Fax: 020 7847 9291**
**Email: info@currenciesdirect.com**
**Web: www.currenciesdirct.com**

# RETIREMENT PLANNING IS ALL ABOUT…PLANNING

There is a famous TV advert, which says that the product does exactly what it says on the tin. To me, retirement planning is exactly the same; you have to plan in order to be able to retire comfortably.

How many of us take the time out to plan though? How many of us really understand how much money we will need when we do retire? And how many of us understand the rules governing pensions?

So, how much do you need to put aside in order to have a comfortable retirement? If you are going to retire at 65, there is a very quick way to work out what you will need, simply multiply the income that you would like by 25. An example will probably help. If you want an income of £10,000, you multiply this by 25, meaning that you'll need a fund of £250,000.

There is, however, some good news. Last year on 6 April 2006, 'A' Day, the Government introduced new pension legislation.

For far too long, pensions law has been very complicated and to a certain extent it meant that the easiest option was to do nothing.

The Government, quite rightly, decided that it was time to simplify pensions. From 'A' Day, the previous eight legal frameworks that governed pensions were replaced by one set of rules. These changes have made it easier for us all to understand.

*The main changes were:*

- A Lifetime Allowance of a total fund of £1.5m, increasing to £1.8m by 2010
- Contributions limited to 100% of salary, with a maximum of £215,000 per year, increasing to £255,000 by 2010
- The earliest that you'll be able to retire from 2010 will be age 55
- 25% of your fund will be available as Tax Free Cash
- Increased flexibility at retirement

Everyone who has a pension will have been affected, to some extent, by the 'A' Day changes. How much you are affected will depend on your individual circumstances.

Since 'A' Day, we are seeing individuals taking positive action to decide how they are going to fund their pensions in order to ensure that when they choose to retire they will have sufficient money.

One of the advantages of pension planning today is that any contribution you make will be relieved at the highest rate of tax that you pay. Therefore, if you are a higher rate taxpayer, any contribution you make to a pension scheme will get tax relief at 40%.

For example, if your income is in excess of £100,000 per annum and you pay in £100,000 per year to your pension, the net contribution to you would be £60,000. If you compare this net contribution to the gross contribution this is a 67% increase on your net contribution before any growth, and remember the growth is on the gross contribution.

As you can see, the tax advantages of funding a pension are very attractive.

So, how can 'A' Day changes help you to plan your retirement?

One client recently decided that they were going to fund their pension over three years. How can this be done? Well, the individual is aged 40, earns in excess of £215,000 per annum and can afford to pay in £215,000 for the next three years.

*What is the process?*
- The gross contribution over three years will be £215,000 x 3=£645,000.
- The net contribution will be £129,000 x 3=£387,000.
- If we assume that the fund is going to increase at 7% per annum, by the time the client reaches age 55, they will have a fund of £1.8m *(obviously it is important to recognise that unit linked funds can fall as well as rise).*
- At retirement (age 55), they can take 25% of the fund as Tax Free Cash, which in this example would be £450,000.

Therefore, this client would have managed to fund up to the Lifetime Allowance of £1.8m, by only funding contributions over three years. The Tax Free Cash of £450,000 is in fact greater than the net contribution of £387,000!

As you can see, the 'A' Day changes have significantly increased the flexibility of our retirement planning options.

One of the other changes that came about as a result of 'A' Day is that you can use other assets to fund your pension. Not everybody has spare cash to fund their pension, but they might, for example, have a share portfolio. Under the new rules, you can transfer an asset that you currently own into a pension fund. Since 'A' Day, we have seen many individuals consider this option. The following example illustrates how this might work.

Mr Smith has shares currently worth £78,000. He is earning in excess of £100,000, so what can he do with them . . .

**Step 1**
By using a Stock Transfer Form, he transfers the ownership of the shares from himself into a Self Invested Pension Plan (SIPP).

### Step 2

Any CGT on the shares that he owns would become payable on transfer.

### Step 3

The transfer of £78,000 worth of shares into a SIPP is treated like a net contribution to a pension scheme. This means that it would be grossed up by a basic rate tax of 22%, making the gross contribution £100,000. Straight away, the £78,000 becomes £100,000.

### Step 4

As Mr Smith is a higher rate taxpayer, he can reclaim the difference between basic rate tax of 22% and higher rate tax of 40% (i.e. 18%). In this case, he would claim back £18,000 from the HMRC.

### Step 5

Mr Smith would receive a cheque from HMRC of £18,000.

Therefore, Mr Smith has transferred his shares of £78,000, they have been grossed up and he now has a SIPP containing £78,000 of shares and £22,000 of cash. He will also receive a cheque to the value of £18,000. *It is important to remember that any CGT on the shares would be payable.*

The great news about a pension fund is that once the shares are in that fund, there is no future CGT to pay.

Using existing shares can really enhance your retirement planning, but it is crucial to take the right advice at the right time in order to make sure that transferring the asset from personal ownership into a pension scheme is the best move.

When looking at planning for retirement, there are some key factors that you need to consider. Firstly, at what age do you want to retire? Secondly what level of income will you need at retirement? And thirdly how long do you expect to live once you have retired?

On average we are living much longer than ever before. A recent survey highlighted that for a married couple, aged 65 respectively, there is now a 50% chance that one of them will live until they are 90. This is good news, however, it means that we will all need more money at retirement, simply because it will have to last longer. So it is important to start as early as possible and take advice as to how much you should be funding.

All of us deserve a comfortable retirement; we just need to make sure that that is what we get!

Longevity is great news for all of us, but it does mean that we will need to put more money aside for retirement, whenever that is, to make sure that we have sufficient income to provide for us in our old age.

# Introduction

Wealth, like beauty, is in the eye of the beholder. A million pounds sterling, US dollars or euros may represent significant wealth in the abstract to most people, but what matters is as much the form that it takes as the absolute value. Residential property to a value of one million pounds or more is commonplace in Central London today, but owners whose principal asset is their home would not consider themselves wealthy in an investment sense unless they were planning to relocate to some remote area where house prices are at a fraction of London values.

The same is true of high-earners in employment who are accumulating substantial pension pots for retirement but whose current income is matched by their household expenditure, school fees and those luxuries that they regard as essentials. These are the group who may be classified as 'rich' rather than 'wealthy'.

In the context of this book, high net worth individuals (HNWs) are those whose marketable assets, unencumbered by debt, can be released and reinvested or whose disposable income significantly exceeds expenditure and is available for investment. At one end of the scale, this definition encompasses the beneficiaries of inherited wealth, captains of industry, successful entrepreneurs, the partners of leading professional firms, hedge fund managers and other senior managers in financial services who qualify for six- or seven-figure year-end bonuses. Also among the mega-income earners who accumulate wealth are pop musicians, movie stars and other figures promoted by the media from the fields of fashion, sport and lifestyle activities. At the other end of the scale are the windfall winners from lotteries and TV quiz games and the more modest recipients of lump sums from inheritance, maturing pension pots and equity release schemes. The value of the disposable funds available for investment may vary from, say, savings of £1,000 or less a month to lump sums of £20,000 or much more.

This book is intended for all those within this broad range of categories who are inexperienced investors or who want to widen the range of their investments from conventional securities into more challenging fields of varying risk. The common ground is a desire to invest prudently for the future at least a part of the wealth that they have gained or are continuing to accumulate.

# Scope of this edition

This third edition of *The Handbook of Personal Wealth Management* revisits much of the same ground as the previous edition but with some important changes in emphasis. Some of the previous authors have written again, updating their previous contributions in light of the changes that have taken place in the past year in the investment climate or their particular investment field. However, most chapters have been written by new authors whose contributions provide fresh and welcome new content to the book.

In Part 1, 'Approaches to portfolio management', the focus is more firmly on the alternative strategies to the delegation and management of investors' portfolios. Of those with significant wealth, only investment professionals, or those who fancy themselves as gifted amateurs, are likely to opt for managing their investments unaided.

Part 2, 'Selective investment from securities alternatives', follows on from Part 1 with a more detailed look at types of investment and investment strategy with less didactic descriptions than in previous editions. Part 3 is devoted entirely to pension issues and Part 4 to real estate and forestry investments, ranging from land and UK and overseas residential property to forestry in the UK and the Baltics and the benefits of real estate investment trusts (REITs).

In Part 5, 'Investments that sparkle', the four chapters from the last edition on investing and trading in coloured diamonds and on diamond exploration and mining investment in Canada have been carefully updated and extended by the same contributor experts. Part 6, 'Investments to live with', brings together the specialist fields of gold, art, antiques and collectables, fine wines and racehorse ownership and investment in bloodstock, each included in the last edition but updated for developments in its respective market during 2006. To this grouping we have added a thought-provoking contribution from the Charities Aid Foundation, entitled 'Engaged philanthropy', which explores the extensive array of options for effective giving by those who wish to make a difference by sharing some part of their good fortune.

No edition of *The Handbook of Personal Wealth Management* would be complete without the chapters of Part 7 on taxation issues and estate planning, again updated from the previous edition to address the additional hurdles that our ever-zealous Chancellor of the Exchequer has introduced in the past year. I am grateful to the Mazars taxation practice for revising their existing chapters, supplemented this time by contributions from KSB Law and Dickinson Dees, Dawsons Solicitors on the use of trusts, and the team at Forsters on inheritance tax, in the context of wills and estate planning.

The publication of this book is made possible by the financial support of our three front-cover sponsors, DiaMine Explorations, Inc., Pastor-Genève BVBA and Taylor Young Investment Management, together with that of the advertisers. My own personal thanks are due to all the authors who have provided such readable and informative contributions.

Personal circumstances and appetites for risk will determine which investment alternatives are the most appropriate for individual investors. Whatever your preferences may be, I hope that you will find in this book useful advice that will help you in making your selections.

*Jonathan Reuvid*

# Part 1

# Approaches to portfolio management

# Money
## is boring

What you can do with it – now that is interesting

wealthmanagement@insinger.com

# Are you getting your wealth's worth?

**For those in the fortunate position of having substantial wealth, a new problem emerges; who to trust with managing it. Neal Churchill and Mike Worsley advise.**

Initially, it may be tempting to leave the money in a bank or move it to a high interest building society account. Then there may be a surprising rash of 'exciting' investment ideas coming from all sides; properties In exotic locations, lavishly marketed investment funds, exciting business start-ups. Maybe your existing bank kindly arranges a meeting with an in-house private banker who suggests a raft of conveniently in-house products for you to buy. An IFA may helpfully suggest you invest in a tax-efficient onshore bond and build up your pension fund. Finally, a lawyer friend asks you if you have updated your will. Suddenly, it all feels rather complex and uncomfortable.

In the face of many choices and conflicting advice, it may be tempting to treat cash as a safe haven. However, when you take into account the relatively low interest rates available, the tax to be paid and the impact of inflation, your capital will actually be shrinking in real terms. The power of compounding means that this dilution of value will have a surprisingly rapid and significant impact on your wealth.

### Eyes on the prize

You are likely to need to invest in other asset classes beyond cash, such as equities, and bonds. This needs to be done to a plan to achieve a suitable asset allocation and an appropriate level of diversification. Diversification is the key to successful asset allocation and when applied properly is likely to involve the inclusion of traditional asset classes such as cash, equities and bonds, as well as alternative asset classes such as commercial property, private equity and hedge funds. The selection of an asset allocation is the single most important decision made in designing an investment strategy.

It is sad to see how often lip-service is paid to asset allocation at the outset and subsequently rarely reviewed. Though the science (and art) behind designing an asset allocation that matches a client's needs are relatively new, there is an increasing number of advisers trained to employ them. The science behind such techniques as "mean variance optimisation"[1] is now well developed and readily applied. However, the results need to be applied with the benefit of experience and a fair amount of common sense. The result will be a framework for your investment plan, designed to produce a satisfactory balance between risk and return, achieved through a diversification of exposure to asset classes.

The single biggest mistake investors make is to try and guess the way markets will perform and time their entry or withdrawal from investments. Market timing is a mug's game and success is only achieved by accident. The only successful strategy, over the long term, is to invest according to a plan and stay invested. It is all too easy to call a market top or bottom early or late.

Despite what many professionals in this industry would have you believe, their ability to predict the future is no better than the average fortune teller. They may tell a good story and it may be entertaining, but it will not make you any money. Accept it for what it is: entertainment. The world of investment is full of uncertainties and the honest investor will work within this uncertainty to build a resilient investment strategy.

Investments are probably the only area where people enjoy buying expensive assets. It is better to react to a temporary decline in an asset class to buy more, to restore your selected asset allocation. Similarly, strict adherence to asset allocation forces the investor to sell as the asset value rises relative to other assets to maintain the selected allocation.[2]

### Let your banker sweat the small stuff

The next level down, below the asset allocation, is the selection of suitable investments either at fund or individual stock level to populate each asset class. Many investors (and portfolio managers) mainly focus on investment selection, probably within one asset class, at the expense of the bigger picture. This is probably because the managers and investors are relatively comfortable with the concept of stock selection but find asset allocation a more difficult concept. However, it is the latter that will largely determine the success or failure of your investment plan. Your

---

1 This investment jargon refers to a computer-aided technique for attempting to produce an optimum portfolio design, based on estimates of asset class risk, returns and correlations. Along with a few other terms mentioned here, you do not need to understand them but your investment adviser should! Ask him or her about them when you next meet.

2 This approach is followed by many of the most consistently successful investors such as David Swenson of the Yale Foundation, who has achieved over 16% average returns over the past two decades.
Ref http://en.wikipedia.org/wiki/David_Swensen

private bank will need to have access to skilled analytical coverage across all the asset classes to be included in your investment plan.

It is likely that you will opt for a 'discretionary' approach, allowing your private banker to make decisions within the mandate you agree, rather than 'advisory' where he/she gives you advice on each potential change. The latter approach is likely to become onerous and time consuming, adding little value where you have agreed a comprehensive plan up-front. On the other hand, you may be offered this approach where deal-by-deal trading is being suggested for your investments. However, this is unlikely to be combined with a top-down asset allocation approach and may be a reason to be wary.

### Beware the cult of personality (mostly)

Among the hundreds of wealth managers, brokers and private banks keen to look after your wealth, many will claim to be able to deliver superior performance in-house. Similarly, thousands of funds are actively marketed on the skill and success of their managers. It will be obvious that not all these investment managers can be stars! Indeed, many are consistently disappointing.[3] The range of returns achieved by fund managers varies by the asset class, geographic exposure and style of the funds they manage. In some asset classes, the range is quite narrow and one might be tempted to suggest skill is unimportant and that it is only exposure to the underlying asset class that is being achieved. In these cases, there may be cheaper ways of achieving similar asset class exposure. Equally, in some asset classes skill is clearly important; some, such as hedge funds, are arguably, *entirely* about manager skill!

The industry is required constantly to remind investors that past performance is no guarantee of future performance. While this is correct, without a track record of past performance, it is difficult to believe that a manager has talent to apply in the future. Finding out whether the manager has talent or luck, what any talent is based on and whether it might be sustainable, is a skilled activity involving a fair amount of due diligence as well as a certain amount of behavioural insight! This due diligence is impossible for a private investor to do themselves.

---

3 Many studies have shown that most actively managed funds underperform a passive index. For example, one study of US funds showed that between 15% and 28% of funds managed to outperform over a 10-year period. In addition, those that did manage to outperform showed little persistence in this outperformance.

The Journal of Financial Planning, The Difficulty of Selecting Superior Mutual Fund Performance by Thomas P. McGuigan, CFP ref http://www.fpanet.org/journal/articles/2006_Issues/jfp0206-art6.cfm

**Tax and timidity: two enemies of wealth**

While the number of wealthy individuals and families is rapidly increasing, the turnover of that wealth is also dramatic. The wealthy come and go. The seriously wealthy often fail to diversify their wealth, sticking to what they know and to what produced their original wealth. They also tend to spend too much of the relatively low real returns achievable in today's investment environment. Finally, tax, particularly when wealth is passed between generations, can have a major impact on wealth.

Though the UK tax regime is increasingly complex and punitive, there are still opportunities for tax-efficient investment. Inheritance tax is largely a voluntary tax for the wealthy but careful advice is required at an early stage to produce an effective succession plan. Similarly, the use of pensions, offshore bonds and other structures can mitigate the impact of tax on net returns. All of this planning needs to be conducted alongside the design of an investment strategy.

We are now likely to be in an era of relatively low real returns and so control of costs becomes more important than ever. It is all too easy to suffer charges on buying and selling investments, as well as on an ongoing basis. With the power of compounding, the impact of small extra charges will make a big difference over time. It is wise, therefore, to invest through a private banker who can negotiate favourable terms with selected managers. Similarly, the use of investment trusts to access talented managers can be a cost-effective alternative to the equivalent unit trusts, and there are tax efficient strategies which can be employed for collecting fees for investment management.

**Plan to change the plan**

A skilled private banker will coordinate and draw on specialist advice as necessary and will be able to work with you to match your needs and circumstances with an investment and structuring plan which will only be implemented when you are happy that it is both suitable and practicable. Unfortunately, no plan survives prolonged contact with reality! Your circumstances will change, gradually or perhaps suddenly, and your investment plan should be regularly reviewed. You should agree with your private banker a regular cycle of Plan, Do, Review. The latter should involve a clear, comprehensive report on the performance (and risk) of your investments, comparing it with your latest plan, reviewing your circumstances and agreeing any changes. These are likely to be infrequent but may involve changes to the risk taken on by the portfolio by adjusting the asset allocation. They may also involve preparing for planned withdrawals to fund major capital expenditure or as part of estate planning, for example.

In order to monitor the progress of your investment portfolio against your plan, your adviser will need to be able to produce clear and informative reports showing investment performance, risk, asset class performance and benchmark performance.

Even if there are no changes to be made in your investment plan, it is important that you review these reports regularly to confirm where and how value is being added to your investments, whether through asset allocation or stock selection, what risk is being run in your portfolio and the degree to which the investments are following the agreed plan. You will also need accurate tax reporting so that you can account to HMRC for any liabilities to capital gains and income on investments.

### Choose your adviser wisely

With as many as 200 firms offering wealth management or private banking services in UK, the selection of someone to plan and implement an effective strategy for your investments is not likely to be easy. The first major decision is probably whether you want a pure wealth manager, who will probably not be concerned about tax-efficient investment or other aspects of structuring your investments, or whether you want a full-service private bank offering access to specialist advice and investment structuring.

By definition, a private bank is likely to be able to offer currency services and lending facilities. Whether it is actually useful to have a fancy cheque book is another matter; many tire of the expense of such a dressed-up commodity product and instead continue to use the free current accounts offered by their high street bank, topped up by payments from their private bank. The larger private banks associated with clearing banks or Swiss banks are likely to be encouraged to sell their own products, while the smaller private banks are more likely to source the better products from across the market. Independence is an important characteristic to seek out; not only will it mean objective use of other firms' products, but it will also mean being ready to access specialist advice from outside the firm for tax, trust structuring, protection and other services.

*The following may be a useful checklist when reviewing your current or anticipated private banking service provider.*

Do they take the time to get to know me and my family, our needs, interests and aspirations?

Do they understand what I want to do with my wealth, offer alternative solutions and discuss these until we reach agreement on a preferred solution?

Do they confirm that my needs for succession planning, tax mitigation, protection and retirement planning are being addressed and, if they are not, do they arrange for me to receive the appropriate advice?

Do they provide a clear and comprehensive plan covering all my financial planning needs, including tax-efficient investing, asset allocation, risk mitigation, succession planning and my anticipated capital and cash flow requirements?

Do they provide regular, clear and informative reports, explaining progress to our agreed plan?

Can I get in contact with them easily and do they give me the time to discuss my ideas and any concerns?

Do they operate independently, accessing where necessary the best talent to meet my needs?

Do they avoid the common tendency of pushing in-house products into my portfolio?

Do they offer to help me with preparing the next generation for taking on the responsibilities of the family's wealth?

Do I like them and trust them? Do they share my views concerning the balance of money for its own sake and money as a means to an end?

Finding the people you can work with has always been difficult; never more so than when finding someone to trust with your hard-earned wealth. We hope that the issues outlined have provided food for thought and, in particular, that the questions above are useful. Given the importance of the advice and management you need to select, it is worth spending the time and effort choosing carefully. You are likely to be entrusting your wealth to your chosen private bank for many years and it is worth getting it right first time. If you don't, it's worth moving!

Insinger de Beaufort is a member of the London Stock Exchange and ICMA.
Authorised and regulated by the Financial Services Authority.
Registered in England and Wales No. 2479169
131 Finsbury Pavement London EC2A 1NT

INSINGER $^{de}$BEAUFORT

# RowanDartington

espoke investment solutions for affluent private clients

Bespoke Portfolio Management, SIPP's, ISA's, PEP's, Inheritance Tax Solutions

For further information, contact -
Richard Mann

**Rowan Dartington & Co. Limited**
**Colston Tower, Colston Street, Bristol BS1 4RD**
**Tel: (0117) 927 7273 / Facsimile (0117) 933 0009**
**Email: assetmanagement@rowandartington.co.uk**

Rowan Dartington is a subsidary of BlueOar PLC

*Member of the London Stock Exchange plc. Authorised and regulated*
*by the Financial Services Authority*

# RowanDartington

## Asset Management for affluent private clients

Rowan Dartington offers a comprehensive range of bespoke investment management solutions to meet the specific financial circumstances and objectives of affluent private clients.

The Rowan Dartington Asset Management service allows you to hand over responsibility for your investments to professionals. The service is tailored to individuals who recognise the need for speed and flexibility, and prefer not to have an active role in the day to day administration of their investments. You agree a strategy with the team of investment managers which combines risk tolerance, investment time horizons and underlying financial needs.

The rigorous approach to investment management starts with asset allocation which will determine the proportions invested in equities, fixed interest, cash, property and alternative investments, and instruments. Your investment manager will then make day to day decisions on which investments are most appropriate using our access to global market information and research.

Your portfolio will be managed in the context of your tax position. Your investment manager will take into consideration your views on capital gains tax and make use of your annual exemptions. You will receive an annual tax package incorporating interest on cash, dividend statements and a full breakdown of capital gains realised in the tax year.

Rowan Dartington Asset Management is always seeking to innovate and brings its clients the latest investment products in the global marketplace. These include structured products and a newly launched Inheritance Tax portfolio service which aims to take advantage of business asset taper relief for capital gains tax purposes and business property relief for IHT purposes

The key executives in the Asset Management department, Andrew Morris, Mark Sevier and Richard Mann, have over 70 years of combined experience in providing best advice based on sound analysis of clients' financial requirements.

Rowan Dartington is a subsidiary of BlueOar Securities a leading corporate finance and institutional stockbroking firm who advises some of the UK's largest investment management groups and pension funds.

# Advisory or discretionary management? – a multiple choice question

*Peter Hearn, Ashcourt Group*

In 40 years' experience of the world of investment management, it has been hard to ignore the evolution of services made available to the individual as an investor. 'It's all so different from my day', 'Far too technical for me', says the client. 'Clients are much more sophisticated', 'You have to keep up with the changes', says the provider of investment services. Of course, underpinning all of this is the attempt to supply the level of personal service to the client on a cost-effective basis. On the face of it, there seems an element of mismatch between the two.

## Then and now

Going back as far as the late 1960s, the investment world has been dominated by the introduction of new technology replacing old manual records, extending massively the amount of information and data that can be provided to investors at an ever faster pace. The provision of this information and data is proffered as an improvement in service for which additional charges can be levied. Prior to this, it was not unusual for the client to be largely ignored in the process of making investment decisions and the provision of data etc, with only the seriously wealthy having the privilege of personal meetings with their stockbroker. The mass market was serviced predominantly by a door-to-door system where the famous man from the insurance company called to collect the premiums under a very long-term endowment savings plan. The supporting investment management was the province of the in-house investment team whose remit was largely to grow the underlying reversionary bonus attaching. This did not in any way involve recourse to the client, and most clients would be blissfully ignorant of the underlying investments.

Within the institutional world, the typical investment portfolio comprised a substantial holding in government stock and other fixed interest investments with a relatively small amount allocated to the shares of the top 30 companies quoted on the stock exchange. In a low-inflation period, it was not essential to take the risks associated with shares, given that government stocks provided a real return together with underlying security to capital at the redemption date.

This investment philosophy was replicated in the world of wealthier investors, who received their advice and recommendations from their friendly stockbroker on an ad hoc basis. Old wisdom dictated that younger investors should be exposed as to 80 per cent in shares and 20 per cent in fixed interest. Following marriage and children this balance would shift to 50 per cent and 50 per cent, finally becoming 20 per cent shares and 80 per cent fixed interest as investors moved to their retirement years.

# The first impact of technology

The introduction of technology was seized upon in the early 1970s as the need to respond to the pressures of high inflation built and the stock markets came under severe pressure in the period leading to the crash of 1974. Government stock could no longer be relied upon to provide a real return, and shares proved to be as volatile as the harbingers of doom had predicted. It was necessary to diversify investments within portfolios, whether they were institutional or private.

This period saw the introduction of different asset classes, most notably commercial property and gradually the external world of share investing into portfolios. Technology allowed the institutional investment manager to keep in touch with overseas markets. The radical introduction of unit-linked life assurance allowed this development to be introduced to the wider world of investors desperate to avoid the high levels of personal tax on both income and capital gains. Whilst the tax planning opportunities have been hunted down by the authorities, the extension of choice in the asset class arena has seen no such limitation, and modern opportunities have proved bewildering even for long-standing practitioners.

# Advisory vs discretionary management

It is this proliferation of choice within the investment world that has, in my view, been a major factor in determining the choice between advisory and discretionary

# ● ASHCOURT

## **Partners** for capital growth and protection

" We are mandated by institutions, trusts and the private investor.
For big or small investor alike, the service is a very personal one. "

Peter Hearn, Ashcourt Group

The Ashcourt Group provides high quality financial planning
advice and investment expertise to private and corporate clients.
Comprising two principal companies:
Ashcourt Financial Planning (AFP) and Ashcourt Asset Management (AAM).

**Flexible strategies that put our
investors in control.**

AAM's investment strategies cover all major
asset classes with a tailored
and independent service. This meets the
needs and aspirations of the individual and
offers a truly universal investment scope.

**A bespoke, traditional and customer
focused approach.**

AFP provides a complete financial
management service to private and corporate
clients, trusts, pension funds and charities.
Advice covers the full range of today's
investment vehicles including IHT, trusts, life
assurance, SIPPs and property.

Our absolute priority is to ensure the advice we offer
makes a positive material difference to each of our clients.

## www.ashcourt.uk.com

For further information please contact Peter Hearn:
Email peterhearn@ashcourt.uk.com. Tel 020 7269 7550

management services. Before commenting further on this, we need to consider the effects of the Financial Services Act introduced in 1986. Together with 'Big Bang' in 1987, these events have been the major influence on the investment businesses that have subsequently survived and prospered in the years to date. Huge additional costs were incurred in improving systems of accounting and reporting, which surely played a major role in the expansion of private client investment business, not least of which was the tremendous improvement in the security and soundness of both the investment provider and the investment adviser.

Nevertheless, the choice between discretionary and advisory services was not of itself affected by the events. More relevant was the approach taken by the bigger providers of investment services that the cost of 'poor advice' to the client was not acceptable within their business models, and this decision has been supported by the series of heavy fines levied by the FSA on providers and advisers alike. The safety-first approach has now become the norm in investment management services, with discretionary services offered by 'account managers' themselves not allowed to discuss the underlying investment portfolio. This seems to me to be a reversion to the old system of separating the investment management from the client although there is a much more realistic approach to communicating with the client by way of relevant improvement. The investment magazine and the intro- duction of the upmarket valuation have bridged the divide.

## Current practice

This system has been adopted also by the larger stockbrokers, who themselves have had to respond to the wider legal and technology changes with the introduction of discretionary management services that compete against the big banks and insurance/pension companies. They have, however, been the mainstay of the advisory management services in the format of long-standing individual stock- brokers dealing with their client banks on a deal-by-deal basis. This advisory service copes with clients who genuinely have the ability to understand the investment data, the workings of the markets and the wider economic circum- stances in which to come to an appropriate decision suiting their own risk profile and investment objectives. It also copes with less qualified clients who in the main rely upon the knowledge of the stockbroker of their own individual circumstances to make the decisions for them. This latter group are in effect deemed to be discre- tionary clients in the event that advice proves inappropriate. I am sure, however, that this rarely occurs. Again, the modern advisory service seems to replicate the traditional system of dealing with your stockbroker in the old-fashioned way.

## Service parameters for stockbrokers

So overall and despite the introduction of new technology, which now extends to the internet, as well as the requirements of new legislation, now including evidence of identity and proceeds of crime reporting, the system fundamentally remains range-bound within its old parameters. The attempt by the main investment management businesses to address the needs of the new breed of investor who does not want advice or management and purely requires a cheap execution-only dealing service has largely evaporated in the face of cheaper and cheaper dealing costs. The internet-based dealing world has spawned huge growth in alternative investments, including options, futures, contracts for difference (CFDs) and hedge funds. The perceived high-risk profile of these vehicles, together with the technical nature of derivatives generally, has deterred the bulk of traditional advisers from extending their services into these areas.

It has to be accepted that the menu of investment options must be restricted for the majority of investors if the provider is to offer a service that:

- is affordable;
- can be expanded with confidence through its team of advisers;
- can meet all the regulatory requirements of offering such a service to private clients;
- offers a sensible range of investment services.

## Living with the limitations

In light of this, there is more and more pressure being applied to clients to accept these limitations – effectively to shoehorn them into a 'one size fits all' regime. Good, but is it good enough? Clearly not all clients who require assistance with their financial affairs want to be treated this way. Is there room for the provision of genuinely bespoke services to the private client market?

Client-focused investment services that combine the role of investment management and adviser on a client-by-client basis have been provided for a very long time by private banks, but more recently they themselves have been under pressure to reduce their scope and quality of service in the face of market forces. This therefore leaves the smaller investment management companies to fill the gap and carve out for themselves the quality niche that seeks to offer an all-embracing personal service to those clients who wish to deal on a personal basis with one or two people with whom they can build a relationship over the long term that extends into their family unit as a whole.

Needless to say, this requires a depth of experience from the advisers and an approach that combines the aspects of investment management and financial services into a well-defined business model. At the hub of the service is the investment management process, which is model-based on blue chip equities but with the opportunity to add on a variety of alternatives drawn from the wider world of shares to meet personal preferences, if any, and specific shorter-term opportunities. Further diversification can be provided by extending into overseas markets, either directly or preferably by the use of collective vehicles. Added value can be sought from specific stock selections drawn from the smaller markets, and extended diversification is provided by allocation to investments that provide an absolute return and/or are structured to provide some underlying protection. Investment into commodities, commercial property and other assets complete the process. Each allocation is set for the client on an individual basis.

The client's circumstances are then reviewed from a financial services aspect and shaped to take as much advantage as possible, being held within pension or individual savings accounts as well as into the world of trusts and inheritance tax vehicles and any other products that offer tax advantages to the client. These products, where applicable, sit on top of the investment portfolio and accordingly the underlying investments are not duplicated, which is often the case when products are sold first.

## Back to the future

As to the future, it is clear that modern portfolio management for private clients will need to take full account of the widest available range of investment opportunities and in particular to take diversification several stages further such that the client's portfolio includes an allocation to assets that are not necessarily correlated to the performance of the stock market. Absolute return investments aiming to achieve performance in both rising and falling markets, as well as structured products that build an element of protection to underlying capital in order to 'lock in' gains and/or return original capital in the event of falling markets, are now becoming readily available.

These new areas of investment are still at early-stage development in the private client world but have been used for some years within institutional fund management and have entered the financial services arena of the major banks promoted to clients as individual products. The key is to build these into a client portfolio as part of a coordinated strategy that combines the investment portfolio with the product advice available from a combined team of appropriately qualified persons working together in support of the client's objectives. For that team to be the cornerstone of the relationship between the client and the firm is for the firm to show a commitment to the long-term support of private client business in a fair and reasonable fee-charging structure.

# Portfolio construction for the high net worth individual

*Nicholas Lambert, Sarasin Chiswell*

## The role of investments and cash in your life cycle

Do you own your house because it is a comfortable home for your family to enjoy, to act as a quasi-pension fund or to make a tax-free profit? The same question can and should be asked of your overall asset base. As one cannot live in an investment portfolio, so one needs to decide the role that your investments and cash are required to play through your life cycle.

What are the major considerations and likely requirements for capital:

- the down payment for your home;
- to supplement the payment of school fees;
- to assist with retirement and medical support;
- to provide assistance to get children into the housing market?

Against this background, we all enter the world of employment with the expectation of a continuous and rising stream of income to cover day-to-day expenses, mortgage repayment and the funding of a pension. Before reaching the age of 40, few of us are in any position to provide for the above and have sufficient surplus to start building up reserves to create an investment portfolio. ISA rules allow each adult to invest £7,000 a year in a tax-free environment, so £14,000 for a married couple, which equates to saving from taxed income of some £23,300.

So where do the assets for a portfolio come from? There are two main sources. First, there is the result of helping to create a business from which a full or partial 'equity' exit provides a capital lump sum. The second source is that of capital inherited upon the death of one's parents. For the fortunate, there is inheritance during one's parents' lifetime.

# Preserving capital's real value

The traditional view of capital in the UK is that it can be enjoyed as a provider of an additional source of income but that the capital should be passed on to the next generation. Most trusts create this situation. On rainy days, some of the capital can be deployed. On this basis the time horizon for investment is long, perhaps two or three decades. The minimum aim for such investment is to preserve the purchasing power of that capital. This may not seem too difficult after living through a period of 15 years when inflation has averaged 2.665 per cent. It was rather more difficult over the previous 15 years when purchasing power was reduced by 8.025 per cent each year. These are very different hurdles, but they demonstrate how important it is to decide what a portfolio needs to achieve before undertaking any investment. The logical approach would be to ask an investment manager to ensure that, over reasonable time frames, the capital grows by the rate of inflation while providing a level of income that can also grow by the rate of inflation, thus 'in real terms'. The starting income could be the income return offered by index-linked gilts, say 2.5 per cent.

## *Time frame*

The time horizon has two aspects. We have discussed the long-term horizon, say 20 years. The problem arises when we need also to provide for rainy days. Rainy days most often arise when conditions are difficult in the economy as a whole, perhaps because interest rates are high – making mortgages expensive – or because being unemployed is more likely. In both environments, investment conditions can be difficult and it is almost adding insult to injury when one has to raise capital just when the portfolio value has fallen by 10 or 20 per cent. For this reason, a shorter-term horizon should be considered, possibly three years.

The last consideration is that the above returns should be achieved after the costs of managing and accounting for the asset base, in this instance the investment portfolio. Ideally, asset class and individual investments should be able to be changed while minimizing short-term tax liabilities. Thus, to grow the capital in real terms, to provide some income and to do this net of expenses, we are asking the investment manager to provide annual returns of some 7 per cent per annum or 22.5 per cent over each rolling three-year period. This is an approach that is being used increasingly in the management of SIPP and other pension portfolios where some measure of liability matching is required.

## Asset class management

The long-term (100 years) average returns from the main asset classes in the UK are 5 per cent for cash, 5.2 per cent for gilts and 9.5 per cent for equities, all for a period when inflation has averaged 3.9 per cent. At first sight, a portfolio divided equally between gilts and equities should provide our 7 per cent. However, one must see what the worst years look like to see what the rainy-day years might hold. Since 1955, the worst return on cash has been 3.5 per cent (1955), for gilts –10.5 per cent (1974, with –9.5 per cent in 1994) and for equities –43.6 per cent (also 1974, with –22.7 per cent in 2002). There are clearly years when one needs the flexibility to avoid some asset classes. Those with portfolios of individual equity holdings in 1999 may remember the thought of paying large capital gains tax bills to switch out of equities, even just to switch from highly valued equities to those trading on less demanding multiples of their earnings. Plainly, holding the core of one's investments in a vehicle that allows for the buying and selling of individual equity and bond holdings without incurring tax liabilities is sensible.

# Investing on a global basis

We believe that today's leading companies have global strategies and that the place of origin or of the listing of a company's shares is increasingly irrelevant. Changes in technology and the internet have meant that companies have undergone a period of disintermediation and price transparency. Add to this the increase in cross-border mergers and we are in a situation where the world's largest semiconductor maker is Korean, the largest cement company is Mexican and the largest steel maker is Indian. There is now no UK-listed company in any of these three sectors.

Investors need to understand how an investment manager chooses its equity holdings. Ideally a manager should not feel obliged to invest in any company simply because it occupies a significant weighting of the portfolio's benchmark. At Sarasin Chiswell, we identify global themes that we believe will drive global growth and deliver enhanced investment returns. This is a five-stage process:

1. Identify key global trends that have a disproportionate effect on world growth.
2. Develop these trends into definable themes by seeing how they will benefit selected areas and industries within the global economy.
3. Ensure that these themes can be reflected and monitored in the long-term profitability or revenue growth of large-cap global companies.
4. Confirm whether any new theme is likely to have a low or even adverse correlation with other existing themes.
5. Create a checklist that allows analysts to evaluate a company on the various criteria that define a theme.

## Currency management

In all the above, we have assumed that inflation or liabilities are in sterling. A level of diversification is prudent in all portfolio management. Within bonds, this is usually diversification of counterparty risk with non-sterling assets held only when one believes that sterling will be weak against one or more major currencies. In equity, the London market is becoming increasingly international in scope but only in a narrow range of sectors like minerals. Indeed, 25 per cent of the index's dividend is now paid in US dollars.

## Creating investment returns

We now need a benchmark, a time horizon, a portfolio yield target and the desire to minimize tax. The first consideration for a high net worth individual (HNWI) is to find an investment manager that has the management of such mandates at the core of its business. The second is to understand how it creates such investment returns. There are two main methods. First, there is investing in the right equities and bonds within their asset classes. For equities this might have the effect of raising the average return on equities from 9.5 per cent to 12.5 per cent for the best managers. However, this does not mean that they will avoid the −10 per cent years. This is achieved by reducing exposure to equities in favour of other asset classes. In 2002, equities returned −22.7 per cent while gilts provided +9.2 per cent. In 1974, cash yielded 12.6 per cent when equities fell by 43.7 per cent.

Second, movement of investments between asset classes is described as active asset allocation, and clearly many pitfalls can be avoided by astute work in this field. In an ideal world one should find an investment manager that can add value, alpha, both from stock selection and from active asset allocation.

## Managing the impact of taxation

The management of tax means that a unit trust or OEIC structure should be used, unless the monies are in an ISA, a PEP, a SIPP or another tax-efficient structure. In order not to be penalized for switching between asset classes, a multi-asset class or 'portfolio' fund is sensible. Ideally a UCITS III OEIC structure should be sought as this allows the inclusion of other, or alternative, asset classes – property, private equity funds, hedge funds or commodity exposure. It is unusual that one investment manager will have in-house expertise in managing investment in all traditional as well as alternative asset classes. Indeed, many experts in the alternative asset classes do not provide portfolio management services for HNWIs. Your investment manager will need a dedicated process for deciding the best method of sourcing such expertise for its clients.

Thus, for an HNWI, an investment portfolio should logically be based around a holding of the 'portfolio' fund of the chosen investment manager. This can be supplemented with a holding of one or two funds that specialize in individual asset classes, in order to personalize one's asset allocation, income demands or time horizon. Typically, this would be equity-based in one's 40s and 50s, while moving to bonds or other income-generating assets during one's retirement. In the UK, an annual capital gains tax allowance permits a gradual switch between these supplementary funds as one's time horizon or rainy-day demands dictate. The allowance is not normally sufficient to allow wholesale changes between asset classes if one holds a best-of-breed fund for each individual asset class.

## Generation of 'income'

With regard to income, HNWIs in the UK should ensure, where possible, that they minimize income tax payments. If we assume that most HNWIs who have an investment portfolio are 40 per cent rate taxpayers, a 4 per cent yield in one's bank is a 2.4 per cent yield after HM Revenue and Customs takes its share. This is raising the performance hurdle by a further 1.6 per cent each year. For a £0.5 million portfolio with £100,000 of unrealized capital gains, and a 2005/06 CGT allowance of £8,800, one could withdraw £44,000 a year from a portfolio fund without paying tax. A 2.5 per cent income requirement is £12,500, which would use just £2,500 of the allowance, leaving the remainder, £6,600, to use for switches between 'supplementary' fund holdings.

## Evaluating providers of 'portfolio' funds

How do you evaluate which 'portfolio' fund should form the core of an HNWI's investment portfolio. If you are persuaded that the rolling three-year 'real' return scenario of, say, 7 per cent per annum meets your expectations, you need a chart that shows the 10- or 20-year returns and volatility for such portfolio funds. You will be seeking funds in the north-west quadrant of the chart – above-average returns with below-average volatility. You will want to ascertain whether that performance record has been achieved by the same investment process and philosophy with the same core individuals still at the helm. Lastly, it is important that the management of such a portfolio fund for HNWIs is of consequence to the investment management business itself. If that is the case and performance slips, the full resource of the business will be used to ensure the investment engine is returned to optimal performance.

## Portfolio funds – the benefits of wider investment powers

Delivery of a suitable HNWI portfolio in a single fund has become much easier. Born out of European Union financial services legislation in 2002 for 'Undertakings for Collective Investments in Transferable Securities' (UCITS), UCITS III compliant funds can now invest in a comprehensive range of asset classes and use more sophisticated techniques of investment that until now have been the preserve of the very largest investors. Importantly, it allows for the creation of funds that can permanently occupy the north-west frontier and achieve an RPI mandate in all investment environments.

## Three-dimensional investing

In May 2006, Sarasin Chiswell launched two funds of a new pioneering family of funds: IIID. The first of these, GlobalSar IIID, is based on the thematic investment process of GlobalSar, the house portfolio fund, which has been tried and tested over 20 years. It offers investors a new and ground-breaking investment proposition that takes our complete portfolio solution to a new level: a global fund that invests across the spectrum of all asset classes, but also uses the flexibility allowed by UCITS III to optimize the fund's risk return profile. Combining low volatility with a focus on capital preservation and a real return target, the fund offers a total portfolio solution, including access to the most specialized asset classes, and is delivered in a tax-efficient vehicle for UK investors.

UCITS III allows managers access to a new investment 'toolkit'. This enables fund managers to use financial instruments, until now largely the preserve of the hedge fund community, to structure downside protection strategies, to reduce volatility and to access new specialized asset classes and trading strategies to enhance returns. Furthermore, after talking to many clients, it became clear that the 2000–03 bear market is still very much in their minds, and many would favour a 'real' return rather than a 'relative' objective. In recognition of this, GlobalSar IIID seeks to beat a benchmark of RPI +3.5 per cent over a rolling three-year period.

We believe that UCITS III will have a huge effect on the investment landscape and that, as the market realizes this, others will follow down the trail blazed by GlobalSar IIID. UCITS III extends the use of derivatives: these no longer have to be used for efficient portfolio management purposes only. Included in derivatives, crucially, are contracts for differences (CFDs). This means that, while funds are still not allowed to 'short' stocks, they can take on short exposure through CFDs.

UCITS III allows much more flexible access to third-party funds. This has allowed us to apply our highly successful open architecture approach to specialist funds and asset classes within a quoted vehicle. Financial instruments can also be constructed to give the fund exposure to baskets of shares or whole asset classes that have previously been relatively inaccessible, such as commodities, private equity or real estate. This dramatically broadens the range of assets available to the fund manager.

Lastly, funds no longer have to be run on a 100 per cent invested basis; they can hold unlimited cash weightings if the manager is expecting uncertain times. This is important as it means that selling units, thus creating taxable gains, is not required in order to protect hard-earned gains.

We believe that Sarasin's global thematic framework adapts particularly well to this broader investment flexibility. Within our theme categories we are able to identify theme outperformers and underperformers, often in different business sectors, and to construct pair strategies. We also look to identify bearish market themes and to establish short positions in either individual companies or baskets of shares that we expect to be negatively affected by these themes.

An alternative for some clients was to invest in an absolute return hedge fund. While many of these performed well in the bear market, from a client's point of view, this came with a cost: a loss of liquidity (most hedge funds trade monthly), less transparency and higher fees. GlobalSar IIID addresses all of these issues. The broader range of assets available and the ability to hold cash freely and to manage the fund's net market exposure give much more credibility to a real return investment objective. GlobalSar IIID also offers daily liquidity and total transparency and only charges a performance fee after the objective of RPI +3.5 per cent is achieved in any given year.

GlobalSar IIID is positioned precisely where traditional long only and hedge fund absolute returns meet. By combining the strengths of a thematic investment approach with downside protection and alpha generation techniques previously used only by hedge funds, we believe that GlobalSar III offers clients the best of both worlds, or an innovative third dimension to their investment approach.

# The Yale investment management model

*Stan Miranda, Partners Capital Investment Group LLC*

You studied hard in school to get into a top university. You worked hard and, despite perhaps playing hard at university, managed to graduate towards the top of your class. You secured an entry-level position with a brand-name employer that made your parents proud. You worked late hours and weekends to learn all you could and to get ahead. You made social sacrifices throughout your career including, later in life, with your family and friends. But it was all worth it as you have been both professionally and financially successful.

Given the time it has taken to earn and accumulate this wealth, you are reluctant, at best, to take chances that present the risk of you losing it. Cash is safe, but there must be an investment strategy that can give you and your family confidence that it can grow more significantly and still be there when you need it.

You struggle to trust the private banks, which appear to be the most typical advisers to people like you. Private bankers struggle to push anything other than their own in-house investment products. They charge extraordinary fees and do not have the detailed knowledge of their own products that you expect them to. These advisers all appear to be focused much more on growing their own profits rather than yours. And you have a keen perspective on how large financial corporations behave. Profit maximization for the company will always win out over value added for the client. So what do you do?

I cannot know whether this conundrum is familiar to you, but it describes exactly where I was in late 2001. I had worked hard for what wealth I had accumulated and I did not want to see it just in cash, nor did I want to see it decline by 40 per cent, which is what it would have done if it had been fully invested in the equity market between April 1999 and that date. I was advised by Goldman Sachs, UBS and Citibank. It wasn't working.

I was confident that there was indeed a 'right' way of investing, a proven approach that the leading institutional investors follow. Who really knows what they are doing in the investment world and can I not simply emulate them? How do the smart super-wealthy families in the world invest their capital? Having worked in the private equity world, I had many connections with wealthy families and institutional investors and set out to find the 'holy grail' of the investment world: the 'right way' to invest for long-term secure growth in capital.

My own investigations sliced the most successful investors into two camps: the opportunistic, highly concentrated investors in 'deals' and, secondly, the systematic investors in best-of-breed asset managers highly diversified across all asset classes. The opportunistic concentrated investors are best exemplified by the Robert Bass family office and Richard Rainwater, two of the most highly respected investors known best to the inner circles of the wealthy in New York. They invest in a highly opportunistic way in 'deals', not so much giving their money to other asset managers, but managing it themselves by investing one year, for example, into Argentine debt, and the next year in the Lukoil Russian oil company, and in US power plants in another year. This approach is not for the faint-hearted and depends on a handful of very expensive individuals. The 'single manager risk' that this embodies would not be acceptable to most of us.

The second approach of more systematic diversification is most prominently identified with the Yale University Endowment and its Chief Investment Officer, David Swensen. But many sophisticated wealthy families, foundations and other university endowments (including Princeton, Cornell, Stanford and Harvard) have long employed a close variant of this approach. However, it is best known in the vernacular of the wealth management world as 'the Yale approach'. In 2000, David Swensen published his first book, *Pioneering Portfolio Management*, which illuminated the Yale model in detail to help other large institutional investors to adopt that approach. Swensen's second book, which came out in 2005, was initially intended to instruct wealthy individuals in how they could adopt the principles of the Yale approach. When the book ultimately came out, David Swensen argued that there were too many practical limitations for individuals and his approach was unworkable for all but the super-wealthy. We have a different point of view based on my own family's investment portfolio over the past 20 years and based on the success of our clients, since our company, Partners Capital, was set up five years ago. (Please note that Partners Capital has no formal or informal affiliation with the Yale Investment Office or the Yale University Endowment. Yale is merely one example among many institutional investors deploying this general investment approach. David Swensen has simply made the Yale approach more transparent to us and others through his very articulate and understandable publications on its strategy.)

# The Yale investment philosophy

The Yale Investment Office has delivered a 16.1 per cent average annual return for the Yale Endowment over the last 20 years under David Swensen's leadership. This places Yale in the top 1 per cent of institutional investors over this time frame. There are four components to the Yale model, all of which are relevant to wealthy individuals and families, including those who do not have sufficient scale to build their own family investment office.

## Rule 1: Clearly distinguish between investment strategy (asset allocation) and asset management (eg security selection)

Asset allocation (including asset manager selection) has historically been responsible for between 80 and 90 per cent of investment portfolio performance, with the remainder being attributed to security selection.[1] The Yale Investment Office's primary role is determining the endowment's investment strategy, which comprises asset allocation and manager selection. It does not manage any assets itself. It leaves asset management (or individual security selection) to specialist asset managers.

The investment world has evolved into a complex array of asset classes where specialization is critical for the asset manager to excel. It is highly unlikely that any one asset manager will be best of breed across numerous asset classes, thus enabling it to fulfil both roles. This mandates that any given investment portfolio has its strategy (asset allocation and asset manager selection) determined by an independent internal or external investment management resource with no incentive to appoint itself as asset manager in any one area. Yale believes that any institution that fulfils both roles is conflicted. In Figure 1.3.1, we illustrate the distinct roles of the two layers of investment resource.

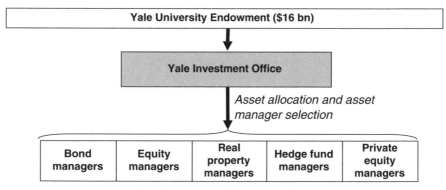

**Figure 1.3.1**   Yale asset managers' securities selection process

1. Asset allocation is frequently cited by academic studies as the primary contributor to portfolio performance. One fairly recent Goldman Sachs report illustrated that 91.5 per cent of portfolio return was attributed to asset allocation (Goldman Sachs report, December 2002; Brinson and Hood, 'Determinants of portfolio performance', *Financial Analyst Journal*, May/June 1991).

For investors with assets of $500 million and below, it is likely that the Yale investment role is performed by an independent investment adviser who has a breadth of expertise that enables it to select the best asset manager across all five asset classes.

## Rule 2: Diversify across a broad array of unrelated asset classes

The equity market is one of the most competitive, volatile and high-risk asset classes in the investment world. The competitiveness of the equity market makes it very difficult for even the most talented equity managers to beat the market from one year to the next. Yale began in 1986 to diversify its US equity-dominated portfolio into all five major asset classes. Today Yale's asset allocation targets fixed income at 5 per cent of the total, public equities 28 per cent, real assets 25 per cent, private equity 17 per cent and absolute return strategies (hedge funds) 25 per cent. Yale's 2004 actual asset allocation is shown in Figure 1.3.2 alongside those of Harvard and Stanford.

This leaves Yale much more concentrated in the less competitive or inefficient sectors of the investment world, where talented asset managers can and do generate exceptional risk-adjusted returns for their investors. The result is a robust portfolio not overly exposed to the vicissitudes of the global equity market, and spread across a broad array of specialist asset managers, most of whom are investing in the less efficient corners of the financial markets. As you can see from Figure 1.3.3, when the equity market declined by 40 per cent in 2000–02, the Yale portfolio continued to generate positive returns every year, totalling over 30 per cent.

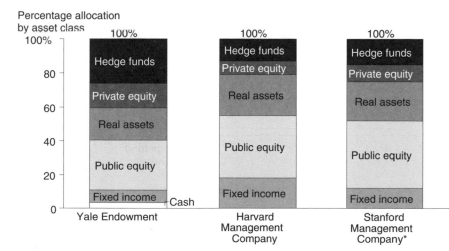

*Source:* 2004 Annual Report for Yale and SMC, 2005 Annual Report for HMC. HMC allocation ignores negative cash balance (borrowing) and pro-rates this to other asset classes. Stanford allocation is a target (vs actual for Yale and Harvard).

**Figure 1.3.2**  Allocation by asset class

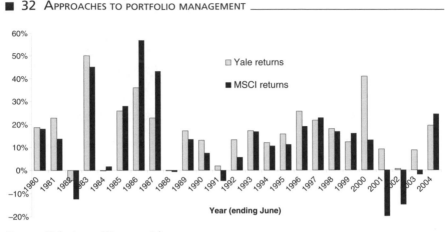

*Source:* Yale Annual Reports, Lipper.
*Notes:* World Equity returns are the MSCI world total return in USD.
**Figure 1.3.3** Historic growth rates of Yale Endowment and world equities

The 1986–2005 average annual performance for Yale was 16 per cent, in contrast to 11 per cent for the global equity market (as measured by the MSCI world index). Importantly, the range of returns for Yale has been much narrower, with no loss-making years in that 20-year period. As you can see from Figure 1.3.4, the US university endowments that follow this approach have significantly outperformed the equity market on its own, as well as the conventional 70 per cent equities and 30 per cent bond portfolio.

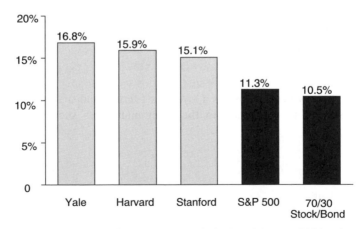

*Notes:* All performance data are for the 10-year period July 1994 – June 2004 and are nominal.
*Sources:* 2004 Annual Reports for Yale, HMC, SMC, S&P and Lehman Government Bond Index.
**Figure 1.3.4** Ten-year annualized returns (1994–2004)

## Rule 3: Invest in rigorous asset manager due diligence

The financial world is plagued with a raft of conflicts of interest and outright deceptions surrounding what may be truly sustainable performance. The grandest deception is that your private bank or financial adviser can pick stocks and bonds for you in a way that will consistently beat the market. Today, Warren Buffett is struggling even to do this and some of the smartest minds in the world fail to consistently beat the market. Most of those that do succeed with a better approach over a small number of years quickly attract such huge quantities of capital that they dilute their own efforts and ultimately revert to the mean, or worse. The truly smart asset managers refuse to take additional capital as they know that size is the enemy of high consistent returns. Hence the small numbers of great asset managers are often closed to new investment capital, and you and I will only ever gain access to them if we are there at the start, before they have proven they can do what they set out to do.

Identifying the asset managers that will outperform their peers requires a combination of art and science, rooted in years of experience and learning from good and bad decisions. The best asset managers cannot be chosen in isolation but must be grouped with relevant peers for direct comparison of their teams, strategies, past performance and risks. In performing due diligence on a given asset manager, specialists in, or ideally veterans of, each asset class must make these tough decisions, informed by a deep understanding of the specific sector of the investment world and the critical requirements for success in those sectors. The best asset managers will also be specialists in their asset class, will be passionate about their strategy and will have a significant portion of their own personal assets aligned with their performance.

## Rule 4: Secure access to the best asset managers through your network and the prospect of adding value to the asset managers

As suggested above, many if not most of the best proven asset managers are closed to new capital and new investors. Knowing who the best are is only half the battle. Access is the real challenge. Yale secures superior access simply because of who it is. The Yale Endowment represents a loyal, long-term, sophisticated investor that has the potential to contribute to the asset manager's success through its endorsement of that manager. Other leading investors will seek to emulate this approach by exploiting their personal relationships with asset managers and by being in some way value added to the asset manager. This value added can come in the form of providing the managers with investment ideas, opportunities or information. Or it can come in the form of strategic, financial and operational assistance to the newer asset manager. The alternative approach is to be exceptional at spotting talent in new asset managers and be at the door when it is opened for capital. Again, Yale and other leading investors seek to build such 'emerging manager' spotting capabilities to add to their manager stables.

> The result of deploying these four core principles is a stable of top-performing asset managers across a broadly diversified set of asset classes. This establishes a portfolio with a high degree of protection against a multitude of market scenarios but with the ability to generate relatively consistent year-on-year returns not overly dependent upon the broader equity market's performance.

## How can you deploy the Yale model?

Unfortunately, Yale is not yet managing money for investors such as you and me, unless we plan to leave it with them permanently. So how can we benefit from this approach today?

As you seek to employ the first of the Yale principles, distinguishing between investment strategy and asset management, you will quickly recognize that there are two layers of advisers in the investment world today: independent investment advisers who focus on asset allocation and asset manager selection, and asset managers who focus on specialist areas of picking individual securities. You should never hire asset managers to advise on asset allocation. Their asset allocation will naturally skew towards their area of expertise and they are unlikely to fire themselves if they underperform their peers. There are an increasing number of competent independent investment advisers who will follow the Yale model and can deploy it within your balance sheet with a stable of entirely independent asset managers. Your checklist for evaluating those advisers follows the four Yale principles:

## 1. Is the adviser truly independent of any asset managers?

They should not pick stocks, bonds, property or any other investment on their own. They should be selecting independent best-of-breed asset managers who have no economic affiliation with them. All of the large banks (Swiss as well as global investment banks) have large in-house asset management shops that swamp the profits of their private banking arms. The incentives for these banks will always lean in the direction of pitching their in-house products. To be guaranteed truly independent advice, look for advisers who are completely unaffiliated with asset managers.

The strong investment advisory firm will have great familiarity with mean-variance optimization tools for providing asset allocation recommendations.[2]

---

2. Most portfolio allocation decisions made by professional managers today rely on Harry Markowitz mean-variance optimization or variants of the method detailed in his book *Portfolio Selection: Efficient diversification of investment* (1959), John Wiley & Sons, New York. The results of mean-variance analysis are often presented in the context of the efficient frontier, which shows expected portfolio return as a strict function of risk. The approach relies on three quantitative inputs – asset returns, measurable asset risk and correlation between different assets.

Finally, any rebates, commissions or fee reductions that the adviser extracts from asset managers should go back to you to ensure the adviser's objectivity in asset manager selection.

## 2. Does the independent adviser's investment philosophy shy away from timing entry into and out of different asset classes, but rather seek to diversify across a broad array of unrelated asset classes over the long term?

Timing markets is a losing game. The financial markets are among the most competitive and efficient of markets. Yale has proven the value of not timing markets, but rather being in most asset classes with demonstrated long-term growth potential. The independent investment adviser's asset allocation toolkit should include allocation model inputs including expected returns, risk and cross-correlation of asset classes covering the five major asset classes and their sub-asset classes:

- Fixed income (focusing on government bonds).
- Public equities (long only):
  - European large-cap;
  - North American large-cap;
  - Asian large-cap;
  - global small-cap;
  - emerging markets.
- Hedge funds (all strategies).
- Private equity:
  - venture capital;
  - leveraged buyouts.
- Real assets:
  - commodities;
  - commercial property;
  - inflation-linked bonds.

## 3. Does the investment adviser have sufficient specialist analytical research resources covering all major asset classes, including hedge funds, private equity and real assets, as well as public equities and fixed income?

Many advisers will specialize in one asset class. Be certain the firm is of sufficient scale to have resources crossing all asset classes. It may have certain external strategic relationships that it can leverage to minimize resource requirements, such as funds of funds or family offices sharing research and manager recommendations with it. In Figure 1.3.5 we illustrate (with a typical asset allocation model) the breadth of asset class knowledge that an investment adviser must have in order to diversify you appropriately. Each of the five asset classes constitutes two or more sub-asset classes that diversify you within those asset classes.

## 4. Can the investment adviser truly gain access to many of the best and often closed asset managers?

This is the toughest and most important criterion. Size can often be the enemy of access as advisers try to place such large amounts of capital that they have to go to second-tier asset managers. While size is critical to fund internal research resources, it often dilutes quality. The ideal size of independent investment advisory firm therefore will be in the $1 billion to $4 billion range where it can afford sufficient internal staff, but not find itself with such large amounts of capital to place that it has to lower its quality threshold to put the capital to work.

But even the 'right-sized' investment adviser can struggle with access. Be certain to cross-check the quality of its stable of asset managers with third parties in the investment world who have insights into this area (family offices, private equity professionals, etc).

This screen will narrow down the field considerably, but the universe of strong independent advisers is growing rapidly to enlarge the field.

## Conclusion

You have worked hard to earn the wealth you hold. Fight the temptation to give in and hand your assets to the conflicted and economically misaligned traditional investment advisers merely because of their brand names and long histories. Trust your own judgement as a business person and ensure that you are properly

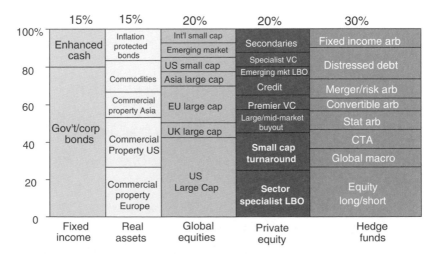

**Figure 1.3.5** Percentage allocation by asset class

advised by those independent firms that embrace the Yale model for all of its logical strengths and proven track record. I hope this chapter helps you down that path and sees your wealth protected and growing for your family today and for generations to follow.

# Portfolio construction and management

*Tony Munson, Fortis Private Investment Management*

## Introduction

This chapter considers the construction and management of a portfolio of financial assets within the context of your overall wealth management. You have a career, a salary that goes with it, perhaps a stake in your company, a property or two, various other assets and maybe even some expectation of an inheritance when dear Aunt Jemima sheds her mortal coil. You receive income from various sources – your salary, some interest, perhaps some dividends – and you have outgoings. Basically, you have a personal balance sheet and a P&L. And, hopefully, you have some plans: how you are going to progress your career and your business, how you are going to set the children up for life, what you are going to do when you retire and finally, because you can't take it with you, how you are going to pass on what is left in your estate when you are eventually reunited with Aunt Jemima.

So, where does a portfolio come into your planning? Well, the answer of course varies from individual to individual. You might be looking at building your own personal pension pot; you might have a trust fund for young Johnny; you might simply be looking for a better return on the funds you are accumulating – surely there must be something better than that derisory rate you are getting from your high street bank! We now have the two essential ingredients for a portfolio: financial needs to meet and assets to deploy to meet those needs. This leads us into the first major question: *what is the objective of the portfolio?* This is the expression of your investment strategy and is of fundamental importance; you wouldn't run a company without a business plan; without a plan you have nothing against which to measure its success or failure.

Within the portfolio objectives there are three key facets to consider: time horizon; risk/reward profile; and cash flow/income requirements. For a managed portfolio, these constitute the essential features of the investment mandate.

The second major question is: *what assets should form the portfolio?* Here, we are focusing on the range of financial assets most commonly used within investment portfolios. They can be classified in four major asset classes:

- cash;
- fixed interest securities;
- equities;
- alternatives.

The first three classes have been the traditional mainstays of the investor for decades. 'Alternatives' is a convenient box in which to hold those new kids on the block: hedge funds, private equity, property, structured products, commodities and so on.

## Investment process

Having set those two questions, we will explore some of the key issues involved in the construction and management of a portfolio. First, under the heading 'Methodology' we will remind ourselves of some of the approaches that will fundamentally influence the way a portfolio is run. Second, we will cover in broad outline asset allocation and stock selection. Third, we will look at how these work together in a portfolio. And finally we will look at some aspects of performance measurement and how that can be used in the management process.

You will often hear the style of investment process referred to as either 'top-down' or 'bottom-up'. These emphasize asset allocation and stock selection respectively. It should be borne in mind that both approaches must be reconciled and expressed in a portfolio. Our aim is simply to meet the investment objectives and we do this by stacking the odds of success in our favour. We adopt an appropriate asset allocation structure and we try to fill the portfolio with securities that will deliver the required performance.

## *Methodology*

There are two traditional schools of investment analysis: fundamental and technical. We can perhaps regard quantitative analysis as a third force:

- fundamental – detailed analysis of company data, and business environment;
- technical – chart-based approach;
- quantitative – intensive computer analysis of market data.

There are also two broad approaches to portfolio management: 1) modern portfolio theory (MPT); and 2) stockpicking. These terms should be readily understood except perhaps for MPT. In the 1950s, Harry Markowitz looked at how the risk of holding a number of securities could be reduced by considering the correlation between individual stock movements. The mathematics involved meant that it was impossible to put the theory into practice until fast computers became available. And until then, most investors built their portfolios by adding stocks they liked and selling stocks they didn't like.

Neither of these two approaches and none of the forms of analysis has any proven consistent superiority. Each has its drawbacks; there is no right path other than the one that suits you.

Most portfolio managers combine both approaches and will draw on each type of analysis. The degree to which they subscribe to each approach and the weight they ascribe to each type of analysis will determine not just the shape of the portfolio, but what drives change in the portfolio.

## Top-down: asset allocation and strategy

*This land is populated by people with high foreheads and very thick spectacles. They have very big computers. Their best friends are pension consultants and actuaries. When they get it right, it matters: most research suggests that asset allocation is the key determinant of performance. When they get it wrong, they huddle together under thick piles of academic research.*

Economic, business and market data are taken as inputs to an appraisal process that captures the salient features of the global economy from both a geographic and an industrial sector basis. Then an assessment is made of the likely performance of the various different asset classes under a range of likely future scenarios.

For example, the Japanese economy may appear to be emerging from a decade-long hibernation. How does this fit with the expansion of China? The likely path of oil prices? The demographics of a greying population that is not supplemented by immigration to anything like the extent of Western economies? Is inflation about to take off? How will this affect Japanese bonds, equities and the yen? The assessment may be negative on the yen and bond markets but more optimistic on the equity markets, perhaps favouring the larger capitalized exporters.

These views are captured in a matrix that, reduced to its simplest level, provides a positive, neutral or negative stance for each asset class. And these stances will be translated into overweight, neutral or underweight positions in the portfolio. At this point you might wonder 'Overweight relative to *what*?' The short answer is: relative to an asset allocation structure that accords with your long-term investment strategy – your neutral strategic asset allocation position.

At this stage, we have a long-term neutral portfolio strategy with weights in various asset classes, let's say 40–60 per cent UK equities and 40–60 per cent UK government stock (gilts) with 50 per cent in each class taken as the long-term neutral position. Let's also assume that we believe gilts are currently poor value and that equities offer better value over the next 12 months. Those views translate to negative and positive stances respectively and we may take a tactical asset allocation decision to adopt portfolio weights of 55 per cent UK equities and 45 per cent gilts.

We now have a matrix of weights for our chosen assets that is consistent with both our strategic objectives and our current view of the prospects for those asset classes. What remains is to select securities to populate that matrix.

# Bottom-up: stock selection

*This land is populated by people with a knowing look. There are two castes, one a rather hairy people, the Rolexei, the other a rather saintly people, the Gurui. When they get things right, they are hailed as gods. When things go wrong, they are expelled from the land and quickly forgotten.*

There are countless thousands of securities listed on the various exchanges around the world. From these, we need to select those that will make up the portfolio. How one sets about that task depends on the chosen investment policy.

The investment policy may be passive. At its simplest, this means selecting an asset mix that meets the investment strategy and not changing that mix unless the strategy changes. In this case, the stock selection process is straightforward. The aim will be to purchase securities that offer the most direct and cost-effective means by which to gain exposure to the chosen asset classes. This is the realm of the trackers, typified in the past by mutual fund and unit trust managers who would seek to replicate the performance of an index (the extent to which they fail to match the performance of the index is termed the 'tracking error'). Recent years have seen the advent of exchange traded funds (ETFs) that minimize the tracking error, leaving cost as the main selection criterion.

If the investment policy is active, it can be active in several ways: greater emphasis on market timing, shorter-term trades, taking active 'bets' against the long-term strategic benchmark at the asset or sector level and simply by seeking to 'pick winners'. And each of these involves stock selection combined with ongoing monitoring.

At Fortis we adopt an approach that will serve to illustrate the stock selection process. For each asset class a reference list of securities is established, each subdivided as necessary. For example, the fixed interest list is split into currency bands, government and corporate, by credit rating and yield. For equities, the splits are by region, country and industrial sector. Separate reference lists are maintained for collective instruments across different asset classes.

Those reference lists are populated by filtering out from the enormous number of available securities those that are most likely to suit our clients' needs. They will include most benchmark government stocks, major corporate bonds and leading equities (some 800 globally). The lists are supplemented by further securities that our analysts believe have compelling merit, in the case of equities perhaps growth prospects that appear to be undervalued by the market, and in the case of fixed interest securities perhaps a corporate bond with an inappropriate credit rating.

The constituents of the reference lists are subject to constant monitoring of price action and news flow, supplemented by company meetings – and, for collectives, scheduled meetings with fund managers.

The reference list constituents change relatively infrequently and form a working universe. A final filtering process undertaken on a very regular basis selects from the reference lists those securities we currently favour and these are used to create 'focus' lists, the core building blocks of 'best ideas' for the portfolio manager.

## Putting it together: running the portfolio

*This land is populated by people with good intentions. They look rather like you and me. When things go well, that's business as usual. When things go wrong, they blame the others.*

How many securities should you have in your portfolio? Well, that obviously depends to an extent on the asset allocation designed to meet your investment objectives. But more significantly, it depends on your risk profile; diversification is the aim or, as your granny said, 'Don't put all your eggs in one basket.' It also depends on whether you are using individual securities or collective instruments that may each hold 50 or more securities. For equities, studies have shown that much of the riskiness of a portfolio can be diversified away with as few as 10–15 securities. The reduction in risk from going much beyond 50 holdings is small. The benefits in risk reduction by holding a large number of securities should be balanced against the transaction costs that are inversely linked to the size of each holding.

What structure should be adopted? Revisit the investment strategy and the asset allocation parameters and assess the specific requirements:

■ Are there any tax considerations that may suggest a particular structure or vehicle should be used or that will cause specific securities to be more or less tax-efficient?

■ Are there any currency considerations?

■ What level of cash yield is required? This is likely to affect the balance between fixed interest and equities.

■ What instruments are permitted or prohibited?

■ To what extent should collectives rather than individual securities be used? This may be driven by the size of the portfolio, but also by the need to obtain sufficient diversity in smaller segments of the portfolio. For example, strategy may dictate 3 per cent of the portfolio is held in Chinese stocks but that might translate to the choice of a single risky holding or a fund that holds a much greater number of stocks.

■ What is the risk tolerance? Again, this will affect the balance between equities and fixed interest stocks, but also whether higher-yielding bonds with lower credit ratings may be used, whether smaller company exposure is warranted, whether alternative investments should be included and, again, whether collective vehicles should be used.

■ Is the investment aim a relative or an absolute one?

■ Are there any ongoing tax considerations such as capital gains tax that should be taken into account?

The quintessential lazy way of managing a portfolio is to adopt a 'buy and hold' approach. There are only two things in its favour: 1) the costs of management are low; and 2) you avoid the danger of making decisions based on market 'noise' or short-term movements.

Against this approach is the simple fact that a portfolio that was constructed in the light of one set of market conditions and expectations must surely be re-examined, and if necessary adjusted, in the face of change.

The balance between action and inaction is important. In practice this typically results in changes at the asset allocation level being made less frequently than at the individual security level. The drivers for change will be both top-down and bottom-up, typically top-down driven by reconsideration of macroeconomic factors and bottom-up driven by reappraisal of individual securities – perhaps following a company's results.

The portfolio manager will need to review the portfolio on a regular basis to ensure that it reflects the current top-down views, that the securities held in the portfolio are sound both individually and collectively and, above all, that the portfolio is doing its job of performing in line with the agreed strategy.

## Performance measurement

There are three periods over which to measure the performance of the portfolio:

∎ Long-term – is the portfolio on track to meet its strategic objectives?
∎ Medium-term – how is the portfolio currently performing?
∎ Short-term – how are the individual securities performing?

This is a rather artificial scheme, but serves to bring out some salient points.

For the long-term, the portfolio must be monitored to ensure that it is still aligned with the strategy. There are two sides to this coin: both the portfolio and the strategy itself should be reappraised from time to time. Depending on the overall aims, strategy should not need to be revisited more frequently than annually.

Short-term measurements may be week to week or even intra-day. What is being measured will depend on the particular approach being taken. A technical approach may flag a security whose price momentum is falling or where a significant chart level has been achieved; a quantitative system may trigger a raft of signals following an unexpected interest rate move; a fundamental system may simply report a change in view following a company meeting.

The medium-term is when the main performance measurement takes place, often performed quarterly or half-yearly.

Given that you have adopted a benchmark by which to gauge your portfolio's performance, you have a simple calculation to perform: subtract the portfolio return from the benchmark return and look at the result. If it is positive the portfolio did well; if it is negative it didn't. Simple. But hold on – what exactly do we mean by the portfolio return? Well, the return on an investment may come from two sources: income or capital, and often both. The combination of the two is known as the total return. So we measure our portfolio return on a total return basis and make sure that we are comparing apples with apples by choosing an appropriate total return benchmark. And if we have outperformed – that's good. But how good is it? How much risk did we have to take to achieve that return? Was it consistent with the mandate? If not, then how bad might things get when the portfolio underperforms? We should really consider our risk-adjusted return, but that is a story for another time.

The medium-term performance measurement presents an opportunity to take a deeper look at how the underlying constituents are performing. The overall return can be disaggregated at the asset class level, the sector level and right down to the individual security, so that you can see the contribution made by each constituent to the total. That's interesting, but by performing a similar exercise on the benchmark itself you can compare the equivalent returns in an attribution analysis. This will show, for example, just how much of the portfolio return was due to a stance taken at the asset allocation level, how much from sector strategy and how much from stock selection. Used properly, performance measurement is an essential part of a feedback loop that starts with strategy and ends with delivery.

## Wealth warning

There is no shortage of people selling their products and services in the investment markets. One of the greatest dangers facing any investor is to get drawn into the latest investment fad. The book *Extraordinary Popular Delusions and the Madness of Crowds* written by Charles Mackay over 150 years ago should be required reading.

The underlying principle of this chapter is basically the same as that we adopt at Fortis: the portfolio you have, and the way it is managed, must centre on *your* needs.

# Creating and preserving wealth – advisory and discretionary portfolios

*Simon Gibson, Atkinson Bolton Consulting Ltd*

Within any handbook such as this, the reader can expect to find very worthy, and often weighty, views on everything from investment markets to tax considerations, from charitable giving to starting a business. As a reader, I would personally not be without that content – it is all a vital part of personal wealth management. However, there is a place for a more light-hearted chapter, albeit with a serious message, and I'd like to think this is it. In an attempt to deliver this to you, I shall use the analogy of making arrangements for, and indeed booking and taking, a holiday, combining the elements of service and delivery that are part of both an advisory and a discretionary portfolio. It is *not* the case that one is necessarily better than the other, just different.

## Where are you trying to get to for this holiday?

This might seem completely unrelated to the topic. However, over 20 years or so of advising private clients, I have found that many people are trying to get somewhere, often somewhere quite specific, but are simply not starting from a place that has any hope of delivering them there, or they have not given due consideration to all of the possibilities on the journey. In the analogy, this might mean they are in the car park at Stansted Airport, but that their plane flies from Manchester, in two hours'

# Thoroughbred Wealth Management™

## Creating and Preserving Wealth

**Thoroughbred Wealth Management™ is a comprehensive service, designed to assist our clients in the creation and preservation of their wealth.** The service is individual, personalised, and bespoke for each client, and works for and with individuals, companies, pension schemes and trusts. It is a focused approach to the management of our clients' wealth.

*"**Atkinson Bolton Consulting** is one of the most progressive, professional and diligent advisory businesses that we have come across operating in the UK financial services market place today. Their 'client focused' approach is consistent with our own and it has been a pleasure to deal with them and watch their company develop."*
**Leading UK Fund Management Group**

*"Very personal, friendly and professional service has been provided over several years."* **Private Client, Norfolk**

*"We are pleased to be with **ABC** and have confidence in the way our portfolio is being dealt with. It is also gratifying to see their personal service continuing as they expand."*
**Private Client, Suffolk**

*"Since first allowing **Atkinson Bolton** to handle our investments a few years ago, we have been more than satisfied with the advice and the return on our investments. It has allowed us to retire in comfort, and without any money worries."*
**Private Client, Scotland**

*"In the short time that we have been involved with **Atkinson Bolton**, we feel confident that our financial affairs are under control. In particular, the investment expertise shown has impressed us."* **Private Client, London**

**Thoroughbred** Wealth Management™ is a trademark of **Atkinson Bolton Consulting Ltd**

Cheveley House, Fordham Road, Newmarket, Suffolk, CB8 7XN
**Tel: 0845 458 1223**
www.atkinsonbolton.co.uk          info@atkinsonbolton.co.uk

time. So, the first thing to sort out is where they are and then where they are trying to get to. This can occasionally cause short-term pain, but is worth it every time when you see the look of delight on their arrival.

Next, we need to establish, assuming they are not do-it-yourself backpackers, the finer points of the service they expect, risks that they are prepared to take whilst travelling, and all of the other related 'baggage', not forgetting the ideal itinerary. First, let us understand what are the main differences before considering, for both options, the things to look out for.

## Advisory

In the analogy, the advisory portfolio service is essentially that of the normal travel agent – you can look at all of the holiday brochures you like (coming back to investing, this means fund fact sheets, adverts quoting performance figures, articles about fund managers, tip sheets, etc), but, as a traveller, you will be looking for someone at least to hold your hand, to talk you through why you want what you think you want and then, most importantly, to help you get what you want. If anything changes or needs amending, then you need the travel agent to help. It may be at the travel agent's behest that the change happens, it may be needed as a result of changed circumstances, positive or negative, or it may simply be that what you wanted hasn't been or can't be delivered. Throughout, however, you will have to confirm each action and respond to each request to take action, and all because your advisory fund manager (AFM) cannot act without your explicit agreement. Again, not necessarily a bad thing, just different.

## Discretionary

If not a 'normal' travel agent, then what? Well, if such a thing exists, the holiday equivalent of a personal shopper or, in business, the business planning guru – you can't literally do nothing, but you are handing over all of your requirements to the specialist, who will 'make it happen'. You may not speak the 'language' needed for your journey (through the investment markets), but your discretionary fund manager (DFM) will be 'multilingual', as well as being well versed in changing the jargon into your own language. With the AFM you get a huge pack of documents at every stage; you will never move without knowing the next step. With the DFM, you will get less paperwork regularly, but will receive, if you like, an 'executive summary' of what's been going on, as well as up-to-the-minute advice about what might be around the corner. This leads on to my favourite part of the analogy (can you see me smiling?), the nature of the itinerary, and indeed how we got to that point.

# When you go on holiday, is it on a whim or with at least some thought?

For most people, of course, the latter is the case, and that is where I concentrate in this section. When I use this analogy with clients (which is not just written for this chapter, but often forms a part of my description in initial client meetings), I ask: *what do you expect or need to know about the 'journey'?* Clients say:

■ I need to know whether I am in a five-star or a three-star hotel – either is fine, but I need to have my expectations managed (I don't expect to pay the same, or receive the same benefits).

■ How long can I expect this journey to be? Indeed, how long do I want it to be, before reaching my destination?

■ How comfortable will I be? What is the mode of transport – is there more than one? Will you switch between modes of transport if appropriate? Will I have to agree or, as the specialist, will you make the necessary arrangements with the minimum of fuss for me (and those travelling with me – families often take these journeys together)?

■ Will you have checked with the appropriate department about the risks involved in the proposed journey?

■ If something does go wrong, is there a parachute? Are you the only pilot, or is there an experienced co-pilot, with a great team backing you up?

■ Are there any local taxes I should know about? If so, when are they due, and how much might they be?

■ I expect to know a little about the reputation of all parties involved, including you as my adviser on this journey.

■ Will I need sun cream and, if so, which factor? Can I buy postcards there?

■ What if I want to take a break during my journey?

■ Even if all is going well (which I set out expecting!), I would like regular updates on the progress.

Do these seem fair enough to you? What's that? Enough of the holiday analogy – tell me what it means? Fair enough – please read on...

## Managing expectations

This may even come down to you, the investor, and how much time you have or wish to spend on the portfolio. How 'pampered' do you want to be? There are great AFMs and great DFMs – both can keep you happy, but you must understand (and they must glean from you at the very first opportunity) what your expectations are.

### Time frame

How long have I got? There must always be a time frame – it could be quite specific (must be available for me to do what I want to do in 2012, when I retire, just in time to watch every single minute of the London Olympics), or vague (it's a long-term portfolio, at least 10 years). There may of course be a mix of elements here, so timing is vital.

## Asset allocation – yes, no or maybe?

An 'ordinary' AFM may well say 'no', or even 'maybe'. I believe that anyone worth his or her salt, specializing in investments, must be prepared to discuss and implement an asset allocation over your portfolio. Whether this is some computer-generated, back-tested, multiple choice version, or a very personal option, I say the answer should be 'yes' every time. Otherwise, why is the advice being sought? This leads on neatly to the next point.

## Risk

Absolutely, definitely, completely and utterly *not* 'What's your risk then, between 1 and 10?' An appropriate amount of thought must be given to the conditions, both of the client and of the market(s) being considered. In addition, the link between this and timescales must be made. I am personally a high-risk investor, in my own terminology. But I would add the rider 'currently'; when I am 75 and in full retirement, probably with my 'earning potential' at an end, I suspect I will be somewhere nearer a 'balanced or balanced/cautious' chap.

## Taxation

Of course, we must not let the tax tail wag the investment dog but, without consideration, more harm than good might be done by either the advisory or the discretionary fund manager. It may well be that other professionals are needed (our firm works very closely with excellent accountants, solicitors and other specialist professionals, such as land agents), and it would indeed be unusual if at least one were not involved with each of our clients at least annually.

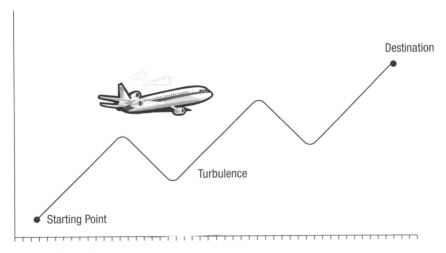

**Figure 1.5.1**   Know where you are going

## Back-up if something happens to the adviser, plus how do you do what you do?

It is unlikely, as you read this, that you are contemplating investing your £50,000 or indeed £5,000,000 with either an advisory or a discretionary 'adviser' or fund manager who has no back-up – maybe a one-person firm. This is absolutely *not* to say that this person would not do a great job for you, most of the time. However, despite all of the advantages of the 'personal touch', the local nature of the business and possibly even other synergies, you will surely want to know the strength of the support system, for when something goes awry, as it undoubtedly will. So what should this look like? We believe that there must be at least two individuals capable of providing you with the investment advice, and at least two people backing *each* of those two. We also think that being able to tell a client how we do what we do is essential – we do it every day; it is like second nature to us. But, going back to managing expectations, if our client doesn't understand, we may disappoint in the future.

I head an investment committee within our business. We do all of our own in-depth research; indeed, in our words, we like to 'look into the whites of their eyes' when we meet people in whose companies or funds we may be considering investing. The investment committee is made up of five individuals, at least two of whom, in some cases three, have to be present for actions or recommendations to be implemented. This is regardless of whether we are dealing with an advisory or a discretionary client.

Finally in this section, whom will you see, as the investor? Will you only see the investment manager, or will it be a 'client relationship manager', or someone else? It doesn't necessarily matter, as long as you are comfortable with the person concerned. Make sure you 'get on' early on; this is important – you don't want just to 'put up' with someone with whom you can't connect.

## The 'soft' facts

You should expect to be asked, and you should be prepared to provide the answers to, many questions aimed at eliciting some 'soft' as well as the hard facts. Hard-fact questions include 'How long?', 'How much?' and 'How frequently?' Soft facts are more likely to be found in answer to the questions 'What if?' and 'Suppose' or 'Can you see a situation when?'

## Things change…

As referred to in the previous point, 'What if' really does become 'Now that so-and-so has happened', and you need to be prepared. If you keep all of your eggs in one basket, it had better be a strong one! Cash is a very valuable part of any portfolio – it must simply be managed as one would manage any other asset (and be kept in appropriate proportions based on timescales and risk strategy).

# Communication

'When will I see you again?' should not be a question you should have to ask. I will talk a little about personal service standards and expectations in a moment. Suffice it to say that your AFM or DFM should be in contact with you as regularly as required based on your expectations and the agreed parameters, and you should agree what this will 'look' like before a single investment has been made.

# Personal service – just what can you expect?

You need to know about efficiency, ease (or otherwise) of administration, and what service standards can be expected. It is one thing to know that your portfolio has risen by 11.2 per cent this year. It is quite another to know that you will get a response when you write, call or e-mail, that you will understand the report you have received, because it looks and 'feels' like those you've had each time, and that it is written in plain English. Go one stage further; see if you can find world-class service, to go alongside the fantastic fund manager that you have found to invest and manage your money. It can all be part of the same experience; great service and great fund management are not mutually exclusive.

# How do I choose then? What are the differentiating factors?

I don't have the answer to that question for certain, but I can tell you what I and my colleagues do. As you will have read in the title to this chapter, we believe in creating and preserving wealth. Every element of what we do is encompassed in that belief. We try to provide world-class service – yes, occasionally it slips, but if it slips from world-class it is usually still much better than the service of those that have 'good service' as their highest aim. Finally, don't believe the hype. Make sure that the people you deal with are grounded in reality, as I think our company is. One of my favourite expressions when explaining to a client how we will deal with those little (sometimes big) unexpected changes in fortune is 'I am 100 per cent honest, and right as often as possible.'

# Part 2

# Selective investment from securities alternatives

# Alternative investments and risk in securities

*Cathy Dixon, Cunningham Coates*

## Introduction

Over the past 20 years the investment world has changed beyond all recognition. The City regarded 'Big Bang', which took place in October 1986, as a step into the unknown. Essentially, it was brought about by changes in the rules of the Stock Exchange when fixed commissions were abolished, precipitating a complete restructuring of the stock market. For the first time the relatively closed world was opened up to outside ownership, and firms that had been trading under the same name for decades were taken over by large international corporations. There was a frenzy of takeovers, with the great divide between stockjobbers and stockbrokers being bridged as they came together to operate under the same corporate umbrella.

It was the start of major changes to the UK's main financial centre. The ground-breaking Financial Services Act 1986 heralded a complete change in the way the investment industry is regulated, and since then this has been developed further, with closer and more structured monitoring. This has resulted in the birth of a completely new industry in the last 20 years. The actual mechanics of stock market trading have also changed out of all recognition. Long gone are the days of the Stock Exchange trading floor: nowadays dealing is all done on an electronic basis and location makes no difference.

As well as structural changes this marked the start of a more subtle but nevertheless dramatic shift in investment. The flotation of the first tranche of British Telecom in 1984 (BT1) heralded the start of the expansion of share ownership from the privileged few to a much wider base. This widening of share ownership has continued apace, through numerous utility privatizations and building society demutualizations and on to the tech boom at the end of the 20th century. However, even the stock market correction in 2000 and the subsequent three-year bear market did not halt the inexorable change in attitude to risk. Investors' increased appetite for risk has developed over the last two decades and has been equally reflected in the variety of stock market investment vehicles available to individual investors. The risk spectrum used to range from cash to equities, but with so many derivative instruments the relative risk of equities is perceived to be lower.

# Cash

Although there are numerous definitions pertaining to risk, there are few people who would dispute that cash is the ultimate in carrying minimal capital risk. It does, of course, face inflation, which erodes its value over time, but the safety aspect is clearly very appealing as part of any individual's investment planning. As a very basic rule of thumb it is important to have sufficient cash to cover short-term needs that might arise, such as the washing machine breaking down. We have experienced a period of low inflation and also low interest rates, which means that the return on cash on deposit is currently relatively low in terms of real return (interest after inflation); with a base rate of 5.25 per cent and the retail price index standing at 3.6 per cent real return is a modest 1.95 per cent.

# Gilts

Next up the risk spectrum are gilt-edged stocks, commonly known as gilts. These are bonds issued by the UK government and are generally regarded as high-quality investments, just as the name implies. Conventional gilts can be issued over a range of time periods, classified as shorts if they have a redemption date up to five years away, mediums if they have five to 10 years to run, and long gilts if they have over 10 years. There are also undated gilts, which have no maturity date; they could theoretically be redeemed if the government is able to obtain financing at a lower cost, but in practice the undated stocks usually pay a low rate of interest. The best known of these is probably the 3.5 per cent War Loan, which was originally issued in the First World War. The rate of interest or coupon of a gilt very much reflects interest rates at the time of issue; one of the most recent issues was Treasury 4 per cent 2016.

Gilts are traded on the London Stock Exchange, which means that the price can go up and down. More recently there has been a high demand from pension funds that have sought to reduce their risk/liability ratio, and prices have therefore been driven up, resulting in the majority of stocks trading at a level above par, the value at which they will be redeemed. The inclusion of gilts in an investment portfolio is important; they offer a fixed return, capital protection and a far lower level of volatility than equities. There are also benefits, such as their exemption from capital gains tax, but their inclusion in personal equity plans and individual savings accounts (PEPs and ISAs) is subject to them having a redemption date longer than five years at the time of purchase.

The yield curve shown in Figure 2.1.1, which shows the yield plotted against maturity, indicates the return that will be received depending on the maturity of the bond. The price of gilts is strongly influenced by interest rates and expectations surrounding interest rates; at a basic level, if interest rates go up gilt prices should go down (all other things being equal).

In 1981 the government issued a new type of gilt, one linked to the inflation rate: index-linked gilts. Arguably, these have an even lower risk than cash; both income payments and capital repayment are linked to the rate of inflation, as measured by the retail price index. In theory you are all but guaranteed a real return from 'linkers' but they are still subject to price fluctuations, influenced primarily by inflation expectations.

## Bonds

In addition to UK government-issued bonds there are a number of other debt instruments. They are a contract to pay the holder a fixed principal amount on a stated future date and (usually) interest payments during its life. When a company issues debt, it is termed a corporate bond and essentially is a method whereby the company can borrow funds. There is a higher inherent risk with these bonds, as compared with government debt, as they are more dependent on the operating environment and the standing of the issuing company; thus corporate bonds usually offer a higher rate of interest than gilts, which increases as the perceived risk rises. For the purposes of assessment, corporate bonds are graded in terms of quality by various credit agencies. Traditionally, they have been less well used in the UK but, with the low interest rate environment and favourable changes in accountancy rules, they have been growing in popularity, although liquidity in some issues can still be a problem.

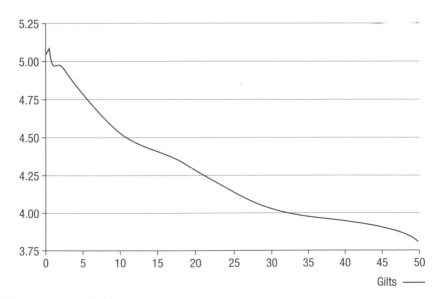

**Figure 2.1.1**   Yield curve

There is another type of bond which, conversely, has been falling in popularity: the convertible bond. This is a sort of halfway house between equities and bonds, as it gives the option to convert the debt into equity at regular intervals throughout its life and ultimately it will be converted at a fixed ratio or redeemed. This type of bond is assessed in terms of future income streams as to whether it is worth converting and in particular its impact on the capital value of the ordinary shares, but it is somewhat complex to value, being a hybrid, and the market has shrunk as other forms of derivatives take its place.

## Collective funds

Collective funds can fall into any category of risk, depending on the constitution of the underlying investments. They can be closed-ended (usually investment trusts) or open-ended (unit trusts or open-ended investment companies – OEICs). Collective investment vehicles pool the money of individual investors to provide a spread of risk by investing in a range of securities. They may have a fairly wide brief, such as global growth, or they may be confined to a narrower field, such as a particular sector of the market; for example, there are trusts that invest in biotechnology or energy. They may also cover a range of different investment instruments, from bonds to equities to derivatives. They are a useful way of gaining investment exposure to areas that are specialized or outside an adviser's area of expertise; overseas markets, for example, or small companies are often used to complement a diversified UK equity portfolio. The managers of such funds often build up a reputation over many years and are a vital factor in deciding the fund in which to invest. Performance figures are published on all collective funds and ratings are given to individual funds, all of which help in the decision-making process.

The essential difference between investment trusts and unit trusts or OEICs is that investment trusts are listed companies on the Stock Exchange and shares in them are bought and sold in the usual way. Unit trusts and OIECs are priced only once a day and dealt through the manager, and they can often be divided into income and accumulation units, referring to the amount of dividend that is paid out. Structures vary and can be very complex, but the most important factor is performance over the longer term.

## Equities

As already intimated, shares are more widely held now than they have ever been and are no longer the province of the privileged few. Ordinary shareholders are in essence the owners of the company, but although the shares usually carry voting rights they also carry with them an element of risk and rank below most other forms of debt and equity (such as preference shares) in the event of insolvency and assets being distributed. Thus in theory shareholders could face losing their entire investment, although in practice this is the extreme exception rather than the rule.

There is no doubt that equities carry risk with them: the warnings that shares go down as well as up are everywhere now, and this was only too obvious in 2000 when the technology bubble finally burst. Managing risk is seen as an important component in the overall management of a portfolio. Total risk can be divided into two categories. Specific or unsystematic risk relates to the variability in the returns of an investment as a result of factors specific to that investment only and can be significantly reduced by diversification across the various sectors and stocks. Market or systematic risk relates to general market influences leading to volatility in the investment and indeed in all investments. This cannot be eliminated, but it can be mitigated by focusing on areas where considerable experience and expertise are offered, thus reducing the impact as much as possible. Although the risk may act as a deterrent for some potential investors, it is the attraction of the long-term returns that equities have traditionally shown that continues to draw investors. The opportunity of a short-term gain is also an attraction, particularly for those investors looking to trade the market.

The other very important distinction between fixed interest instruments, such as gilts or bonds, and equities is the rate of dividends paid. Companies determine how much they pay out in terms of dividends and it is usual for a successful company to have a progressive dividend policy whereby the amount paid out increases on an annual basis. This is not guaranteed, but it can provide protection against inflation if the payment exceeds the rate of price increases. Strong growth in the rate of dividend paid is usually reflected in a growing share price.

The London stock market is one of the most highly developed on a global basis and provides a very effective framework through which to trade shares. The largest 100 companies constitute the FTSE 100 index, the most high profile measure of the market. These stocks are highly liquid and equally a huge volume of information about them is in the public domain. The next 250 companies in terms of size make up the FTSE 250, which are also reasonably liquid and well researched by analysts. At the smaller end of the market there are more opportunities to identify a stock that is not factoring in its prospects, but along with the potential greater returns comes a higher degree of risk. Smaller companies are not as well researched as the larger end of the market and often information is only released when results are announced.

The alternative to a main market listing is the Alternative Investment Market (AIM), which is specifically targeted at the smaller end of the market and is renowned worldwide for having a regulatory framework that is uniquely suited to smaller companies. It is much more flexible than the main market in that it does not stipulate minimum requirements for company size, track record, number of shares in public hands or market capitalization. Its success – a number of companies actively choose AIM rather than a main market listing – is indicative of the increasing appetite for risk amongst investors.

The whole subject of equities is vast and somewhat complex; discussing methods of evaluation could fill a book by itself. In addition, the stock market is prone to very subjective influences, but this often results in opportunities rather than limitations. Frequently, there is a 'herd' mentality amongst professional investors, but the way to make money is often to move against the tide.

## Exchange traded funds

A relatively new financial vehicle, exchange traded funds (ETFs) are essentially index funds that are traded like securities on stock exchanges. They have expanded to cover a number of areas, including a range of indices, both UK and abroad, as well as soft and hard commodities. They have several advantages in that they avoid many of the charges levied by unit trust/OEIC managers and yet spread risk in the same way. They also cover a variety of markets and hence may vary in terms of risk profile.

## Traded options

These are among the oldest forms of derivatives, with the traded options market established in 1978. A traded option offers the right, but not the obligation, to buy or sell a specific number of shares at a specified price at a specific date. An investor can buy calls (the right to buy) or puts (the right to sell) in a number of stocks, which include most of the FTSE 100 shares and others (usually ex-FTSE 100 stocks). In practice the right to buy or sell is rarely exercised and those using the traded options market tend to use it when, for example, they expect the price of a particular share to rise and, rather than buying the underlying shares, for a much smaller consideration they can participate in the increase (and gear up) by buying call options. The risk is theoretically lower than buying underlying shares, as the amount of money that could be lost is limited to the premium paid for the option. Options trading can be more complex, as there are a number of different strategies that can be devised as well as writing (or selling) options. The latter can result in unlimited losses if the price moves sharply against the investor, a point illustrated in 1987 when an individual incurred a debt well into seven figures through options trading. They can also be used to reduce risk by hedging or guarding against an adverse share price movement.

## Futures

Futures work on a very similar principle to traded options, as an investor pays for the right to buy or sell at some point in the future, but rather than individual stocks it usually relates to commodities, market indices, gilts, interest rates and bonds. Futures are traded on the London International Financial Futures Exchange (LIFFE) and are really aimed at the larger institutional investors.

## Hedge funds

Hedge funds are a more recent phenomenon; hedge fund managers use aggressive strategies such as short selling and derivatives to target absolute performance. Although in theory such funds utilize strategies to reduce risk, they are not subject to the same regulatory controls as most other investment vehicles and lack transparency. In addition, they tended to perform well when they first came into being, mostly at the beginning of the century, but since the marketplace has become more crowded performance has notably languished.

## Contracts for difference

Another relatively new investment instrument, the contract for difference (CFD) is aimed at sophisticated investors who want to have extra leverage in their share trading. Instead of paying for share trades in full, a margin is deposited with a broker and that margin will go up or down in line with the rise and fall of the share portfolio. In effect it enables investors to speculate with more capital than they actually have by borrowing money to purchase a larger amount of shares.

## Conclusion

The above account by no means covers an exhaustive range of investment instruments; nowadays the most sophisticated trader is well catered for together with the more conservative investor. There is little doubt that appetite for risk amongst both institutional and retail investors has risen sharply over the past two decades, but there is little evidence that the use of such complex instruments dramatically changes gains over the long term. In short, there are few substitutes for good advice and thorough research into the best means of investment to suit the individual.

# independent, agile & proactive investment management

**TAYLOR YOUNG**
*Investment Management*

## SERVICING THE NEEDS OF OUR CLIENTS
Private Clients, Trusts, Charities, SIPPs, SSASs, Private Offices

Wealth Preservation
Income Generation
Wealth Creation

Absolute Return Portfolios -
Combining the traditional and the alternative

Balanced, Income, Growth and Opportunistic Portfolios -
Single or multiple asset classes UK and International markets

---

For further information please contact the Chief Investment Officer at
Taylor Young Investment Management Limited,

Tower Bridge Court, 224-226 Tower Bridge Road, London, SE1 2UL.

Telephone: 020 7378 4500  Fax: 020 7378 4501
Email: invest@tyim.co.uk

Website: www.tayloryoung.com

# Thematic investment management

*Nicholas Rundle, Taylor Young Investment Management*

One of the core investment beliefs at Taylor Young Investment Management is in thematic investment – we believe that, by identifying themes and investing in companies relevant to those themes, we will be able, over the medium term, to outperform market indices. Investment themes naturally come in various shapes and forms; for example, the emergence in economic significance of China and India as potential global superpowers over the past five years has had a major impact on international capital markets, particularly in the form of increased demand for primary mineral resources such as iron ore and coal. Companies exposed to this area have benefited from this strength in demand, and their share prices have tended to appreciate. Another more specialist theme is the trend for major companies to outsource many of their activities, particularly in areas such as IT, catering, customer service and payroll activities. This has led to increased valuations being attributed to a number of companies with expertise in these areas as business levels over the past five years have increased incrementally.

The above are two macroeconomic examples of investment themes. By their very nature, such themes are not short-term in duration, and it is particularly important to be able to identify them and maintain confidence in them, given the amount of volatility that exists in the capital markets of today. It is also part of the job of a thematic investment manager to re-examine these themes on a regular basis and evaluate whether any fundamentals have changed that could render a theme either less or more attractive as an investment proposition. One of the major advantages of a focused thematic investment process is that it enables the investment manager to concentrate on a narrower range of stocks than a conventional investment manager would necessarily need to do. For example, there may be a large number of relatively large stocks within an index that do not suit the most important thematic considerations that are in place when constructing an investment portfolio at that time. Although a watching brief is necessarily kept on these stocks, a lot of time may be saved by concentrating on what is important within a relatively narrow range of stocks and not spreading one's investment universe too broadly.

It is for this reason that we at Taylor Young believe that a focused thematic investment approach should, over time, be more successful in outperforming a general benchmark index than a process that to some extent necessarily replicates the various index weights of the stocks within that index. Of course, given the fact that a thematic portfolio will necessarily be more concentrated in nature, it is possible that there will be more volatility of performance against a fixed benchmark index, but it is to be hoped that, over time, the positives from the process will outweigh any short-term negatives that may be experienced. It is also the case that a truly thematic investment process is the domain of only a relatively small number of investment managers. Most investors who opt for an actively managed portfolio are seeking a return over and above that of an index by the very selection of this active management process. However, it is generally observed to be the case that most managers adopting a portfolio strategy of, to a large extent, replicating index weighting of stocks in the portfolio will most likely underperform that index over time owing to frictional costs such as the payment of commissions, stamp duty and the buy/sell spread experienced when dealing. Thematic investment cannot offset these costs, but the longer timescale that a thematic investor possesses can mean that trading is less frequent.

In order to appreciate the impact that a thematic investment process can make on the management of an investment portfolio, it is perhaps helpful to examine in closer detail a key investment theme that Taylor Young has pursued for the past three years and continues to support. This is our belief in the investment attractions of companies involved in the investment and development of real estate. Why have we been so positive on this area for the past three years? There are a number of reasons.

## Institutional diversification

First, large investment funds, including pension funds, have been under some pressure from their actuaries and fund advisers to diversify their asset base, which was previously heavily biased towards equities. In the 1970s and 1980s, funds typically held well over 10 per cent of their assets in direct property but, over time and given the long bull equity market that developed from the mid-1970s until 1999, the percentage of their portfolios invested in property had tended to diminish. Similarly, the overall size of the quoted sector within the overall market fell and, given the rise of benchmarking against industrial sectors, overall exposure towards property fell considerably over this period. However, property has a number of defensive characteristics and its returns over time tend to be somewhat uncorrelated against the returns from equities and fixed interest. To this end, institutions have been rebuilding their weightings in direct property and also where possible in the quoted property sector. In many ways, it is easier to invest in the quoted sector as it is considerably more liquid and cost-effective than investment directly. For instance, individual buildings can be costly to buy and sell given agents' fees, stamp duty and liquidity issues, and also tend to require maintenance. A share in, for example, Land Securities can be bought and sold on a daily basis. There are, however, some tax considerations that are particularly relevant.

## Interest levels

Second, a major consideration is the persistence of the relatively low level of interest rates worldwide over the past 10 years. This has allowed investors to leverage up their portfolios considerably. Against a background of generally rising capital values, together with an income stream often higher than the cost of borrowing, leverage has made a lot of sense to those prepared to borrow. To some extent, this has been mirrored in the residential market by the explosive growth of buy-to-let over the past 10 years.

## Inflow of overseas money into UK property

Third, there has been a dramatic inflow of money into the UK property market from overseas. For various reasons, investors in Russia, China and the EU have seen the UK as a solid and reliable base in which to invest. Planning restrictions have tended to keep capital values high, and the development of London as a premier centre of world capital markets has encouraged significant new inward investment particularly into London and the South-East.

## Changes in the tax basis

Last, and of particular importance over the last year, the tax basis of the quoted sector is set to change. This change comes from the introduction of real estate investment trusts (REITs) introduced in the Budget in spring 2006. Nothing is as yet set in stone for this legislation and indeed a number of changes are still being made, following consultation between the industry and the Treasury, but the key outline is that, for a one-off conversion charge of round about 2 per cent of assets, property companies will be able to relieve themselves of the restrictions of capital gains tax on their estates, provided that they distribute a high level of their earnings to their investors. This has a major impact on a number of the well-established companies, who have built up considerable capital gains tax liabilities over the past 30 or 40 years. It is notable that under the current regime the majority of our domestically quoted property companies trade at a discount to net asset value, whereas where REITs have been introduced the companies tend to trade at a significant premium. We envisage that a similar pattern of investor activity will occur once REITs are introduced and the companies convert in 2007. Also, there is a global pool of investor capital that is orientated towards the global REIT market and that currently is unable to invest in our property companies as currently constituted. This pool of capital will be open for investment in the sector once the companies convert.

As an example of the position that we have taken in the real estate sector, one of our OEIC investment funds has held the position of approximately 10 per cent of equities by value in the real estate sector compared with a benchmark weighting in the All-Share Index of around 2.5 per cent. This is represented by three key companies: Land Securities, Hammerson and British Land. All three companies have indicated that they will change their investment status and move to become REITs when legislation permits in 2007 and this will, in our view, unlock further value within these companies, particularly the value of their outsourcing interests, and in the case of Hammerson a development portfolio particularly strong in Western Europe.

## The commercial property market today

As an indication of the strength of the current commercial property market, it might be useful to give one or two examples. In the West End of London, five-yearly rent reviews for space previously assessed in 2001 at around £40 a square foot came in, during the late autumn of 2006, at between £75 and £80 a square foot for relatively prime sites. A number of trophy buildings in the City of London have been placed on the market by Middle East investors recently and already it appears that at least a couple of these have found firm interest within two or three weeks of being placed on the market. An example of the enthusiasm towards slightly less central Home Counties property came recently with the sale by Hammerson of a supermarket site with car park attached in Romford for the sum of £380 million to a group of Irish investors. This demonstrates that two of the key factors driving the commercial market at the moment are the low level of interest rates within the EU and the keenness of overseas investors to gain exposure towards property in the London area.

The question we naturally have to ask ourselves, and this process forms part of the continual thematic investment process, is will this boom continue? Of course, were interest rates to rise significantly from current levels this would tend to put a dampener on commercial activity, as would a rise in stamp duty from the current 4 per cent level. However, it remains our view that institutions will continue to diversify their portfolios into assets away from equities and that property and property companies are, in many ways, a better match for a number of corporate liabilities over the long term, given that property provides a sound stream of income coupled with some protection against inflation.

## London's role as a financial centre

London's role as a financial centre is of paramount importance, and another key driver of this has been the number of overseas companies, particularly from Russia, that have listed on the London Stock Exchange in preference to New York, given the current onerous corporate regulatory regime that exists in the United

States. It has been observed that any large aspirant Russian company, particularly if it enters the FTSE directly, aspires to a substantial London base, and this fact has contributed to significant uplift in demand for prime space within London and the West End. In our view, this is also an attractive area for private client investment, given its transparency and asset backing. The major companies, too, are unlikely to provide any unwelcome profit warnings, as their asset bases and liquidity remain relatively stable.

The analysis above illustrates the rigorous examination and re-examination of the themes that make up our thematic process. It is flexible, agile and non-dogmatic and is the cornerstone of our methodology of building portfolios for our clients.

# welcoming
# private clients

Our private client teams are
equipped with a modern investment
process and a proven track record.
Our independence and flexibility,
reinforced by direct contact with
your fund managers, make sure that
investment solutions are dovetailed to
your specific requirements.

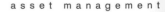

# Equity investment for the private investor

*Alan McIntosh, Cheviot Asset Management*

## The case for equities

### Can go down as well as up

There is one simple maxim that participants in the market should remember – equities should be treated as a long-term investment. In this context an investment is defined as a purchase that, over time, produces a return above the rate of inflation, ie a real return. What constitutes the long term is a moot point but, in the case of equities, holding periods of 10 years plus should certainly be considered. That is not to say that large amounts of money cannot be made over much shorter time horizons, but such gains can be swiftly lost in a sudden market reversal. Recent history bears testimony to this. Having reached an all-time high of 6,930 at the end of December 1999, UK equities (as measured by the FTSE 100 index) fell to a low of 3,300 in March 2003 following the bursting of the internet bubble and the subsequent bear market. The FTSE 100 has still not recovered all of its losses.

As a result of this, equities have lost something of their shine as an asset class. Over the past few years many investors have re-evaluated their portfolios and, in some cases, reduced their exposure to equities, replacing them with an increased commitment to bonds as well as alternative asset classes such as private equity, property and hedge funds. Diversification is, of course, important within a portfolio, but the timing of any switch between asset classes will greatly affect the future returns that can be expected.

It was undoubtedly the case that a very positive disposition towards equities was built up during the 1980s and 1990s. In the UK, the total return (capital gain plus reinvested dividend income) generated by shares averaged 18.9 per cent per annum in the years 1983–99. This was substantially ahead of the returns enjoyed by government bonds and by cash, and served to reinforce the view that equities were indeed the asset class of choice. However, after three years of falling share prices over the period 2000–02 the pendulum, unsurprisingly, began to swing the other way, with equities seen as risky and volatile and, for some long-term investors, even deemed as an inappropriate asset class.

## Good long-term returns

There is a danger, however, that a period of bad experience can change expectations unduly and lead to discouragement. What is important, therefore, is to try to determine what return can be reasonably expected from equities, compared with other asset classes, and decide whether there is a place for them in a portfolio, depending upon the investor's time horizon and appetite for risk.

There have been a number of studies that have looked at the returns of various asset classes over time. The most relevant of these tend to look at real total return, ie both capital appreciation and income generation after adjusting for inflation. This is particularly important for long-term investors, as the purchasing power of the investment can be substantially eroded by inflation. Figure 2.3.1 shows the results of one of the most comprehensive long-term studies conducted in the UK.

As can be seen, equities have produced a better long-term return than either bonds or cash. Why should this be the case? There are two main factors that influence the rate of return on equities. First, the return required by an investor is directly linked to the risk-free rate of return that can be earned, for example on a government bond. In theory, investors should be willing to accept a lower rate of return from an investment whose future value is easily predictable, such as bonds and cash, and expect a higher return from an asset class that is characterized by

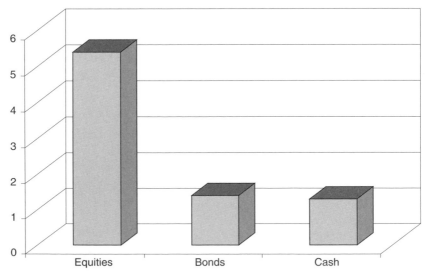

*Source:* Barclays Capital

**Figure 2.3.1**   Real returns (percentage per annum) 1900–2005)

greater uncertainty. In the case of equities, this uncertainty includes the fact that dividends and future capital values are not known in advance. A period of rising interest rates would generally have a negative effect on share prices as the expected rate of return adjusts along with the risk-free rate of return. Of course, the converse should be true during a period of falling interest rates.

Secondly, the return on equities is influenced by corporate profits. Over long periods of time, corporate profits should grow broadly in line with nominal GDP. In the UK, the trend rate of real GDP growth is seen at around 2.5 per cent per annum and this is deemed to be consistent with an inflation target of 2 per cent. This gives a nominal GDP figure of 4.5 per cent. If, however, the 3 per cent received by way of dividends is also factored in, the real return expected from UK equities is 4.5 per cent + 3 per cent − 2 per cent = 5.5 per cent. There are, however, times when the proportion of GDP represented by corporate profits will be rising, perhaps during a period of improving productivity, and this would generally be expected to provide a more favourable background for equities. Similarly, in recessionary times, if corporate profits are under pressure, equities might be expected to fare less well.

It can be argued that the period between 1983 and 1999, when annual equity returns were particularly high, benefited from the dual effects of falling interest rates (as inflationary pressures within the economy became more subdued) and labour market reforms, which helped to improve productivity and the GDP share of profits. Furthermore, such favourable factors are unlikely to recur imminently and it would thus be foolhardy to extrapolate the equity returns enjoyed over that period into the future.

Equities should still produce a long-term return above that of bonds and cash. Notwithstanding, investors should remain realistic in their expectations.

# Constructing an equity portfolio

There is a variety of ways in which an equity portfolio can be constructed. This may include the incorporation of collective vehicles such as open-ended funds and investment trusts, the use of index trackers or active funds, or direct equity investment.

## Collectives – index tracking or active investment?

In theory, the value of index tracker funds (or passive funds) – as the name suggests – will rise and fall exactly in line with movements in the market. Depending on the way in which the portfolio is constructed (faithful replication of index or representative sample selection) and the level of charges, the tracking error should be relatively low. However, an index tracker will not outperform a rising market and – owing to the inability to hold cash within the fund – will not outperform a falling market.

Another problem with the index tracking approach is that, at certain times, there can be tremendous areas of concentration in the market. A good example of this was the time of the TMT (technology, media and telecoms) boom in the late 1990s. At the market's peak at the end of 1999, TMT represented over 25 per cent of the FT All-Share Index and nearly 30 per cent of the FTSE 100. As these stocks were pushed ever higher, index funds had no choice but to keep buying them since they have to maintain the exact weightings of stocks and sectors as they appear in the index. Even if these stocks are perceived as overvalued, the fund manager has no choice but to buy them.

Concentration can also take place at the individual stock level. Table 2.3.1 shows the top 10 stocks by market value in the FTSE 100 at the end of 1999. Thus, 10 stocks represented nearly half of the index. This is not just a quirk of that period, however. The top 10 stocks in November 2006 (Table 2.3.2) once again represented half the value of the index. For many investors, this may constitute an undesirable concentration of risk.

Actively managed funds seek to outperform the market through superior stock selection. Not only will the investor pay higher charges to participate within an actively managed fund, compared to an index fund, but regular studies show that

**Table 2.3.1** Top 10 FTSE stocks by market value (1999)

| Stock | % of FTSE |
|---|---|
| BP Amoco | 8.7 |
| British Telecom | 7.0 |
| Vodafone Airtouch | 6.8 |
| HSBC Holdings | 5.2 |
| Glaxo Wellcome | 4.6 |
| Shell T&T | 3.7 |
| AstraZeneca | 3.3 |
| SmithKline Beecham | 3.2 |
| Lloyds TSB Group | 3.0 |
| Marconi | 2.1 |
| **Total** | **47.6** |

*Source:* Datastream

**Table 2.3.2** Top 10 FTSE stocks by market value (November 2006)

| Stock | % of FTSE |
|---|---|
| Royal Dutch Shell | 8.5 |
| BP | 8.1 |
| HSBC | 8.0 |
| GlaxoSmithKline | 5.4 |
| Vodafone | 4.9 |
| Royal Bank of Scotland | 4.1 |
| AstraZeneca | 3.2 |
| Barclays | 3.2 |
| HBOS | 2.8 |
| Anglo American | 2.6 |
| **Total** | **50.8** |

*Source*: Datastream

relatively few funds consistently outperform the market. One of the main problems with open-ended funds is that, as they become larger, there is a tendency to increase the number of stocks held and thus the larger fund may take on the characteristics of a passive fund, but with higher charges. Moreover, cash flows can create further distortions. In a market downturn, if investors sell their units, managers may have to sell investments held within the portfolio in order to meet redemptions. They may have to sell the most liquid holdings irrespective of whether they believe these to be better-quality investments. Similarly, if the fund attracts new money, the manager may feel obliged to buy more stock rather than hold a large amount of cash.

Investment trusts are also collective vehicles, but are quoted companies in their own right. The purchase and sale of shares in an investment trust has no effect on the value of the trust's underlying portfolio (unlike open-ended funds, where the purchase or sale of units adds to or reduces the value of the portfolio). This means that the share price can move out of line with the value of the underlying investments, giving the investor an opportunity to pick up a portfolio of stocks at a discount to the net asset value.

Collective investments, be they closed-ended or open-ended, do have their place in an equity portfolio, particularly in the case of smaller portfolios where a reasonable spread of direct equities is impractical. More specialized funds can also be used to gain exposure to areas, such as emerging markets, where it may be difficult to choose suitable investments without particular local knowledge.

## Active management using direct equities

### How many stocks?

As the name suggests, this approach involves putting together a portfolio of individual stocks. With this approach, however, careful attention should be paid to diversification so that there are not areas of unnecessary risk within the portfolio. The first consideration is the optimal number of stocks. The risk in a portfolio comprises systematic risk and specific risk. Systematic risk is that which is common to all stocks, ie market risk. Specific risk is associated with individual equities but can be minimized by having an optimal number of stocks. Modern portfolio theory suggests that such optimal diversification can be achieved by holding approximately 15–20 stocks.

Once the right number of stocks has been decided on, there are further ways that an equity portfolio can be refined, namely by sector, by geographical considerations and by investment style.

### Don't put all your eggs in one basket

There are clearly considerable risks associated with the strategy of single sector investment. For example, a portfolio composed entirely of water and electricity companies is potentially vulnerable to an adverse change in the regulatory regime affecting the utilities. Investors with portfolios composed chiefly of technology stocks were left exposed at the start of 2000 when the TMT bubble subsequently burst.

## Going overseas

Another way of achieving diversification in an equity portfolio is through geographical selection. Traditionally, investment in overseas markets was to obtain exposure to industries not readily accessible in the home market. More commonly, overseas investment is seen as a way of taking advantage of countries where growth is faster than that of the UK, in anticipation of this being reflected in more rapidly rising equity prices. Investing in overseas markets also gives rise to currency risk, however, and this may impact on the returns available to a sterling investor, since a rise in the value of sterling reduces the value of non-UK investments. Notwithstanding, the benefits of geographical diversification would be felt if, for example, wage growth in the UK were to rise sharply, undermining company profits and competitiveness and thereby negatively impacting on the exchange rate. This would increase the value of overseas equity holdings.

## Showing some style

Active management can also be divided by investment style. The two most common styles are usually described as *value* and *growth*. Value investing was perhaps best expounded by Benjamin Graham, who in turn inspired one of the most famous contemporary investors, Warren Buffett. The basic premise is to buy companies where the market value is less than the net current asset value. In periods of strong market performance, however, such bargains may be more difficult to find. More modern interpretations of value investing include buying companies with an above-average dividend yield – often these have depressed share prices or sell on sub-market price/earnings ratios because they are perceived as having fairly pedestrian prospects.

Growth investing, on the other hand typically, involves identifying companies with above-average earnings growth potential either relative to their peers or in a fast-growing industry or sector. Today, it often simply means focusing on capital growth rather than income. Growth companies often sell at a large premium to their net asset value (NAV), but the assumption is that the NAV will grow over time and should exceed the current valuation. Growth companies are often relatively young companies, and value companies are often very mature companies.

The difference in styles was easy to observe in the run-up to the market peak on 31 December 1999. The best- and worst-performing sectors over the previous 12 months are shown in Table 2.3.3.

**Table 2.3.3**  Best- and worst-performing sectors in 1999

|  | Change relative to the UK All-Share Index (%) |
| --- | --- |
| Information technology hardware | +593.7 |
| Software and computer services | +112.5 |
| Tobacco | −43.9 |
| Water | −46.5 |

*Source:* Datastream

Technology stocks were in great demand because the perception was that the new information age promised enormous growth opportunities. Mature industries, by comparison, were seen as relics of the 'old economy'. However, these fortunes were soon reversed after the dotcom bubble burst, with technology stocks suffering dramatically, while the previously underperforming, low-growth sectors recovered sharply.

Proponents in both camps will argue that their style delivers the best long-term returns. The data behind this are ambiguous, and success can depend very much on where we are within the economic cycle.

# Summary

The bear market of 2000–02 forced many investors to reassess their expectations about equity markets. Nevertheless, long-term data still suggest that equities should produce a better return than bonds and cash over time.

The construction of an equity portfolio will partly depend on whether the investor wishes to buy individual stocks or collectives, or indeed a combination of both. Collectives have a role to play, particularly as a way of gaining exposure to specialized areas such as emerging markets.

However, the active investor should not be put off the idea of having a portfolio of individual stocks. This can offer flexibility and, with a sensible spread of equities, extremes of valuation, or sector and stock concentration, can be avoided. Whichever approach the investor chooses, it is important to remember the simple maxim that equities should be treated as a long-term investment.

# ARC FUND MANAGEMENT LIMITED

*Do you have capital gains or income to shelter
from the Taxman?*

*Do you want to have the opportunity to invest in early
stage smaller companies?*

*Arc Fund Management Ltd. may have the answers you need*

Arc is one of the market leaders in offering HMR&C approved Enterprise Investment Scheme ("EIS") funds which offer investors a chance to invest in a diversified portfolio of smaller unquoted companies, spreading the risk of investing in these less established and potentially more risky investments. Investments are made prior to companies' flotation on a public market, such as AIM, adding to the potential of the investment. Investment in an EIS qualifying fund qualifies for unlimited deferral of capital gains tax.

Arc manages the Arc Growth Company VCT plc a Venture Capital Trust which invests in smaller unquoted companies. Investment in a VCT provides income tax relief at 30%.

*The performance of our funds speaks for itself.*

If you need more information or think we can help you
then contact **info@arcfundmanagement.com** or visit our website at
**www.arcfundmanagement.com**

Arc Fund Management Ltd. is authorised and regulated by the FSA (registered number 190860).

# The Enterprise Investment Scheme

*Chris Powell, Arc Fund Management Ltd*

The Enterprise Investment Scheme (EIS) has been around since replacing the Business Expansion Scheme (BES) in January 1994 and was launched with similar ambitions: to aid smaller companies raise funds for growth by offering a series of tax concessions to investors. It is worth stressing that the EIS applies to investment in qualifying companies and these are by definition small, often at an early stage of development and deemed high-risk.

To mitigate the intrinsic risks in EIS companies, several EIS funds are offered each year by specialist fund managers, such as Arc Fund Management, which use a portfolio approach to spread investors' funds across a range of separate qualifying companies. However, it should be noted that the investor remains the beneficial owner of the individual underlying shareholdings, thereby satisfying the requirement of investing directly into individual companies.

Despite the EIS having been around for more than a decade, details of the EIS and EIS funds are less well known and attract considerably less press coverage than venture capital trusts (VCTs), which share similar investment rules but offer a different and complementary set of tax breaks.

All too frequently, comment on EIS funds as investment vehicles focuses first on the potential tax benefits and second on the underlying merits of the companies, which is evidently the wrong order, as the performance of the investment has a substantially greater impact on total returns than do the tax concessions.

In this under-researched and little-known sector, it is important to explain Arc's credentials. Arc Fund Management Ltd is a niche fund management business specializing in identifying and assisting pre-IPO enterprises to raise funds for growth. It is a strongly held belief within Arc that these pre-IPO companies offer the greatest opportunity for capital appreciation. Accordingly, it has developed and manages a number of different schemes that invest in the exciting opportunities presented.

Over the past few years Arc has been a major player in the EIS fund field and anticipates that, through the launch of its EIS6 Fund, it will capture around a fifth of the money committed to this sector during the 2006/07 fiscal year. The company's success with its EIS products has been built upon the performance, skills and knowledge of the fund managers and its ability to attract sufficient quality investment propositions.

## Qualifying investments

For a company to qualify as an EIS approved investment, through which individuals can claim valuable tax concessions, it has to satisfy Her Majesty's Revenue and Customs (HMRC) that it meets the many qualifying criteria.

The intention of the EIS is to encourage individuals to support financially small companies, and to ensure that the funds are received into the business the investment must be made through an issue of new shares. At the time of issue, the company must not be listed on a recognized stock exchange, and there must not be arrangements in place for it to become quoted, though trading on AIM and PLUS markets is permitted.

First, it is useful to define a small company and, for the purpose of the EIS, HMRC uses a gross assets test. To qualify, the company should have no more than £7 million prior to the issue or £8 million immediately after, which is the same as for VCTs.

While there are, unsurprisingly, many more specific conditions, the only others worth mentioning here are that the enterprise must carry out trade in a qualifying activity, wholly or mainly in the UK, on a commercial basis and with a view to the realization of profit.

In addition to the criteria for qualifying companies, there are separate issues for approved EIS funds, which confer benefits on fund holders, notably that the various reliefs can be obtained for the tax year in which the offer closes rather than once the investments have been made. Again the HMRC has specific requirements for approval, which include that at least 90 per cent of the available funds are invested into a minimum of four qualifying companies within six months.

## EIS tax concessions

As with all tax concessions, the Treasury giveth and the Treasury taketh away, and readers should bear this in mind. At the time of writing, and after the changes in the Budget of 2006, the tax benefits associated with EIS qualifying investments fall into five separate categories, and are offered against income tax, capital gains tax (CGT) and inheritance tax (IHT).

While the detail and allocation rules are complex, demanding that proper tax advice is sought, the key benefits are relatively straightforward and consist of the following:

■ *Income tax relief* of 20 per cent is available on investment up to £400,000 per annum on shares held for a period of at least three years. The relief is against an individual's income tax bill in the fiscal year of investment, though up to half can be carried back against the previous year's liability if the purchase is made on or before 5 October, to a maximum of £50,000.
■ *Capital gains tax deferral relief* – a CGT liability can be deferred on unlimited taxable profits made in the previous three years or in the subsequent 12 months. The CGT becomes due once again when the EIS shares are sold.
■ *Capital gains tax freedom* – subject to an initial investment of not more than the £400,000 annual limit, any profits made on the EIS investment are free from CGT provided that the shares have been held for at least three years.
■ *Loss relief* – capital losses net of EIS relief attributable to the investment can be set against capital gains or income in the fiscal year of disposal. The net effect of this is to limit the investment exposure to 48p in the pound for a 40 per cent taxpayer should the shares become worthless.
■ *Inheritance tax exemption* – 100 per cent relief is available in the event of the death of an investor provided that the investment has been held for a minimum of two years.

Apart from being attractive to individual investors who are UK resident for tax purposes, the EIS offers excellent tax planning opportunities to trustees of certain trusts.

Where the beneficiaries of a trust are individuals, the trust will usually qualify for unlimited CGT deferral, capital gains taper relief, loss relief (limited to capital gains) and IHT relief. However, it must be remembered that neither EIS relief nor exemption from CGT is available to trustees.

# Risks

Qualifying companies, by their very nature small and often unquoted, attract little, if any, independent research and analysis, which makes it difficult for the majority of investors to follow and assess their investment merits, inevitably adding to their already high level of risk.

While it is clearly prudent to moderate the level of risk by diversifying their exposure across a range of suitable qualifying investments, most investors will not have direct access to sufficient EIS opportunities. To obtain the risk-reducing spread, many investors sensibly either allow a specialist fund manager, like Arc Fund Management, to source, investigate and administer their exposure through one of its EIS funds or allow their regular investment adviser to perform a similar function on a limited part of their portfolio.

Even in the best EIS funds and portfolios, it is more or less inevitable that over the qualifying period for relief a proportion will diminish in value or, worse, fail and become worthless, making stock selection a critical factor for success. This alone highlights the value added by the specialist skills and knowledge of the fund manager, and the importance of a continual flow of investment opportunities, from which to choose the most suitable and, potentially, the most profitable.

The role of the EIS fund's manager often extends beyond pure stock selection into actively participating and advising on the governance of the company, thereby further protecting investors' interests.

While the inherent risks associated with individual small, early-stage companies and illiquid investments remain high, the expertise and knowledge of a specialist fund manager, together with the element of diversification offered by an EIS fund, act to moderate risk to a level that is acceptable to a wider audience of potential investors.

Additionally, the tax breaks offered through the EIS help to further improve the risk/reward profile of investment, by significantly reducing the net cost of the investments (risk) and increasing the net reward.

Though an investor's risk can be effectively managed through diversification and asset allocation, the one area that is outside the investor's control and that has a bearing on returns is the medium- to long-term tax regime. Look no further than the decline in the attractiveness of VCTs following the 2006 Budget changes.

# EIS vs VCT

Historically, VCTs have been the subject of substantially more press coverage than the EIS, with many articles highlighting the specific benefits and shortcomings of one or the other. However, there are few that analyse the differences between the two investments, and those that do seem, almost exclusively, to focus on the various tax breaks. However, the differences and similarities go far deeper than tax alone.

One of the most striking differences is the total size of the VCT sector and the volume of new issues, which dwarfs the EIS. One of the consequences or, perhaps, one of the reasons for this is the ready availability of reliable performance data and analysis carried out by independent research houses.

Though the EIS collective is referred to as a fund it is much more akin to a discretionary portfolio made up of qualifying shares, where all holders have the same proportion of their investments committed to the same companies. Indeed, the investor remains the beneficial owner of the underlying securities, whereas a VCT investor buys shares in the company whose only assets are the underlying shares, similar to an investment trust. Consequently, the structure of the EIS fund can increase the administrative burden on the investor as the acquisitions and disposal of the underlying securities have to be tracked individually, although this burden can be lightened if the fund manager uses an experienced administrator.

Liquidity is an issue for both but more so for the EIS as the investor has to consider the disposal of individual holdings, which could prove difficult, time-consuming and expensive; VCT investors should be better able to sell their shares in the VCT through a normal market transaction. However, even in this case marketability can still prove an issue.

The key tax differences are expressed in Table 2.4.1 and, while the EIS offers more reliefs than the VCT, there are differences that will impact on its suitability and attractiveness for various investors. In essence the EIS is focused toward capital performance whereas VCTs concentrate on income tax concessions.

Accordingly, different classes of investors will favour one more than the other, but overall the tax benefits associated with the EIS will be particularly valuable for those with large incomes, portfolios with gains and substantial estates but less attractive to those seeking income from their investments, as dividends are not tax-free as is the case with VCTs.

The changes in the 2006 Budget for VCTs strongly suggest that a large proportion of VCT portfolios have been constructed to take advantage of the tax concessions rather than to provide funding to small enterprises. Furthermore, investors in a VCT have less reason to follow and understand the individual constituents of the portfolio, whereas the collective approach for an EIS fund promotes a more transparent and closer relationship between the investor, the company and investment.

The changes in the 2006 Budget considerably increased the risk of VCT investment through the lowering of the tax benefits, reducing the size of allowable companies and prolonging the holding time. The effect of these changes has been a reduction in the attractiveness of VCTs, which can be seen in the generally held view that the total funds raised in 2006/07 will be significantly lower than the £750 million raised in 2005/06. However, there is no indication that the decline in the VCT sector will be made up for by an increase in EIS investment.

## Summary

EIS has been around for more than a decade, with the objective of encouraging investors to help provide much-needed equity financing to small, developing

**Table 2.4.1**  Comparative tax relief

|  | EIS | VCT |
| --- | --- | --- |
| Annual investment limit | £400,000* | £200,000 |
| Income tax relief for subscribers | 20% | 30% |
| Clawback if held for less than | 3 years | 5 years |
| Reinvestment relief period: |  |  |
| Before gain is made | 1 year | n/a |
| After gain is made | 3 years | n/a |
| Tax-free dividends | No | Yes |
| Tax-free capital gains | Yes (after 3 years) | Yes |
| Tax relief for losses | Yes (after 3 years) | No |
| IHT business property relief | Yes | No |

* no limit on CGT deferral

businesses. Despite its long history, it remains relatively unknown and poorly understood by many of the investors it was designed to attract, with most preferring the higher-profile and wider-researched VCT.

With both VCT and EIS funds committing funds to similar opportunities, the deciding factor for investors should be the suitability of the tax breaks and their willingness, or not, to invest in illiquid assets.

There is no question but that the EIS is a very effective tool for tax planning purposes but it should not be used in isolation, as it is imperative that a holistic approach is taken to the overall investment profile and tax position of the investor. Accordingly, the significant tax incentives attached should not be seen as the reason to invest, but as a way of altering the risk profile of investing in small, early-stage and illiquid companies.

Stock selection is important to any portfolio but given the enhanced risk of EIS qualifying companies this is even more critical; so, ideally, investors need to have access to a range of suitable enterprises from which to choose. However, the majority of investors will not be able to gain the necessary diversification them-selves and this, coupled with the specialized knowledge required for success, generally demands that exposure is gained through a managed portfolio, either in an EIS fund or as part of a professionally managed portfolio.

The skill and experience of the fund manager are crucial, so it is essential that investors undertake the same kind of analysis for EIS funds as they would for any other collective scheme; while past performance is no guarantee for the future it is a useful starting point. However, EIS funds are unlike other better-researched products in that comparative performance data and independent comment are light on the ground, so investors will have to do much of the legwork themselves or rely on their professional advisers to do it on their behalf.

Finally, the EIS should represent an important element of a diversified port-folio for those sophisticated investors seeking to gain an exposure to an exciting market sector, with the additional benefit of a reduced tax bill. Furthermore, investors can draw satisfaction from the knowledge that they are helping to promote and support the UK's 'enterprise culture'.

# Tempting tax breaks with a venture capital trust

*Jeff Cornish, Beringea*

## Introduction

The VCT market has enjoyed a renaissance over the last couple of years. In 2004 Gordon Brown announced an increase in the tax relief received from 20 per cent to 40 per cent when investing into a VCT (for the tax years 2004/05 and 2005/06). This relief has now decreased to 30 per cent, but are they still worth considering?

Although not a definitive guide to VCTs, this chapter attempts to explain what they are and what they invest in and briefly looks at some of the considerations that need to be taken into account when incorporating them into a portfolio. The obvious attractions of the upfront tax relief can easily tempt investors into over-allocating funds into this sector purely owing to the seductive effect of mitigating tax – thus increasing the overall risk profile of their investment portfolio.

## VCTs – what they are

A strong base for growing entrepreneurial businesses is one of the key drivers behind a nation's wealth. Now that's a pretty strong statement, but the BVCA (the UK's venture capital association) conducted a survey about the impact that companies backed by VCTs have had relative to other sectors of the economy. Broadly speaking, as you can see from Figures 2.5.1 and 2.5.2, these companies grew comparatively more quickly than their FTSE counterparts in terms of growth in employment and sales.

# UP TO 30% TAX REBATE

## VENTURE CAPITAL TRUSTS
- what to buy - up to date research and newsletters - visit www.H-L.co.uk/VCT

" ProVen had a great year in 2006 with the disposal of one of their underlying companies for fourteen times the original cost...we believe they have the potential to be one of the top performers over the medium to long term."

**Hargreaves Lansdown VCT Survey 2007**

Tax reliefs are subject to change, the exact amount of any rebate will depend on your circumstances. VCTs are higher risk investments, you could get back less than you invest. We do not offer advice, if you are unsure of an investments suitability, obtain your own advice.

## WE ARE THE BIGGEST DIRECT:

### VCT Broker - Savings of up to 3.5%
### Fund Supermarket - Savings of up to 5.5% and annual savings up to 0.5%
### SIPP Provider - Savings of up to 5.5%

## *LAST YEAR WE SAVED OUR CLIENTS £75 MILLION IN CHARGES*

### Some recent awards won by Hargreaves Lansdown

- Best ISA Funds Provider - Consumer Finance Awards 2005
- Best Online Broker - Investors Chronicle 2006
- Pensions IFA of the year - Money Marketing 2006
- IFA of the year - Money Marketing 2006
- Best Income Multi Manager Fund - Real Advisor 2006

For more information on any of our products or services, please telephone **0117 900 9000 (Monday - Friday 8.30am - 6pm)** or visit www.H-L.co.uk

## HARGREAVES LANSDOWN

Hargreaves Lansdown Asset Management
Kendal House | 4 Brighton Mews | Clifton | Bristol | BS8
Authorised and Regulated by the Financial Services Auth...

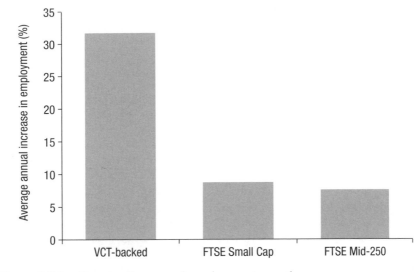

**Figure 2.5.1**    Comparative annual employment growth

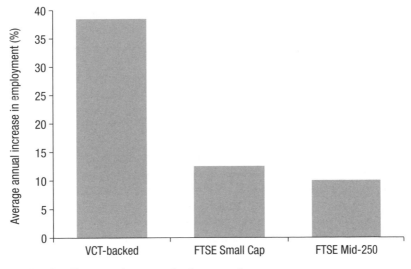

**Figure 2.5.2**    Comparative annual sales growth

Venture capital trusts (VCTs) were first established by the government in 1995 to encourage investment into these smaller, often fast-growing, companies. As many of you will know through personal experience, there comes a time when a company faces a situation where it requires capital either to expand and grow or to fund the buy-out of owners wishing to retire.

Obtaining funding between £250,000 and £5 million can be difficult – too much for a bank to consider and too little for an institutional private equity firm to bother itself with – and many companies have trouble finding the required finance to fund their business expansion plans. This is the 'equity gap' that VCTs were designed to fill and have filled with great effect, supporting many organizations in their growth aspirations. As you can see from Figures 2.5.1 and 2.5.2, VCTs have contributed greatly from an economic viewpoint. Investors who put money into VCTs have also enjoyed some very generous tax breaks; the initial VCTs offered a 20 per cent tax break and deferral of capital gains tax (CGT). This relief was then increased to 40 per cent and the deferral of CGT dropped for the 2004/05 and 2005/06 tax years but was reduced for the 2006/07 tax year to a still very generous 30 per cent upfront income tax relief; other tax benefits are mentioned in more detail later in the chapter.

A venture capital trust can therefore be best defined as an investment trust whose stocks are traded on the London Stock Exchange and that invests in a portfolio of those companies that generally are not listed on any stock market (although VCT rules do allow investment into new issues on AIM). Consequently, VCTs can be a great way for a private investor to access this part of the private equity and venture capital markets – ordinarily the domain of institutional investors. Through VCTs, private investors can benefit from the skills of a professional manager as well as getting an enhanced return through the generous tax breaks on offer.

Beringea, one of the leading VCT providers, will look at the business plans of hundreds of these companies every year, all of which are seeking funding to further finance their businesses. Of these, the fund managers will have initial meetings with between 20 and 40 management teams and will generally invest in only perhaps one or two deals per month. VCT rules stipulate that any funds raised must be invested within three years to comply with the regulations. As the investee companies are normally not quoted on a stock exchange, they may be deemed as being higher-risk, but they do offer the potential to offer a higher reward. Almost all of these companies are ones that you have never heard of. However, every large company has to start somewhere, and investing early generally provides higher growth potential. For example, restaurant chain Loch Fyne was backed by Beringea to help expand its business to become a successful fish restaurant chain with an outlet in most large towns or cities. Clothes retailer Fat Face, which specializes in surf wear, was similarly backed by the Baronsmead VCTs and, although once small and specialist, has now expanded on to most major high streets around the country. When fully invested, a VCT will typically have 25–35 investments and this helps to mitigate risk.

## Mergermarket case study

Mergermarket is typical of the companies VCTs invest in. Mergermarket had created an online subscription business providing a business intelligence service for advisers active in mergers and acquisitions. Wanting to expand their business into different geographical locations and publications they approached Beringea Ltd, managers of the ProVen range of VCTs, for funding. Investment was made into the company and Mergermarket's highly skilled management team rapidly grew the business, culminating in its sale to the Pearson Group in September 2006 for £120 million. ProVen's VCTs return was 14 times that of their original investment and resulted in a 31p and 50p tax-free dividend per share paid out on ProVen VCT and PGI VCT shareholdings respectively. Although not necessarily typical of VCT investing, it does demonstrate what can be achieved from investing in these small high-growth companies. However, one must be mindful of the fact that small companies have a greater likelihood of failure than large companies.

The investment process for each investment is lengthy and it can often take up to six months to complete a deal as lawyers, accountants and industry specialists go through the company with a fine-tooth comb. This is known as 'due diligence' and is an important part of the process. The major reason for this detail is that, unlike investing in a quoted company such as Vodafone, if you invest in an unquoted company it is very difficult to exit if you get it wrong. At least with Vodafone you can always sell your shares through the stock market, regardless of the size of your holding.

Once an investment has been made, the investment process, unlike that of quoted shares, does not end there. The investment team has a close relationship with these companies and often takes a position on the board (if unquoted) and therefore has a direct influence on the strategic direction of the company. This means that the level of control the investment managers can exert on their position is much greater than that of an investor in a listed stock. Figure 2.5.3, from the BVCA study of the economic impact of VCTs in the UK, shows some of the added-value services that can be obtained, as well as the obvious benefit of funding.

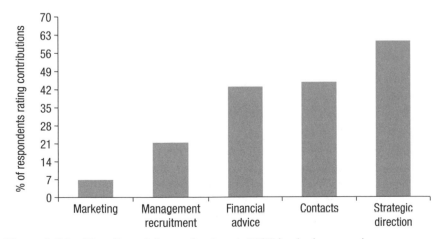

**Figure 2.5.3**   Non-financial contributions to VCT-backed companies

Investment returns are derived from the income the VCT receives on its investments but more significantly from the profits that it makes when it sells one of its investment companies. VCTs distribute these profits to their shareholders as an additional **tax-free dividend**. VCT shares have the potential to increase in value over time and any capital made on their sale is also free of tax.

## What are the tax breaks?

As you have probably concluded already, VCTs do exist at the higher end of the risk spectrum and obviously one of the ways of attracting money into this sector is by offering some very attractive tax incentives, which the Chancellor has done over the last 10 or so years, culminating in a £750 million VCT market in 2005/06. The tax advantages are outlined below and, as well as good upfront tax relief, VCTs can also be a good source of tax-free dividends.

Investment in a VCT offers a number of very attractive tax reliefs to investors:

■ Income tax relief of 30 per cent is given on the amount invested, subject to a ceiling of £200,000 per tax year per person (provided the shares are held for at least five years).
■ Dividends paid by the VCT are tax-free.
■ Disposals of VCT shares are not liable to CGT.

You can invest £10,000 in a VCT and the next day you are eligible for a £3,000 reduction in your tax bill.

You don't even have to be a higher-rate taxpayer to benefit. People paying the standard rate of 22 per cent are eligible for the 30 per cent tax rebate. The tax benefits are not only upfront. Any dividends that the VCT pays out are tax-exempt and, what's more, any profits made when you come to sell your VCT are free of CGT. VCT rulings stipulate that shares must be held for at least five years, and this rule has two crucial implications. First, VCT investment should be viewed as a medium- to long-term investment and not just for five years. Second, the tax rules mean that your VCT could perform very poorly indeed and still leave you no worse off than you were before. If it does well, it will knock many other investments into a cocked hat.

## How to claim tax reliefs

Once investment has been made into a VCT, the VCT manager will issue a certificate entitling you to claim income tax relief when the share certificate is issued. At the end of the tax year you should enter the details of your investment on your tax return and the tax office will deal with any repayment due. The relief reduces your income tax liability for the tax year in which the VCT shares are issued. Alternatively, HMRC can adjust your tax code so that less income tax is deducted at source during the financial year.

# Different types of VCTs

As discussed earlier, a VCT will invest in a portfolio of unquoted and/or AIM-traded companies that are at an earlier stage of development than listed companies, and VCTs are generally categorized as follows:

- *generalist* – as a rule invest primarily in the unquoted sector across a broad range of sectors;
- *AIM* – invest in new issues launched on to the AIM market;
- *specialist* – tend to be sector-specific and have historically been early-stage investments;
- *asset-backed* – a few VCTs offer an asset-backed, lower-risk approach;
- *limited life* – VCTs that look to wind up and return capital and profits within a five- to seven-year time period.

# Portfolio considerations

Investments should never be made just for the purposes of mitigating tax. Although the tax considerations are attractive, the investment should always stack up on its own merits. Investment should be made because it is suitable in the context of the investment portfolio, and the risks associated with it should be acceptable to the investor. VCTs should be considered by investors with significant investment portfolios who can afford to take a long-term view and are comfortable with the risks of investing in smaller companies. VCTs are therefore not suitable for all investors.

However, that said, VCTs can play an important role in a diversified portfolio, as they can provide a tax-efficient investment in a portfolio of potentially high-growth smaller companies. Investment IFAs Best Invest and Hargreaves Lansdown suggest that VCTs should account for 5–10 per cent of your equity portfolio and can be very useful for replacing part of your UK small-cap portfolio with a tax-efficient one. Obviously if you can afford, and are prepared, to take more risk this percentage can be increased.

It is also probably best to take advice from an investment specialist who knows about VCTs and their applications. This is important, as many advisers do not have the requisite knowledge to advise on these specialist investments and may simply advise you not to invest in them. A good investment adviser will be able to assist you not only in indicating how much of your funds should be allocated to VCTs without upsetting the risk profile of your investment portfolio, but also in giving some guidance in constructing a portfolio of VCTs suitable for your objectives.

As you may have guessed, as they are higher-risk investments it is probably not the best idea to back just one VCT but to hedge bets and consider spreading your subscription across more than one VCT with a number of different managers in a number of different sectors of VCTs. For example, in the 2005/06 tax year, Martin Churchill, editor of *Tax Efficient Review*, advised a portfolio consisting of 60 per cent into generalist VCTs, 30 per cent into AIM VCTs and 10 per cent into specialist VCTs, although he states this is likely to change in the 2006/07 tax year owing to a couple of regulation changes that came into effect in April 2006.

If you are insistent on making your own choices, as many people understandably are, there are a number of very useful resources where information on VCTs is available online, from which an informed decision based upon information available can be made. A sample of these resources is outlined in the box.

---

## VCT resources and discount brokers

- *Tax Efficient Review*: www.taxefficientreview.com
- *Tax Shelter Report*: www.taxshelterreport.co.uk
- Hargreaves Lansdown: www.h-l.co.uk/
- Best Invest: www.bestinvest.co.uk
- Chelsea: www.chelseafs.co.uk/

---

## Considerations when investing in a VCT

When the government offers you 30 per cent cashback on an investment it's bound to grab your attention; so it is important to understand the risks and understand why VCTs are deemed to be high-risk investments. These risks primarily fall into two categories: investment risk and liquidity risk.

### Investment risk

First, small unquoted companies do fail, and investing in an unquoted or AIM-listed company is riskier than putting it into its blue chip counterpart. However, VCT managers are aware of this, and there are a number of ways to reduce risk. A portfolio approach reduces this risk by spreading the funds over a collection of these companies. Most managers also invest 15–30 per cent of the fund into lower-risk investments such as cash, liquidity funds and fixed interest securities, which helps to lower the overall investment profile of the VCT. Moreover, VCTs have the ability to invest into other non-equity instruments such as loan notes and preferences shares, which also help to lower the overall risk of the investment. As described earlier, professional managers undertake an intense process of research and due diligence before investing into a company, and with a VCT manager taking a position on the board the fund is able to take an active interest in the strategic direction of the company and will be alerted to issues with the company as soon as they arise.

### Liquidity risk

VCT shares must be held for a minimum of five years if investors are to retain the 30 per cent income tax relief. The sale of shares before this point may result in investors having their tax relief revoked. Even after the five-year holding period, VCT shares may not be easy to sell at full value and usually trade at a large discount to their net asset value, thus having wide bid–offer spreads. This is primarily because there is no secondary market: why purchase a second-hand share when you can buy a new one and get 30 per cent tax relief? Good VCT managers will operate a 'buy-back' policy whereby the VCT will purchase shares from investors wanting to sell at a certain buy-back price (typically at a discount of 10–20 per cent to the VCT's NAV), thus reducing the risk of being subject to the vagaries of the market.

## Selecting a VCT

So, if you've decided that you want to invest in VCTs, what are some of the things you should look at when selecting a portfolio of VCTs?

- *Investment strategy.* Not all VCTs have the same risk profile. Understanding whether or not the VCT invests in start-ups or profitable established companies, MBOs or growth opportunities, single or multiple sectors will help in the understanding of their relative risk profile.
- *Track record.* Good performance and consistency of returns are important, especially over different phases of the investment cycle.
- *Depth and breadth of experience.* How long have the managers been in business? A record of success generated by a team who have worked together for a while is much more reliable than short-term stunning performance.
- *Charges.* Charges comprise an upfront charge, the annual fee and performance-related fees. These can then be compared across all VCTs on offer.
- *VCT share buy-back policy.* As there is a very illiquid market in most VCT shares, it is important that VCTs have a strong buy-back policy in place, in order to provide an exit for investors. Particular attention should be paid to how the VCT intends to treat investors who wish to sell their shares.

## Conclusion

VCTs can offer investors a tax-efficient way of accessing the higher-risk market of unquoted investing with the ability to mitigate some of the risk through the 30 per cent tax relief. VCTs are really only a consideration for investors with good-sized investment portfolios who can afford to take a long-term view and are comfortable with the risks of investing in smaller companies. VCTs are therefore not suitable for all investors but, if you have a propensity for adding a little spice to your portfolio, then there could be a place for VCTs in it. And you never know: you may be in line for one of the windfalls that these funds can provide.

# Katalyst Ventures

## capital and expertise
## creating wealth

Katalyst Ventures brings together private investors to invest in early stage and small business opportunities. We are the link between good business ideas, the money to finance them and the advice and support to make them successful.

Katalyst was formed in 1999 when we, Katalyst's Directors, personally found that many good opportunities were financially too demanding for us to undertake on our own. In addition we saw that our shared business experience and knowledge could be put to good use in the companies in which we were investing. Over 150 investors have since now invested with us.

We aim to identify and invest in early stage and small businesses before the wider investment community recognises their potential. In most instances investors secure EIS tax advantages. Alternative transaction structures are also frequently put in place.

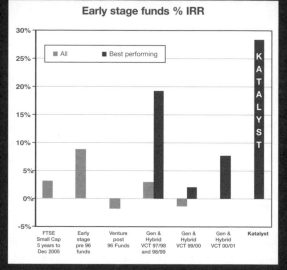

*Source: - PWC BVCA Performance Measurement Survey 2005, Allenbridge VCT Performance June 2006 and Katalyst Ventures Ltd.

Since Katalyst's inception we have always let our performance speak for itself.

- With an annual return ("IRR") of over 25%, Katalyst has become one of the UK's best performing Private Investor Groups.

- Based on publicly available performance data Katalyst has:

  - Beaten the best performing VCT

  - Significantly outperformed the sector average for:

    - Generalist VCT's

    - Venture Capital Early Stage and Development Capital Funds

- With the benefit of full EIS Tax Relief the Investment Portfolio has achieved an IRR of 46%.

Each year we aim to introduce carefully selected opportunities to our Investors. While Katalyst identifies and appraises opportunities, the investors make their own decisions. There is no maximum or minimum investment amount. An Investor can invest in one or a series of investments – or even none.

We are keen to meet like-minded individuals – Entrepreneurs, Businessmen and Professionals – seeking capital growth from investing in young businesses. Becoming a member of Katalyst is straightforward. We will ask you to provide information about your financial standing and expertise in order to meet the requirements of the Financial Services Authority You will also need to provide documentation to satisfy Money Laundering Regulations. If you feel that you are like us please call Anthony Collinson, Chairman – on 01664 823810 to arrange to come to one of our lunchtime presentations in London. Alternatively go to our website www.katalystventures.com/wealthregister for more details about Katalyst and how to invest ahead of the rest.

Please note that past performance is not a guide to future performance and the value of investments and the income from them can go down as well as up. Katalyst cannot guarantee that it will be able to identify business opportunities that will yield the same historical returns. Indeed it should be noted that Investments in shares in private companies carry some significant risks.

Issued by Katalyst Ventures Ltd which is authorised and regulated by the Financial Services Authority, Registered Office: Sulney Fields, Upper Broughton, Melton Mowbray, Leicestershire LE14 3BD, Registered in England number (3843058). Katalyst is a member of the British Venture Capital Association.

# Private equity – an investment model for private investors

*Anthony Collinson, Katalyst Ventures Ltd*

Private equity clearly offers high potential rewards but there can also be considerable risks. An individual investor typically faces several challenges:

- Identifying the best opportunities is far from easy. The first challenge is, metaphorically, finding the pearls on a beach where there is plenty of shingle.
- Then, continuing the metaphor, how do you ensure that these pearls are real not synthetic?
- Early-stage businesses need both capital and management support if they are to realize their potential. Management teams in small companies tend to be young, energetic and committed. But they can be inexperienced in key areas and lack some of the necessary skills. So how does a portfolio private equity investor cover for this?
- It is axiomatic that a balance of risk requires diversity. This normally requires substantial capital unless an investor can co-invest with others.

Katalyst Ventures' investment model enables investors to resolve these issues. According to Alexander Macpherson, Katalyst's CEO, Katalyst's investors are 'like-minded people, seeking similar investments, co-investing to their mutual benefit – and at lower cost and risk than they can achieve on their own'.

Katalyst has become one of the UK's best-performing private investor groups, with an annual return (IRR) of over 25 per cent (46 per cent with EIS tax benefits).

Members of Katalyst's investor group are effectively a 'club' and are typically entrepreneurs, senior executives and wealthy private investors, who can provide expertise as well as capital. The variety and extent of the 'knowledge capital' these investors bring to the businesses they invest in are a resource far beyond the reach of most other small businesses and are an important contributory factor to Katalyst's success.

A typical year will see Katalyst screen some 2,500 opportunities, typically sourced from Katalyst's own investor group, business angels and venture capitalists. Of these, 60 to 70 propositions are evaluated in depth. Key areas of focus include: the market need for the product or service; the business's strategy; its growth potential; and its projections. Particular attention is paid to the strengths of the management team and its ability to exploit the opportunity's potential. The selection process eventually distils the number of opportunities to approximately six per annum, and these are then formally presented to the 'club'.

Once an investment is agreed in principle, Katalyst coordinates the commercial, financial and legal due diligence, leading to completion. All participating investors sign up to a shareholders' agreement, and capital is subscribed by a syndicate of individuals rather than as one investment under the name of Katalyst, thus enabling investors to benefit from EIS and other tax advantages. Each investor makes his or her own decision whether or not to invest. There is no maximum or minimum.

Economic and market conditions and the performance of the businesses themselves determine exit timing, but most investments typically have a timescale of around five years. Katalyst has to date invested in 23 companies and successfully exited five – four through trade sales and one by AIM flotation.

Private equity investment was previously the preserve of venture capital and private equity funds. The emergence of professionally managed business angel groups such as Katalyst has, at last, enabled private investors to participate profitably in this potentially very rewarding sector.

'Early-stage venture capital is not for widows and orphans,' says Macpherson, 'but we do our best to work with our investors in finding good opportunities, maximizing their potential and minimizing the risks. For an individual with a reasonable amount of capital, it can be appropriate for a moderate proportion to be in this asset class, ideally with a good spread to mitigate risk.' He adds, 'Every now and again that pearl on the beach turns out to be a diamond. We believe we have a few. And remember how Microsoft, eBay and Google started!'

# Investing for everyone's benefit

*Stuart Tyler, Lincoln Financial Group*

Stock market investment can often seem selfish, with a glaring conflict between what companies should be doing for the benefit of others and the returns demanded by shareholders. The growing market of socially responsible investing (SRI), also known as green or ethical investing, looks to address this.

Green investing is big business, with around £10 billion in retail funds and £80 billion in occupational pension schemes. Lincoln Financial Group has operated green life and pension funds since 1992.

Green investing takes different forms. One way is 'negative' screening, which avoids companies considered unethical. This however is subjective, particularly for companies deemed unethical! At Lincoln, companies involved in armaments, alcohol, tobacco, pornography, nuclear power and gambling are avoided. Involvement is defined as making 10 per cent of turnover from these activities.

Another approach is to select companies for their positive contributions. The Lincoln Green funds have identified six areas of change, detailed below. Green investing is of course always about good fund management – it is not a case of just buying any green company.

## Clean energy

Climate change concern and energy security have prompted G8 governments to set targets to generate at least 25 per cent of electricity from renewable sources by 2025.

Wind energy is essential if the UK government is to meet its target of a 20 per cent reduction in $CO_2$ emissions by 2010. This sector has averaged 28 per cent annual growth for the past five years. A new growth area is offshore wind power. Gamesa, Vestas and Clipper Windpower are leading developers of wind turbines.

The solar market grew by 60 per cent annually from 2000 to 2004 and is predicted to grow by 30 per cent per year to 2010 and beyond. Solar power systems harness solar energy and convert it into hot water or electricity. Sharp is the world's largest manufacturer of solar cells and is reducing costs through manufacturing efficiency. Carmanah is a world leader in solar lighting. Solar Integrated Technologies and Romag design building materials incorporating solar electric cells, enabling buildings to generate their own electricity.

Fuel cells are regarded as the technology that will deliver the zero-emission vehicle. However, they have other applications. Fuel cells use a chemical reaction between hydrogen and oxygen to create electricity, heat and water vapour. FuelCell Energy produces highly efficient cells that can generate up to 50 mW of electricity. Azure Dynamics and Quantum Fuel Systems develop systems to support hybrid electric, electric and fuel cell-driven vehicles.

## Did you know?

Wind is the closest to being commercially competitive. Current high energy prices mean the most efficient turbines operating in the most favourable conditions are already competitive with oil- or gas-generated electricity.

The largest wind turbines have blades over 50 metres long and a tower higher than 100 metres, and generate over 3 mW of electricity, enough to power up to 2,000 homes.

## Water management

The global water industry is big business and is growing rapidly. Developed countries may need to spend up to $1 trillion by 2026 to upgrade water and waste water treatment systems. Meanwhile China has one of the fastest-growing urban populations and economies in the world. Demand for water from urban areas and industry is expected to grow by 70 per cent and 104 per cent respectively between 2010 and 2030. The Chinese government admits its water infrastructure is inadequate and plans extensive development.

United Nations' figures show 1.1 billion people cannot get clean drinking water and 2.6 billion people – half the developing world – do not have access to even a simple pit latrine. Simultaneously, health concerns are prompting demands for tougher regulation of the water industry, while companies producing food, pharmaceuticals and electronics require water treated to higher standards than drinking water.

Supplying quality water is challenging. Only 0.01 per cent of the Earth's total water is usable, 97.5 per cent is salt water and the rest is locked into glaciers and ice caps. Put simply, if the world's water supply were stored in a 5-litre container, available fresh water would only fill a teaspoon. Currently about 20 per cent of the world's population is facing water shortages, expected to rise to 30 per cent in 2025. China has 22 per cent of the world's population but only 7 per cent of the world's fresh water.

New water treatment technologies have emerged, such as ultrafiltration, which removes microbial contaminations without increasing the concentrations of by-products. As filtration and purification help ease water shortages, these technologies are expected to see significant growth, of 15–30 per cent over the next three to five years.

Kurita Water Industries designs and installs specialized filtration units in the Asian markets. Pall and Zenon Environmental provide similar products and services in the United States and other parts of the world. Zenon also supplies an easily transportable mobile ultrafiltration system, which can be used in drought or emergency conditions. It produces high-quality drinking water regardless of the water source. Utilities such as the Spanish Aguas de Barcelona and the French Veolia Environnement provide the more traditional services of distributing drinking water as well as treating waste water.

# Transport

The introduction of the congestion charge in 2002 has had a hugely positive impact on public transport in London. Bus usage is at its highest level since 1968 and continues to grow. In 2004, light rail services (the DLR and the Croydon Tramlink) recorded a sixfold increase in passenger numbers since 1994. There are now 70,000 fewer vehicle journeys into the congestion charge zone each day. And the number of casualties on London roads has fallen. Transport for London policy has made a difference.

$CO_2$ emissions from transport rose throughout the 1990s and account for around 25 per cent of total UK emissions affecting air quality. The Department of Health estimates that up to 24,000 early deaths annually result from poor air quality in our cities.

Transport noise causes disturbance, with aircraft noise being a key contributor. Road transport is predicted to grow a further 33 per cent in the next 20 years, while demand for air travel is forecast to treble by 2030. Despite technological advances, the environmental impacts of transport will grow unless government, business and individuals act.

UK bus and train operator First is tackling one problem head on – the school run, which adds one in five cars to the morning rush hour. Its 20,000 yellow school buses carry nearly 2 million students a day in the United States, and it launched a UK initiative in 2002. It operates the Croydon Tramlink, carrying approximately 20 million passengers annually, and is trialling three zero-emission fuel cell buses in London. London and South-East bus and train operator Go-Ahead carried nearly 500 million passengers on 3,310 buses in 2004. It is testing hybrid diesel and electric vehicles. Its subsidiary Govia will manage the new Integrated Kent franchise, one of the largest commuter rail franchises. National Express reports continued growth of bus passengers. Its Saver Bus initiative, offering affordable bus fares, launched in 2004 in Birmingham, has resulted in double-digit passenger growth. Speed and convenience are vital if public transport is to expand. The Japanese bullet trains operated by Japan Railway East transport 16 million passengers each day.

# Waste management

Markets for recycled materials demonstrate the value of waste. The United States recycles about 65 per cent of its steel. More steel is recycled than aluminium, paper, glass and plastic combined. Brazil recycled 95 per cent of its aluminium can production in 2004, a volume of 121 thousand tonnes, saving enough energy to power a city with a population of over 1 million. But more markets can be created. For example, selling the plastic bottles currently landfilled in the UK would generate over £27 million. To boost recycling the UK government has provided £420 million for 2003–06, and it has increased the landfill tax.

The UK produces around 400 million tonnes of waste annually – a quarter from households and businesses, with the rest from construction, sewage sludge, farm waste, spoils from mines and dredging of rivers. In England and Wales about 100 million tonnes of waste are landfilled annually – even though landfill space will run out within 5 to 10 years! Recycling and incinerators are seen as the way forward. European directives relevant to waste management will generate a value for waste. Indeed, the UK government's target to increase local authorities' recycling to 25 per cent has doubled UK domestic recycling rates in four years to 23 per cent in 2004/05. Households could recycle up to 60 per cent!

---

## Did you know?

British Airways enables customers to offset the carbon dioxide emissions from their flights by contributing to an environmental trust called Climate Care. The money is invested in sustainable energy projects tackling global warming.

---

Increasing recycling, regulation and pressure on landfill space has spurred businesses to expand in waste collection, treatment and recycling. Technologies that reduce waste or develop recyclable materials are other investment options. Companies such as the UK's Shanks and the United States' Casella provide recycling services as well as collection and disposal. Stericycle has developed technology that uses high temperatures and pressures to kill pathogens. It is used to treat medical waste, much of it plastic, which can then be recycled.

---

## Did you know?

Every year UK households dump the equivalent of 3.5 million double-decker buses (almost 30 million tonnes).

Over half of England's waste is garden waste, paper and board, and kitchen waste.

Around 20 per cent of the food we buy off supermarket shelves goes straight to the bin. Every household dumps £424 of food annually.

## Sustainable living

Concerns over health, nutrition and food safety have increased opportunities in the organic and health food market. In the UK organic food sales have climbed from £100 million in 1993/94 to £1 billion plus in 2003/04.

Strong growth is forecast in the UK and the United States – 11 per cent annually to 2007 in the UK and 9 per cent to 16 per cent up to 2010 in the United States. The 'functional food' market is another growth story, where companies produce foods or dietary components using, for example, plant and vegetable extracts that improve health.

The organic and health food retailer Whole Foods Market is serving the demand for healthier choices in North America and the UK. Whole Foods Market's UK subsidiary Fresh & Wild plans a flagship store in 2007 in London.

French food-testing company Eurofins Scientific can detect genetically modified (GM) content in food, giving manufacturers certainty when offering GM-free foods. Provexis is a functional food company whose products include fruit juices that help to reduce unwanted blood clotting, a critical factor in heart attacks and strokes.

---

### Tips for healthy living

■ Consuming at least five portions of fruit and vegetables a day can reduce the risk from heart disease, stroke and cancer by up to 20 per cent.

■ Regular exercise cuts stress, aids sleep and boosts the immune system. In the long term it reduces the risk of diseases such as stroke, diabetes and heart disease.

■ Cut the distance your food travels – buy from your local farmers' market; www.farmersmarkets.net will show your local market.

■ Read the Soil Association's consumer guide at www.soilassociation.org to learn more about organic food.

---

## Environment policy

Regulation is increasing and enforcement is being stepped up.

Companies such as Mouchel Parkman in the UK and Stantec in North America advise on the implications of legislation for business, environmental impact assessment and provision of water and waste utilities. Companies such as WS Atkins help to develop solutions to meet compliance with environmental regulations. Consultancies such as Waterman and RPS can advise on urban planning, sustainable design and construction best practice to make London 2012 a low-carbon and zero-waste Games.

In addition to environmental legislation, there is health and safety legislation requiring employers to protect staff. Training may be one solution, as is specialist equipment to cut risks. For example, Latchways manufactures safety equipment for people working at heights.

# Part 3

# Pensions planning and products

# The new world of self-invested personal pensions (SIPPs)

*Christine Hallett, Pointon York SIPP Solutions Limited*

We have to become increasingly aware of planning for our own retirement and seek out the numerous tax shelters that are available to ensure that the wealth we have created during our working life and the standard of living we have enjoyed remain with us through the most important years of our life – our retirement!

One thing is sure – we need to take control; we need to work with our advisers and specialists in order to plan proactively to ensure our wealth is not eroded.

Since the inception of SIPPs in 1989, the aim of many clients to meet their own investment targets rather than those of insurance companies has brought about a sea change in retirement planning control by members, and it is thought that this must surely expand under the new and generally more liberal rules.

The wider range of potential investment, although the withdrawal of the much heralded inclusion of residential property has disappointed some, has encouraged others to feel a greater sense of control of their investment strategy and given their advisers more rein in their investment advice.

Asset allocation, the byword of investment over the last few years, can more fully be realized under the new rules. The ability for SIPPs to invest in unquoted shares is seen as a real opportunity to apply expertise and personal experience. However, in this respect we need to identify a dependable and acceptable method of valuation to meet the Revenue's requirements that any transactions, particularly with connected persons, are still evidenced by arm's length market valuations. Everyone also needs to understand the impact of HMRC's rules on tangible moveable property to ensure any tax charges are minimized.

# POINTON YORK SIPP SOLUTIONS LIMITED

Pointon York SIPP Solutions Limited, are a specialist pension service provider and have been since the early seventies when they led the marketplace in the establishment and running of Small Self Administered Schemes. They have been specialising in Self Invested Personal Pensions since their launch in 1990, and are now a company that solely provides services for Self Invested Personal Pensions (SIPPs) to IFA's, Employee Benefit Consultants, Accountants, Solicitors and clients.

Pointon York SIPP Solutions (PYSS) is an independent company that administers the pension wrapper and acts as the trustee for the pension schemes. Enabling the professional connection to add value by advising on the asset allocation within the pension wrapper and selecting the appropriate investment strategy for that.

PYSS provides services for individual high net worth clients, they provide services for groups of individuals that want to club their pension pots together to purchase a joint asset, for professional partnerships who want to purchase their business premises through their pension scheme, and for company'Os who want to provide a company pension scheme.

PYSS have specialist staff working to ensure the experience of working with us is stress free, our staff are constantly trained to deliver the best service they can, and to ensure that the pension assets are administered in accordance with the connection's or client's instructions.

The flexibility of the SIPP framework, and the flexibility of pricing almost makes the SIPP the pension scheme of choice these days, the ability to change investment choices quickly if they are not working without having to change to a new pension provider has got to be a big advantage, a pension scheme for life is here and PYSS can administer it from cradle to grave.

PYSS are specialist in direct commercial property investments within the SIPP making the experience of purchasing the property an exciting and hassle free one. The PY SIPP owns many different types of property from land, retail shops, offices and warehouses in the UK and abroad. The process is simple the SIPP is established, money comes into the SIPP by either contributions or transfers from other pension pots, we are instructed to purchase a particular commercial property, we instruct environmental searches, the solicitors, the bank (if there is borrowing), we liaise with all parties through to exchange an completion when the pension scheme will own the property we then ensure that the terms of the Lease are adhered to by the tenants, and eventually we would sell the property on the client's or their advisers instructions.

Borrowing is allowed for the purchase of an asset within a SIPP, up to a limit of the net fund value.

PYSS own over 700 properties, some individuals have purchased, we have a family that all have SIPPs and the husband, wife and children all own a share of a commercial property, we have a number of barrister chambers who all have SIPPs and their pooled pensions have purchased the building from which they run their chambers.

PYSS are one of the few SIPP service providers, who will allow joint ownership of a commercial property with another third party whether that is the scheme member personally, or a company, or just a friend we will undoubtedly have a solution for the requirement.

PYSS run company pension schemes, advisers to company's no longer want to be establishing insurance company schemes where there is often mediocre performance, restrictions on Investment choices, lack of transparency and hefty exit penalties when transferred, so using the SIPP framework as the base for the company pension scheme with PYSS they are able to build a bespoke pension scheme suitable to the needs of that particular company with improved results.

PYSS will work to provide a solution to an individuals requirement as long as it is within the rules and regulations, so some of the newer investment types now allowable PYSS will consider if requested, we have agreed to some Unquoted share investments, also private equity offers, some loan schemes from SIPPs have been approved, we aim to deliver to the connections and clients requirements.

With the ability now to contribute significant amounts of earnings into pension schemes and the flexibility of investment choices the only option really is utilising a SIPP framework through PYSS.

*If you are:*

An individual reviewing their pension arrangements and retirement plans.

A group of individuals who want to purchase an asset together.

Parents who want to make provision for their children.

A partner in any firm who may currently own a commercial property, but may not have any pension arrangements.

A Director of a company who wants to provide the pension scheme for their staff

Contact us via the details on the next page 106.

The market will open up to those who wish to purchase assets already held personally, which was previously outside the rules controlling 'connected persons' transactions. This particularly applies to those who, reflecting the mindset of the small to medium-sized business proprietor, have purchased the premises housing their business. It will now be possible to put such an asset in the SIPP, using tax-relieved contributions or transfers, and shelter all capital gains and income on rental from tax.

Where does a self-invested personal pension wrapper fit into the plan? Well, for those better informed it has to be an integral part. The self-invested personal pension wrap allows you to enjoy:

- tax relief on 100 per cent of your earnings on contributions made up to the annual allowance, which is currently £225,000, although this will increase each year – 22 per cent reclaimed by the pension's administrator goes into your pension pot and the further 18 per cent is claimed through your self-assessment form for higher-rate taxpayers;
- all growth from the assets held within the pension scheme free from capital gains tax and not generally part of your estate for inheritance tax purposes;
- being able, along with your advisers, to develop a bespoke investment strategy within your pension scheme, allocating funds across the different asset classes in proportions that suit you and utilizing a range of different companies' products;
- a wide range of flexible retirement options to suit you and your beneficiaries without the need to purchase an annuity.

Many people will not be maximizing their pension contributions because they haven't really considered the new rules and what benefits they as high net worth individuals can enjoy. For example, when bonus time comes, you may consider making a bonus sacrifice into your self-invested personal pension either in part or in whole, a 40 per cent tax saving straight away.

You may already own a property from which you are running your business – have you thought about transferring the property into a SIPP by way of contribution? Again, you will enjoy 40 per cent tax relief on that value without having to find any real cash.

You may have a number of different pension pots that need to be consolidated and a more cohesive approach to investments deployed. Well, by considering transferring them all to a self-invested personal pension plan with one company not only will you be starting to take control and be able to plan for that successful retirement but you will also undoubtedly be reducing the costs of the ongoing servicing of those schemes, or you will undoubtedly benefit from the economies of scale from only one set of fees.

You may be an employer running a business and offering a pension scheme to your employees. Well, why should they have second-best? Why not consider a SIPP framework where all employees from the most senior to the most junior can enjoy this level of flexibility and control? This could reintroduce the proactive approach to pension planning as opposed to leaving it with insurance companies where funds are managed without reference to the needs of individuals.

If there has ever been a time to consider your retirement plans it is now; we no longer have the luxury of carry-back and carry-forward, so you need to consider your position for this tax year now and ensure that you maximize the tax available to you.

Pointon York SIPP Solutions are specialists in self-invested personal pensions, and are the pensions' administrators. Our trustee company, Crescent Trustees Limited, holds the assets for the benefit of the individual member schemes.

The majority of our scheme members work with their advisers in order to structure an investment portfolio that suits them and that can be changed as and when required; some clients come direct.

We deal with schemes for high net worth individuals and for professional partnerships such as solicitors, accountants, doctors and dentists; we work with groups of individuals who want to purchase a joint asset through their SIPPs; and we operate company pension schemes.

Please contact us if you wish to discuss any thoughts you might have after reading this chapter.

# The new 'simple' world of pensions

*John Moret, Suffolk Life*

In April 2006 the pensions landscape in the UK changed – and a new simplified world was unveiled. Although ultimately the pensions tax simplification changes were not quite as profound as originally envisaged by their architect, Alan Pickering, nevertheless their impact is already starting to be felt. The full effect of the changes will depend on a whole range of other influences, many of which are politically dependent. What is undeniable is that for many – particularly those financially able to save regularly and materially – the pension saving opportunities have increased enormously.

## Summary of main pension tax changes

The main pensions tax changes introduced with effect from 6 April 2006 are:

- Personal contributions up to the lower of 100 per cent of earnings and the new annual limit of £215,000 (in tax year 2006/07) qualify for tax relief of up to 40 per cent.
- As was the case prior to April 2006, anyone is able to invest up to £3,600 per annum regardless of earnings.
- Both employer's and employee's contributions count towards the annual limit. However, employer contributions are not restricted to the 100 per cent of earnings limit for tax purposes, potentially creating significant tax planning opportunities for owners of small businesses.
- Individuals are now able to belong to an employer's occupational scheme and also contribute to one or more individual pension arrangements – sometimes referred to as 'full concurrency'. Prior to 6 April 2006 this was not allowed.

- Members of any pension scheme can take 25 per cent of their pensions savings as tax-free cash up to a maximum of £375,000 (in 2006/07).
- A new lifetime allowance – £1.5 million for 2006/07 – sets a maximum for the amount of tax-relieved savings that you can accumulate. This will rise to £1.8 million by 2010/11. Any excess assets will be subject to a tax charge of 25 per cent, increased to 55 per cent if the excess assets are taken as cash rather than income.
- Pre-April 2006 pension rights can be protected through either of the following:
  - Primary protection. If by April 2006 your accumulated pension assets exceeded £1.5 million you can register the value. Subsequently you can take benefits up to that value (increased in line with inflation) without paying the excess tax charge. Similarly you can also register any tax-free cash entitlement in excess of £375,000, ie 25 per cent of £1.5 million.
  - Enhanced protection. Alternatively anyone can register for 'enhanced protection' regardless of their total pre-April 2006 pension assets. This will ensure that those assets are protected and can eventually be taken without any excess tax charge. However, importantly in this case you are not able to make any further pension contributions post-April 2006.
  Registration for protection can be made up until April 2008.
- The earliest age at which you will be able to take benefits will rise from 50 to 55 in 2010. However, you are now able to start drawing benefits regardless of whether you have retired.
- The limits on income drawdown (the alternative to purchasing an annuity) have changed. In particular there is now no minimum annual income requirement, and the maximum income limit has increased.
- The requirement to buy an annuity with your pensions savings no later than age 75 has been removed. Now you can elect to take an 'alternatively secured pension' (ASP) – this is similar to income drawdown but with a lower maximum limit. At the time of writing the government have proposed some changes to the regime introduced in April 2006. These changes will be introduced in the Finance Act 2007 and if unaltered will limit the flexibility in income and make the transfer of funds on death relatively unattractive from a tax standpoint. It is unclear whether these changes will be retrospective. However, they reflect the government's continuing belief that purchase of an annuity should be the preferred option for those reaching age 75.
- Many of the previous restrictions on 'permitted' investments have disappeared. The restrictions on transactions with a 'connected' person have also been removed. For example, it is now possible for a company or partnership to purchase its existing business premises through a sale-and-leaseback arrangement with the pension arrangements for the company directors or the partners. It is also possible to transfer certain personally owned assets such as a share portfolio into a pension arrangement in lieu of a cash contribution – and derive full tax relief provided the contribution can be justified based on earnings. However, there are some complex provisions relating to what is called 'taxable property', which is defined as residential property and 'tangible moveable assets'. Whilst such investments are not prohibited, the potential tax charges make such investments very unattractive.

## The growth of the SIPP

One of the consequences of these changes is that we have seen a big growth in a type of individual pension called a self-invested personal pension (SIPP). Once seen as the preserve of the wealthy and financially sophisticated, the SIPP is rapidly becoming the solution of choice for those people who require a more responsive way to plan their finances for retirement.

A SIPP is simply a personal pension under which the investor or the investor's adviser selects the investments, giving wider freedom of choice and control to the individual. As a result it is not necessary to hold a number of different personal pensions to get a wide investment spread because with a SIPP all types of permitted investment can be held under one umbrella – the SIPP.

In 2005 there was enormous publicity around the opportunity to invest in residential property and exotica within a SIPP. That publicity undoubtedly contributed to much greater general awareness of SIPPs. Although the Chancellor effectively killed off many of the 'fringe' investment opportunities – including direct investment in residential property – in the 2006 Finance Act, the more mainstream investment options that have contributed to the growth of the SIPP market since it was launched in 1989 by Nigel Lawson remain. Figure 3.2.1 plots the historical growth of this market.

It is estimated that there were around 180,000 pension investors with SIPPs as at October 2006, with aggregated assets in excess of £30 billion. Those assets will have been invested in a range of investments, primarily:

■ UK and overseas equities;
■ collective investments such as unit trusts and OEICs;

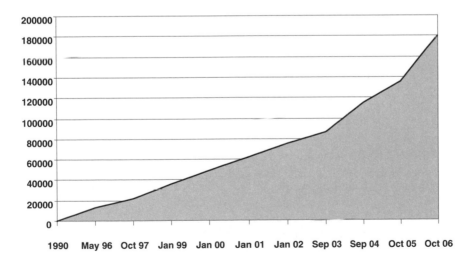

Estimated number of SIPPs at
1.10.06: 180,000 – value *c* £30bn

*Sources:* Trade magazine surveys 1995–2006

**Figure 3.2.1**    The growth in the SIPP market

- insurance company managed and other funds;
- commercial property;
- cash and other deposits.

In addition to the investment flexibility with a SIPP, the component parts of a traditional individual pension are unbundled. Historically, insurance companies have provided all the constituent parts of the individual pension product in one 'bundled' package. This 'one stop shop' approach is effective when each part works well but where this isn't the case investors can be locked into inadequate administration or underperforming investment funds to the detriment of their overall pension fund.

## Managing your SIPP

With a SIPP the various components are 'unbundled' and it is possible to select the best provider of services in a number of key areas:

- *Pensions administration.* One can use a specialist administrator for whom dealing with the not inconsiderable demands of the new pensions tax regime is a core competence.
- *Investment advice.* The opportunity to choose the most appropriate source of investment advice can ensure a more individually tailored pension portfolio.
- *Investment administration.* Under a SIPP the ability of a competent investment administrator to deal with a diverse range of investments is central to making the most of investing for retirement.
- *Cash management.* The effective movement of cash and market rates of interest on cash balances should be readily achievable under a SIPP.
- *Property administration.* Investing in commercial property is one of the options available under a SIPP. The specialist nature of property means that very different processes apply both at the outset and on an ongoing basis when compared to other investments.
- *Payment of benefits.* A SIPP allows optimum flexibility and choice when it comes to taking an income.

Whatever approach is taken to the provision of these various services, the SIPP provider and administrator has a pivotal role in ensuring the seamless exchange of information between the providers of the various components. In some cases the provider will provide the majority of the services; in others a range of different organizations will be utilized. Whatever the model, increasingly technology is the key to providing true added value to the SIPP investor.

As a result, a SIPP will frequently offer more choice, better control and greater flexibility when it comes to investing for retirement. In conjunction with their advisers, SIPP investors can devise a personalized investment strategy and build a diversified portfolio appropriate to their needs. A SIPP provides options that are not available through more traditional types of individual pension – one of the reasons why more and more advisers are recommending a SIPP as the solution to their clients' total pension needs.

Historically, the cost of a SIPP has been higher than for traditional products except for higher levels of contribution – say funds of over £100,000. SIPP charges tend to be flat fees – usually a set-up fee in the region of £300–£400 and an annual fee of around the same amount. In addition there may be transaction fees. There will almost certainly be additional charges for administering income drawdown and for setting up and administering property investments.

However, with the growth in online SIPP providers and improved technology there is some downward pressure on charges and depending on the investment strategy and frequency of trading in some cases SIPP costs will compare favourably with traditional products at contribution levels as low as £10,000.

One of the attractions of a SIPP is that charges are generally clearer and more explicit than for many historical traditional individual pensions. However, it is still important to look at the small print carefully – for example, to check the rates of interest paid on cash deposits within the SIPP.

Also SIPPs are potentially more demanding to administer, particularly where income drawdown is used or property investments undertaken. Consequently service levels and reputation are equally important. That is why most investors considering setting up a SIPP would be well advised to seek professional advice. Running your own investment portfolio can sound attractive but it requires skill, experience, access to up-to-date information and technology, and time.

In April 2007 the establishment and operation of a SIPP will become an FSA-regulated activity. The full implications of this change are still to emerge but it should provide greater protection for SIPP investors and may also lead to some consolidation amongst providers and potentially the emergence of some new 'operators' and new SIPP propositions.

## Likely SIPP investors

Given the various changes mentioned above we can expect to see an increase in the number of investors taking out SIPPs, such as:

- ■ *Professionals* – particularly accountants, solicitors and other partnerships, including those who own their own premises or can benefit from the ability, for example, to invest in unquoted and private company shares – subject to the provisions of the new 'taxable property' regime.
- ■ *Soloists* – these are the 'do it yourself', mainly online, investors who are now benefiting from greater choice of SIPP provider.
- ■ *Aggregators* – investors whose total pension details have emerged as a result of the need to check for 'protection' and lifetime allowance purposes. Some or all of their existing pension entitlements will be consolidated within a SIPP, possibly through assignment or transfers. Clearly each case will need to be assessed on its merits.

Alongside these more traditional SIPP investors it is likely we will see the emergence of several new types of SIPP investors, including:

■ *SIPP on the siders* – individuals who remain in an occupational scheme or another type of pension scheme but who are in a position to take advantage of the new full concurrency rules.
■ *High flyers* – many City and other professionals are ideal candidates for SIPPs. As a result of their job mobility many have several deferred pension entitlements from previous employments. They may also be in a position to contribute substantial sums as a result of bonuses etc by way of salary or bonus sacrifice arrangements, which can be attractive to employees and tax efficient for their employer.
■ *Late starters* – the new contribution rules provide opportunities for those with no or underfunded pensions to correct the position over a short space of time – particularly in the run-up to retirement.
■ *Portfolio shifters* – it is possible for individuals to move personally owned assets such as share portfolios into a SIPP in lieu of cash contributions, possibly over a period of years. This could prove to be very attractive to older individuals with underfunded pensions, although care needs to be exercised over potential capital gains tax liabilities.
■ *Diversifiers* – further investment diversification is possible in some circumstances via direct investment in private company shares and other vehicles such as overseas collectives that were previously not allowed.

## SIPP investment opportunities in property

These are just some of the many opportunities that are now available. What is very clear is that the flexibility offered through a SIPP is likely to be in increasing demand. For those wishing to invest in property, there is still an extensive choice of commercial property to choose from, such as offices, warehouses, shops and other traditional commercial property investments, alongside more unusual ones such as car parking spaces, zoos, airfields, football stadiums or leisure centres. Investing in commercial property can be useful for many individuals such as:

■ self-employed professionals, eg barristers, dentists and architects, who can buy their new practice offices via a SIPP;
■ farmers buying additional land;
■ wealthier individuals investing in commercial or office premises as part of a balanced pension investment portfolio.

Investing in property can be particularly beneficial where the property in question is used for business purposes by the SIPP investor. Since April 2006 it has been possible for the proprietors of small businesses and professional practices to utilize their existing commercial business premises as investments within a SIPP. In some circumstances it may be possible for the premises to be transferred into the SIPP in lieu of contributions, possibly over a period of years.

Holding premises within a SIPP and leasing them back to the business can be attractive for a number of reasons:

■ Rental income and capital growth are tax-free.
■ Rental payments can be treated as business expenses for tax purposes.
■ The monies used to purchase the property will attract tax relief when first invested into the plan.
■ The business's covenant as tenant could add to the investment value of the property.
■ The property may be outside the policyholder's estate for inheritance tax purposes.

Investing in commercial property within a SIPP is a specialist area, and professional advice is essential. It also makes sense to choose a SIPP administrator with both knowledge and experience of acquiring and administering commercial property within a SIPP.

## Conclusion

The wealthier investor's interest in investment for retirement through a pension plan has been conspicuously lacking in recent years with widespread disappointment at the performance of stereotyped with-profits and similar pension plans. As a result a large proportion of such investors did not take advantage of their full tax allowances. On the other hand, the previous contribution limits have been a major drawback for many in a position to contribute more than the basic amount. They should welcome the new simplified pensions tax regime with its new and mostly increased limits.

The recent rule changes also create a range of new investment opportunities that could benefit a wide number of individuals. The case for choosing a SIPP as the vehicle for pensions savings has never been stronger. We have already seen a number of new SIPP products and new providers, and I expect to continue to see many more new 'operators' of SIPPs in the new regulated and simplified pensions world. This will include traditional suppliers such as insurance companies and smaller consultancies, but I believe we will see increasing numbers of wealth managers such as private banks, fund managers and stockbrokers join the fray.

That is good new for investors. However, for the vast majority advice will be essential as, despite the apparent simplification, many of the options require specialist knowledge and skills – particularly in the area of investment. An investment in good-quality and professional advice will be money well spent.

# The case for a self-invested pension plan

*EFG Private Bank Ltd*

The simplification of pensions has opened up a wide variety of opportunities for a large number of people. However, a personal pension scheme for the majority of people who have one, means a packaged, off-the-shelf product from an insurance company. The service can be far from personal, and although your pension fund could well be one of your largest investments, you generally have very little say in its management.

In this chapter the case is made for the benefits of taking the self-invested personal pension (SIPP) route.

Within a SIPP you have greater freedom to determine the investment profile of your pension portfolio. You should be able to select your own independent manager or, indeed, oversee the day-to-day management of the investments yourself.

The better SIPP plans will offer:

■ a transparent, low-cost fee structure;
■ the opportunity to control the investment of your pension fund;
■ the chance to invest in a much broader range of investments;
■ an efficient way to save for your retirement and flexibility over the benefits you want at retirement;
■ the flexibility to adapt to changes in your personal circumstances;
■ the chance to purchase commercial property, which can be used by you or your partnership or business.

Although there are many choices available to the SIPP investor, there are a number of factors the would-be investor should consider:

■ Is your SIPP provider financially sound?
■ Many SIPP providers will avoid investments they regard as difficult, even though they are permitted under the current regulations. How flexible is your proposed provider?
■ Does the team consist of skilled, qualified individuals who know, or will quickly find, the answer to your queries?
■ Does the SIPP provider offer an individual, personal service to SIPP holders? Will you be greeted with automated telephone answering machines and will you know the names of the individuals looking after your plan?
■ Is the administration of a high standard, with the majority of enquiries responded to on the day of receipt?
■ Does the provider rank high in surveys of SIPP plans for its competitiveness on costs and flexibility?
■ Can you gain access to loans, to fund larger investments such as property, and a wide range of investment opportunities?

## The key points at a glance

■ You build up your own individual pension fund.
■ Your personal contributions qualify for full tax relief (within HMRC rules), and no UK income or capital gains tax is levied within the fund.
■ You choose what level of contributions to pay and when to pay them (within HMRC rules).
■ You can pay what you want, when you want – there is no commitment to future payments.
■ You have total flexibility in the appointment of a professional investment manager – or, if you choose, you can manage the investments yourself.
■ Investments can include commercial property, which can be used by your own business (on commercial terms).
■ You can increase the range of investments by consolidating all your existing pension arrangements into one plan.
■ You can take your pension benefits any time after age 50 (rising to 55 from 6 April 2010), and this decision does not have to be made in advance.
■ There is no upper limit on your pension – you get as much as your fund will buy. (However, the size of your fund may affect the taxation of your benefits where your total pension funds exceed the lifetime allowance. The lifetime allowance is a fixed level of benefits members can draw from all their registered pension schemes in their lifetime without triggering certain tax charges. The lifetime allowance is: £1.5 million in 2006/07; £1.6 million in 2007/08; £1.65 million in 2008/09; £1.75 million in 2009/10; £1.8 million in 2010/11.)

- Subject to the lifetime allowance, you can normally take up to 25 per cent of your fund in the form of a tax-free cash lump sum before age 75, the balance being used to provide pension benefits for you and your dependants.
- You do not have to retire from work to draw your pension and cash benefits.
- The income withdrawal facility means that you need not be locked into poor annuity rates when you start drawing a pension.
- Death benefits will normally be paid free of inheritance tax.
- You can retire earlier than expected, stop contributing to the scheme for any reason, or transfer your fund elsewhere. Your fund's full value should always be available for your benefit.

## Eligibility

Most individuals, including those resident overseas, are eligible to join a SIPP, although tax relief is only available on contributions paid by, or on behalf of, a member if that member is a relevant UK individual and under age 75. You can join a SIPP irrespective of whether you are:

- self-employed;
- employed but in non-pensionable service;
- employed and a member of your employer's personal or occupational pension scheme; or
- not in employment, although your contribution will be restricted to a basic amount of £3,600 (for 2006/07).

## Contributions

If you intend to pay contributions no greater than the basic amount (£3,600 in the 2006/07 tax year) in any tax year, you do not need to be in receipt of relevant UK earnings to contribute. Individuals should continue to receive tax relief on contributions of up to £3,600, or 100 per cent of their earnings if higher, subject to the annual allowance (see below). Contributions in excess of the annual allowance will attract a tax charge of 40 per cent.

A good-quality SIPP should give you complete personal choice within the above limits to pay in as much or as little as you want, when you want:

- You can pay regular, set amounts at monthly, quarterly, half-yearly or yearly intervals.
- You can stop making regular payments whenever you wish, without penalty.
- You can restart regular contributions whenever you choose.
- You can reduce or increase the amount of regular payments at any time, or supplement them with additional single sums from time to time.
- If you prefer not to make any regular commitment, you can pay in single sums as and when it suits you.

Your employer can also make a contribution to the SIPP. There is no set limit on the amount of the contribution that can be paid. Your employer will normally receive tax relief where the contribution is considered wholly and exclusively for the purposes of the business.

Persons other than your employer can also make a contribution to the SIPP in respect of you. For tax purposes that contribution will be treated as if it was made by you, and you should be able to claim tax relief on the contribution.

However, total contributions paid by or in respect of a member may result in the annual allowance being exceeded. The annual allowance is effectively a limit on the amount of tax privileges available on pension savings in a given year. The annual allowance for 2006/07 is £215,000; for 2007/08 £225,000; for 2008/09 £235,000; for 2009/10 £245,000; and for 2010/11 £255,000. When the annual allowance is exceeded an annual allowance charge will be charged on the member equal to 40 per cent of the excess above the annual allowance.

## Tax advantages

A SIPP is a registered pension scheme for HMRC purposes. This means that, under current legislation, contributions to the scheme and its investments enjoy the following advantages:

■ Contributions made by you and by others on your behalf (except your employer) are subject to tax relief up to the higher of the basic amount and 100 per cent of your relevant UK earnings, providing you are a relevant UK individual and under the age of 75.
■ The funds in which your contributions are invested are free from UK income and capital gains taxes (except that tax may not be reclaimed on UK dividends, or dividends from shares issued by certain foreign companies).
■ You are normally entitled to take up to a 25 per cent tax-free cash lump sum on taking benefits, subject to the lifetime allowance.
■ Lump sums payable on death normally will not be counted as part of your estate for inheritance tax purposes.
■ Where contributions are paid by an employer and these are below the annual allowance, you should not be taxed on the amount of those contributions as a benefit in kind. Your employer will normally receive tax relief where the contribution is considered wholly and exclusively for the purposes of the business.

If you are a director, an employee or self-employed, you pay contributions using the 'relief at source' method. This means that you pay your own contributions to a SIPP net of basic rate tax. The provider of the SIPP will claim the tax from HMRC and add it to the net amount already invested. If you pay tax at more than the basic rate on your income, you can obtain the higher-rate relief by making a claim on your self-assessment return.

# Investment

Consistent long-term management of your pension scheme investments is extremely important. It is, of course, the size of this fund that will determine the level of future income you get from it.

You should have complete freedom to choose an independent investment manager authorized under the Financial Services and Markets Act 2000 or, if you prefer to retain day-to-day control over the selection of investments in the scheme, you can manage the portfolio yourself.

Holding a high-quality SIPP allows you a wide choice of investments and facilities, and these include:

- Stocks and shares quoted on the London Stock Exchange (eg equities, debentures and gilts), including securities on the Alternative Investments Market (AIM).
- Stocks and shares quoted on an HMRC-recognized overseas exchange.
- Unit trusts and investment trusts.
- Open-ended investment companies (OEICs).
- Insurance company managed funds and unit-linked funds.
- Deposits in interest-bearing bank and building society accounts.
- The purchase of commercial property, including agricultural and development land and commercial forestry. If you control your own business, you can (subject to certain conditions) purchase property that can be leased back to your business on commercial terms. (Loan facilities can sometimes be arranged by the SIPP provider subject to conditions.)
- Trustee borrowing, from a commercial lender, to acquire property.
- Second-hand endowment policies (provided they are purchased through an independent broker specializing in this field).

You should remember that your SIPP provider will accept no responsibility for the performance of any investment or liabilities associated with any investment. The provider's only responsibility will be to ensure that the member understands the relevance for tax and other purposes of any particular investment.

# Administration

SIPPs are usually established under irrevocable trust. You may be a joint trustee of your personal arrangement together with the scheme trustee. You may also be able to appoint an additional trustee if you wish. However, the role of any additional trustee is likely to be restricted to the dispersal of your death benefits under the terms of the discretionary trust. All of the technicalities and paperwork are taken care of by the scheme administrator.

## How it works

Your contributions are paid into an individual private bank account on which you can be a counter-signatory. Monies are paid from the account for investment in accordance with your instructions. Any uninvested cash is part of your fund and earns interest on deposits at market rates. The provider will normally:

■ prepare the legal documents to establish your scheme;
■ maintain records of your contributions, transfers in, transfers out and investments;
■ provide the necessary documentation regarding investments;
■ reclaim basic rate tax on contributions paid by an employee or a self-employed person;
■ reclaim any tax deducted at source on interest payments made by UK banks and building societies;
■ supply an annual valuation of your scheme's assets to whichever date you advise;
■ provide you with information required by HMRC.

# Drawing benefits

A SIPP should offer you the flexibility to take your retirement benefits when it is most convenient to you:

■ You do not need to have retired or stopped working to take the benefits from the scheme and you do not need to have fixed your retirement date when you join.
■ You may defer all or part of your benefits to a later date, although options are more restricted after your 75th birthday.
■ You may take your benefits before you are 50 (55 after 6 April 2010) on production of evidence from a registered medical practitioner that you are (and will continue to be) incapable of carrying on your occupation because of physical or mental impairment and you have actually ceased to carry on your occupation.
■ You do not have to use the entire fund at once. A good SIPP provider will divide your fund into lots of equal segments, and you can take the cash and pension benefits from one or more segments whilst leaving the others until later.
■ You can take part of your benefits but carry on contributing to the scheme to provide extra pension and tax-free cash later on.

# Income withdrawal facility

Pensions from personal pension schemes can be secured by purchasing a lifetime annuity from an insurance company when the pension age is reached. The amount received depends on the size of your fund, your age (and the ages of your spouse and any dependants for whom a pension is being provided), and insurance companies' annuity rates at the time of purchase.

Purchasing a lifetime annuity ensures that your pension is secure and that future payments are guaranteed, but both you and the trustees lose investment control. Annuity rates can fluctuate substantially according to prevailing market conditions (especially returns on long-dated gilts). Unless you can delay taking your pension until annuity rates are attractive – which can mean waiting several years – lower rates will mean you will suffer a reduced income for the rest of your life.

There should be no such problem with better SIPPs. Instead of buying a lifetime annuity contract, you have the choice of drawing an unsecured pension direct from some or all of your fund. Alternatively you should be able to provide your unsecured pension in whole or in part by buying a short-term annuity from an insurance company. The balance of your unsecured pension fund remains invested until better annuity rates might be available. The maximum amount of unsecured pension you can be paid is found in calculation tables produced by the Government Actuary's Department. You will generally be allowed to take a tax-free lump sum payment from your pension fund when funds are used to provide an unsecured pension before age 75 (subject to the lifetime allowance), although this will not apply if your unsecured pension is provided by buying a short-term annuity. There is no requirement for a minimum level of unsecured pension to be paid in any year. The maximum amount of income that can be paid is calculated every five years or earlier on the request of the scheme member. Figure 3.3.1 illustrates this facility.

Income withdrawal can continue after age 75 by way of an alternatively secured pension, although there are more restrictive rules on the maximum pension that can be paid and there are more rigid and frequent reviews of that limit. There is also a minimum amount of income that should be paid. A tax-free cash lump sum payment is not available after age 75. Both unsecured pension funds and (after age 75) alternatively secured pension funds can be used to provide a secured pension by purchasing a lifetime annuity contract.

## Death benefits

If you die before taking your retirement benefits from a SIPP, all of your personal fund can be used to provide a tax-free cash lump sum to your surviving dependants or beneficiaries if you die before age 75 (subject to the lifetime allowance) or a pension for your dependants.

If your provider has established the scheme under irrevocable trust, the fund will not normally be considered as part of your estate for inheritance tax purposes. Furthermore, the provider (acting with any additional trustees) will usually be able to pay the benefits quickly and with a minimum of formalities, because there will be no need to wait for a grant of probate.

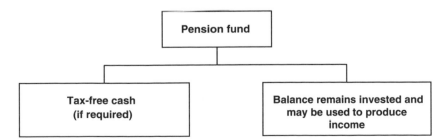

**Figure 3.3.1** Typical pension fund allocation

The reader will see from this chapter that there are potentially many benefits to be enjoyed by utilizing a self-invested personal pension as against more familiar forms of pension arrangement. However, great care is needed in the selection process, and would-be investors should always seek good-quality professional advice.

# Part 4

# Real estate and forestry investments

# Guide to the land investment process

*FortunaLand Investments SL*

## Why invest in land?

History is littered with the names of individuals who amassed great fortunes through the medium of land investment. Some of these you will never have heard of; others are now household names, such as Donald Trump, Howard Hughes and Bob Hope. Bob Hope himself is reported to have amassed a fortune of over $500 million, at one time owning land that made him the largest private landowner in the United States.

These individuals understood the message from one of the UK's all-time great entrepreneurs, Adam Smith: 'Land is the basis of all wealth.' This is because land is a commodity that cannot be manufactured and, if anything, available land is reducing in size and therefore it is always increasing in value.

## Where to buy land?

Regardless of where land is located, it will be a good investment if title is secured properly. It has been said that you can buy land in the back streets of Baghdad and it will make you money, most probably not tomorrow, but over time it *will* make you money.

The key is to ensure that you are actually getting what you are paying for. Paying the lowest price is not always the best option. Buying land in countries where the legal and fiscal systems are stable, eg members of the EU, is often more costly than buying in, say, the Eastern Bloc or Arab countries, but the protection provided by these countries reduces the risk considerably.

With this in mind, the most successful land projects are always going to be in the areas where the economy is strongest. In Europe, for example, the two strongest economies are currently Ireland and Spain, so these represent good opportunities for the astute investor. However, there are many select areas in all countries that, if identified and sourced correctly, will bring the returns required.

## How to make money from land investment

There are two main types of land investment: 1) *plot purchase* – buying a specific piece of land that is clearly identified; and 2) *syndication* – buying into a larger piece of land with others where ownership is proportional. Both types have plus and minus factors. Small specific plots are easily managed but investment return for each plot may vary dramatically on the whole site. Syndication of a major land project requires expert management by an agent but guarantees the same proportional return to all investors, thus reducing the risk to growth.

FortunaLand Investments is just such an expert. It has the in-depth knowledge to manage the syndication of major land tranche negotiations. It is totally versed in acquiring virgin land that will develop into the setting for an appropriate project.

The key is to select the right land and the optimum plan for development. This is land that is not at its development peak right now but is in the path of future development, with a plan that takes account of the economic and logistic factors that maximize the potential for investors.

By achieving this, investors get the land at a point when it is relatively inexpensive and then hold it until the value has risen. Depending on the project, this process can take a few years to achieve but nevertheless it is a foregone conclusion that it will gain value.

If a shorter timescale for financial return is preferred then significant growth can still be realized by purchasing land with imminent or approved planning permission for development. This can be a complex and costly process and requires input from a range of experts, but the rewards are such that the value often rises dramatically once this has been achieved.

FortunaLand has in-depth knowledge of sourcing and acquiring land that is primed for development or has project construction plans already prepared.

To release profit at the end of the programme, regardless of its type, you ultimately need to sell your land to someone else. A quality land investment will be managed by an experienced land agent who will provide this service for you, usually at a pre-specified point in time.

## What are the risks?

All investments have an element of risk. With land investment they are as follows:

■ *Time.* It can take longer than expected for the land value to increase. This is the major risk with any land investment of note that is to a large extent uncontrollable. The realistic way to mitigate this risk is to use an experienced agent who knows the market.

- *Planning restrictions.* The plan for the land may be unacceptable to the authority. This is only likely to apply in cases where the plan is to change some element of the land categorization in order to move the project forward in a shorter space of time. For this the agent or developer must have access to a team of experts who can liaise with the relevant authorities and rectify any problems as and when they occur.
- *Unable to sell.* You may find it difficult to realize your investment. If you have purchased your investment through agents, they will have the required market knowledge to locate a buyer on your behalf and they may have an idea of when this will be achievable.

The bottom line is simple: select your investment from a **reputable agent** and **understand the plan** for the particular project. Land investment is a low-risk, high-return investment, but realizing the profit is dependent on time and knowledge of where to look for the next buyer.

# FortunaLand Investments

Headquartered in Malaga, Spain, FortunaLand is a leader in land investment, having built a reputation for delivering solid real estate opportunities that build wealth for clients. The company's ability to understand growth patterns and identify land prospects in Southern Spain has attracted clients at all economic levels from all parts of the world.

FortunaLand is uniquely positioned to identify and administer land investment opportunities. Its investment projects are researched extensively prior to release. FortunaLand will only undertake projects from the landowners once its own extensive due diligence has been completed.

No other company offers the unique opportunities that FortunaLand offers its clients. Working primarily within the commercial sector of land development, it has developed a programme of investment techniques that bring this highly lucrative sector within the grasp of the ordinary investor. These investment projects offer the astute investor a safe, highly rewarding alternative to traditional investment mediums.

FortunaLand uses its expertise, experience and skill in the selection of the projects it releases direct from the owner. It follows four vital stages to maximize investor return:

- *Identification.* All land offered to Fortuna as a potential investment project is subjected to meticulous research and evaluation by its land acquisition team. Only land that is confirmed as being in the path of feasible future development, and that meets Fortuna's basic criteria, is accepted.
- *Participation.* Profitable investment opportunities are created at modest entry-level costs. Each investor part-owns the tract of land to a greater or lesser degree, according to the number of square metres purchased. Each landholding is legally documented, and a notarized *escritura* is issued in the investor's name.

■ *Adding value.* Based on what has been learnt in appraising the land prior to its release, and on market developments in the intervening period, Fortuna instructs an experienced professional team of affiliates, including architects and market specialists, to prepare scheme proposals. The proposal must satisfy public and social interests, provide employment and income, be environmentally beneficial – and be commercially viable.

■ *Exit strategies.* Following the issue of planning permission and the appropriate technical building permits, the value of the land tract – and of each share within it – will rise dramatically. FortunaLand then puts into action the appropriate asset realization strategy and will invite and undertake discussion with potential purchasers – developers and end users.

It was this formula that led FortunaLand to commence and concentrate its initial projects in the beautiful region of Andalucia in Southern Spain.

## FortunaLand's project history in Spain

With the Spanish economy currently the second strongest in Europe, the shortage of available building land on the coast together with ever-increasing rural tourism has resulted in a dramatic increase in land prices. This increase shows little sign of slowing, as more and more people flock to the region to capitalize on the Mediterranean climate and relaxed lifestyle whilst appreciating the stunning unspoilt countryside.

Having a politically stable environment coupled with an ever-improving infrastructure, Spain represents a safe and lucrative alternative to traditional, underperforming investment mediums.

It was these factors that led to the introduction of Fortuna's signature projects, Bella Fortuna and Sierra Fortuna, being located within the beautiful region of Andalucia, midway between the cities of Malaga and Granada, adjacent to the typically Spanish town of Zafarraya.

Zafarraya is situated just north of the Axarquia at an altitude of 893 metres and has a population of approximately 2,500 inhabitants. Situated at the foot of the Sierra Tejeda mountains, north-facing and surrounded by green pastures and vineyards with pine forests climbing the slopes, Zafarraya has been populated since prehistoric times and relies mainly on market garden produce, which is grown locally and exported worldwide. The village itself contains an old town with a ruined church and whitewashed houses, whereas a newer development with a more contemporary aspect also exists.

Bella Fortuna was first offered to investors in September 2002 at €6.80 per square metre. This 410,000 square metre plot of stunning Andalucian countryside closed to investors at a price of €9.20 per square metre. In October 2004 final planning approval was granted by the local authorities for a four-star hotel, wedding chapel and recreational facility incorporating a full wellness centre and health spa. The project has been subsequently well received by the regional authorities and has progressed substantially.

It was decided to expand on the potential of the region for our second and more ambitious project, Sierra Fortuna. Launched in February 2004 at €10.80 per square metre, this 648,000 square metre land investment closed to investors in December

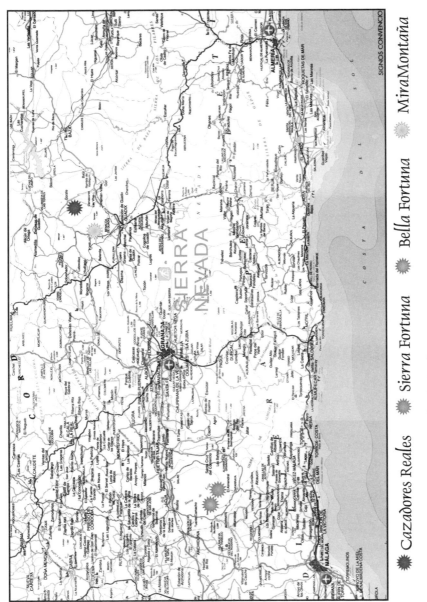

**Figure 4.1.1** FortunaLand's location in Spain

🌟 *Cazadores Reales*   🌟 *Sierra Fortuna*   🌟 *Bella Fortuna*   🌟 *MiraMontaña*

2004 with a final release price of €17.50 per square metre. Proposals are being submitted for a mixed-use development similar in nature to that of Bella Fortuna.

FortunaLand's third offering, Cazadores Reales, features a stunning plot strategically located within the Granada–Almeria–Murcia triangle near the historic village of Gorafe, and just a short drive from the booming city of Granada.

Launched in May 2005, the first release of 250,000 square metres was quickly allocated to existing Fortuna investors at €9.80 per square metre. With subsequent releases selling to the public at €10.40 per square metre and €15.60 per square metre respectively, this has resulted in the final phase price of €18.15 per square metre in line with a recent valuation carried out on the land.

In September 2006 (at an exceptionally advantageous entry-level price of €5.75 per square metre) Fortuna released to investors its latest venture, MiraMontaña, strategically located between the cities of Granada and Almeria near the typically Spanish village of Fonelas. The project is poised to take advantage of the explosive growth currently under way in central Andalucia.

MiraMontaña is within an hour of the booming city of Granada and the Alhambra, with the majestic Sierra Nevada and its renowned ski resort close by, and Fortuna is confident that it will offer investors a rare opportunity to capitalize on the region's growth over the next five to seven years.

## Examples of criteria used to explain why FortunaLand projects, to date, have been located in central Andalucia

■ The popularity of 'New Spain' created by the lack of available building land on the coast means land prices in central Andalucia are set to increase dramatically.

■ As a consequence, Granada and the surrounding area is currently experiencing a huge increase in property and development investment.

■ With some of the most visited tourist destinations in Spain, this vibrant area is well supported by a substantial tourist trade.

■ Granada is home to Andalucia's number one tourist attraction, the Alhambra Palace. This masterpiece of Moorish architecture is one of the most remarkable monuments of the Muslim, Jewish and Christian religions.

■ Minutes from Granada is the Sierra Nevada. Venue for the 1996 World Cup, the skiing resort of SolyNieve offers some of the best snow in Europe and means the region experiences year-round tourism.

■ Granada is also well known for its prestigious university, the Mardraza, and is said to be one of the three best cities in Spain for higher education.

■ This region's potential has been recognized by Ryanair and Monarch airlines. Both now have a scheduled daily service to Granada's airport.

## *Land investment – the 12-point investment procedure*

1. The investor decides the financial level of his or her investment. (All investments are subject to an administration and notary fee, which covers all legal representation at notarization.)

2. FortunaLand issues a contract covering the investment. This is issued by fax or e-mail.

3. This document must be signed, dated and returned to Fortuna immediately upon receipt by fax or e-mail.
4. Payment is expected to be made immediately upon receipt of the contract up to a maximum of three working days of the investment commitment.
5. Fortuna then purchases the land on behalf of the investor from the appropriate land agent. This secures the price of the investment against any increase.
6. Payment is made by international priority swift wire transfer from the investor's bank to the account of FortunaLand.
7. Once funds are received, Fortuna issues a receipt to the investor and instructs the Spanish lawyer to commence notarization.
8. The lawyer then issues a personal details form to the investor, which must be completed and returned to the lawyer. This form gives the lawyer verbal power of attorney in relation to this one investment only. Any further investment must be secured via a separate form.
9. Notarization commences.
10. Title deeds are delivered to FortunaLand and sent to the investor via courier.
11. Upon proof of signed receipt by the investor, Fortuna releases funds to the appropriate land agent.
12. The investor now has full legal title to the investment. The title deeds should be ratified by a public notary or, alternatively, if the investor is visiting Fortuna this can be arranged at no cost during the visit. There is no time penalty for the ratification and it does not affect legal title.

The successful activities of FortunaLand in Spain produced an inordinate number of referrals and enquiries from interested parties in other countries. Referrals are the sign of a successful company, and the growth of FortunaLand internationally is in no small part due to this fact.

A further positive advance of the company's profile is the progress of its joint land and development principle. FortunaLand now works jointly with landowners who wish the company to sell land and developments in tandem, the criteria being that the development is already prepared and the licence applied, ready to progress.

This has marked an exciting development in the company's international expansion. It is currently concerned with projects in Turkey, Germany, France, Italy and the Seychelles.

# Buying tips and considerations for the residential property investor

*Jan Morgan, Grosvenor International*

The press and TV are awash with information, misinformation and generalities about the present and future state of the residential property market. *Caveat emptor* and 'Location, location, location' have never been more relevant.

Estate agents are masters of purple prose, with many richly deserving their doubtful reputations. It therefore behoves all buyers to acquaint themselves as widely as possible with the market, the history and condition of any property being considered and likely changes in the area, and they should also consider how resistant the property would be to a market downturn.

In the current UK market, opportunities for those seeking high short-term asset growth are limited. The most rewarding deals are likely to go to those professionals who can assess the potential of a property at first sight and exchange contracts almost immediately.

Professionals will have built relationships with agents and usually get to hear about 'hot properties' before they are widely exposed to the market.

Property continues to hold its traditional investment position, often outperforming other types of investment in the long term. Many people are drawn to it simply because of the sense of comfort about something entirely tangible. It is virtually impossible to lose one's entire investment in property, unlike stocks and shares, and in almost all cases one has the guarantee of getting one's money back given time.

Long-term investment planning often raises special considerations, particularly if the purchase is to provide for a pension or is for retirement occupation or the future use of children.

Many seek out properties that fulfil those needs rather than current investment criteria. They would do better to consider an easily managed and resaleable property, which could be exchanged for a 'perfect fit' for their eventual needs.

Before venturing into the market it is prudent to consult with one's tax advisers to plan how the property is to be held. If not held personally or in a trust, whether on- or offshore, a single property vehicle (SPV) should be considered. This is a company with only one property as its asset, which can therefore be disposed of very quickly and often with a stamp duty saving.

The benefits of being market-ready cannot be overstated. The key factor is finance. If the funding is on immediate call the buyer is well ahead of the competition.

One should always shop around for mortgages and avoid tied brokerages. The best port of call may well be one's own bank.

Many deals abort as a result of dilatory conveyancing or mortgage processing. It pays not to be bashful about chasing one's solicitor or mortgage broker, if necessary on a daily basis.

Researching the potential investment area fully and befriending one or two reputable and sophisticated agents, who are clearly 'movers and shakers' in the area, are likely to pay dividends.

All agents have their 'special' applicants list to call on immediately there's a 'sniff' of a good deal. Their 'special' applicants are always on site within a few hours, don't need a mortgage, are well informed about the area and the local market, have an established and responsive relationship with their solicitor who will act on instructions over the phone, and generally exchange contracts within 48 hours. They are also happy to pay an acquisition fee (generally *circa* 1 per cent plus VAT of the total purchase consideration) and always re-instruct the introducing agent on any letting or disposal of the property.

Inexperienced investors should not be dispirited: however, they should be extra diligent about their preparation and heed the advice of sound professionals.

## Homework!

Check local transportation and go on foot in the rush hour. Have a pint in the local pub and chat to the locals. Check the availability of good GP practices, dentists and schools. Call the local police station to see if there are 'dodgy' or 'druggy' streets in the vicinity.

Pollution, noise, personal outside space and parks, gymnasiums, public swimming pools and health clubs are all lifestyle factors that can affect the ease of letting. Parking, good local shopping and restaurants play an important part in tenants' choice of property.

When considering the building itself, 'Location, location, location' is all.

Location 1 is the setting – much better to be a lesser property in a very desirable street than the reverse. Never be tempted by a fantastic property in a terrible street – it will be very hard to let to decent tenants.

Location 2 relates to the general amenities in the area and may offer important 'pluses', eg the American School in St John's Wood guarantees a ready supply of high net worth US families at the top end of the local residential market. At the other end of the scale a property for 'sharers' may need to be near the owner's home for ease of management and must be near good transport.

Location 3 relates to the local area within the wider environs. If long-term asset growth within a predicted period is sought it's worth considering an up-and-coming area surrounded by already-improved zones.

Currently there's a 'hot spot' within a two-mile radius of King's Cross in London (the subject of a major urban regeneration programme, with the Eurostar terminal opening in 2007). Already Bloomsbury, Mornington Crescent, Euston, Somerstown, Islington, Fitzrovia and the Lloyd Baker Estate are all seeing above-average rises but with considerable mileage yet.

Other London areas emerging from the doldrums include Shepherd's Bush and White City and, south of the Thames, the London Bridge area, following major infrastructural commercial development schemes; with the newly fashionable Spitalfields and Brick Lane areas, attention is moving to the Petticoat Lane district with the City virtually on its doorstep.

When estate agents, dry cleaners, opticians, coffee shops and florists open up in a new area, it's a pretty safe bet it's on the way up!

The great Olympic catchment area is attracting much attention in the press, but many in the agency world are advising caution in relation to short- or medium-term investment for all but the major corporate developers. Other than in the period immediately leading up to and during the games, an oversupply is predicted until the commercial sectors are fully established – which may be well after the original investors have fled with their fingers burnt.

## Niche investments

'Accidental' investment sometimes occurs in the face of market stagnation with no sales despite dramatic price cuts. Vendors fear or face possible foreclosure but, for those with property in desirable areas, a rescue window of opportunity sometimes exists.

Few, if any, would-be purchasers buy in times of crisis and rent instead, creating an unnatural demand and therefore a comparatively buoyant rental market. The vendors may face the inconvenience of a move to a slightly distant or less smart address for a few years but their asset remains healthy and intact. As the market recovers the owner also benefits from asset value reinstatement and sometimes growth.

Not infrequently such rescue schemes attract people into long-term holdings who otherwise had no plans to enter the investment market.

With the advent of 'live/work' spaces and many small businesses being started in people's homes, many regard the need for slightly more space as a good time to purchase ('invest in') a property in which they can work to save paying rent. This is unwise! While investing in a property is probably an excellent idea, it should be separate from business so that there are no crippling effects if crisis hits or one of the joint owners wishes to move on at a financially inconvenient time. Furthermore, an investment property may be an excellent vehicle for raising capital for the business from time to time.

## Life tenancies

Life tenancies can be the basis of freedom and comfort for the vendors and a great investment for those seeking large long-term asset growth with no need for intermediary income.

Over the last three to four years my firm, Grosvenor International, has identified an increasing interest in life tenancy sales and purchases; the sales are generally among late-middle-aged and elderly people who wish to free themselves from their mortgages, provide for their children or their own care in old age, buy a home abroad, reduce death duties or, in one case where the person was childless, simply have fun instead of always worrying about spending money.

The sale value is established from a combination of the freehold open-market vacant possession value with an actuarial assessment of the life expectancy of the residents, taking into account their age and medical records.

The tenants remain responsible for both the structural good order and the insurance of the building. It is possible to include in the contract permission for the tenants to sub-let all or part of the property for the duration of their lifetime, to pay for nursing help or residential care in a home.

Interest in 'tucking these properties away' for the children has escalated in recent years with the enlargement of City bonuses.

## Worth considering

Anyone can invest in a strong market, and time will conceal any errors and make unwise deals come good, but investment is about safety and as much certainty as possible, so it's worth considering:

- Why? Investment can be simple or complex; it can tie up a few thousands on a holiday timeshare whim or can be one's modus operandi and tie up one's entire wealth and more, so it's worth pausing to consider why, how much, what for and for how long – before jumping into the investment pond.
- When? Is now the right time for me personally and for the market generally? Will the investment be short- or long-term?
- Does my age affect or relate to my investment?
- What happens if there's a downturn?
- Location. Should the property be convenient and best for me or is the maximum return more important?
- Management. Can I manage the property myself and, if not, will the yield accommodate the management costs?

- Saleability. How marketable is the property if I decide to sell?
- Agents. Seek out truly professional agents with a depth of knowledge and experience in the area in which one is planning to operate. Good agents have a huge amount of useful information and expertise, which is available free once one is a regular client!
- Any potential 'added value'. Consider all aspects of the building in case there's a possibility of increasing the asset value or return by incorporating a loft or basement, integrating a garage or building a home office or granny flat in the garden, etc.
- Presentation. 'Would I like to live there myself?' is a useful guide. Aside from the ultra-luxe couture market, which is a world of its own, one should aim for pristine and neutral decor, with white or broken white having finally superseded magnolia, shutters or blinds not curtains, wood or high-grade laminate, at the moment in slightly darker tones than in recent years, rather than carpet in reception areas, and tiles are essential in bathrooms. Oversized stand-alone showers and granite worktops are a bonus if the budget permits. Jacuzzis and saunas are out! The current 'must-haves' at the top end of the market include multi-function coffee machines, five-ring hobs, built-in steamers, real flame fires (now possible without a chimney), sunken trampolines, and ponds being replaced with hot tubs.

It's worth remembering that the secret of business is secret, so when one's found a deal it shouldn't be mentioned to a soul prior to exchange. Every agent has tales of lost deals owing to the buyer chatting freely about them!

# For 2007...

Although general predictions for 2007 show an average rise of 11–12 per cent across the residential market, nothing seems certain and caution is advised.

Whilst rises as high at 26 per cent have occurred in Central London, rises across the country have averaged at 13 per cent in the year to December 2006, with some areas having slowed to 2–4 per cent and a few small areas actually reporting falls in the year. Alongside these house rises there has been a fall in the number of people able to buy under the age of 35.

The situation is unhealthy, the greatest rises having been driven by large bonus-led demand alongside a sharp downturn in supply. In the face of prices predicted to continue rising steeply in 2007, vendors are motivated to wait, thus escalating the shortage and completing the vicious circle, with an ever-widening gap between the top and the bottom of the market.

The US dollar shows signs of instability, UK inflation and interest rates have risen slightly and the world is an unsafe place. Any major world event immediately affects the London market, with some knock-on across the country. No one rings a bell before a crash.

Following dramatic downturns the more fashionable areas generally recover fastest.

Were we investing at present we would probably be looking in quiet streets with good public transport and local shopping in London's inner suburbs.

# Overseas property investment

*Anna Farrugia, Harlon Overseas Property*

## Introduction

Overseas property today is a significant element in personal wealth management. Many fund managers as well as private purchasers include overseas property, both residential and commercial, in their portfolio of investments. Growth in property values in the UK and many other developed economies has given property investment a broader appeal to a large number of investors.

Over the last 30 years, a growing number of homeowners, especially in the United States, Ireland, Australia and the UK, have been investing in second homes. Initially, the UK residents were looking for retirement or second homes in the sun, but the principal motive of owning property abroad has gradually shifted towards investment. UK property prices grew 166 per cent between 1997 and 2005 (*Economist*, December 2005), generating equity, and owning a second home abroad has never been more affordable.

Many UK homeowners capitalized on the equity accumulated on their homes to reinvest in additional property abroad, and more and more young people are jumping on the property ladder through the purchase of relatively affordable homes in Spain, France and Italy, as well as emerging property markets.

Property prices in many EU countries are expected to rise as a result of favourable economic and political conditions brought about by the EU through measures to regenerate the economies of newly elected member states. Other influences, such as the introduction of low-cost flight services and major sporting and other international events, have contributed to price rises in overseas property markets.

# HARLON OVERSEAS PROPERTY
**LONDON OFFICE**
Tel: 020 8942 9558
Fax: 020 8404 7003
Email: property@harlon.co.uk
## www.harlon.co.uk

SPECIALISTS IN:

INVESTMENT PROPERTY
RESIDENTIAL AND COMMERCIAL
HOLIDAY AND RETIREMENT HOMES

*We source commercial property – hotels, leased buildings, shopping malls, restaurants, yacht marinas and tourist resorts – and offer full support and after sales services to Fund Management companies.*

*Luxury apartments to character homes in sunny destinations – Italy, Morocco, Portugal, Spain, Cyprus, Malta, France and cities all over Europe.*

*Finance, Insurance, Foreign Exchange, tax and legal advice assistance on request.*

# Benefits of investing in overseas property

Property ownership abroad allows individuals planning for retirement to diversify their portfolio by adding real estate, along with pensions, endowments, equities and/or other investment instruments.

Key benefits include:

- *The enjoyment of a second home in the sun.* Many homeowners today look for a richer lifestyle. There are many opportunities in idyllic environments that have a choice of outdoor leisure amenities such as golf, yachting, swimming and other activities and sports. Many developments today come with sport and leisure facilities aimed at couples, families and people in other life stages.
- *Rental income.* During the peak tourist seasons properties are rented, the proceeds of which contribute towards the cost of maintaining and owning the property, as well as providing an extra income.
- *Capital appreciation* (especially significant with gearing). Capital appreciation in the property market is a *sine qua non.* Moreover, careful gearing can greatly boost capital gains, especially if finance costs can be offset by rental income (see below).
- *Tax advantages.* Tax advantages in some countries, such as Dubai, Cyprus and Malta, can be an attractive incentive. Double taxation relief agreements with many countries – over 1,300 worldwide – provide protection from being taxed in two countries. However, UK residents, if domiciled in the UK, are still liable to capital gains tax at home. It is important to be fully aware of all tax implications when purchasing property abroad.
- *Future financial security.* Property investment is generally considered to carry lower risk than the stock market. However, **property values can go down as well as up** and it is important to seek sound advice. Research is the key to a good investment, and the property market is a complex vehicle to assess. The level of risk must be determined in order to make an informed decision.

# Investing in overseas property

As with any other asset, property is based on the concept of scarcity – supply and demand. Understanding market forces – predicting people's behaviour and perceptions – is the key to successful decisions when choosing a country in which to invest. It is people who make up markets and their actions that will determine the rise or fall of prices. There is no perfect science to predict future property values, with supply and demand being influenced by both microeconomics, such as local government restrictions on permits, local business activity, employment, population and immigration growth, and macroeconomics, such as income growth (GDP), tax incentives, easy access to mortgages, etc.

These are some of the factors to consider when purchasing a property abroad:

- The economic stability of the country in which to invest is not simple to assess but it is possible to stick to the safest growing economies.

- The location of the property – whether it is in a ski resort, a sunny seaside resort or a city – is important; it should be under an hour's drive away from an airport and have good local transport.
- A conservative level of mortgage, to ensure that the property is not too highly geared.
- A choice of good property management companies.
- A healthy rental market to cover the property running costs and mortgage repayments.
- The rental potential and yield of the property in question.
- Good capital returns against the initial investment and cost of purchase.

## Financing and maximizing returns on the purchase of overseas property

Most banks provide mortgages of 80 per cent or more, and investors could gear property with as high a loan as possible in order to maximize the return on investment. The higher the gearing the more important it is that the property has a high rental potential and yield. Some properties come with a rental guarantee and, provided this is a genuine offer, this will secure mortgage payments and running costs. It is safer to think of property as a long-term investment of, say, five to ten years, which will allow the property market to mature. The higher the mortgage, the greater the risk, and the better the potential returns.

---

### Gearing – an example

On a property of £100,000; initial capital investment 20 per cent, ie £20,000; loan £80,000.

Expected capital growth after five years: 30 per cent of original price, ie £30,000.

Return on capital investment after five years: £30,000/£20,000 = 150 per cent.

During the first five years, the monthly mortgage payments of approximately £400 per month are payable at an assumed rate of 6 per cent over 25 years.

Therefore, for the above investment to be sustainable, it requires a rent return of no less than £400, plus running costs, per month.

---

The general running costs of a property are:

- management costs, normally between 10 per cent and 12 per cent of rent;
- letting fees – one month's rent;
- block management costs (for apartments) and annual maintenance (for houses);
- insurance;
- wear and tear;
- mortgage payments.

*Failure to keep up with your mortgage payments will put your property investment at risk. A smaller mortgage may be easier to pay in the event of a rise in interest rates.*

## Off-plan property investment

Off-plan property investment requires minimum capital. Developers are prepared to sell at a discount in order to promote their project at the initial stages of construction. These properties are generally on the market at prices of 5–15 per cent below the market value during the first few weeks of the project. The reservation fee is between £2,000 and £6,000. When the contract is drawn up a payment of 20 per cent to 30 per cent is generally payable. The balance is then due on delivery around 18 to 24 months later. In most instances, a mortgage can be arranged for this final payment.

A bank guarantee or insurance should preferably be in place to protect your initial payment; however, in many emerging markets this is not possible. It is therefore important to ensure that due diligence has been carried out on each development. It would also be prudent to speak to another buyer in the same development or in a property built by the same developer.

Some off-plan developments have a penalty in place if the property is resold before completion.

## The process and costs of purchase

In most European countries the Napoleonic law applies when purchasing property. A notary appointed by the central government acts as an independent party to register transfer of title from vendor to buyer. It is therefore recommended that you appoint an English-speaking local solicitor or international legal adviser in the UK, or wherever else you are based, for independent legal advice. Surveys are recommended, especially on older resale property.

Every country has its own purchasing charges of:

■ stamp duty;
■ registration fees;
■ legal fees;
■ search fees.

The total cost of purchase could vary from 8 per cent to 12 per cent of the purchase price. Most property abroad is subject to VAT, so be sure to check that property prices quoted include VAT where applicable.

## Popular overseas residential property investments

Research to evaluate the stability of the countries under consideration should also identify the target rental market, the best locations and the market value of property in order to establish the potential capital return. Properties in less stable economies and/or situated on the edge of cities are considered a higher risk, and a longer-term investment.

We have selected a few popular developments, and for the sake of simplification analysed them in the following categories:

- *Location:*
  - Leisure location, such as a holiday resort – the popularity of the resort and the density of development in the area are among the considerations. The length of the rental season will affect the rent return. Ski resorts are known to generate a higher daily rent return than beach resorts.
  - Speculative location is where property prices are increasing without justification, owing to an unprecedented demand by investors. The reason could be the resale of off-plan property before completion. This gives investors a quick return of profit; however, the artificial increase in property values is unsustainable and creates a bubble in the property market.
  - Good or excellent location is when properties are located within the centre of a city or with good transport to the city centre. Other examples are when the property is located close to a ski lift in a ski resort, or front and second row in a beach resort.
- *Price.* Low, medium and high price – the expected capital increase as compared to today's value. If the property price is low, it is generally acknowledged that there is more room for growth.
- *Risk.* Apart from the level of economic and environmental stability in a country, some areas are susceptible to earthquakes or hurricanes. Compromising on any of the above categories will alter the level of risk on your property investment.
- *Term of investment.* Short, medium or long term depends on the demand for a property. Unlike stocks and shares, property cannot be sold within a few days; therefore, it is wiser to invest in a property that is highly appealing to a great number of buyers. For example, a city centre pad is much easier to sell than a home by the beach, since the demand is normally higher and more urgent in cities.

The following is an attempt to classify and assess a range of current opportunities selected by location/price/risk/term, which are interrelated; for example:

- Miami luxury apartments: excellent location, low risk, medium price, short term;
- Northern Cyprus villas and apartments: speculative location, high risk, low price, long term;
- Tuscany renovations: leisure location, low risk, medium price, medium term;
- Morocco off-plan villas and apartments: leisure location, low risk, low price, medium term;
- Dubai Sports City: speculative, medium risk, medium price, short term;
- Dubai Financial City: speculative, medium risk, medium price, short term;
- Dubai The World or Thailand: speculative, high risk, medium price, short term;
- Spain golf resort: leisure location, medium risk, medium price, short term;
- Prague IX exclusive gated development: good location, low risk, low price, short term;

- Prague II renovation: excellent city location, low risk, medium price, short term;
- Budapest city centre: excellent location, low risk, medium price, short term;
- Budapest XIII: good location, low risk, low price, short term;
- Budapest VIII: speculative location, medium risk, low price, long term;
- Gozo five-star residence: leisure location, low risk, medium price, short term.

## Costings and cash flow

Before committing to a purchase the following calculations should be clearly identified as part of your feasibility study:

- the price of the property, including VAT where applicable;
- the costs of purchase;
- the running costs for maintaining the property;
- the mortgage payments;
- the rental income.

### *Foreign exchange*

Once the property is reserved and the payment terms and currency are confirmed, it is time to ensure that you fix the rate of change. A number of FSA-supported foreign exchange companies are available to assist. Your property consultant will normally be able to put you through to a few reputable companies.

### *Insurance*

Building and contents insurance should be in place before delivery of a property for peace of mind. Some insurance companies in the UK are now happy to insure your home and contents abroad. The advantage of being in control should a claim arise is clear, since you will be dealing with an English-speaking agent and a policy you can understand.

## Conclusion

To conclude, we would like to add that you can identify a reputable overseas property consultancy with the recommendation of the UK National Association of Estate Agents by telephoning +44 (0)1926 496800. A property consultant should be able to help you make an informed decision.

Good luck with your next overseas property investment.

# Property and forestry investment in the Baltics

*Felix Karthaus, KMS Baltics*

## Summary

The Baltic countries, Estonia, Latvia and Lithuania, have a turbulent and oppressed history, but beautiful forests.

In 1997 I visited Estonia with a view to starting a forestry business there. Baltic forests are part of the Boreal forest: a belt of coniferous forest circling the globe in the north of this hemisphere. The main species are birch, pine and spruce, but oak, ash, aspen, rowan, juniper, alder and willow also occur. These forests have been managed for centuries, but during the Soviet period those that had been in the private sector were largely left unmanaged.

It was not difficult to find investors for such quality woodlands, and we now manage over 750 woodlands in Estonia and Latvia. Some of our clients have used the cash from timber sales to invest in commercial property, and we have about €12 million worth of real estate under management.

## Baltic history

The Baltic countries were invaded by the Prussian knights in the 13th century and converted to Christianity. These Baltic Germans remained there until 1940 as feudal lords, although the countries were frequently invaded and, in turn, ruled by Sweden, Denmark and Russia. The feudal system was democratized in about

1850, but the Baltic Germans remained the largest landowners, with small tenants working the land. Only in 1920, when the Baltic countries became independent for the first time in their history, was the large estate system broken up and the peasants became owners in their own right. The average property size was seven hectares.

In 1940, the Soviets invaded the Baltics, and private land was collectivized. Only in 1991 did the countries regain their independence through their remarkable 'Singing Revolution'. Those who could prove ownership before the Second World War were given back their land. However, property sizes were still small, because the short period of independence was not enough to create larger holdings through buying and selling.

After independence there was economic turmoil, as free economies were established, each with its own currency. Estonia especially bit the bullet and allowed free trade, at considerable cost to the rural population and the state employees (doctors, teachers, etc). However, this has paid off and it is now the most advanced of the three countries in economic terms. The others have eventually followed suit and all three have 'tiger economies', with double-digit growth recently.

# Property

Since the Soviet era there has been a frenzy of activity in renovating and expanding infrastructure, housing, factories, warehouses and office buildings. Especially since the entry into the EU on 1 April 2004, the pace has increased and prices have risen. However, much remains to be done. This creates opportunities that are often ignored by the many market reports that are published.

## *Commercial*

Since the Soviet period a three-tier system of commercial property has developed:

- Many businesses still survive in the old Soviet offices. They are cheap to purchase and rents are low. However, where they are well situated, they can be a good investment, either to be pulled down or to be renovated.
- Then there are the renovated Soviet-era or pre-Soviet-era offices. They can equal the very best modern buildings, but generally are not quite to the same standard. In the right location, however, they are easily let. The older buildings can have exceptional capital appreciation.
- Third, there are the modern buildings. These are in high demand and at present there are no vacancies in the Tallinn 'Class A' office rental market.

Yields are 6–8 per cent depending on location and quality. However, values and rents are predicted to increase, partly through increasing demand and partly through inflation. The high GDP activity is fuelling inflation, not helped by the many young people who have left to find their fortunes elsewhere, causing labour shortages and thus increasing wages. This is considered to improve yields by 2 per cent.

## Retail

There have been many retail developments in Tallinn and it now has more retail area per capita than Helsinki and Stockholm. Thus, there is unlikely to be much further development. However, local supermarkets in large housing areas or rural towns can still offer very attractive returns.

## Warehouses

There is substantial warehouse development outside Tallinn, as logistics are increasingly important and businesses are moving from small, unsuitable warehouse facilities in town to better-located modern buildings on the Tallinn bypass, with good access to the harbour. Few warehouses are built speculatively, because there are better profits for developers in other markets. However, there are opportunities for investors in funding warehouse developments in conjunction with a developer and a business that prefers to rent. There are also opportunities for smaller warehouses, combined with retail premises and offices for small businesses nearer the town centre. These premises can often be converted from the warehouses that the larger firms are vacating.

## Residential

Generally, Baltic people buy their homes, and the rental market is relatively small. Developers therefore generally sell flats individually prior to or during construction. However, there is a rental demand from students and others who require temporary accommodation. Yields are generally small, in the region of 5 per cent, but capital appreciation is usually very good.

Most towns have large areas of Soviet-era apartment blocks, which initially kept their values very well compared to new-built buildings, simply because of the housing shortages. Also, some of the older flats have been well renovated and offer attractive accommodation. Thus, there are investment opportunities by investing in development sites or suitable buildings for conversion to flats, but these tend to be short-term investments and are best considered in conjunction with a developer.

There are also very many attractive houses, often wooden with large gardens, in the towns. Many of these have doubled or trebled in value over the last few years. They make a good opportunity for a small investment, but finding tenants can be difficult, as they are usually too large for those seeking rental accommodation.

## Forestry in Estonia and Latvia

My business, and hence my detailed knowledge, covers Estonia and Latvia.

During the Soviet occupation, the countryside was emptied of people and abandoned agricultural land seeded up with trees from surrounding forests, producing beautiful natural forests.

The forest laws are very strict, as the forests are an important economic and environmental resource and appreciated as such by the people. Thus, felling is designed to ensure sustainable woodlands, mainly restocked through natural regeneration. Chemicals and fences are not used and only occasionally is planting or seeding necessary.

## Investment returns

When these forests were returned to their pre-war owners, they were often sold to timber merchants for the value of the timber that could be felled immediately, plus a bit more. The new owners mostly no longer had any ties with the countryside and they did not want to, or could not afford to, manage their forests. Also, there is a land tax, a cost the new owners often wanted to avoid. Thus, when the timber merchant bought the mature timber, this often meant acquiring the remaining crops and the land for nothing.

Although this is now much less the case, the timber that cannot be felled for 10 or 15 years is still heavily undervalued and forms the basis of investors' capital growth. Also, forests are often under-managed, as previous harvesting has concentrated on felling the easier areas. The remainder of the forest can often be selectively felled at considerable profit, which is also needed for good forest management. Typically, we have seen 6 per cent annual return from timber sales and 10 per cent to 20 per cent annual capital growth. We think this has some way to go before prices reach those of the Scandinavian neighbours.

The forest land is often still not valued, as are small areas of agricultural land included in the sale, although, increasingly, amenity and development potential is being recognized.

## Ownership

On EU entry in 2004, the East European countries were given permission to restrict ownership of forest and farm land for a period of seven years. However, these restrictions can easily be overcome by creating a local company, which can be wholly owned by foreigners and does not require a local director. Property ownership is run along German lines through a property register or kadaster. Every company and property change is extremely bureaucratic and has to be notarized, but this ensures secure ownership rights. We have now bought over 700 woodlands without significant problems.

## Tax

In Estonia, there is no corporation tax; thus, any profit is tax-free as long as it remains in the company. It can be used to purchase more woodlands or other property. In Latvia, corporation tax is 15 per cent.

Both countries have dual taxation agreements with most European countries, including the UK. Dividends are taxed at 24 per cent, but in Estonia the company is taxed when dividends are paid, and thus this cannot be set against UK tax under the dual taxation agreement. However, there is no capital gains tax if less than 75 per cent of the balance sheet consists of immoveables.

## Risks

A reasonable investment is likely to consist of 100 different small forests, and this reduces any risk in itself. Mostly, our clients do not insure. Devastating disease is far less of a risk in natural forests than in plantation forests with introduced species. Winds are much less strong than in the UK, only occasionally causing damage in localized summer storms. Fire is an occasional hazard in spring, but only affecting small sections of forests, because of their varied species and age structure.

As the Baltics are stable economies and now part of NATO and the EU, politically there also seems to be little risk.

Choosing an overseas property
Do everything *your* way with
# Cavendish Brooke International

## *Why?*

- *Bespoke Property Search covering many countries*
- *Property Investment opportunities identified and qualified*
- *Guaranteed Rental Schemes*
- *SIPP Opportunities in several countries*
- *Above all, we make the process easy for our busy clients*

Our commitment is to offer our clients comprehensive advice and guidance in addition to introducing you to high quality properties and developments. We also introduce a range of qualified professional experts to assist you throughout the process.

So, if you are considering purchasing or investing in UK or overseas property, start with a call to us for a discussion with no obligation. It would be our pleasure to welcome you as a client.

**Cavendish Brooke International Ltd**
**London, England**
**W: +44 (0)20 8868 9330  Mob/Cell: +44 (0)7973 480 204**
**www.cavendishbrookeinternational.com**

Members of FOPDAC (Federation of Overseas Property Developers and Consultants) and Founder Members of AIPP (Association of International Property Professionals)

# Investing in Overseas Property

Many readers will have some experience of property investment here in the UK, usually via buy-to-let ownership and/or the purchase of discounted off-plan apartments. The principles used to determine the viability of such an investment are largely similar when deciding on exploring opportunities further afield. As with any property investment decision, location is paramount and suitable professional advice should always be sought to deal with the aspects of law and taxation.

Overseas Property is already being acknowledged as an asset class in its own right and as with any form of investment, one's 'Attitude to Risk' should accurately match the profile of the property, taking into account geography, political stability, age of the market and many other factors. It is important to decide just how much exposure to risk feels comfortable and how the overseas property sector fits within your existing investment portfolio. Ask yourself whether you prefer to own properties directly or should you instead be looking at one of the international real estate funds being launched by some of the large investment banks and insurance companies. As with any collective investment vehicle, these funds spread the risk and negotiate reduced costs as well as being hassle-free. You are however relinquishing control over the timing and nature of the investment decisions.

Whatever your assessment, unless you are prepared to undertake your own thorough research and allocate the amount of time required to do this, it would be wise to work with an adviser who will establish an understanding as to your objectives and make an appropriate recommendation.

Let us look below at some of the options available to you.

**Established Markets**

Some assume that because a market is firmly established, it does not offer opportunity for interesting investment gains. As with the UK, this is not always the case and indeed some of the more established markets such as Portugal, Florida and Cyprus can offer reasonable rental yields and very good capital growth too. The security and peace of mind that accompanies investment in these regions appeals to many investors, especially those who prefer to place their capital in areas that they are familiar with. French Leaseback schemes are very popular and always worth considering. There are also guaranteed rental schemes in countries such as Spain, Portugal and Cyprus. (It is essential to check the small print of such schemes as they may not always be quite as good as they seem.)

One potential opportunity to consider is that of providing key worker housing in the established EU countries. As many of these areas have attracted high immigration from new member states, pressure is building on their domestic housing markets. In some cases, governments are even offering guaranteed rental schemes to try and attract investors in order to solve the problem. Given our experience of the boom in the buy-to-let market in the UK over the past ten years, we should perhaps look at applying some of the lessons we have learnt here, to other European markets. Investing in property that is designed and intended for the local market is likely to be more secure than putting our faith in properties that rely upon demand from tourists or foreign buyers.

### Emerging Markets

The emerging markets attract a large amount of attention predominantly because of the lower entry prices and expectations of high capital growth. Whilst in many cases this interest is justified and investors make exciting profits, in others it must be said that the investor is often too late and misses the opportunity of the significant gains for which he was hoping. As with any investment decision, thorough research and knowledge of the market is essential before making a commitment and this is perhaps especially true of the Emerging Markets.

However, it is fair to say of many of the Emerging Markets that personal research can be difficult. This is because much of the relevant information and statistical data required is not easily available. Many factors need to be taken into account when selecting a location and the fact that regions may be offering outstanding value for money is not sufficient reason in itself to justify buying there. It is important to consider the political stability and economic climate as well as assessing who your market is going to be. Who will buy or rent the finished product from you? If the prices, as is often the case, are likely to be out of range of the locals, is the foreign or tourist market really likely to take off there or is this going to just be a fad? Many people are left with properties that they can neither rent nor sell simply because they did not consider the end-user market when they made their investment decision.

There are highly reputable companies who specialize in specific Emerging Markets and who will offer honest and appropriate advice as to the region and type of property that will most meet your objectives. The potential of the Emerging Markets should not be ignored but you would be well advised to approach one of the experts before parting with any money.

## SIPPs (Self Invested Personal Pension plans)

When the proposed legislation allowing the inclusion of residential properties within SIPPs was withdrawn, many people were extremely disappointed as they had already created liquid funds within their pensions with a view to investing not only in the UK but overseas as well. The opportunity to invest in residential property abroad still exists as long as the investor has no personal use of the property and is following an approved process. In some cases the purchases are made via syndicates and specially designed SIPP schemes are available to cover areas such as Bulgaria and Cyprus. French leaseback properties are allowable within SIPPs and are proving a popular choice for those wanting to invest directly. Please be aware though that SIPP rules can be complex and expert advice should be sought in all cases. Indeed many SIPP providers will not allow the inclusion of overseas properties within their plans but do not be put off, this is a legitimate area and the attractions of the tax free growth and tax reliefs are very valuable to the serious pension investor.

## Finance

It is essential to consider how one will finance the purchase of the property. Will you be buying this outright or will you decide to take a mortgage? If via a mortgage, will you withdraw equity from property here in the UK or do you prefer to look for a mortgage in the country of purchase?

An important consideration is that of the currency in which to take the mortgage. It is often possible to obtain a lower lending rate in the country of purchase, especially if euro based, but if you are making the mortgage payments from the UK you should take into account the currency fluctuations and costs of transferring money as well. A good mortgage broker who deals in the international market should be able to help you here.

You will also need to consider how best to transfer your deposit and other relevant payments. There are many foreign exchange companies who offer very competitive rates and an excellent hassle-free service. It is worth using them as their rates will almost always be lower than those offered by your bank and most of them do not charge fees or commission.

## Regulation

Given the increasing popularity of the overseas property market you may find it surprising that there is no compulsory regulation in place to protect and guide the consumer. Many overseas investors are confused as to which companies will offer an honest and professional service and this can often put people off exploring this area further. Another concern is that there is no official avenue for complaint or compensation should incorrect advice be given or unprofessional methods adopted by a company operating in this market.

The move towards voluntary regulation has already started and there are bodies in place that agents and companies can join. These include FOPDAC (Federation of Overseas Property Developers, Agents and Consultants) and the AIPP (Association of International Property Professionals). Membership of these bodies is restricted to companies or individuals who act ethically and honestly and demonstrate integrity in their dealings with the public and each other.

Investing within any unregulated sector carries additional risks and it would be prudent only to deal with those companies or individuals who are members of either of the above organizations. Membership not only demonstrates a commitment to good practice but also offers the consumer access to a disciplinary process should anything go wrong.

So, in conclusion, overseas property offers an interesting and exciting dimension within an investment portfolio but it should be approached with the same amount of research and care as any other financial decision. Be clear on your objectives, decide how you will fund the purchase, identify your market, conduct sufficient research and then find your property. Above all, enjoy your experience and good luck!

# Forestry as an investment

*Alan Guy, fountains plc*

## Introduction

The forestry investment sector has seen exciting changes in the last few years, both in the UK and elsewhere. In the United States, some major paper producers have sold their forestry assets as part of strategic realignments. These assets have been purchased by new investors, particularly timber investment management organizations (TIMOs), real estate investment trusts (REITs) and pension funds, motivated by falling bond yields and a broadening interest in real estate in the United States.

Meanwhile, in the UK, the successful financial and property sectors have produced a new influx of investors. These investors are attracted by an investment combining steady long-term growth, low volatility and tax shelter possibilities with good risk diversification qualities. The end result has been consistently strong demand and rising forestry prices over the past three years.

In this chapter we look at the nature of forestry assets, their long-term performance and the tax advantages. I will explain how to select the most suitable asset when entering the market, how to minimize risk and maximize value, and finally some possible exit strategies.

## The nature of the forestry investment class

The forestry asset class can be looked at in several ways:

- Forestry is a physical asset, like other properties, yet it does not generate a significant leasing income – although it may contain other income generators such as wind farms or holiday chalets. It does, however, require management and maintenance like other property.

■ Investment in forestry in the case of pure 'industrial' plantations is mainly a commodity play, driven by the international price of timber, currently in high demand from China, as well as all the established industrial economies.

■ By contrast, much of the value in the lowland woods of England, and increasingly Wales and Scotland, is derived from their perceived value as an amenity and recreational asset. The value of timber is less important to the value of such woods.

■ Some commentators such as Mark Campanale[1] have likened forestry investment to a bond, as it is long-term and independent of financial markets, and can be structured to produce regular income. It should be noted, however, that only very large forestry portfolios and TIMOs have a sufficient spread of differently aged forests to produce timber, and so income, every year!

■ As equity – there are few options for taking equity stakes in forestry in the UK, but far more in the United States, Scandinavia and Australasia, through TIMOs and REITs, mentioned earlier.

■ Increasingly, investment in woodlands is gaining an environmental subsidy aspect, with new woodlands attracting grants from government and from certain intermediaries in the voluntary emissions reduction sector for their environmental and carbon offset benefits.[2] This element of return is based on current government grant schemes and current prices paid for credits in the carbon trading markets but these income streams can be locked in via grant contracts.

One major feature of forestry investments is that they have been shown to have a negative correlation with stocks and bonds.[3] They also have lower volatility, although values of commercial woodlands are affected significantly by timber prices. These features are particularly attractive to pension funds, which are major investors, particularly in the United States.

In summary, forestry returns are characteristically less volatile than those of other low-risk investments such as gifts or bonds. This characteristic, along with the low correlation with equities, gifts and commercial property, gives the asset class an important diversifying and risk-hedging quality that can be exploited in multi-asset portfolios.

## How UK and US forestry have performed in recent years

The Investment Property Databank (IPD) Forestry Index for the period 1992 to 2005 showed an annualized return of 2.2 per cent for UK forestry against 9.4 per cent for

1. M. Campanale of Henderson Global Investors, *FT Investment Adviser* magazine, 15 May 2006.
2. The voluntary emissions reduction market is one of the non-Kyoto-compliant project-based credit schemes. See Department of Trade and Industry, 'Carbon prices – a climate change projects office guide', April 2005.
3. RG Ibbotson and CL Fall (1979) 'The United States market wealth portfolio: components of capital market values and returns 1947–1978', *Journal of Portfolio Management*, **6** (1), pp 82–92.

equities. This return was maintained despite a fall in timber prices over that period to under half their real value in 1992 (see Figure 4.5.1). The performance of UK forestry for the three years to December 2005 was considerably better at an annualized 8.2 per cent.

Performance varied considerably between individual forests, reflecting site quality, age and closeness to timber-processing mills. For example, the top quartile of mature (over 30 years) forestry in the IPD sample averaged a return of 24.4 per cent against 0.7 per cent for the lower quartile over the period 2000 to 2005! The weighted average was 7.6 per cent for that age class (see Figure 4.5.2).

Meanwhile, in the United States, the NCREIF Timberland Index showed timberland investments between 1990 and 2005 achieving an annual compounded return of 12.49 per cent, against 10.55 per cent for top US stocks, represented by the Standard & Poor's 500 Index.

The range of returns above highlights the advantage of maintaining a portfolio of forestry investments in order to spread risk. It also shows that it is prudent to obtain professional advice before purchase, in order to identify quality woodland and to value it correctly.

## Recent trends in forestry prices

Over the last three years, we have seen UK forestry prices increase steadily, well in advance of inflation, by at least 10 per cent per annum. There are several possible explanations.

Firstly, the UK forestry market is relatively small in area compared with the country's population and wealth, amounting to under £40 million in 2005.[4] This situation is exacerbated by the fact that the Forestry Commission, the government's

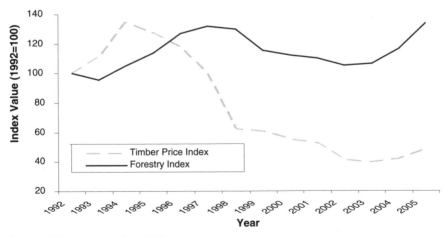

*Source:* IPD Forestry Index 2006

**Figure 4.5.1**  IPD comparison of timber and forestry prices 1992–2005

---

4. UPM Tilhill and Savills Forest Market Report, Spring 2006.

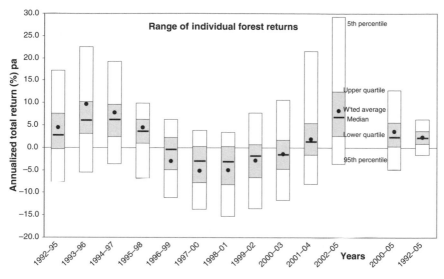

Source: IPD Forestry Index 2006

**Figure 4.5.2**  Range of individual forest returns in UK commercial forestry

commercial forestry arm, still owns well over half of the larger commercial properties and is only now bringing a small proportion of these to the market, on a strategic basis.

A further factor is the booming financial and property sectors in the UK producing a large number of new investors, as mentioned earlier.

# Commercial forestry

This chapter refers primarily to investment in commercial forestry. In the UK, this consists of fast-growing conifers in upland areas, which are typically 'rotated' (felled and restocked) every 40 to 50 years; broadleaf woodlands are mostly amenity assets and are therefore excluded. In the United States, I refer to 'timberland', whose value lies primarily in a range of native hardwoods, which are typically rotated every 80 to 120 years, using natural regeneration rather than restocking.

## Risks in forestry investment

### Economic

These are risks arising from markets and the political environment. The value of commercial forestry is primarily determined by UK and international timber markets. Until recently, timber and wood fibre demand in the UK came almost exclusively from the construction, DIY, furniture and paper industries and was subject to their cycles, thus affecting forestry returns.

Fears of future energy shortages and fears of climate change have placed a new emphasis on the importance of biomass, including forest by-products, as a renewable and carbon-neutral source of energy. Several large power plants in the UK are already co-firing or exclusively burning biomass. At a local and micro level, boilers burning woodchip or pellets are becoming widespread, as competitive fossil fuel sources increase in price.

This increase in the number of markets for timber and associated products must spread market risk, reducing the potential for a major slump in demand and hence price. Nevertheless, the return from a particular forest in a particular country may be affected adversely in the short term by external economic factors.

## Natural

Certain 'natural' risks can affect the health and productivity of a forest, and hence its value. These include windthrow (areas of forest uprooted by high winds), pest, disease, drought and fire. Fire and storm damage can be insured against. Pest and disease – particularly deer, rabbit and squirrel damage – can be predicted in certain conditions and appropriate protections and management regimes implemented.

## Political

Political risks to forestry investment include changes in forestry grants and changes in fiscal regimes. Regarding grants, risks can be mitigated by good planning. As for possible changes in the tax treatment of forestry, these would certainly have a marked effect on the value of properties that do not have under-lying timber viability but rely heavily on their amenity and perceived tax advantages for their value.

## Managing risk

There are tactical responses to short-term economic downturns; in particular the sale of a timber crop can generally be delayed for several years until prices recover, with no harm to the crop.

There are many strategic steps that can be taken to minimize risk:

■ Ensure that investments are not dependent upon the maintenance of current grant regimes for their viability. Challenge your valuer on this point before purchase.
■ Make forestry part of a mixed investment portfolio.
■ Maximize the range of income streams coming from each woodland.
■ Hold a portfolio of forestry with a spread of age classes, species and national locations, eg note the relative performance of US hardwood forests versus UK conifer forests between 1990 and 2005, referred to earlier.

## *Tax treatment of forestry*

The tax treatment of forestry investment in the UK recognizes the long-term nature of the investment. All income from timber sales and other income generated from ownership of commercial woodlands is free of income and corporation tax. Growing timber is exempt from capital gains tax (CGT); moreover, CGT liabilities arising from the sale of business assets can be 'rolled over' into commercial woodland purchases.

For individuals investing with the ultimate benefit of their children in mind, forestry is particularly attractive as, after two years of ownership, it qualifies for 100 per cent business property relief from UK inheritance tax.

The definition of 'commercial woodlands' as set out in the legislation has yet to be fully tested in the courts. However, most tax inspectors apparently seek evidence of ongoing professional management, proper accounts and an effort to derive income from the timber crops being grown. The area of forestry management is one in which my own company, fountains plc, provides services to a wide range of individual and institutional forest owners.

## Maximizing the value of forestry assets

As with other property, the value of forestry assets can be greatly influenced by the actions of the owner, usually with the professional assistance of a forestry manager. Examples include:

■ *Strategic purchasing of properties.* The value of a given property can often be increased by the purchase of an adjoining property or properties. So-called 'marriage value' is obtained from factors such as shared road access, economies of management and operation, and improved amenity such as larger-scale or better-structured deer-stalking ground.

■ *Good forestry management and planning.* There are often management options to choose from, which can potentially increase forest value. Just a few examples are:
  – Thinning of conifer crops to increase average tree volume (and hence price per tonne) when felled. This is not always economic to carry out.
  – Selective thinning of hardwood (broadleaf) crops to select the species and trees of the greatest quality and value, and to increase girth and sawlog value.
  – Fertilizing conifer crops on poor, nutrient-deficient soils.
  – Restructuring of the site by selective felling and possible planting with different tree species. This can be done to improve sporting value, increase conservation and landscape value and/or increase ultimate crop value.
  – In some situations, there are strong grant incentives to replace felled non-native conifer crops with native tree species. This can also, in the right locations, give the woodland an additional conservation and amenity value.
  – Installation of good internal roads to facilitate forestry operations and transport of timber from the site.
  – Certification of the management plan to the UK Woodland Assurance Standard, which confirms environmentally sustainable management. While incurring fairly modest registration and audit costs, the owner can apply the internationally recognized Forestry Stewardship Council (FSC) stamp to the

timber. Already, timber carrying this mark gains access to markets in the UK and Europe, as major buyers such as B&Q demand it.

■ *Recreation and sporting.* Additional income can be earned from recreational facilities, eg for paintballing and mountain biking. Proximity to population centres and major roads is a key factor here. Sporting rights normally come along with freehold forestry ownership. Deer stalking, game shooting and fishing can be developed in appropriate locations; these often provide a modest but useful regular income.

■ *Installing income-earning assets.* Forests can accommodate other assets that can provide additional income streams, subject to planning controls and a suitable location. These include:

– Wind farms and mobile phone masts. Even fairly small wind farms can provide substantial annual rental of £8,000 or more per turbine per annum, far exceeding potential timber income. Phone masts can also provide regular income.

– Holiday or sporting chalets.

– Residential buildings. These are only permitted by planning legislation in very special cases, eg where forests are adjacent to expanding population centres. Potential returns from obtaining planning consent to build are substantial.

## Other motives for forestry investment

Investment in forest property is unlike other property investments in that the owner can derive benefits from use of the forest property whilst still maintaining it as a commercial operation.

These potential benefits include recreation, nature conservation and, for those so inclined, deer stalking and rough shooting. In certain cases, game shooting can also be developed around the woodland.

In the environmental field, the sequestration of atmospheric carbon is increasingly seen as a particular benefit from the establishment of new woodland. Together with a technical partner, fountains is able to calculate the carbon dioxide output from an investor's activities – or 'carbon footprint' – and to propose various new woodland options for offsetting that impact. This could be anything from a new native Scots pine forest in Inverness-shire to a new oak woodland in the National Forest (East Midlands).

Alternatively, woodland investors can gain funding for planting projects from the voluntary carbon credit market by agreeing to establish woodland on their land, which will offset a third party's carbon impact. We are now doing this for clients on a regular basis, using carbon market intermediaries who broker these deals for us.

## Selection and valuation of a forestry investment

Before approaching a forestry agent for available properties, investors should decide clearly on their investment objectives as this will largely determine the type of woodland they should invest in. The optimal choice of forestry investment depends on the investment profile and the objectives of the purchaser:

■ *If one of the investor's objectives is tax-free income, or at least a positive cash flow, from an early stage of ownership:* The investor should consider buying a property with a crop at or near maturity, which can be felled in the near future for timber income. Competition for properties is greatest in this part of the market and investors should be aware they may get a lower long-term return than from investing the same amount in younger woodland.

■ *If the investor's main objective is to acquire an asset exempt from inheritance tax, and if income from the woodland is not a significant issue:* People in their 50s or younger should consider buying a young or mid-rotation (say up to 20-year-old) conifer woodland. This is because the investors will buy a woodland at a stage when the timber is at a low value. They will experience a steady, long-term increase in the value of the crop, which can be passed on to their children without inheritance tax, offering them a valuable asset carrying a renewable source of tax-free income. They will, however, have to fund the annual costs of management and insurance themselves. Older investors could look at a more mature property of up to 30 years old.

■ *If the investor's main aims are to combine tax protection with amenity, and if the level of return is not important:* The investor may be prepared to consider purchasing a woodland that will not provide a positive cash flow at any time during its ownership. There are many lowland woods in England and Wales that are priced well beyond a level reflecting their income-earning potential; the excess consists of the market's assessment of amenity and underlying land value. Table 4.5.1 and Figure 4.5.3 contrast these investments with commercial woodlands. Buyers should ensure that such woodland is managed in accordance with a commercially based forest management plan if they do not want to put potential tax protections at risk. Moreover, there are a large number of small (under 15 hectares or 40 acres) amenity-based woodlands in lowland England and Wales that are not economically viable forestry units, for various reasons, and where it might be difficult to convince the tax inspector that commercial forestry is being carried on, even with a professional forester managing the site.

Whatever the objectives of the investor, the buyer should certainly obtain independent advice from a forestry agent or professional forester who is experienced in valuing properties. There are only a handful of forestry agencies of significant turnover in the UK, easily found on the internet, and about the same number of sizeable forestry management companies, including fountains, that you can rely on to have this expertise in-house.

## Selecting possible targets

An experienced forestry valuer will select properties currently on the market which fit the financial and other objectives you have specified. You will help narrow the range by stating preferences for region (if any) and your budget.

**Table 4.5.1**   Types of forestry in the UK

| Type | Scale | Character | Investment Status | Typical Price* |
|------|-------|-----------|-------------------|----------------|
| Upland forestry | ≥100ha non-native conifer | Large efficient units. More limited landscape and conservation value. May be certified to UKWAS (FSC) standards. Can be structured to promote amenity, eg deer stalking. | Gives long-term return comparable with low-risk investments (4–8% real annual return). May have development potential, eg wind farms. | £1,000–£4,500/ha |
| Lowland amenity | 5–100ha broadleaf or conifer | High in amenity. Good landscape and conservation value. Often on ancient woodland sites. | Low or negative commercial return (less than 4% pa). High capital growth allied to agricultural property market. | £2,000–£7,000/ha |

*Upland forestry prices are influenced primarily by geographical location, size of unit, maturity and quality of crop. Lowland amenity prices are influenced by attractiveness, character, amenity, conservation value and proximity to population centres.

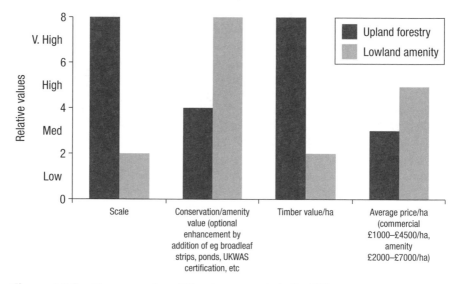

**Figure 4.5.3**   Two examples of forestry property in the UK

The cost of a woodland valuation depends on the level of detail and accuracy required. A very broad estimate of crop value and a brief summary of risk factors and major capital expenditure items might cost under £500, while a detailed valuation, including cash flows based on sample timber volume measurements on the site, is likely to cost between £1,000 and £2,000 for a straightforward site. If amenity is one of your objectives, you should arrange to visit your target site with a forester.

## Assessing risk and return

The valuer will calculate the volume of timber likely to come off the site at the optimum point in the future, and will use knowledge of local timber prices, combined with predictions of price escalation, to value the future crop to be harvested. A cash flow showing all areas of income and cost over a given period is prepared, and discount factors applied. Finally, adjustments are made for amenity and sporting and other benefits to come to a likely range of values.

The valuer should also advise the investor concerning the current property market, recent price comparisons and the level of interest in the property. In a market such as the current one, with demand well exceeding supply, the expected range of offers for a property may well exceed the commercial value that might be calculated using low-risk assumptions. A discussion with the investor concerning market sentiment and forecast movements in timber prices is likely to precede a final decision on the price to offer.

The current level of interest in forestry investment is leading to most properties being sold by competitive bids at a closing date. This means that good market intelligence is required regarding the likely level of the successful bid. But it is essential to go through a 'reality check' with your valuer and to consider the downside risks, as with any investment.

As current demand in the UK well exceeds supply, forestry prices are rising ahead of timber prices and expected returns are inevitably falling. You may well consider it is time to look at forestry overseas that is offering better value at present; an easy starting point is the United States. For example, our colleagues at fountains real estate inc broker properties across the enormous hardwood belt stretching over a thousand miles in length from Maine to Tennessee.

## Exit strategies and liquidity

The market for commercial woodlands is currently very liquid in the UK. This is particularly true of the more mature woodlands, which are often present on the market for only six weeks or so before going to bidding. It is certainly much easier to sell a quality woodland at present than it is to buy one!

What are some of the possible exit strategies that can be considered?

- *Hold the property until death.* Any capital gain in the land value will be written off upon death. The asset will be passed on, exempt from IHT.
- *Long-term hold.* Harvest timber (tax-free income) and restock, maintaining a continuing family asset and income source.
- *Short- to medium-term hold.* Maximize the value of the asset. Take any timber income but time the sale according to the peak in the property market. Sell and roll over the capital gain into another forestry property or business/agricultural property asset.

■ *Short- to medium-term hold.* Maximize the value of the asset and give it during lifetime to the children. The investor will have a CGT liability on the increase in land value, not timber. Consider transfer into a trust to avoid CGT and IHT liability.

■ *Short-term hold.* Buy mature property; harvest timber to take early tax-free forestry income. Sell with limited (or negative) capital gain on the land value.

## Summary

Commercial forestry is an investment that, on average, provides returns over the medium to long term on a par with other low- to medium-risk investments. It is a useful diversifying element to a multi-asset portfolio and enjoys several valuable tax exemptions. There are also opportunities for buying either forestry property or forestry stocks in overseas markets, particularly the United States.

When buying forestry property, it is essential to obtain valuation advice from a reputable forestry firm.

After purchase, the value of the asset should be maintained and maximized by taking on good professional forestry management support. There are opportunities for developing additional income streams, although these opportunities will usually have been discounted into the prices offered for a property.

In closing, it should be emphasized that forestry investment has many benefits in addition to those of a financial kind. These include a range of environmental and recreational benefits, and many investors gain a great deal of pleasure from owning their own forest.

# Property – will UK real estate investment trusts (REITs) be the investment for the smart investor?

*Avril Whitfield, Mazars*

## History

Those who have had dealings within the property sector as fund managers or investors will already know that REITs have been in the marketplace for some time at a global level. Both Australia and the United States have had legislation in place for several decades that, over time and in reaction to economic trends, has developed into a sound foundation for their respective property investment markets. Europe has been some way behind in developing a similar strategy.

For those unfamiliar with the concept, REITs are collective investment vehicles designed to allow small private investors access to the property market without the administrative and other burdens that would accompany direct investment.

A campaign to introduce a UK REITs structure began in the late 1990s and was rejected by the government in 2000 as being unworkable. However, a different discussion was taking place in France, which successfully introduced its SIIC structures in 2003. On the back of this, and heavily influenced by France, the discussion was revived in 2002. The machinery of change does not move quickly in the UK though, and it was not until March 2004 that the UK issued its first consultation paper on the subject, then known as property investment funds (PIFs). A Treasury discussion paper followed in March 2005, with draft legislation released to the public in December 2005 at the time of the pre-Budget report. The term 'PIF' is notably replaced by 'REIT' in both these papers.

At long last in the UK though, REITs are with us and went 'live' on 1 January 2007. The industry is breathing a sigh of relief, aware of the long journey it has had to take to get us here. Following the Budget in March 2006, share prices in listed property companies rose dramatically. Does this signify that an investment in a REIT will be better than any other investment though?

## Will REITs resurrect the property sector?

In the main, there has always been strong support for a REITs structure to be adopted in the UK. With property still being a key influencer for growth, a REITs market should provide increased financial stability. The global economy has seen a bull market now for several years (since the late 1990s), and economists the world over are asking when this will change. In Australia, for example, 70 per cent of the holdings in unlisted property trusts are owned by ordinary people for their children and grandchildren. It is quite possible this will be mirrored in the UK.

But will the UK REITs revolution revitalize the industry as many expect? I firmly believe that, although it will sit alongside the current offering in the listed property market, it is unlikely to be substantially different from it in reality. The same economic influences will still apply to both. What I think will be different will be the type of investors attracted to REITs. Whatever my views, the new regime will undoubtedly help stabilize volatility in the marketplace and will therefore be an alternative investment to individuals and pension funds.

We have seen through various consultations (including those on REITs) that the government is indeed willing to listen to the industry and move. If we take the United States as an example, it has been working on and amending its REITs legislation for 45 years. Clearly the UK government has the benefit of this and, whilst our legislation will not be perfect on day one, it can be equated to having already got to the 30-year stage out of that 45-year period.

The UK government is adamant that the legislation should be both European Union (EU) and double taxation agreement (DTA) compliant. Just how big will the UK market and appetite be? Globally, the current property industry has a $680 billion market cap. Merrill Lynch has suggested that we are likely to see a market cap increase to $1.3 trillion within the next five years for just the UK, Germany and Japan! There is doubt though as to whether the UK can actually achieve the growth needed within the next five years to get to a market share of $50 billion from its current starting point of about $30 billion market cap. Certainly, economists will continue to debate this whilst the legislation clarifies and solidifies over the next 12 months or so.

What is abundantly clear is that doing nothing was no longer an option that the UK could afford to take.

# Key features

There has been a dramatic landscape change since 2000 when only the United States and Australia had any form of REITs legislation. As with most new legislation, the pitfalls are in the detail. What follows is an outline only of the key features that an investor will need to consider and the main issues that will be facing practitioners and the industry in the immediate future.

With effect from 1 January 2007, a UK REIT is a UK tax-resident company carrying on a 'property rental business' that satisfies conditions relating to:

■ the company and its share structure;
■ its activities; and
■ its 'balance of business' activities.

Subject to meeting these conditions, the effect will be that:

■ income and capital gains from the qualifying activities will be tax-exempt within the REIT;
■ 90 per cent of profits will need to be distributed annually from the qualifying activities;
■ investors will receive their dividend income gross and be taxed on it as though it were income from their own property rental business; but
■ subject to payments to exempt investors (eg pension funds), withholding taxes of 22 per cent will be imposed on distributions arising from non-qualifying activities.

The whole object of the legislation is to allow investors a similar profile to someone who has invested directly into property so that they are not disadvantaged. In fact an investor in a REIT could be in a better tax position than someone who invests directly in property. This is because the direct investor will always face capital gains tax legislation on a disposal of a property, even if the proceeds are to be reinvested in another property. Although the tax treatment of capital distributions from a REIT is still uncertain, it is clear that such distributions are unlikely to be mandatory and that, subject to meeting certain restriction tests, capital transactions within the REIT will not be subject to a tax charge (providing those capital transactions relate directly to the tax-exempt part of the business within the REIT). This allows the property portfolio to be managed without worrying about the tax impact.

## The company

There are six key conditions to be satisfied by the company. It must:

1. be tax-resident only in the UK;
2. not be an open-ended investment company (OEIC); and
3. be listed on a recognized stock exchange.

Before looking at the remaining three conditions, it is important to note that these three conditions must be met before the company converts to a REIT. Meeting these conditions only on conversion does not appear to be an option. This may well impact on potential initial public offerings (IPOs). Note also that dual-resident companies are likely to be automatically barred from joining the regime even if taxing rights rest only with the UK under DTAs.

The remaining conditions that must be met by the company are that:

4. it must not be a 'close' company;
5. it must only have one class of share capital in issue; and
6. there should be no 'non-commercial' loans.

Both at the time of conversion and throughout each subsequent accounting period, there must be 'reasonable belief' that these final conditions will indeed be met by the company.

The requirement to list on a recognized stock exchange excludes companies wishing to enter the AIM market. Quite rightly, the London Stock Exchange is keen that it should not lose out through potentially lucrative deals going to foreign exchanges such as those in Ireland or the Channel Islands. It is currently reviewing its listing rules to see how it can capture any advantages arising.

## The qualifying activities

There are four issues here:

1. The REIT must hold at least three properties.
2. No single property should account for more than 40 per cent of the total value of the portfolio.
3. Owner-occupied properties and stapled stock arrangements are specifically excluded.
4. Subject to a specific override by company law, 90 per cent of the profits from these activities (which will be tax-exempt) must be distributed to the investors (excluding distribution of capital gains).

These conditions are in order to provide the investor with some level of protection, but do they go far enough?

## Balance of business conditions

This will include both an asset and an income test. The two conditions are: 1) at least 75 per cent of the total income must relate to qualifying property rental business; and 2) at least 75 per cent of the total value of the company's assets must relate to qualifying property rental business.

A word of warning though: in determining the income test, capital allowances, loan relationships, embedded derivatives and hedging all need to be taken into account.

## What is still missing though?

### The 10 per cent rule

It was originally suggested that, where one person was able to exercise control of 10 per cent or more (either directly or indirectly) of the shares or voting rights in a

REIT, then the rules would be breached if dividends were paid to that person. As such, the company would not be a REIT. Thankfully, the government has mellowed in its views and bowed to industry pressure. Whilst a penalty will arise for breaching the 10 per cent rule, companies may be able to avoid such a penalty if they can demonstrate that they have taken 'reasonable steps' to ensure there was no breach. Further guidance is eagerly awaited as to what might or might not be construed as 'reasonable steps', and I wait to see if it focuses on issues such as: identification of 10 per cent shareholders; and what happens when dividends are paid to a 10 per cent shareholder through ignorance or mistake.

Critics may argue that there are already adequate disclosure regulations in place for identifying existing shareholders. This may be so. However, what is not regulated for disclosure is where there is an entitlement to dividend rights. Because of this, will a company really be able to adequately police with any accuracy who the 10 per cent persons are?

## Non-commercial loans

In the run-up to the March 2006 Budget there was much debate over gearing and interest cover as outlined by the draft legislation. The UK government has taken the unusual step of restricting the gearing by reference to interest cover, which should be in the ratio of 1.25:1. This will be determined by a fixed formula. As many people in business know, whilst your gearing might be adequate in one period, market forces could cause a temporary 'blip' in cash flow. Solid monitoring throughout each accounting period will be vital here, as a breach could mean an unexpected tax charge of 30 per cent!

Table 4.6.1 illustrates this and assumes a constant rental income yield of 6.5 per cent and a constant interest rate of 6.25 per cent.

It is easy to see how a slight change in the variables relating to interest rates or rental income yield could cause companies problems. Issues such as property flooding or shortage of property could therefore have a substantial impact upon the number of companies remaining within a REITs structure during the whole of the accounting period.

One must bear in mind that the interest cover test is largely an anti-avoidance-driven test rather than an EU-driven test. It is highly likely that, as the new legislation

**Table 4.6.1**  Interest cover restriction

| Asset | £1,000,000 | £1,000,000 | £1,000,000 | £1,000,000 | £1,000,000 |
|---|---|---|---|---|---|
| Loan as percentage of value | 75% | 65% | 55% | 45% | 35% |
|  | £750,000 | £650,000 | £550,000 | £450,000 | £350,000 |
| Rental income yield | 6.5% | 6.5% | 6.5% | 6.5% | 6.5% |
| Interest rate | 6.25% | 6.25% | 6.25% | 6.25% | 6.25% |
| Rent | £65,000 | £65,000 | £65,000 | £65,000 | £65,000 |
| Interest | −£46,875 | −£40,625 | −£34,375 | −£28,125 | £21,875 |
| Profit | £18,125 | £24,375 | £30,625 | £36,875 | £43,125 |
| **Cover** | **1.39** | **1.6** | **1.89** | **2.31** | **2.97** |

adapts to the marketplace (and vice versa), there will be a prohibition on gearing up at the investor level to get round the interest cover test. This could bring with it potential streaming legislation and further anti-avoidance rules. In any case, gearing up at investor level is generally an unsound commercial practice.

## Entry charge

Now clarified is the level of the entry charge for conversion to a REIT. This is set at 2 per cent of the gross market value of the investment properties at the time of conversion. The charge can be paid over a four-year period (subject to election), but if done this way the conversion charge equates to 2.19 per cent.

Whilst this is good news for those companies that have held properties for a number of years, representations from the industry continue to be made where it is felt that a reduction in the conversion charge, coupled with a zero stamp duty rate, would trigger the incentivized growth hoped for. By leaving matters as they are, companies that have made recent acquisitions could face a conversion charge higher than the inherent capital gains on their balance sheet at the conversion date.

## Global comparisons

So just how will the UK proposed structure compare with what is already in the global marketplace? See Table 4.6.2.

A word of warning: this table gives just a brief flavour of the global comparisons and should not be used as a definitive guide to what those comparisons actually are. Each country has its own tests and mandatory conditions and, as can be seen, there are benefits and losses in each jurisdiction.

## Conclusion

Is it possible at this time to say whether REITs will be the success that many in the property industry want them to be? In the end, it is the investor who drives the market forces. The perceived attraction of a REITs investment for a pension fund has already evaporated against the current FTSE100 average yield, which is running at a rate of 3.2 per cent. It is also interesting to note that some US REITs have gone private in recent years!

Have we missed the bandwagon in the UK? Should we prepare ourselves for a REIT boom-and-bust such as we saw with the dotcom era?

Whatever the answer, and I refrain from giving any personal opinion here, the government has clearly worked very hard with advisers and with the industry to ensure that this new regime hits the ground running and is not stillborn. Despite reservations, what is very clear is that UK REITs are intended to bring greater opportunities to investors to access the property market. Let us hope the economists and the forecasters are right.

**Table 4.6.2**   REIT global comparison

| | USA | Canada | Australia | France | UK (proposed) | Germany (proposed) |
|---|---|---|---|---|---|---|
| **Entity:** | | | | | | |
| Vehicle used | Does not need to be a company | Not a company | Trust | Entity that can be listed | Listed company | Corporation or stapled stock |
| Shareholding | 100+ investors | 150+ unit holders | No minimum | N/A | 10% test | Widely held |
| Listing | N/A | Listed | None | Listed | Listed | Listed |
| **Asset test** | 75% test | Cannot carry on a trade | Predominant rental test | 60% test | 75% test | Must be real estate investment |
| **Gearing** | No gearing limits | No gearing limits | No gearing limits but thin-cap rules apply | No thin-cap rules | Fixed formula P+I/I | Unlimited |
| **Conversion charge** | Tax calculated but deferred | None | None | 16.5% of gains spread over four years | 2% of market value of assets spread over four years on election | Similar to France |
| **Transfer taxes, ie stamp duty etc** | Applies in most states | May apply in some states | Applied | Applied | Applied | Applied |
| **Tax treatment of vehicle** | Dividends deductible; 90% distribution policy taxed at 10% | Payments distributed deductible and remainder taxed | Not taxed | 85% distribution policy on income and 50% on gains; tax-exempt | 90% distribution policy, remainder taxed at 30% | 90% distribution policy and remainder tax-exempt |
| **Tax treatment of investors** | Income and capital distribution taxed as normal; withholding tax applied to overseas investors | Tax depends on residence and withholding tax issues | Some taxation applies subject to units held; withholding tax applied to overseas investors | Return of capital tax-free; standard tax rates apply to income distributions but exemptions apply; withholding tax applied to overseas investors | Taxed as though rental income; gains taxed as income; withholding tax applied to overseas investors | Withholding tax applied on all distributions |

# A practical guide to overseas property purchase

## Ian Hunter, Sun Kissed Homes Limited

## Background

The trend of overseas property ownership is a phenomenon mainly peculiar to Northern Europeans, originally fuelled by a high level of affluence and a desire to escape to sunnier climes. This trend was accelerated by the introduction of package holidays in the 1960s and now the growing availability of cheap flights. Countries that were once the domain of the 'jet set' are now becoming the province of the 'jet to let' set. No more obvious is this trend than in the UK, where it is said that more than two-thirds of the population would like to buy an overseas property for investment, holiday home or retirement, and this model can be found throughout other parts of Northern Europe.

With the impact of growing prosperity in their home countries, there is an ever-increasing stream of enthusiastic purchasers in search of a better climate, cheap cost of living, lifestyle and of course the legendary returns on investment, especially as in the traditional home markets the continual rise in property values is slowing when compared to those in the emerging markets. This has meant that purchasers are now ready to take advantage of perceived great-value property and investment opportunities. In turn, this has been further fuelled by the present low cost of borrowing – even lower in the euro zone than in the UK – which means the trend for buying property overseas is expected to accelerate.

There has been a shift from a second home being regarded as a luxury to it being something attainable by most people, made possible by a buoyant property market at home. This is illustrated as follows: in 1995, the average price paid for a second home overseas was 65 per cent of the average UK property price but by 2005 it had fallen to 37 per cent, reflecting in part steeper house price inflation in home markets.

A recent study by the market research group Mintel has found that the number of British householders who own a property overseas has risen by 45 per cent in the past two years, with almost 3 per cent of the UK population now owning a home abroad. Another piece of research indicates that, contrary to belief, people purchasing overseas homes are doing so as an investment, seeking to outstrip the home market, rather than as a holiday home purchase. It also found that nearly half of prospective overseas property buyers were looking for a villa by the sea (49 per cent), followed by 19 per cent looking for a house in the countryside, with only 5 per cent of buyers considering an apartment in a city. This ties in with the desire to purchase property that gives a strong return and the opportunity to occasionally escape a busy lifestyle.

## The purchase process

Before you make the decision to purchase, to ensure long-term success, undertake research. The first task is to identify a potential target country or region. Ideally make a number of visits and whilst you are there collect copies of the local English-language newspapers and magazines. This will give you a feel for the place and assist with an understanding of local issues. Check the small ads to see how active the local property rental market is. Take out an overseas subscription to publications to keep a handle on what is going on in your chosen location and, of course, use the internet.

Remember that you are about to enter a new cultural and legal environment. It may seem that in many countries the systems look remarkably similar to that in your own country. But don't be lulled into a false sense of security. The legal system varies from country to country and, in some locations, region to region. In most cases so do property ownership laws, and for a foreign national this can include the inability to own freehold property except through a corporate entity (Bulgaria), being unable to purchase within specific areas (Turkey) or being unable automatically to reside there 365 days per year (the United States). These are just three simple illustrations.

Equally, owning overseas homes can present tax issues. Purchasing an overseas property has important tax implications. Contrary to popular belief, you are often still subject to tax on your offshore income and capital gains if you are resident and domiciled in your native country. Also remember, if your own country's tax system is not complicated enough, then when you purchase overseas you will have to cope with local tax systems that may be culturally dissimilar to ones you are familiar with, so always seek professional advice.

Buying through an offshore company to avoid certain taxes, expenses and laws is sometimes an option open to an individual interested in purchasing overseas. Whether this route is actually the best is open to debate. First, it depends on the country in which you're buying. Second, local agents may be incorrectly advising foreigners by basing their advice on the local situation. This method of approach can be beneficial, but take care. There are specialist companies that can advise you based on your individual situation and, as it's not a case of one method fits all, be careful and be informed. Find out the following. If you do buy through an offshore company and wish to take the property out of that company in the future, how easy will that be to do? Will you incur an expense? Will there be further tax liabilities if you decide to sell your company-owned property, and what happens if you try to take the profit from the sale? Will you be taxed? Also consider the taxation situation from the point of view of where you are domiciled and the local situation in your chosen country.

At the first opportunity organize a *will* to cover local inheritance tax laws, and make sure your overseas property is also detailed in the *will* held in your country of residence/domicile. Specialist legal advice should always be sought when you hold property in more than one country, as not only do inheritance laws differ greatly depending on the country, but certain local inheritance laws can completely contradict and invalidate your main *will*.

Most importantly, engage the services of a reputable lawyer with expertise in your chosen country and location. These can be found through your local embassy or consulate (they all hold lists of reputable professional service providers, although they will not recommend any individual company). Alternatively, engage the services of a country-specialist lawyer at home, of which there are a growing number. The benefit of appointing a lawyer in your own country is that he or she will normally carry professional indemnity insurance.

Make sure you, or your advisers, get key documents translated, and remember ignorance is never a valid excuse! Not understanding the language in which your key legal contracts are written is a problem; don't ignore it! Don't blindly sign on the dotted line; it's your responsibility to be informed. In many cases both developers and agents will tell you that a lawyer with local and/or country knowledge is not necessary. It is! And don't be confused between a notary (or notary public) and a lawyer, as there is a fundamental difference.

Notaries are not authorized to give advice and guidance, as they are only state-licensed public officials authorized to attest to the signing of documents, such as deeds or mortgages. Notaries public certify that they have witnessed the signing of the document by also signing the document and affixing their official seal. Lawyers, on the other hand, are there to give you advice and guidance through the whole of the purchase process, ultimately giving peace of mind.

As I have explained, investing in an overseas property portfolio has its risks, as with all investment, but with a little forethought and planning it can also provide huge returns for the astute investor.

The problem is that, while stories of house prices soaring 40 or 50 per cent in a year are not uncommon, inevitably by the time these stories are in the media price growth has begun to slow. So if you are looking for an investment opportunity the secret is to identify the places that are set to boom – rather than those that are already increasing in value.

# Ten pointers to a potential property hotspot

1. *Property prices.* Many people will tell you that location is the most important aspect. Well, if a location offers lower-priced property, it opens up the market to a far broader profile of potential buyers and therefore presents a far greater opportunity. But do some research and ensure that you are paying a competitive price for your 'great-value' investment, as value can all be down to perception. It is often the case that in emerging markets property prices for overseas buyers are 'picked from the sky' and are often negotiated (remember the cultural thing).

2. *An expanding economy and increase in tourism.* This is a key 'driver'. Countries with a developing economy will witness an increase in tourism and popularity, leading to high rental demand and increasing the returns on capital invested.

3. *Recent or projected entry to the European Union.* This brings the expectation of inward investment and the easing of restrictions on the movement of capital and trade. Many of the new EU member states, such as the Eastern European states, have performed well.

4. *Simplified house-buying process for foreigners.* Keeping abreast of legal issues surrounding foreigners' access to the housing market or removal of purchasing restrictions allows you to move in and take advantage of the lower property prices ahead of the rush.

5. *Political stability.* It is important to research and understand the political environment of the country you are planning to invest in, so as to assess the risk and balance that against reward in the short, medium and long term.

6. *Government and private investment in the area.* Investment encourages improvements in the local infrastructure and amenities and brings money into the area, always pushing house prices upwards.

7. *Improvements in local transport links.* Accessibility is a major factor with new or expanded airports. Look out for extension of international flight periods, from summer months only to year-round services, and the upgrading of general transport infrastructure, ie roads and railways, as this will inevitably give access to previously less developed areas and regions even in the most mature markets, which in turn leads to investment opportunities.

8. *The opening up of low-cost flight routes.* Low-cost carriers and charter flights always herald the arrival of a noticeable property price increase. When the companies decide to fly directly into an area, the increase in demand for second homes and rental accommodation immediately begins to climb by a considerable factor.

9. *The construction of large-scale leisure facilities.* Ski runs, golf courses, marinas and hotels increase property prices and drive demand.

10. *Hosting an international sporting event.* Major events on the sporting calendar, such as the Olympic Games, the World Cup (to be held in Durban, South Africa in 2010) or golf tournaments, encourage development, regeneration and attract tourists to the area, boosting house prices.

# Things to consider before you buy

The first group of questions you should ask yourself are what your drivers are and what you want from an overseas property investment. There are three initial questions:

■ Do you want to buy for purely investment purposes? If so, is it a short- or long-term investment? Do you want to generate income from rental and/or capital from value growth?
■ Do you want a holiday home with the opportunity for some rental return?
■ Are you looking for relocation and a lifestyle change?

It could be combination of objectives.

Having decided on your investment drivers, the next question is what you want to buy. At this stage, forget the accommodation size and style. There are more fundamental questions to address.

The investor is faced with another group of choices: at what stage of the build cycle to buy:

■ *Off plan*, as the term implies, is a property that is yet to be built or that is part-constructed. This will potentially deliver the largest return, and it delivers the best use of capital, as you can secure and benefit from your investment without having to pay the total amount until completion. But a word of caution: remember, if your plan is to sell or 'flip' on or just prior to completion, look around at the developments in the area and consider the opportunity to sell. If this is your intention, check that this is an available option, as many developers include a clause prohibiting this practice. Also bear in mind that you don't want to attempt a sale in a market flooded with similar investment opportunities, which has recently happened in the Costa del Sol and could occur in Dubai. Finally, remember you won't normally have the use of the property for up to two years.
■ *Key ready* is a newly built property that has been completed and is ready to move into. The benefit is that the property is for immediate use either for rental or for relocation or holidays. The upside is that you know what you are getting; the downside is that there is no opportunity to personalize it and, more importantly, you are paying the 'at time of purchase' market price.
■ Finally there is the *resale* property, normally in a mature setting, but remember, having purchased it, you will normally want to undertake some level of renovation, from a simple redecoration through to a complete rebuild, so make sure you have a contingency budget in anticipation of some additional expenditure.

Now is the time to choose the type of property and the location. If it's for your personal use, consider how often you are proposing to visit each year and for how long. Travel time eats into short breaks, so consider closer locations with a maximum two- to three-hour travel time in each direction. For those longer breaks, destinations further afield can be considered. For property investments undertaken across the world, it is prudent to consider appointing a local trusted agent/lawyer to take care of your interests. It is difficult and expensive to get a problem solved from the other side of the world, and even if you are closer to home it is advisable to appoint a local professional representative to ensure bills are paid and repairs undertaken. There is nothing worse than arriving at your destination to find the electricity and phones are cut off or worse!

If you are considering a renovation project, get a good grasp of the local language before you start, as miscommunication can be very expensive and frustrating for all parties. Check labour and material costs and appoint quality professional service providers to ensure a smooth planning and build process. As always, preparation is all.

For the pure investor who is keeping property for the medium to long term it is necessary to consider the business model based on rental. There are three types of rental opportunities:

1. *The local long-term market.* Consider the local salary structure. Normally if property prices are low this is reflected in the earning capability of the local population.
2. *Long-term rental to inbound expats.* Often when people make the decision to relocate overseas they want to rent initially whilst their new home is under construction. But check the back pages of the local English-language papers because if there are lots of rentals available then the chance for yours renting could be uncertain. Consider advertising your property in your home market to secure your tenants before they leave.
3. *The holiday rental market.* This often seems the most lucrative. The less scrupulous sales agent will entice you with rental rate figures that are positively exciting but may not be as certain as indicated. Check the market out, look at present availability and look at the travel trends to your chosen location. But most importantly consider how you are going to generate the rentals. You will need to market your property. This can be done through online services such as www.skhvillas.com or www.holidaylets.net, which charge a fee for posting your property. Alternatively you will need to proactively market yourself, with the associated time and marketing costs.

Another major question is where, or from whom, do you purchase? There are hundreds if not thousands of overseas property agents and developers all providing what they consider a professional service; but some are more professional than others. I would always recommend dealing with an accredited professional company. In the UK there are two professional associations: the Federation of Overseas Property Developers, Agents and Consultants (FOPDAC), the oldest and most established with years of experience and expertise and members that are always happy assist where possible, and the Association of International Property Professionals (AIPP). Both operate strict codes of conduct and carry professional indemnity insurance. Members display their membership on their websites, and promotional material can be found via the associations' websites, www.fopdac.com and www.aipp.org.uk respectively. For those purchasing 'off plan', also check whether the developer has some type of insurance, bank guarantee or bonding to secure your payments during the construction period.

So you have chosen your property and now you have to fund your purchase. There are many options depending on your personal circumstances, so speak to an independent professional adviser with specialist knowledge and keep an open mind.

Once the finance has been organized, if you are transferring funds overseas don't automatically transfer via your bank. As with most things there is a market and you may well find that you achieve more advantageous rates through the services of a foreign exchange specialist.

## In conclusion

It is all too easy to be seduced and carried along by the media extolling the attractions of overseas property ownership. There *are* proven, great opportunities to accumulate significant capital assists and wealth through careful planning and prudent investment. Unlike many investment opportunities, overseas property investment offers the opportunity to truly 'spread' risk through countries, locations and property types, so offering the potential investor the opportunity of a secure investment portfolio. To sum up, the three key words to remember are *research*, *knowledge* and *preparation*.

# Investing In Overseas Property

## Are you an investor?

The property market has evolved over the last few years. With 10 years experience in the business McLaren Investments Ltd have experts on hand who specialise in investment portfolios. Hand picking our projects globally enables us to build portfolios for our clients, with deposit only and nothing to pay until completion.

**We can give you** One to One Personal Appointments. **Let us show you how easy it is to make your money go further.**

Why pay for information from other companies when McLaren will give you this for free?

* Clients who come to us with, for example: 50,000GBP-100,000GBP to spend on a property abroad.
* We advise our clients on the best investments. Properties with Guaranteed Income. Locations with potential for High Capital Growth. Properties in countries with low mortgage rates.
* We provide excellent after sales service and an exit strategy on all properties.
* We work in conjunction with The International Law Centre and many Financial Institutions in the UK and Overseas. We are also members of the Association of International Property Professionals.

£50,000 Investment Option

* Three properties worth £182,900
* Require £54,500 worth of deposits from the investor
* In five years these properties could be worth up to £406,300
* These properties are based on 20-40% deposits, nothing to pay till completion
* Estimated Annual Capital Growth: Cyprus – 20%, Bulgaria– 15%, Italy – 15%

**Net Profit of £243,880 in 5 years from £54,500 of deposits**
**R.O.I = 447% over 5 years**

McLaren Investments Ltd.
Charter House, Sandford St. Lichfield WS13 6QA

Tel: 01543 268333
www.mclarenproperties.com

# £1000 Investment Scheme

## Purchase a Property in:

## Barbados, Dominican Republic & St Vincent for £1000

**McLaren Investment Limited** are pleased to announce an excellent opportunity to invest in a brand new property in any of the above locations with only £1000 required. See the example process below:

- £1000 non-refundable reservation fee required for reservation of a specific property.

- 30% deposit required (less £1000) within 45 days of reservation. Should you choose to borrow the 30% deposit from your bank on your behalf, the developer will pay the loan repayments, including interest, for the 30% deposit until completion of the specific unit you have reserved. These payments will then be added to the purchase price upon completion.

- Example (Sterling): Property price £200,000. £1000 reservation fee paid.

The deposit = 30% of £200,000 = £60,000 – £1000 (reservation fee) = £59,000. Interest on £59,000 @ 6% p.a. = £295 per month, paid for 24 months by the developer = £7,080 added to the purchase price upon completion.

Due to the significantly discounted off-plan contract price and the capital appreciation during the construction phase, it is anticipated that the £200,000 purchase price will have grown to a property value at completion of circa £325,000.

At this point a 70% loan to value guaranteed mortgage is available and therefore you will be able to borrow up to £227,500. This is clearly ample to pay for the £199,000 (purchase price less £1000 reservation fee) that you owe as well as the accrued interest of £7,080 – from the above example.

Assuming you borrowed the maximum loan to value mortgage, available from the example above, you would borrow £227,500 on which the annual interest payment would be £18,200 based on a rate of 8%. The rental guarantee of 10% of your purchase price of £200,000 will generate you an income of £20,000 each year, should cover your mortgage payments.

If you wish you could retain the £59,000 loan you took out for the deposit, pay the interest yourself each month, from completion onwards, and use the money to invest in a further investment property purchase.

We would be delighted to answer any further questions you have regarding the exciting opportunity as well as helping you to make your reservation in the Caribbean.

Subject to status and conditions apply – please contact John McLaren on **01543 268333** for further information. If cases where the developer is unable to obtain finance for you, they will be prepared to refund the £1,000 reservation fee.

# Investments that sparkle

# Understanding coloured diamonds

*Stephen Hershoff, Pastor-Genève BVBA*

## Introduction

Diamonds have long been considered the ultimate form of concentrated wealth – a private and easily transportable international currency. The coloured diamond market in particular can be traced back centuries to Indian merchants and European kings. These rare items have always adorned royalty and the wealthy merchant classes as symbols of power and prestige. Elizabeth Taylor and the Sultan of Brunei can be counted amongst those who have developed a passion for rare coloured diamonds.

Usually small and subtle, coloured diamonds possess a sophisticated, low-key glamour that only the wearer, or another elite connoisseur, can understand.

Although coloured diamonds continue to evoke images of wealth and prestige, collectors and investors now recognize the powerful investment fundamentals driving this closely held market. Few markets offer the price stability, concentration of wealth and growth prospects of coloured diamonds.

According to coloured diamond expert Stephen Hofer, author of *Collecting and Classifying Coloured Diamonds*, 'Supply is down and should decrease further, demand is up significantly and as a result prices are expected to continue to go up, especially for the highest graded stones, such as the intense and deep colours.'[1]

That is why, in the last three years, 38 of the 40 highest prices paid for gemstones and jewellery at the major auction houses around the globe have been for coloured diamonds, with prices often reaching hundreds of thousands of dollars per carat.[2]

---

1. 'Global investment', *Sovereign Individual*, March 2006, pp 6, 7.
2. Russell Shor (2005) 'Fancy color diamonds catch public fancy', *Loupe*, GIA Publications.

As sophisticated international investors continue to seek portable, tangible wealth in these uncertain times, the potential of investing in rare coloured diamonds has never been stronger.

## Grading diamonds

As with any collectable, the initial price of a diamond and its ability to increase in value are determined by its rarity. The main factors that influence diamond prices are its colour, cut, carat weight and clarity, all being factors of rarity.

### Colour

The single most important factor in grading and valuing coloured diamonds is the colour of the stone. The colour saturation of the diamond is compared to the lightness or darkness of the colour to determine the grading, or quality, of the stone (see Table 5.1.1). The stones at the top end of the grading spectrum, such as the intense and vivid grades, are the rarest pieces in the marketplace with the strongest colour saturation and the highest values. Furthermore, the rarer colours that appear less frequently in nature will command a higher value than the more common colours.

### Cut

Cut has the strongest influence on the diamond's brilliance. In a well-cut stone, rays of light entering the diamond reflect back to the eye of the observer. In a coloured diamond, the unique mixture of colour that the viewer experiences is termed 'face-up colour'. The cutter of fancy coloured diamonds is an artist using the coloured diamond rough material to create individual masterpieces with perfectly faceted dimensions and a vibrant colour composition. Radiant and brilliant cuts in rectangle, asscher, oval, heart and pear shapes are often used to maximize the colour saturation and enhance the sparkle of the stone, as Figure 5.1.1 illustrates.

### Carat weight

The size of a diamond has an impact on its price and is a major factor of rarity. The metric carat, which equals 0.20 gram, is the standard unit of weight for diamonds and most other gems. Coloured diamonds tend to appear naturally in smaller sizes compared to other diamonds and gemstones. In fact, very few pink diamonds from the Argyle mine in Australia are over 1 carat in size. At last year's Argyle tender, the largest pink diamond was 2.31 carats and most of the stones were between 0.5 carat

**Table 5.1.1**  GIA colour grading scale

| Faint | Very Light | Light | Fancy Light | Fancy | Fancy Dark | Fancy Intense | Fancy Deep | Fancy Vivid |
|-------|-----------|-------|-------------|-------|-----------|---------------|------------|-------------|

**Diamond and gemstone shapes**

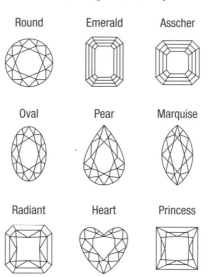

**Figure 5.1.1**    Coloured diamond cuts

and 1 carat in size.[3] Because coloured diamonds have a higher price tag and are more readily available in smaller sizes, there is an active sub-carat collector market for these stones (see Figure 5.1.2).

## Clarity

Diamonds contain minute imperfections called inclusions. The majority of coloured diamonds contain inclusions because of the chemical structure and pressure required to create one. Coloured diamond connoisseurs will acquire a stone based on the colour saturation and consider clarity as a secondary issue. Instead of using a loupe to examine the stone, they use different light sources as their guide. The question they ask is: how does the stone look in natural sunlight as opposed to artificial light? The most expensive stone ever sold was a 0.95 carat red

**Carat weight scale**

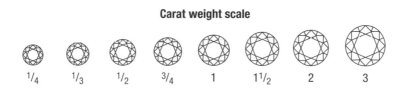

$^1/_4$      $^1/_3$      $^1/_2$      $^3/_4$      1      $1^1/_2$      2      3

While diamonds are not actual size, the increase in proportion between each is to scale.

**Figure 5.1.2**    Carat weight scale

3. Robert Genis, 'Pink diamonds', *Rapaport News*, 11 November 2004.

diamond for $926,000 per carat in 1987.[4] This stone was heavily included, but because of its rich strawberry colour it sold for a world record price. A comparable D-flawless diamond would sell for $17,000 per carat.

## Evaluating coloured diamonds

The actual grading of coloured diamonds is very straightforward and simple to understand but it requires sophisticated laboratory equipment and years of experience to become an expert. It is based on both colour saturation and the appearance of colour.

Figure 5.1.3 illustrates the four general categories of colour: pale, bright, dull and deep. This is determined by how light or dark the colour of the stone is and how weak or strong the colour saturation is. Note that the light and faint colour grades will be plotted into the pale quadrant while the brighter stones with stronger colour saturation are classified as the intense and vivid stones. The coloured diamonds plotted in the bright and deep categories (Fancy Intense, Fancy Deep, Fancy Dark, Fancy Vivid) represent the smallest percentage of the overall coloured diamond market and are considered the rarest and most sought-after coloured diamonds. According to Stephen Hofer, a polished coloured diamond exhibits a unique impression of coloured reflections that appear deceptive and mysterious as the stone is turned in the light.

It is important to understand that coloured diamonds often appear in nature with a dominant colour and a colour modifier, or secondary colour. On a certificate, colour modifiers will appear with the suffix '-ish'. For example, a coloured diamond with a dominant colour of purple and traces of pink may be certified as follows: 'Fancy Intense pinkish Purple'. The term 'Fancy Intense' indicates a medium amount of colour saturation and a brighter colour tone. In this example, the dominant colour Purple appears last and is capitalized while the secondary trace colour of pink appears first and is in lower case. If the secondary colour appears stronger in the stone, ie approximately one-third pink and two-thirds purple, the

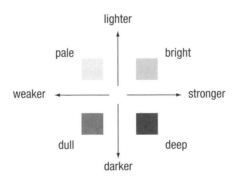

**Figure 5.1.3**   General categories of coloured diamonds

4. http://www.bankrate.com/brm/news/investing/20031103a1.asp

grading will be as follows: 'Fancy Intense Pink Purple'. In this case, the pink still appears first but is capitalized because it appears in stronger amounts while the dominant colour remains the same.

Over the years specialists in the coloured diamond market have developed the use of common colour names to help collectors and investors understand and visualize the colour. These common colour names incorporate terms like 'strawberry red' and 'pumpkin orange' to help illustrate the colour to potential buyers.

In fact, the National Colored Diamond Association (NCDIA) is working with the International Gemmological Institute (IGI) to develop a certificate that will include common colour names. These attributes are significant because they provide a common language for describing a diamond's colour between buyers and sellers, and use colour terms that enable the consumer to experience the colour on both an emotional and a personal level.

Each analysis is performed by an expert graduate gemmologist using state-of-the-art spectral analysis to determine the origin of colour.[5] The reports were launched in the summer of 2005 and have already helped expand consumer knowledge and appreciation of natural coloured diamonds.

## Coloured diamond rarity

While it is true that all natural coloured diamonds are rare occurrences, the astute investor knows that there are differences in rarity among different colours. In other words, certain colours are more or less rare than other colours.

In addition, investors must also understand which diamond colours are perceived in the commercial marketplace as being more rare than others. Table 5.1.2 offers a guide.

Table 5.1.2 is designed to explain different levels of rarity. However, there are exceptions, such as pure orange diamonds, which are almost as rare as reds or blues. Orange is more common with secondary colours of brown or yellow, whereas blue and red rarely appear as secondary colours.

It is important to understand that stones that are classified as modestly rare, such as yellow diamonds and brown diamonds, have also seen dramatic sales increases because of their affordability, beauty and rarity relative to colourless

**Table 5.1.2**   Perceived rarity of coloured diamonds

| Extremely Rare | Notably Rare | Modestly Rare |
| --- | --- | --- |
| Red | Orange | Yellow |
| Violet | Purple | Grey |
| Green | Pink | Brown |
| Blue | Olive | Black |
|  | White |  |

5. www.diamondintelligenceonline.com/magazine/magazine.asp?id=845&searchunderscoretext=

diamonds. Canary yellows and cognac browns are two of the most popular offerings in the market.

Conversely, stones classified as extremely rare are truly one-of-a-kind pieces and are available in the open market only a few times a year. These stones continue to set new record prices at auction on an annual basis and will often see several buyers competing for the same stone. Both scenarios have a positive impact on the market and add to the continuing demand and appeal of coloured diamonds.

In the coloured diamond marketplace – where buyers compete against one another to own the so-called 'best' stones for their collection and/or portfolio – knowing the order of coloured diamond rarity from 'least rare' to 'more rare' is an important step in determining a diamond's present and potential value.

## Certificates and reports

When purchasing a fancy coloured diamond, it is essential that the stone have an origin-of-colour report from the GIA or one of the other qualified gemmological laboratories. The most identified laboratory in the world for grading and certifying coloured diamonds is the GIA. The GIA will analyse the stone and create a colour-only report, which identifies the colour, the weight, the measurements and the colour grade. This report will also determine whether or not the diamond's colour is natural and unaltered, which is the single most important information on the report. The GIA also produces more detailed full certificates, which include the clarity, a measurement of the fluorescence of the stone and an analysis of the shape and polish of the stone. The other laboratories used for grading and certification are: the IGI, EGL, Gubelin and the HRD. A Stephen Hofer report is also a valuable coloured diamond document. Mr Hofer analyses and measures the colour, provides a historical reference for that type of stone and explains why that particular piece is a rare and unique collector's item.

## The science behind coloured diamonds

To appreciate the extreme rarity of coloured diamonds, it is important to understand the unusual process behind coloured diamond formation. Created millions of years ago, these colourful gems crystallized under relatively similar geological conditions as the well-known colourless variety, yet with a slight twist of fate, endowing each of them with exciting and unusual colours.

For example, an intense canary yellow diamond is caused by nature's addition of nitrogen atoms to a diamond. But these are not just any nitrogen atoms; they are the more volatile isolated nitrogen atoms. If the crystallized formation is exposed to too much heat or pressure, as is often the case as the volcanic ascent exposes the crystal to temperatures in excess of 1,400 degrees Celsius, the nitrogen atoms move around inside the crystal formation, which alters the colour from an intense canary yellow to a pale cape yellow. In more rare instances, the isolated, nitrogen-containing diamond is not exposed to temperatures above 1,300 degrees Celsius, which results in a more saturated, canary yellow colour. It is these sets of unique physical and chemical circumstances that define true rarity for coloured diamonds.[6]

Every coloured diamond has its own story. Green diamonds are exposed to natural irradiation, blue diamonds contain trace amounts of boron, and pink diamonds are created by extreme amounts of pressure that leave structural defects in the crystal and cause a pink colouration.

It is these unusual circumstances in nature that lead to the creation of coloured diamonds. Only a small percentage of the Earth contains diamond deposits. Within these deposits, only ideal conditions of temperature, pressure and chemical exposure will lead to the formation of coloured diamonds. What is critical to understand is that, of these coloured diamond formations, very few have the colour saturation, colour composition and consistency of the top-graded coloured diamonds. The science behind coloured diamond formation dictates that very few will appear in nature as the mining cycle continues in the future.

## Coloured diamond supply

Coloured diamonds appear infrequently in nature. In fact, for every 10,000 carats of colourless diamonds mined, only 1 carat will turn out to be a fancy coloured diamond.[7] Of the estimated 160 million carats of diamonds mined in 2005, only a few thousand carats will be cut and polished coloured diamonds (excluding browns and blacks).[8]

Consider the Argyle mine in Australia, which is the largest source of pink diamonds in the world. 'They may recover 25 million carats of diamonds in a year, but only 10,000 carats of pink, of which fewer than 1,000 will be larger than a quarter of a carat in the rough.'[9]

Anyone involved in the diamond market should understand that important long-term developments are occurring in diamond-producing countries around the world that will have a direct impact on prices over the next decade. Although these developments have been unfolding over the last two years, they are now coming to the forefront as dealers, jewellers and consumers struggle with the reality of the market fundamentals: the global supply of diamonds is decreasing for the first time in 25 years.[10]

The first announcements came out of Australia in 2003, when Rio Tinto Diamonds, owner of the largest diamond mine in the world, the Argyle mine, announced that they would no longer be mining the alluvial deposits surrounding the main open-pit mine. Another announcement quickly followed indicating that Argyle was doing a feasibility study to determine how much longer reserves could support current mining rates.

6. Stephen C. Hofer (1998) *Collecting and Classifying Coloured Diamonds*, Ashland Press, New York, p 102.
7. http://money.guardian.co.uk/print/0,3858,4532840–110138,00.html
8. David Markum, Gemmologist, 'Coloured diamond price forecast 2010: a report prepared exclusively for Sovereign Society members'.
9. *Scotsman*, February 2006, http://living.scotsman.com/index.cfm?id=195862006.
10. 'Diamonds to outpace metals as scarcity, Asia sales boost prices', Bloomberg News, 7 August 2006.

In late 2005, after millions of dollars of research and a lucrative financial package from the Australian government, Argyle decided to take the mine underground in 2008 and close the open-pit mine, but the supply is expected to decrease by at least 40 per cent a year, and the quality of the diamond ore will drop considerably for the next decade.[11]

During this time, De Beers announced that they would be closing the oldest diamond mine in the world, the Kimberley mine in South Africa, along with two smaller mines. This was another indication of where the supply in the market is headed. As South Africa is the primary source of yellow diamonds, the supply of certain types of coloured diamonds began to come under pressure.

As recently as the summer of 2006, a number of diamond-producing countries have been reporting their first-half production and a number of them have reported decreases:

- For the first time ever, Russia reported its annual diamond production. In the past, experts had to estimate its production but Russia is trying to comply with international standards so it has increased its disclosure. It reported production of 23 million carats in 2005, down from an estimated 35 million carats in 2004.[12]
- For the first half of 2006, Rio Tinto's diamond production fell 25 per cent to 15.5 million carats. Australia's Argyle diamond production for the first half of 2006 declined 30 per cent to 12.7 million carats. Of this, less than 35,000 carats were sorted gem-quality. The value of rough diamond exports dropped 14 per cent to $115.9 million from $135 million in 2005.[13]
- Diamond exports from Sierra Leone for the first half of fiscal 2006 dropped some 20 per cent according to officials. Diamond exports from January to June fell $63 million, down from $75 million in 2005.[14]
- De Beers' South Africa unit expects diamond production in that country to fall 2.6 per cent in 2006 to 14.7 million carats. The production drop was not entirely related to the closure of the Koffiefontein mine. The company's Cullinan production is about one-third less than one year ago as well.[15]
- Botswana, the largest diamond producer in the world by value and by carats, said 2006 rough production would fall 10 per cent.[16]

Dr Steve Sjuggerud, editor of *True Wealth* newsletter, recently reported that by 2008 the world would be facing a diamond shortage. If you examine the supply figures from the first half of 2006, the decreasing supply developments in the global diamond market are occurring at a much faster pace than anticipated.

---

11. 'Argyle open pit mining to cease in 2008', *Rapaport Diamond News*, November 2006.
12. 'Russian diamond exports at $1.7B', *Rapaport Diamond News*, 16 June 2006.
13. Rio Tinto Diamonds, www.riotintodiamonds.com.
14. 'Sierra Leone diamond exports – 20% in first half', *Rapaport Diamond News*, 14 July 2006.
15. 'De Beers lowers S. Africa production est. for 2006', *Rapaport News*, 26 May 2006.
16. 'De Beers lowers S. Africa production est. for 2006', *Rapaport News*, 26 May 2006.

# Buying the right colours

Although there is no such thing as a coloured diamond mine, certain mines are known to produce small quantities of specific types of coloured diamonds. For example, Australia is recognized for its beautiful pink and cognac diamonds. South Africa and Botswana produce fine yellow diamonds and an occasional blue diamond. Central Africa and Brazil produce orange diamonds and a small selection of chameleon and green diamonds. It is important to consider which colours will be most affected by the imminent supply crisis in the diamond market before acquiring rare coloured diamonds for your portfolio.

# Demand for coloured diamonds

Over the last decade, demand for coloured diamonds has increased considerably. This is due to a number of important factors. First and foremost, international investors and collectors have recognized their beauty, rarity and value. Coloured diamonds are the rarest gemstones in the world, and collectors consider their beauty unsurpassed in the marketplace. In addition, very few asset classes offer the price stability, long-term appreciation, portability and privacy that coloured diamonds possess.

Until very recently an occasional rarity, coloured diamonds have become a staple, taking an increasing share of trade show and independent jeweller counter space. A recent *Wall Street Journal* article advised adding a large yellow diamond to every well-rounded investment portfolio. Many jewellers and dealers believe that demand is the real question because supply is finite.

Historically, coloured diamonds have been for collectors and investors because they have consistently grown in value while maintaining price stability over time. At the annual Basel show in Switzerland in 2003, a number of dealers began showing coloured diamonds for the first time for their jewellery clients. Today, few booths will not have a piece or two.

A growing trend in the jewellery market is retail buyers seeking coloured diamonds to add to their jewellery and estate holdings. Recently, the National Colored Diamond Association (NCDIA) in the United States and Rio Tinto Mining in Australia sponsored a US consumer survey. Chief among the findings: 58.8 per cent of respondents are interested in natural colour diamonds, with many reporting that they are likely to buy or own jewellery containing them, and that most of these purchases would be for themselves. However, there are still fairly low levels of consumer exposure to these diamonds, which means the growth potential is unprecedented.[17]

For example, the growth of right-hand ring sales and three-stone ring sales in the United States has corresponded with a rise in demand for coloured diamonds because a number of these buyers are looking for second or third jewellery pieces with coloured diamonds incorporated in the design. During the past five years,

---

17. 'Marketing colored diamonds gets results', *National Jeweler*, 5 April 2005.

three-stone diamond jewellery sales growth has risen almost 35 per cent, according to the Diamond Information Center.

François Curiel, Christie's International head of jewellery, agrees that Middle Eastern buyers are the biggest consumers of coloured diamonds in today's market, followed by Asian collectors. 'The market for coloured diamonds is as strong as it has ever been', he says.

> In our Geneva jewellery sale in November, a fancy intense blue diamond, of 3.71 carats, that had been unsold, at $850,000 in New York in 2002, sold for $1.3 million. Good coloured diamonds are so scarce, that they fetch 10 times the price of a colourless D flawless stone. Plus there is a lot of money around looking for good jewellery.

Furthermore, as the supply of diamonds continues to decrease, Figure 5.1.4 illustrates that the price of polished colourless and coloured diamonds will grow significantly over the next decade.[18]

The market has already seen selected coloured diamonds selling for double and triple their reserve estimates at the major auction houses. Dealers are reporting that the price of pink, yellow, cognac and blue rough is up by at least 20 per cent over the last year. As fewer rare coloured diamonds appear on the market and as demand continues to accelerate, collectors who act now will position themselves to enjoy a robust period of growth in the coloured diamond market.

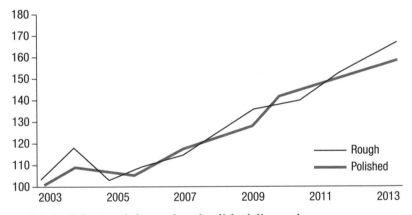

**Figure 5.1.4** Price trends in rough and polished diamonds

---

18. Vivienne Barber, 'The ultimate jewel of jewels', *International Herald Tribune*, December 2005.

# Investing in coloured diamonds

*Stephen Hershoff, Pastor-Genève BVBA*

In terms of both value and growth, coloured diamonds are offering perhaps the best return in the gemstone market. Since formal records were first kept at the beginning of the 1970s, prices for the highest grades of coloured diamonds have increased in value by an average of between 10 per cent and 15 per cent a year, with rarer colours and higher grades enjoying the greatest appreciation. In addition, this appreciation has statistically been non-correlated to the stock and bond markets, an important consideration for investors seeking a diversified portfolio.[1]

Since 1970 natural fancy blue diamonds have doubled in price every five years, natural fancy pink diamonds have doubled in price every six to seven years (see Figure 5.2.1) and natural fancy yellow diamonds have doubled in price every eight to 10 years. During recessions, coloured diamonds tend to retain their value, and in stable or healthy economies they appreciate in price.[2]

While there are no performance guarantees, the consensus of coloured diamond dealers is that continued long-term conservative appreciation of 7–10 per cent annually is a reasonable prospect, with the rarer colours appreciating in excess of this range.[3] Investors should consider starting a collection by investing £5,000 to £10,000 in one or two coloured diamonds.

1. 'Global investment', *Sovereign Individual*, March 2006, pp 6, 7.
2. http://www.webguru.com/investing-diamonds.htm
3. http://www.europeanbusiness.eu.com/features/2005/jul/world_diamonds.html

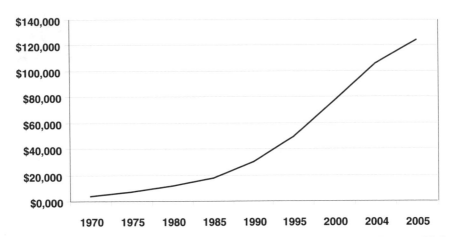

**Figure 5.2.1**   Average prices of a highly saturated 1-carat Fancy Intense Pink diamond since 1970, eye-clean stones

There are five main reasons why investors purchase coloured diamonds:

■ *Privacy.* Most countries do not require the ownership of coloured diamonds to be disclosed to any government authority. The certificates are in bearer form, there are no names or serial numbers and there are no registration requirements for coloured diamonds.
■ *Portability.* Coloured diamonds are considered the most concentrated form of wealth in the world. A multimillion-dollar portfolio can be discreetly placed in a small envelope.
■ *Estate planning.* Consider the acquisition of a small cache of coloured diamonds that can be discreetly passed from one generation to the next. Depending on the number of heirs, more stones with less unit value may be needed.
■ *Price stability.* The majority of the important coloured diamonds are in strong financial hands, whether it be the dealers/jewellers or the investors/collectors who own them. Even in a severe recession, owners of fine coloured diamonds who need money will sacrifice or discount their common merchandise or other

UK penny versus $1 million in coloured diamonds.
Courtesy of the 'Colour Variety Collection'

**Figure 5.2.2**   Diamonds as concentrated wealth

assets first. Fine coloured diamonds are so hard to substitute that anything that can be replaced more readily will be sold first. These two fundamentals combine to lead to remarkable price stability and consistency.[4]

■ *Long-term growth.* Because of the rarity, decline in supply and steady increase in demand for quality coloured diamonds, prices should continue to rise for the next decade. It is important to recognize that coloured diamonds are still new to the general public and the potential for new buyers in the next decade is significant, while the supply stream is finite.

## Acquisition

When purchasing a coloured diamond, consumers have a number of options:

■ *Retail jeweller.* Retailers normally have a limited inventory of coloured diamonds. However, they can take requests and acquire stones in the secondary market. Although coloured diamonds are very popular at the retail level and the more prestigious retailers maintain an inventory of quality goods, you will be paying established retail prices.

■ *Auction houses.* If you are planning to acquire a piece at one of the major auctions, you are required to provide information of financial suitability in order to enter into the bidding process. Although you may be able to bid on a number of different stones, auctions are a sellers' market, and the top pieces usually see a number of buyers competing for the same stone. However, astute buyers have been successful at selectively acquiring pieces at auction.

■ *Speciality dealers.* A third method is through a small group of international speciality dealers. Although most speciality dealers only work with a select client base, they are often in possession of rare coloured diamonds unavailable at the retail level and at a more reasonable price than one would find at auction. Speciality dealers have contacts directly at the mines and are often in communication with any private estate sales offering coloured diamonds. The advice you will receive from a speciality dealer will be more personal and will give you a better gauge of the overall trends in the market. More importantly, speciality dealers are obliged to maintain both discretion and confidentiality for their clients.

## Key trends in the market

■ *Orange diamonds.* People don't realize how rare orange diamonds are. They are very undervalued relative to their rarity as they are priced at a deep discount to blue, green and red diamonds even though they are almost as rare. One should attempt to find an orange diamond that looks like a pumpkin, tangerine or citrus orange.[5]

---

4. Zurich Club Communiqué, UK, August 2002.
5. Robert Genis, 'The pumpkin diamond', *Rapaport Diamond Report*, 7 November 2003.

■ *Chameleon diamonds*. These possess the ability to change colour under different lighting conditions. Most chameleon diamonds have a greyish-yellowish-green colour. They are one of the great mysteries of the diamond world. According to Ariel Friedman, 'with chameleons, you will own something clearly unique among the fancy colours'.[6]

■ *Pink diamonds*. The Argyle mine in Australia produces only a few hundred a year. With demand for pink diamonds growing dramatically and the mine seeing the supply decrease, pink diamonds offer strong fundamental growth prospects. The owners of the Argyle mine have announced that they expect the last year of open-pit mining to be in 2008, and the first-half supply in 2006 decreased 30 per cent at the Argyle mine. If that pace continues, an investment in Argyle pink diamonds today could double in value in the next 36 months. Bubblegum, rose and lilac pinks are the most popular.[7]

■ *Yellow diamonds*. True canaries continue to set new record prices at the world's auction houses. They are also experiencing dramatic growth at the retail level. With the pending supply decreases in Botswana and South Africa, quality canary and daffodil yellows offer very good long-term prospects.

■ *Special stones*. Any time a red, green, violet or blue can be acquired at the right price, it is always a worthwhile purchase. Only one or two greens and reds are available for sale each year.

## Taking possession vs offshore storage

Investors have the option of taking possession of their coloured diamonds or leaving them in an offshore storage facility. If you take physical possession, diamonds can be delivered to any major city in the world by a bonded and insured delivery service. It is advised that investors have their diamonds insured, which may require an appraisal from a recognized laboratory, such as the EGL. Appraisals usually cost £50 to £100 and insurance premiums are inexpensive, usually well below 1 per cent of the value per year. If you choose to leave your diamonds in a bonded and insured storage facility, the fees vary from a flat rate every year to a small percentage of the value of the stones annually. Investors have full authority and control of these accounts. In either case, the owner will take possession of the laboratory certificate. Overseas storage facilities are available in the Caribbean, Switzerland, Dubai and the free trade zones in Asia. Your private dealer will be able to advise you on your options when it comes to both storage and insurance.

## Monitoring the market

Monitoring prices is similar to the property market and requires a comparison of prices achieved for comparable stones on a per-carat basis. Auction results, retail

---

6. Diana Jarett, 'A phenomenon', *Rapaport News*, April 2006.
7. 'Global investment', *Sovereign Individual*, March 2006, pp 6, 7.

sales figures and dealer prices are used to gauge the general price level. Individual stones can sell for premiums or discounts depending on the buyer's preference.

## The sales process

Like the real estate or art market, the coloured diamond market is considered a decentralized market because there are no specific bids and offers on stones and there is not one central market where the majority of transactions take place. The advantages of a market like this are that buyers working with experts can take advantage of inexperience, lack of knowledge, distress sales and economies of scale to achieve discounted prices of specific pieces. For example, a seller of an uncertified stone may misidentify the stone for a fancy grade when in fact the laboratory may certify the stone as an intense diamond, thereby significantly increasing the value for the purchaser upon certification. However, it is essential to work with experienced firms that can source top-quality stones at various levels of the wholesale market and that can acquire the relevant certification and documentation to ensure authenticity and quality standards.

Fancy coloured diamonds have among the most liquid and sophisticated markets for any collectable asset. They can be transported quietly and legally and sold globally in most major cities. There are thousands of participants in the market, from collectors and investors to dealers and jewellery buyers.

However, you should view them as a mid- to long-term investment with a time horizon of five years or longer from acquisition to liquidation. When you do want to sell, you should contact your dealer at least 90 days before you need the money. This will give your dealer the chance to accurately gauge the expected market price. Coloured diamonds are similar to real estate and require time to find the right buyer.

Be realistic in your investment outlook; while coloured diamonds have historically been an exceptional investment, they are not as liquid as most securities investments and they are subject to higher mark-ups.

## The auction process

When the time comes to buy and sell rare coloured diamonds, among the most prominent levels of marketing are the major auctions, held globally in the spring and autumn and selectively throughout the year. The major auction houses have an international clientele of wealthy collectors and investors who are attracted to rare pieces that represent good value. Because the coloured diamond market is narrow in size and scope owing to the supply restrictions, it can be difficult to source stones categorized as extremely and notably rare through the retail sector. In addition, many buyers don't have the benefit of working with a speciality dealer who exclusively handles rare coloured diamonds. Consequently, they turn to the public auctions because of the access and the contacts they have developed.

The auction houses primarily sell estate jewellery, along with selective loose coloured diamonds.

Although the auction houses prominently market the truly one-of-a-kind pieces, such as a 4-carat vivid pink or a true red diamond, they also handle more moderately priced pieces that have inherent rarity and natural beauty. These pieces also sell particularly well and have been shown to achieve prices well above the estimates. Examples of prices achieved are shown in Tables 5.2.1 to 5.2.5.

The auction houses will charge a percentage of the selling price, depending on the value of the sale. The higher the selling price, the lower the commission will be. However, the auction houses have the advantage of getting the kind of exposure that brings out buyers through their global marketing efforts and extensive list of wealthy clients.[8] The minimum offering prices they accept are in the range of £3,000–£5,000, with top lots selling in the millions (see Tables 5.2.4 and 5.2.5).

Experts agree that auction sales will continue to grow as new buyers in Europe, Asia, the Middle East and United States learn to appreciate the beauty and rarity of coloured diamonds. HSBC private banking has already worked with Sotheby's on three auctions in the UAE, and major European private banks are advising their customers on rare coloured diamond purchases.[9] As wealthy global investors are introduced to the benefits of investing in coloured diamonds, the auction houses will continue to see new record prices and strong sales for fancy coloured diamonds.

**Table 5.2.1**   Geneva, November 2005

| Lot | House | Size | Colour Grade | Shape | Estimated Price | Actual Price |
|-----|-------|------|--------------|-------|-----------------|--------------|
| 344 | Sotheby's | 2.01 | Fancy Intense Yellow | Cushion | 20,000–30,000 CHF | 48,000 CHF |

**Table 5.2.2**   Hong Kong, June 2006

| Lot | House | Size | Colour Grade | Shape | Estimated Price | Actual Price |
|-----|-------|------|--------------|-------|-----------------|--------------|
| 2274 | Christie's | 2.08 | Deep Brown Orange | Heart | $5,200–$8,450 | $29,640 |
| 2283 | Christie's | 1.08 | Fancy Yellow Green | Pear | $20,800–$31,200 | $40,560 |

**Table 5.2.3**   New York, April 2006

| Lot | House | Size | Colour Grade | Shape | Estimated Price | Actual Price |
|-----|-------|------|--------------|-------|-----------------|--------------|
| 289 | Sotheby's | 0. 61 | Light Pink | Round | $8,100–$10,000 | $19,200 |

8. 'When the hammer comes down', *Rapaport Diamond Report*, New York, 6 May 2005.
9. *Jewelers Circular Keystone*, 11 May 2005.

**Table 5.2.4**   New York, April 2006

| Lot | House | Size | Colour Grade | Shape | Estimated Price | Actual Price |
|-----|-------|------|--------------|-------|-----------------|--------------|
| 302 | Christie's | 3.17 | Intense Blue | Rectangle | $500,000–$700,000 | $1,012,800 |

**Table 5.2.5**   Geneva, May 2006

| Lot | House | Size | Colour Grade | Shape | Estimated Price | Actual Price |
|-----|-------|------|--------------|-------|-----------------|--------------|
| 357 | Sotheby's | 5.57 | Intense orangy Pink | Pear | 460,000–720,000 CHF | 1,140,000 CHF |

## Summary

In these times of world economic and political uncertainty, investors are looking for alternative asset classes. Many turn to investing in collectables as a means of diversifying their portfolios away from traditional investments.

The coloured diamond market offers investors the chance to achieve long-term growth, wealth preservation, financial privacy and portfolio diversification. They have proven to be one of the safest and most profitable long-term investments. However, before you buy your first diamond, research the market and always work with a dealer that specializes in coloured diamonds. It is important to learn the subtle nuances of the market so that you can make informed decisions and plan your portfolio to meet your financial goals realistically.

# Diamond exploration

*H John Stollery, DiaMine Explorations, Inc.*

## History of diamonds

The history of diamonds dates back thousands of years to India, where diamonds were valued for their ability to reflect light. The primary purpose of diamonds was for decorative purposes and also as talismans to ward off evil spirits and to provide protection during battle.

During the Dark Ages, diamonds were also used as a medical aid. Deeply superstitious religious figures used diamonds to cure illness. For example, Pope Clement ingested small diamonds to cure an ailment from which he suffered.[1]

As history moved into the Middle Ages, the focus shifted away from the supposed powers diamonds possessed to their value. During this period, the popularity of diamonds surged. Mines in India produced the famous Hope diamond and the one-of-a-kind Koh-I-Noor, a 108-carat round brilliant stone rumoured to be found in the Godaveri river thousands of years ago and currently part of the Crown jewels in London.[2]

It wasn't until the 15th and 16th centuries that diamonds found their way to the West. When trade with the East finally opened up, Europeans and later Americans were astonished by the power and beauty represented in diamonds.

As the supply of Indian diamonds came to an end, small mines began to spring up in places as far-flung as Borneo and Brazil, but there was not enough supply to meet the increasing demand for diamonds. In the mid-19th century, prospectors discovered diamonds near the Orange river in Africa and created the biggest flurry of diamond exploration the world had ever seen until the 21st century. Soon diamonds were being sourced throughout Africa.[3]

1. http://www.costellos.com.au/diamonds/history.html
2. http://www.suevematsu.com/famousdia.html
3. Matthew Hart (2001) *Diamond*, Penguin, Toronto.

With these discoveries, the great diamond boom of the 20th century exploded. Cecil Rhodes formed the De Beers mining company in 1880.[4] This company would go on to control over 80 per cent of the world diamond supply until the late 20th century and develop arguably the most famous marketing campaign in the world, 'A Diamond is Forever'.

However, the foundation of diamonds' allure has always been their beauty and mystique as a symbol of value and wealth. Their durability along with their ability to sparkle and reflect light captivates the viewer and drives consumers to purchase these rare and beautiful stones.

This is what leads prospectors and exploration companies to travel to the four corners of the Earth, so that they can meet the insatiable demand for these scarce geological formations.

It is important to understand how diamonds are formed to know what regions are likely to contain diamond deposits and which areas are worth the investment of surveying and exploration.

## The geology of diamonds

Diamond is a natural crystalline mineral. It is carbon in its most concentrated form and it is widely recognized as the hardest mineral on the planet.[5]

Kimberlite is a rare form of peridotite that can contain diamonds. Although not all kimberlite contains diamonds, all diamonds are found within kimberlite formations called pipes, or in the secondary deposits of washed-away materials called alluvial deposits.

The structure of the Earth is divided into distinct layers, shown in Figure 5.3.1. Diamonds occur at the bottom of the upper mantle (also known as the lithosphere), where it is particularly deep and thick.

Kimberlite begins in the much deeper region of the Earth known as the asthenosphere (the mantle in Figure 5.3.1, also known as the lower mantle). The temperature and pressure are much higher here and, for reasons not entirely understood, sometimes the rock liquefies to form kimberlite magma. This hot magma begins to rise, in bubble-like globules, through the Earth's layers. While these pulses pass through the lithosphere some, but not all, pick up diamonds that have formed in this layer.[6]

Once the first pulse reaches the outer layer, it passes through the cold brittle crust and breaks the surface violently in a volcanic explosion. All of the rock is blown out of the surrounding area, creating the characteristic crater. As more of the kimberlite bubbles reach the surface, they break through in a quieter and much less explosive fire fountain.

The matter that is released in the fire fountain falls back and begins to fill the hole. This magma begins to cool quickly and solidifies to form a kimberlite pipe, typically in a carrot-shaped formation.

4. Matthew Hart (2001) *Diamond*, Penguin, Toronto.
5. http://education.jlab.org/itselemental/ele006.html
6. http://en.wikipedia.org/wiki/Kimberlite

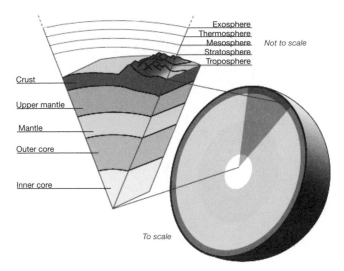

**Figure 5.3.1**  The layers of the Earth

Thousands of years of erosion and glacial activity work to remove the top of the kimberlite pipe. Any diamonds within this section of the pipe can be scattered throughout a large area.

## The world cratons

A craton is an old and stable part of the continental crust that has survived the merging and splitting of continents and supercontinents for a minimum of 500 million years. Identifying cratons is essential because favourable pressures and temperatures for the formation and preservation of diamonds are found beneath them. They are generally found in the interior of continents and formed from light-weight rock (for example, granite) that is attached to a section of the upper mantle. The craton can reach depths of 200 kilometres. Cratons are subdivided geographi-cally (see Figure 5.3.2 for the North American craton), and these geological provinces are classified as archons, protons or tectons according to their age:

- ■ *archons:* consist of rocks from the Archaean era (more than 2.5 billion years old);
- ■ *protons:* consist of rocks from the early to middle Proterozoic era (more than 1.6 billion years old);
- ■ *tectons:* consist of rocks from the late Proterozoic era (more than 800 million years old).[7]

Since minerals, such as the diamond, in the Earth's crust tend to become separated over time, the oldest cratons are the most interesting to mining companies. Cratons are still being discovered as more and more prospecting is done around the globe.

---

7. http://en.wikipedia.org/wiki/Craton

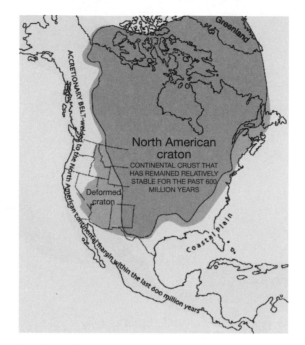

**Figure 5.3.2**   The North American craton

# Diamond mining

Modern exploration and survey techniques require sophisticated geological equipment and an understanding of the science behind diamond formation. The first stage requires the targeting of areas with a high potential for kimberlite formation. These are areas located on cratons with strong geological characteristics associated with diamond formations. The most commonly used technique is airborne magnetic surveys, which are completed by flying over the surveyed area with sophisticated equipment to test for magnetic anomalies present on the property. Surveying companies have found that areas that reported no kimberlite activity may in fact contain kimberlite anomalies, using new surveying equipment and flying at lower levels to receive a stronger read of magnetic activity.

After critical areas of discovery have been targeted and claims have been staked, explorers look to locate indicator minerals, such as garnet, that were dispersed like volcanic ash in the vicinity of the pipe's surface. No matter how far these colourful, glassy minerals have travelled, diamond prospectors can often trace their trails back to the source from which they came. Prospectors are also looking for the right kind of indicator minerals; otherwise a pipe can prove to be of no value.

The next step is to determine drill targets by pinpointing the pipe's location. This is where the science of geophysics comes into play. Airborne electromagnetic surveys and gravity surveys reveal different physical properties for kimberlites when compared to the surrounding ground in the area. These kimberlitic anomalies stand out as small circular features in the ground. Drilling will only take place if the right indicator minerals exist in the target area (see Figure 5.3.3).[8]

If drilling reveals the presence of macrodiamonds (greater than 0.5 millimetres) and microdiamonds (less than 0.5 millimetres) in sufficient quantities, then the next stage of exploration, a mini-bulk sample, may be initiated. This is accomplished by recovering at least five tons of kimberlitic rock. Using this sample, the scientists will have a preliminary idea of what the grade of the deposit might be.

One key difference between diamond exploration and the search for metals is that not all carats are equal in value, whereas one ounce of gold is worth the same as any other ounce of gold. This is one reason why the process from discovery to production is longer: diamond mining requires more thorough analysis.

If the results of the mini-bulk sample are favourable, the next step is to take a bulk sample in the range of 10,000 to 20,000 tons. These samples are costly but necessary to determine the grade of the deposit and the quality of the pipe's diamonds.[9] The cycle from initial discovery to production is long and only one in five pipes tend to contain diamonds. In addition, only 1 per cent of pipes worldwide are economic.

However, investors and mining companies continue to invest in diamond exploration because the returns are considered the highest in the mining industry. A small company with nominal landholdings could be sitting on billions of dollars; the potential is enormous.

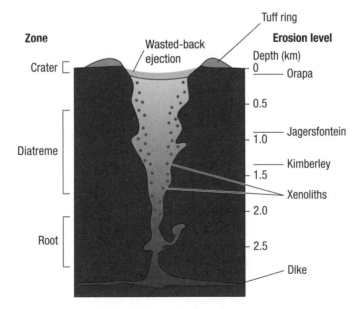

**Figure 5.3.3** Kimberlite anomalies

8. http://www.diamondex.net/s/DiamondExplorationProcess.asp
9. 'Mining explained', Glossary of terms, *Northern Miner*, Toronto, 2004.

For example, Canada's Ekati mine in the Northwest Territories has a valuation of over \$2.5 billion and its reserves are over 60 million carats, making it one of the most valuable mines in the world.[10]

# World diamond industry

## Global diamond supply

The production of diamonds globally in 2005 was estimated to be a total of 160 million carats, with an estimated value (rough diamonds) of US\$13.4 billion.[11] This is an increase of only 2.5 per cent from 2004. However, *Bloomberg News* recently reported that, for the first time in 25 years, global diamond supply is expected to decrease.

De Beers remains the largest producer of diamonds, by value and by caratage, but has seen its stranglehold on the industry significantly decrease in recent years. In 2005 its mines in Botswana, South Africa, Tanzania and Namibia produced an estimated US\$6.54 billion, or 48 per cent of the world production by value, and 49 million carats, or 30 per cent by volume.[12]

The discovery of mines in regions not controlled by De Beers has allowed companies to establish themselves and successfully compete against De Beers. Rio Tinto and BHP Billiton are two of the largest examples of companies successfully competing with De Beers. The Lev Leviev Group and the Steinmetz Group have also established mining operations that have increased global competition.

## Diamond-producing countries

Diamond-producing countries are listed in Table 5.3.1. Botswana continues to be the largest diamond-producing country in terms of value and in terms of carats. Australia ranks number two in the number of carats mined, but ranks eighth in terms of value mined.

South Africa remains one of De Beers' dominant areas. Mines owned by De Beers produce 97 per cent of the 15.2 million carats. However, De Beers recently announced they will be closing three of their mines in South Africa, including the world-famous Kimberley mine. These three mines were responsible for 2.33 million carats in 2004. Although Botswana produces more than South Africa, the four operating mines are owned by Debswana, a 50/50 joint venture between De Beers and the Botswana government. A fifth mine has opened in the area, with 2003 as the first full year of operation. Botswana recently estimated that 2006 production would decrease by as much as 10 per cent. De Beers holdings in Namibia produced 1.8 million carats in 2005, a decrease of 5 per cent.[13]

10. http://www.nnsl.com/ops/ekati.html
11. 'Diamonds to outpace metals', *Bloomberg News*, 7 August 2006.
12. De Beers Group 2005 Annual Report.
13. www.northernminer.com/Diamonds/pdfs/SourcingCanada.pdf

**Table 5.3.1** Estimated 2005 diamond production by country

| Country | Number of Carats Produced | Value of Diamonds Produced |
|---|---|---|
| Botswana | 31.9 million | $3.08 billion |
| Russia | 23 million | $2.54 billion |
| South Africa | 15.2 million | $1.61 billion |
| Canada | 12 million | $1.47 billion |
| Angola | 7 million | $1.21 billion |
| DR Congo | 30.4 million | $1.07 billion |
| Namibia | 1.8 million | $1.07 billion |
| Others | 8 million | $804 million |
| Australia | 30.5 million | $536 million |

*Sources:* WWW International Diamond Consultants, Rio Tinto, BHP Billiton, De Beers

The Russian state company Alrosa's mining ventures grew to $2.26 billion in 2005, and Alrosa owns all of Russia's active mines.[14] This places Russia second in terms of value. However, many of the open pits in the diamond-producing region of Yakutia are almost mined out. Alrosa reported 2005 production at 23 million carats, significantly lower than the estimated 35 million carats in 2004. Alrosa is investing heavily to mine these deposits underground and actively prospecting new diamond deposits but it can be expected that Russia's production will decrease in the near future unless diamond-producing veins can be identified.

Canada is a recent entrant into the club of diamond-producing nations and has redefined the organization, stepping almost immediately into the number three spot in terms of value. With the mines in Russia and the Argyle mine in Australia reaching their productive limits, many in the international diamond community are looking to Canada to keep the global supply steady. Canada's latest diamond mine in Jericho came online in the spring of 2006, and two new mines will start production by 2009, increasing Canada's annual diamond production to an expected 17 million carats a year and over $2.3 billion a year in annual sales based on current diamond prices. Canada also has many exploration projects under way that will continue to develop the diamond industry in the future, which means Canada can be relied upon to be the country to fill part of the expected global production gap.

## Global diamond demand

In 1983, worldwide diamond jewellery sales were $20 billion; today that figure is over $70 billion. Demand for diamonds globally continues to outpace the available supply. In the United States, retail sales of diamond jewellery grew by 7 per cent in 2005 to $33.7 billion.[15] That is an increase of $2.2 billion over 2004 sales, a sum equal to roughly 50 per cent of the country's annual engagement ring sales. This is the 10th consecutive year of growth in US retail diamond sales.

---

14. *Rapaport Diamond News*, 10 April 2006, 26 May 2006.
15. 'Diamonds to outpace metals', *Bloomberg News*, 7 August 2006.

Fuelled by strong sales in China, India and the Middle East, global diamond sales grew almost 10 per cent in 2005. In fact, Dubai's rough diamond trade increased 46 per cent in 2005 to $3.7 billion, according to the Dubai Diamond Exchange.[16]

In China, where rough diamond sales were $1.32 billion in 2005, experts predict the market will grow by at least 15–20 per cent per year. Jewellery sales are expected to rise by over 40 per cent in the next five years, with the most significant sales increases expected for diamond jewellery. China's gold, platinum and diamond jewellery sales reached $17.5 billion in 2005, a 15 per cent increase. Shanghai is expected to become a sizeable trading centre in the world's diamond-processing and -trading field in the next decade. By then, in Shanghai alone sales revenue of diamonds and jewellery will come to US$3 billion–$5 billion, and the number of people engaged in the industry will rise to 100,000.[17]

Because of the growing demand for diamonds and the limited supply, experts and retailers claim that wholesale prices are already up by a third since 2003, and De Beers raised its prices twice at its diamond tenders in 2005 for a total increase of 9.5 per cent (see Figure 5.3.4).

According to James Picton, an analyst with WH Ireland, rough diamond demand is expected to grow 6 per cent a year to $23 billion by 2015 from $13.4 billion in 2005. Prices will rise by one-third, and he estimated by 2015 there should be a shortfall of $10 billion of unfulfilled demand. Several fund managers agree. Trevor Steel of Baker Street Capital Managers in London believes diamond investments will experience above-average returns in the next several years, and Andrew Ferguson of New City Investment Managers Ltd in London believes diamonds will outperform base metals.[18]

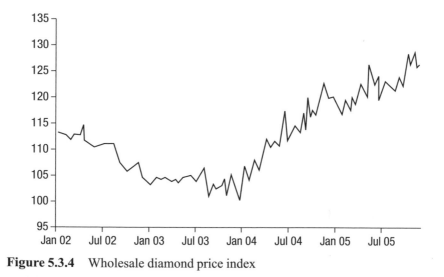

**Figure 5.3.4**  Wholesale diamond price index

16. *Rapaport News*, 14 April 2006.
17. 'International giants strive for China's diamond consumption', China Economic Net, 3 November 2004.
18. 'Diamonds to outpace metals', *Bloomberg News*, 7 August 2006.

Retail diamond demand is expected to grow by at least 5 per cent a year over the next decade as new buyers from Asia purchase diamonds and US buyers increase their jewellery holdings. That means that a mine equivalent to $500 million of diamond production must open every year for the next 10 years to meet the increasing demand from consumers. Because it takes 8 to 10 years to get a mine into full production, a significant increase in exploration must occur to meet the increasing demand for diamonds.

# Canadian diamond mining

*H John Stollery, DiaMine Explorations, Inc.*

The Canadian diamond mining industry began in the late 1980s with two prospectors from British Columbia, Chuck Fipke and Stewart Blusson. In the 1980s Fipke became convinced the Northwest Territories was prime diamond property. In a story that is now folklore, Fipke chartered a helicopter to an unnamed lake about 300 kilometres north-east of Yellowknife. He had been following a trail of glacial run-off that led to the lake's shores. The patch of sediment was full of diamond indicators, such as garnets and chrome diopsides. The site, on the shores of Lac de Gras, became Ekati, Canada's first diamond mine. Dia Met and BHP Billiton own the mine.[1]

Fipke's discovery sparked the largest staking rush in Canadian history, perhaps the largest in the world up to that point. Some 50 million acres were claimed in a frantic rush over the next two years.

One of the first on the scene was Grenville Thomas, a Welshman based in Vancouver who had been prospecting in the Territories since the mid-1960s. He teamed up with the experienced South African diamond explorer Chris Jennings. In the early 1990s, they decided to stake claims south-east of the Ekati mine because De Beers was already staking claims to the north-east of the area. This decision proved a shrewd move for Thomas's company, Aber Resources, because in 1994 a group of geologists headed by Thomas's daughter Eira was examining the last rock-core samples before wrapping up the season when one of the three-inch tubes of kimberlite broke off, revealing a 1.8-carat diamond. It was a phenomenal find, considering that kimberlite normally yields an average of 1 carat (equivalent to one-fifth of a gram) per metric ton of rock.[2]

1. Vernon Frolick (2000) *Fire into Ice: Charles Fipke and the great diamond hunt*, Raincoast, Vancouver.
2. http://www.canadianarcticdiamond.com/03_history/history.html

This discovery became the Diavik mine owned by Aber Resources and Rio Tinto Mining, worth over $2.5 billion. Together the two mines produced 12 million carats valued at $1.669 billion, or approximately 12.5 per cent of the world supply by value in 2005. Canada exports over 90 per cent of its diamonds to the UK and Belgium, where stable demand and a well-developed diamond infrastructure have been present for over a hundred years.[3] The growth in annual Canadian production value is illustrated in Figure 5.4.1.

# Why Canada is an important diamond producer

It has long been known that, when a mining company discovers diamonds, its share price will grow significantly. However, investors have had difficulty investing in diamond companies because privately held De Beers used to control over 80 per cent of supply, and new diamond discoveries in the 20th century were in areas of turmoil, such as Sierra Leone and Angola.[4]

Canada offers investors the chance to profit from the enormous growth of diamond consumption while enjoying the political and economic stability of an established democracy.

## Political stability

Unlike Africa and Russia, where corruption is rampant and corporate oversight is minimal, Canada, industry analysts say, holds companies to high levels of accountability and they are subject to strict environmental regulations.

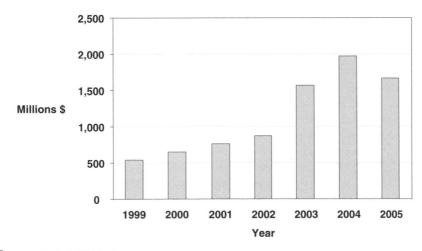

*Source:* www.statscan.ca

**Figure 5.4.1**   Annual Canadian production value

3. www.statcan.ca/english/research/
4. *Sovereign Society A-Letter*, February 2006.

The high standards, in turn, have earned Canadian diamonds a reputation for being 'ethically clean', standing in stark contrast to African gems, which continue to be mentioned in the same breath as child labour and blood diamonds – the illicit gems used to finance murderous civil wars in the Congo and Sierra Leone.

## Profitability

Canadian mines are amongst the most profitable diamond mining ventures in the world. *Bloomberg News* reported that every $1 of sales from the Ekati mine in the Northwest Territories results in 56 cents of profits.[5]

According to analysts, the Diavik mine is even more profitable, with a gross operating margin of 82 per cent compared to less than 10 per cent for a base metal mine.[6]

Indeed, the now-famous A154S pipe from the Diavik mine is thought to be the richest in the world. It yields an average of 4.8 carats per ton, a large proportion of which are high-quality gems, and now forms part of the Diavik mine, which began operations in 2005. Along with Ekati, in production since 1998, it claims to mine three of the world's six richest pipes.

## Efficiency

The ratio of diamond-producing kimberlites is also much higher in Canada. It has been reported that 3.1 per cent of the 540 kimberlites found in Canada prior to 2003 were worth mining. By comparison, only 0.7 per cent of the 6,395 kimberlites found across the globe were worth mining. That means Canadian mines are four times more likely to be successful.[7]

## Pricing

Canadian rough tends to have much better colour, and buyers for these goods are plentiful. That is why Canadian rough is more expensive than De Beers'. Buyers like the fact that there are few surprises. Canada produces a consistent supply of large, commercial-quality goods that are most in demand in the major diamond markets.[8]

Playing off the dubious origins of some stones in Africa, Canada created a certificate of authenticity that guarantees its diamonds have been mined, cut and polished locally. To date it has spent millions marketing the virtues of its trademark 'Canadian Arctic Diamonds' in the United States, Europe and Japan.

Laser-inscribed with tiny polar bears and maple leaves and bearing up to three certificates of authenticity, Canadian stones sold in Canada are reportedly garnering premiums of between 5 and 30 per cent over other comparable diamonds.[9] Canada has a consistent supply of good-quality rough at a time when major sources of supply are dwindling. This means that, as demand for diamonds increases, it is expected that Canadian diamonds will continue to garner premium prices.

5. Ketan Tanna, 'Ekati earnings to fall to historic levels', *Rapaport*, 28 October 2005.
6. http://www.diamineexplorations.com/=Diamond_Information/ca_diamond_history.php
7. *Northern Miner News*, February 2004.
8. 'Canadian rough gives edge in polished', *Rapaport Diamond Report*, 4 February 2005.
9. http://www.diamineexplorations.com/=Diamond_Information/ca_diamond_history.php

## Areas of active exploration

The race to find diamond-bearing kimberlitic pipes remains in full force around the world. But nowhere is it more active than in Canada, which has maintained its position as one of the most promising new locations for diamond mining, as is illustrated in Figure 5.4.2. The diamond giant De Beers has discovered more than 200 kimberlites in 12 different areas of Canada. It estimates that well over half of these are diamondiferous. In 2004, over 30 per cent of De Beers' exploration budget was spent on the search for diamondiferous kimberlites in Canada.[10]

## *Ontario*

One of the most talked-about areas is the Attawapiskat region in Northern Ontario. De Beers Canada and other exploration companies have quietly invested heavily in the Attawapiskat region and to date have discovered 21 diamondiferous kimberlite pipes. De Beers' main project is the Victor pipe, which is set to begin production in 2008 and will have an estimated annual production of 600,000 carats of 'high-value diamonds', which is expected to add $6.7 billion to the Northern Ontario gross domestic product over the 12-year life of the mine.[11]

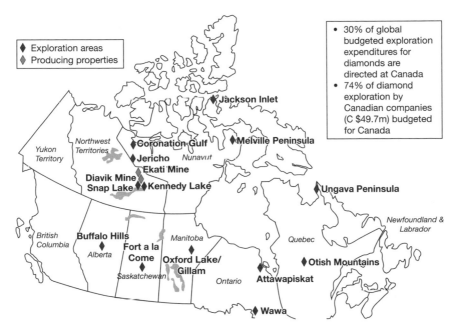

*Source: Dimensions of Canada's Diamond Mining Industry.* Minerals and Metals Sector, Natural Resources at The Economic National Roundtable on Canada's Diamond Industry, Edmonton, AB. 20 May, 2003.

**Figure 5.4.2**   Map of Canadian mining activity

10. 'Who's up next?', *Rapaport Diamond Report*, 4 February 2005, p 37.
11. Angela Pacienza, *Toronto Star*, 19 June 2006

There are several other significant activities in the region. For example, Metallex, owned by Charles Fipke, who is famous for discovering the Ekati mine, has been sampling and surveying in the area. Mr Fipke believes the Attawapiskat region has as much potential as the Northwest Territories.

The Attawapiskat region lies on the Eastern Canadian Shield, which has recently seen a surge in exploration. The geology indicates strong potential for diamond discovery based on the presence of an Archaean craton, which is a thick and cool lithosphere. There are also well-developed, deep structures favourable for the ascent of kimberlite magma. Investors who act now may jointly own a part of what is rapidly becoming the main source of diamond supply in the 21st century and reap the benefits of the vast wealth created from diamond mining.

Another area of active exploration is the Wawa district. Exploration companies have shifted their focus away from volcanic rock to a thick conglomerate body that extends some 1.5 kilometres. The diamonds in the area tend to be smaller, high-quality gems. The Temagami region near Kirkland lake in north-eastern Ontario also hosts a number of exploration companies and promising prospects based on preliminary analysis.

## Quebec

The main location for diamonds is the Otish Mountains region, east of James Bay, 400 kilometres from Chibougamau.

In 2001, a drill programme on the Foxtrot property discovered Renard 1 and 2, which proved to be diamondiferous. Programmes in 2003 identified an additional eight kimberlite locations. As a result, the total number of kimberlitic bodies thus far discovered in the Renard cluster stands at nine. The modelled value of US$88 per carat at the Renard properties was reported on 26 April 2005. Modelling by WWW International Diamond Consultants pegged the entire parcel's minimum value at $76 per carat and its high value at $104 per carat.[12]

The discovery of the Hibou dyke, a WNW-trending kimberlite dyke, adds to the diamond exploration frenzy in the area. The Renard cluster and the Lac Beaver and Tichegami kimberlite clusters are associated with the Mistassini-Lemoyne structural zone (MLZ), a major corridor roughly 30 kilometres wide characterized by late faults and fractures.

Recent kimberlitic discoveries within the MLZ continue to confirm the tremendous diamond potential of the Superior Craton in Quebec.

## Northwest Territories

The Snap Lake Project, located 220 kilometres north-east of Yellowknife, began construction in 2006. The mine should begin production in late 2007 and is expected to be fully operational for over 20 years, with an expected annual production of 1.5 million carats. It is wholly owned by De Beers Canada and will be its first operational mine outside of Africa.[13]

---

12. *Sovereign Society A-Letter*, February 2006.
13. 'Who's up next?', *Rapaport Diamond Report*, 4 February 2005, pp 38, 39.

The region can also lay claim to the Gahcho Kue, a joint venture between De Beers Canada Explorations Inc and two Canadian junior exploration companies. Eight diamondiferous kimberlite occurrences have already been found on the property and two of the kimberlite bodies are currently undergoing a $20 million technical study to determine whether or not they are economically viable.

This area is rich in kimberlite and is considered one of the strongest diamond-bearing regions of Canada. That is why De Beers is spending a large percentage of its exploration budget in this region.

## Saskatchewan

There have been 73 kimberlites located in the north of Saskatchewan, 63 of which are covered in the Fort a la Carne claims, together forming one of the largest diamondiferous kimberlite clusters in the world.[14] The goal in this region over the next three years is to analyse the most economically feasible way of mining the estimated 70 to 100 million carats. The kimberlites in this region appear to be large and tend to have broad glass forms lying under 100 metres of glacial cover. The area also has the Star property kimberlite, which has seen very successful sampling in 2005, including a 45 ton sample that yielded 0.2328 carats per ton.

## Alberta

Alberta's Buffalo Hills region in north central Alberta has so far located 38 kimberlite bodies. The most promising kimberlite formation has indicated a diamond concentration of 0.55 carats per ton. Some of the kimberlites in this region were discovered with virtually no magnetic signature and have proven to yield the best grades.

## Nunavut

This region of Northern Canada already has a diamond mine that began production in 2006. The Jericho project is expected to be operational for at least eight years, and Tiffany & Co Jewellers will purchase or market all of the diamond production from the Jericho project.

The main area of activity is the Coronation Gulf diamond district, approximately 200 kilometres from the Lac de Gras camp. Kimberlites occur here mainly as a sequence of echelyn dykes, as well as a number of pipes, along four distinct structural trends. A number of diamondiferous kimberlites have been found on the Melville Peninsula and at the Churchill Diamond Project, where 10 diamondiferous kimberlites have been found. BHP Billiton has used significant amounts of capital exploring for diamonds in this area because of its potential.[15]

14. 'Who's up next?', *Rapaport Diamond Report*, 4 February 2005, p 39.
15. 'Who's up next?', *Rapaport Diamond Report*, 4 February 2005, p 39.

# Diamond-mining companies – shareholder value

Diamond exploration companies can take years to develop a viable revenue source, like that of Aber Resources. However, there are a number of proven ways for a new mining company to increase its long-term value and position itself to develop sustainable profitability in the future, identified in Figure 5.4.3.

## *Active exploration*

The first step requires continuous acquisition of claims and properties of merit in proven mining areas along with developing a grass-roots exploration programme in underdeveloped areas. This will develop a diversified and balanced property portfolio in critical areas of discovery. As new diamond discoveries develop in surrounding areas and as more exploration companies stake claims in the area, the value of property claims will rise.

## *Surveying*

Properties will undergo geological mapping, surveying and line cutting in order to establish high-probability targets. Airborne electromagnetic surveys and gravity surveys reveal different physical properties for kimberlites when compared to the surrounding ground in the area. Drilling and sampling are an important way of determining the viability and value of a property. All of these announcements on surveying developments will have an impact on the value of the company's property holdings.

## *Joint ventures*

Pursuing relationships with other companies is a cost-effective way of gaining a position in an important area of discovery. It gives companies the opportunity to pool their resources through joint financing arrangements, and it allows experts from both camps to look at projects from different angles and help develop a more thorough long-term plan for surveying and sampling. All of the major discoveries in Canada involved junior mining companies working closely with larger, well-funded companies to develop the site properly. This strategy also includes a company selling off parts of its property portfolio to other resource companies for cash, stock and net smelter interests that are standard to the industry.

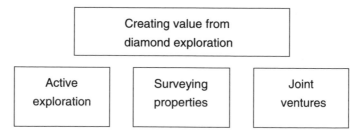

**Figure 5.4.3**   Developing shareholder value

# Diamond exploration financing

In order to finance exploration, surveying and joint ventures, junior mining companies generally raise capital through brokered and non-brokered private placements. The shares are sold to accredited investors interested in investing in diamond exploration companies. These offerings usually include warrants attached to the shares, which can be exercised for an additional common share or half a common share at a predetermined price in the future. These securities are also usually restricted for a period of time before being sold back on to exchanges.

# Diamond exploration investors

There have been numerous success stories in the Canadian diamond business. A number of new, junior exploration companies have developed into mature companies raising millions of dollars on organized exchanges, developing consistent revenue streams and generating value for their investors. Two examples of successful Canadian diamond exploration companies are as follows:

■ Aber Resources was selling for approximately $7.00 in 2001. Since then the share price has risen to over $35.74 in late 2006.[16]
■ Tahera Diamond Corporation was available for sale in 2003 for between $0.10 and $0.15 and in late 2006 its shares traded for $1.02.[17]

## *Investment expectations*

Investing in junior diamond exploration companies can potentially be one of the most profitable segments of the equity market. However, investors in new mining companies should be prepared for share-price volatility. Because the cycle from exploration to production is a long one and announcements of progress from companies during this period are not made regularly, the share price will fluctuate. Speculation in the junior mining stock sector should only be attempted by experienced traders and only with a limited portion of discretionary trading capital. Further, you should research the company or seek professional advice before making any equity investments.

Investors can purchase private placements of new stock from the company or acquire stock listed and traded on an organized exchange. Private placement stock is restricted from trading for a predetermined period of time. It can usually be acquired at a discount to the expected selling price but requires longer holding periods. These shares are exempt from registration under local and relevant national securities acts. These shares can only be marketed through 'over the counter' trading systems.

Shares acquired on an organized exchange are purchased at established market prices through brokers. Investors have the ability to trade these shares on the

---

16. uk.finance.yahoo.com/q?s=ABER
17. www.tahera.com/Investors/StockPerformance/default.aspx

exchange but they will not be buying at a discount. The major exchanges where junior diamond exploration companies trade are:

- Vancouver Stock Exchange (Canada);
- Toronto Stock Exchange – Venture Exchange (Canada);
- Pink Sheets – Over-the-Counter Market (United States);
- London Alternative Investment Market Exchange (AIM) (UK);
- NASDAQ Penny Stocks (United States);
- Neuer Markt, Frankfurt Stock Exchange (Germany).

## Summary

All forecasts indicate that in 2010 Canada should be mining about 20 per cent of global diamond output by value. This 20 per cent should account for the best-quality stones in one of the most stable socio-political environments. Today, diamond rough is rare and Canadian rough is essential for production.[18]

Canadian rough is expected to play a more prominent role because the output from Australia's Argyle mine is declining, Botswana and South Africa are expecting production decreases and Russia's main pipes are starting to show signs of strain. New growth markets in China and India will continue to drive demand forward at a time when supply restrictions mean that Canada is one of the only viable new sources for consistent diamond supply.

Some of the largest cutting houses in the world, such as India's Rosy Blue and New York's E Schreiber, have set up operations in Yellowknife, Northwest Territories. The entire diamond industry has changed the landscape of the region and helped drive the local economy significantly higher over the last few years.

Considering that the Northwest Territories produces almost 10 per cent of the world's diamond supply and some of the highest-quality diamonds in the world, the continued growth of the Canadian diamond industry in critical areas of discovery will benefit astute mining investors looking to get in on the ground floor.

The conditions in Canada are ideal for large-scale mining operations and high-quality diamond deposits. Investors who act now may jointly own a part of what is rapidly becoming the main source of diamond supply in the 21st century and reap the benefits of the vast wealth created from diamond mining.

---

18. 'Is Canada the answer?', *Rapaport Diamond Report*, 4 February 2005, p 87.

# Part 6

# Investments
# to live with

# Lyxor Gold Bullion Securities

## Simply Gold
Traded just like a share

**Discover how to trade gold like a share on the London Stock Exchange**

For both professional and retail investors seeking a high-performing investment linked to physical gold. Easily traded and transparent, **Lyxor GBS** closely tracks the performance of this precious metal.

It is a safe and cost-effective way to easily diversify your portfolio with a single asset: **gold.**

- Guaranteed daily liquidity from Société Générale
- 0.40% annual management fee
- ISIN GB00B00FHZ82
- Trade through any UK broker
- Reuters code GBSx.L

**www.lyxorgbs.com** ■ **For any enquiries contact Dan Draper at Lyxor Finance on** +44 (0) 20 7762 5581

## LYXOR FINANCE

SOCIETE GENERALE GROUP

# Gold

*Katharine Pulvermacher, World Gold Council*

## Introduction

Gold has long been considered one of the most precious metals, and its value has been used as the standard for many currencies in times gone by. Gold, owing to its rarity and durability, has historically been used as a method of payment, and is used today in the portfolios of fund managers and private investors alike because of its unique investment properties. In today's sophisticated financial markets, investors seek exposure to gold for a range of reasons and have access to a variety of investment options suited to their profiles. This chapter takes a closer look at this range of reasons and the investment options that match them.

## Gold price

Up until 1973 the dollar price of gold was fixed as part of the international monetary system established in the wake of the Second World War. Under this system, sometimes referred to as the Bretton Woods Agreement, the values of different currencies were held constant in terms of gold – and so gold formed the basis of the fixed exchange rate regime that prevailed internationally. Through the dollar, each currency was indirectly convertible into gold. The intent was to create a system that would be stable and resistant to the runaway credit and debt expansion that had been part of the build-up to the war. In the wake of the hyperinflation that had plagued Germany in the 1920s, there was a deep concern to create a system where currency could not be created by government fiat, and would therefore be safe as a store of wealth against inflation. This was intended to reduce currency uncertainty, keep the credit of the issuing monetary authority sound, and thus contribute to the rebuilding of Europe.

# INVESTING IN GOLD

We believe that gold related investments have an important part to play in most investment portfolios. Unfortunately, it is an asset class overlooked by the majority of investors and wealth advisers, although – hang on – surely that means the opportunity is still there!

As an active discretionary investment manager, RH Asset Management has included gold related investments in clients' portfolios since early 2001.

The rationale behind the original purchases was two-fold. Firstly, the rising deficits in the US would lead to a major devaluation of the US dollar and gold prices are negatively correlated to the US dollar. Secondly, our concern was for a financial 'shock' which manifested itself in the bear market for equities from 2000 to 2003. (Perversely it was also when Gordon Brown pinpointed the bottom for the gold price at around $250 when he sold the majority of our nations gold reserves).

So in 2007, has the investment position changed, are the fundamentals for gold, moving forward from here, as attractive? After all, since our first purchases back in 2001, the bullion price at February 2007 is 147% higher in US dollars, 90% higher in pound sterling and investment in gold mining shares 440% higher.

Without doubt, as far as we are concerned, the answer is a categoric YES.

## A golden opportunity?

We believe investors should be holding a proportion of their assets in gold related investments, for diversification, for the safe haven it represents, because of its non-correlation to other asset classes, but most importantly it still represents an enormous investment opportunity:

- Demand for gold hit a record US $65bn in 2006
- Supply fell 13% in tonnage terms in 2006
- China gold reserves only represent 1.1% of their $1tr foreign exchange reserves (compared to 61% for the US). China could diversify up to 2.5% of its foreign exchange reserves and buy gold which would represent a $14bn investment into gold, similar to the entire gold Exchange Traded Funds (ETFs) issued to date
- ETF demand is growing and the potential for an Indian gold ETF is currently underestimated. This will provide pro-gold Indian investors easy access to

the market, demand would be high and the gold price would almost certainly soar

- The potential for a financial 'shock' increases day by day. The huge expansion in liquidity over recent years, has fuelled the so called "carry trade" of borrowing in low interest rate currencies and investing in other higher returning assets is likely, at some point, to fail: triggering a flight to quality, away from fiat money, into gold

- Volatility is at multi-decade lows and complacency is at record lows across the financial markets. This reminds us of the wisdom of Sun Tzu: "At times of peace, prepare for war. At times of war prepare for peace"

- Gold is the ultimate inflation hedge

- Gold is still trading some 20% below its all-time high set in 1980. Adjusted for inflation, that price today would be in excess of $2000/oz – some three times higher than today's price

## How to obtain exposure

There are numerous ways to gain exposure to gold related investments. For example, the following are three suitable areas for personal investors:

- **Exchange Traded Funds (ETFs):** These securities are 100% backed by physical gold and track the bullion price; they offer a cost-effective route to owning gold

- **Gold related investment funds:** This is our favoured approach as it provides a return, historically, at a rate of two to three times the increase in the bullion price whilst providing an element of currency diversification

- **Geared Bullion:** A higher risk approach to trade gold bullion is now available with non-recourse borrowing. Only collateral of 24% is required. In effect, this enables investors to take out an undated futures contract whilst minimising investment risk to the level of capital invested

In a world of growing uncertainty, gold offers investors the opportunity to invest in the ultimate store of wealth. Gold is precious, it is scarce, its monetary qualities are inscribed in history but most importantly, it is impossible for governments to dilute it through their misguided actions.

R H ASSET MANAGEMENT LIMITED
**www.rhasset.co.uk**

By the time inflationary pressures led to the suspension of dollar convertibility to gold in 1971, the average annual gold price was US$41.17 per ounce (£16.91 in money-of-the-day terms). By 1973, these pressures had become so severe that the international fixed exchange rate regime broke down, and we have lived in a floating exchange rate world ever since, with any form of gold standard replaced completely by fiat money: legal tender, or promissory notes, issued by governments.

With the backdrop of dollar inflation, a shortage of oil and tension with the Arab nations in the Middle East, the gold price escalated from an average of $200 in 1978 to over $300 in 1979 and to more than $600 in 1980. It peaked in January 1980, at $850 per ounce. The following 20 years saw the gold price decline, coinciding with a booming equities market, culminating in a low price of $256 in July 1999.

Over the past four years, with a combination of declining equity markets, geopolitical tensions and inflationary fears, the dollar price of gold has soared and with it we have witnessed renewed interest in the yellow metal as an investment. Gold, traditionally seen as a safe haven against uncertainty, has proved very attractive to investors. At the end of 2005 the gold price broke $500 per ounce, rising to $540 in December 2005 and breaking through a 25-year high point in early 2006.

## Gold as an investment – why?

### *Portfolio diversification*

Most investment portfolios are invested primarily in traditional financial assets such as stocks and bonds. The reason for holding diverse investments is to protect the portfolio against fluctuations in the value of any single asset class. Portfolios

*Source: Global Insight*

**Figure 6.1.1**    Gold price, US dollars and euros, 2006

**Annual average price of gold (US$ and £) 1900–2006**

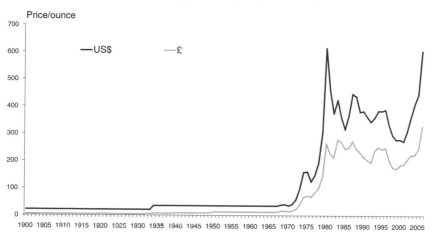

*Source:* World Gold Council, *Global Insight*
**Figure 6.1.2**    Price performance – long-term

**Gold price 2000–06**

*Source:* World Gold Council, *Global Insight*
**Figure 6.1.3**    Price performance – short-term

that contain gold are generally more robust and better able to cope with market uncertainties than those that don't.

Adding gold to a portfolio introduces an entirely different class of asset. Gold is unusual because it is both a commodity and a monetary asset and is an effective diversifier because its performance tends to move independently of other investments and key economic indicators.

Independent studies have shown that traditional diversifiers (such as bonds and alternative assets) often fail during times of market stress or instability. Even a small allocation of gold has been proven to improve significantly the consistency of portfolio performance during both stable and unstable financial periods. Gold improves the stability and predictability of returns. The performance of gold is not correlated with other assets because the gold price is not driven by the same factors that drive the performance of other assets.

## Dollar hedge

Gold is often cited as being an effective hedge against fluctuations in the US dollar, the world's main trading currency. If the dollar appreciates, the dollar gold price falls, and similarly a fall in the dollar relative to the other main currencies produces a rise in the gold price.

In a recent study by leading metals consultancy GFMS, the strength of the link between 22 commodities and the US dollar was examined. The results clearly suggested that not only is gold a more potent hedge against the dollar than other commodities, but also that protection is provided when most needed (when the dollar is losing value), with relatively little upside forgone during a period of dollar appreciation.

Like all physical commodities, gold is an asset that bears no credit risk. Holding assets in the yellow metal involves no counterparty and is no one's liability. In addition to that, the physical properties of the metal make it an excellent alternative to money. Gold is durable. It is unlike many of the other commodities examined in that, other things remaining equal (ie assuming no changes in price), there is no depreciation in the value of gold, other than any storage costs that might apply. Gold is fungible. It is, at least in theory, infinitely divisible with virtually no losses (other than any operational costs the process might incur). Furthermore, gold has a high value-to-volume ratio, which makes it easily transferable, with low transport and storage costs. Moreover, gold is one of the deepest commodity markets with the highest levels of liquidity, second only to oil.

## Inflation

The purchasing power of gold has not diminished since biblical times. According to the Old Testament, during the reign of King Nebuchadnezzar, an ounce of gold bought 350 loaves of bread. Today, an ounce of gold still buys 350 loaves. The value of gold therefore, in terms of real goods and services that it can buy, has remained remarkably stable. In contrast, the purchasing power of many currencies has generally declined. There is a growing body of research to bolster gold's reputation as a protector of wealth against the ravages of inflation. Market cycles come and go, but gold has maintained its long-term value.

So gold is often bought to counter the effects of inflation and currency fluctuations. In fact, extensive research from a range of economists has consistently shown that, in spite of price fluctuations, gold has consistently reverted to its historical purchasing power parity; and during periods of financial, economic and social turmoil, gold has been a safe refuge when the value of other assets has been all but destroyed.

## Safe haven

In volatile and uncertain times, we often witness a 'flight to quality', when investors seek to protect their capital by moving it into assets considered to be safer stores of value.

Gold is among only a handful of financial assets that is not matched by a liability. It can provide insurance against the extreme movements in the value of traditional asset classes that can happen in unsettled times.

In fact, statistical analysis shows that, over a period of 30 years, the correlation between gold and the Dow Jones Industrial Average actually declined during the worst 36 months of the equity index – an indication that investors in gold had the protection they sought when they needed it the most.

Some recent examples of the refuge afforded by gold include the following:

■ In 1997/98 the government of South Korea asked its citizens to allow it to buy their gold holdings in exchange for local currency debt instruments. The government raised over 5 million ounces of gold in this way, which it sold for hard currency. As a result it was able to service its external debt.
■ Fearful of the implications of the forecast electronic and communications disaster surrounding Y2K, there was a flight to gold in 1999.
■ The first quarter of 2002 saw a flight to gold by Japanese investors as they awaited the withdrawal of government guarantees on bank deposits.

## Liquidity

Amid the uncertainty surrounding mainstream asset classes, risk management has become a hot topic. Alternative investments, by definition, skirt the constraints of rigorous benchmarking. As a result, a variety of alternative assets are being promoted as portfolio diversifiers. Among them may be found hedge funds, private equity, commodities, real estate, timber and agricultural land, fine art and so on. But

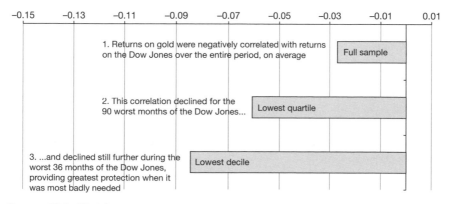

*Source: Global Insight*

**Figure 6.1.4** Correlation of monthly returns on gold and Dow Jones, April 1975 to March 2005

when people talk of their portfolio diversification benefits it should be remembered that buying them is one thing. Selling them when one needs the cash is quite another.

Gold's liquidity is one of its critical investment attributes. Gold can be traded around the clock in larger size, at narrower spreads and more rapidly than many competing diversifiers or mainstream investments.

## Gold as an investment – how?

There are a number of alternative ways to invest in gold, including bullion coins and bars, exchange traded products and special funds. The attractiveness of each of these depends on a number of factors. Does the investor want to own gold or simply want exposure to gold price fluctuations? Is the investor comfortable with the idea of leverage and margin calls or not? Does the investor understand the fee structures attendant upon each type of product? Regulatory constraints may also restrict access to certain types of investment, and this is something else to take into consideration. These apply regardless of the particular set of reasons driving an investment strategy.

### Coins and bars

Bullion coins and small gold bars, for example, which each contain a minimum of 99.5 per cent fine gold, are appropriate for private investors wishing to buy small amounts. In many countries, including all member states of the European Union, gold purchased for investment purposes is exempt from VAT.

Bullion, which is legal tender in its country of origin for its face value, should not, however, be confused with commemorative or numismatic coins.

### Gold accounts

There are two types of gold accounts: allocated and unallocated.

Holding gold in an allocated account is rather like keeping it in a safety deposit box. Specific bars (or coins, where appropriate), which are numbered and identified by hallmark, weight and fineness, are allocated to each particular investor, who has to pay the custodian for storage and insurance.

Many investors prefer to hold gold in unallocated accounts, which are conceptually similar to foreign exchange accounts. Unless investors take delivery of their gold (usually within two working days), they do not have specific bars ascribed to them. An advantage of unallocated accounts is that investors do not incur storage and insurance charges. However, they are exposed to the creditworthiness of the bank or dealer providing the service in the same way that they would be if they had any other type of account.

As a general rule, bullion banks do not deal in quantities under 1,000 ounces. In this sense, they can be thought of as wholesalers or business-to-business entities. Their customers are institutional investors, private banks acting on behalf of their clients, central banks and gold market participants wishing to buy or borrow large quantities of gold. Major bullion banks are members of the London Bullion Market

Association (LBMA), and their contact details are available on the 'List of Members' section of the LBMA website.

However, other opportunities exist for investors wishing to open gold accounts representing less than 1,000 ounces. The minimum investment requirement of the Perth Mint Certificate Program is US$10,000 (approximately 32 ounces), while the minimum investment requirement for gold pool accounts is 1 ounce. More information about the Perth Mint Certificate Program is available from the Perth Mint and Kitco, an online dealer, as well as other approved dealers of the programme. The Bullion Vault, an internet-based trading platform, takes orders for as little as 1 gram and has no limit on maximum size.

## Exchange traded funds

The newest way of investing in gold is through exchange traded funds. Gold is traded in the form of securities on stock exchanges in Australia, France, Mexico, Singapore, South Africa, Switzerland, Turkey, the United Kingdom and the United States. By design, this form of securitized gold investment is expected to track the gold price almost perfectly. Unlike derivative products, the securities are 100 per cent backed by physical gold held mainly in allocated form, and are generically referred to as 'exchange traded gold'. The securities are all regulated financial products.

Exchange traded gold provides retail and institutional investors with an efficient and cost-effective way to invest in gold. It aims to overcome the existing barriers to gold as a practical asset and trading tool. For many investors, costs associated with buying and selling the securities are expected to be less than the costs associated with buying, selling, storing and insuring gold bullion in a traditional allocated gold bullion account. Furthermore, exchange traded gold can be traded as easily as any other security listed on a stock exchange.

Financial advisers and other investment professionals can provide further details about these products.

## Futures and options

Investors seeking leverage may prefer futures contracts or options. Both operate like their counterparts in other marketplaces. The price of gold futures is determined by the market's perceived value of what the carrying costs ought to be, and consequently is typically higher than the spot price.

Both futures and options can be traded through brokers on regulated commodity exchanges, such as the New York Mercantile Exchange Comex Division, CBOT and TOCOM. Gold futures are also traded in India. Forward contracts are agreements to exchange gold at an agreed price at a future date, and can be used either to manage risk or for speculative purposes.

These contracts are negotiated directly with counterparts and consequently, unlike standard futures contracts, are tailor-made. However, unlike futures, which are guaranteed by the exchanges on which they are traded, there is a degree of counterparty risk with forwards. They are also less liquid. Warrants give investors the right to buy gold at a specific price on a specific day in the future. Investors pay a premium for this right. Warrants are usually leveraged to the price of the under-lying asset, but gearing can be on a one-for-one basis.

## Gold certificates

Gold certificates are a type of warrant issued predominantly by banks in Germany and Switzerland. Some certificates are traded on exchanges, others are available only 'over the counter'. Some represent one-for-one ownership of gold held by the issuing bank on the client's behalf, whilst others are closer to deriv-ative-type products like options, offering clients geared exposure to the gold price. Given the range of products to which the term 'certificates' is applied, investors should check structures carefully with their advisers before committing funds.

## Gold-mining equities

Although investment in the shares of gold-mining companies does not strictly represent investment in gold bullion per se, the conventional wisdom is that the shares of many mining companies represent geared exposure to the gold price because the intrinsic value of these companies derives at least in part from the gold they are entitled to mine in the future. If the gold price rises, the profits of the gold-mining company could be expected to rise and as a result the share price may rise. Investing in equities generally augurs benefits such as dividend yields, a type of return that gold itself cannot provide (returns on gold being essentially derived through capital gain). But investing in gold-mining equities is not the same as investing in gold, and investors should take a number of factors into account in addition to the outlook for the yellow metal. Has the company already sold its future gold production, through forward sales? Is the company already producing gold, or is it mainly exploring for gold? Does the company make a profit? How many years of ore reserves are left in the mines before they have to be closed down? What p/e ratio and dividend yield does the company have now and in the following years? Are the mines subject to political or economic risks?

## Gold investment funds

A number of collective investment vehicles specialize in investing in the shares of gold-mining companies. The term 'collective investment vehicles' as used here should be taken to include mutual funds, open-ended investment companies (OEICs), closed-end funds, unit trusts and so on.

A wide range of such funds exists and they are domiciled in a number of different countries. These funds are regulated financial products and as such it is not possible to go into any details on specific funds.

Funds are likely to differ in their structure – some may invest simply in mining stocks, some may invest in companies that mine minerals other than gold, some may invest in futures as well as mining equities and some may invest partly in mining equities and partly in the underlying metal.

## Gold-linked structured products

This type of investment, which typically entails some kind of fixed income with limited exposure to the gold price and some degree of principal protection, is available over the counter (is not exchange-based) to larger-scale investors.

Derivative in nature, this type of product is extremely flexible and can be tailored to suit the requirements and outlook of individual clients (subject to a substantial minimum investment). Typically, structured notes use part of the investment funds to purchase put or call options, depending on whether the product is designed for gold bulls or bears. The balance is investment in fixed income products to generate a yield.

# Conclusion

It has never been easier for investors to access gold, ranging from the traditional coins and bars to the relatively recent addition of exchange traded funds. With gold's role as a portfolio diversifier and a hedge against inflation and exposure to the dollar, there are several compelling arguments for investing a portion of one's portfolio in the yellow metal. The real value of gold is not that it provides a quick, speculative fix, but its capacity to provide a sure and steady means of protecting wealth and to enhance the consistency of returns whilst maintaining low portfolio risk.

 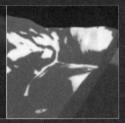

# Practical collecting

*Spencer Ewen, Seymour Management*

Does this sound familiar? You've bought a property. It took you weeks, maybe months, to find. Then you get the experts in: first a surveyor and then a lawyer. Maybe you get some quotes for remedial work too. A month or two down the line, once you're sure the property and the area are all right, you finally put your money down. All that advice cost money but you know it was worth it and you would never buy a house without it. So if you are buying a house, or filing company returns, you use an expert and take advice. But when it comes to buying art, many people, with little information, pay many thousands of pounds without asking an expert's opinion. This can often lead to huge mistakes, and expensive work can immediately decrease in value once it has left the gallery wall.

Now, of course, it's fine to buy art and possessions that way, but there is an alternative. The commercial art world is a minefield, so be careful and get help, independent help. Dealers have a vested interest in talking up their artists, so find out what other informed people think and know. Quality in art is much less subjective than you might think. A good starting point is a solid grounding in art history – you really can't have enough of this. Even with a fairly basic understanding, you'll be able to root out the plagiarists and see them for the dull copyists they are. You may also begin to discern the big issues that have driven the development of art over the last few centuries. With this knowledge comes understanding and, with that, profound pleasure. Next find out about your artist: make sure that the work is original, not derivative. Read books if there are any or, failing that, exhibition catalogues. Look at the artist's CV – has his or her work been in museum shows or retrospectives, and is it in important collections? From your research, ascertain when the artist stopped copying other people and found a unique style. Often artists will spend time working through other artists' idioms before finding what is, somewhat patronizingly, called their mature style. Of course, some, in fact most, never do and they're the ones you'll never be able to sell. But of those who do, only buy works that are in the artist's true style, unless you're a real connoisseur of the artist.

So now you've got a picture by this artist and you know it fits the criteria. Next, if this picture is by a famous artist, establish its authenticity. When buying from auction or a reputable dealer, they will be able to give you binding assurances based on the piece's provenance. If they turn out to be wrong, they will give you your money back. Let's assume it's right; now you need to check the condition. Again, an auctioneer or reputable dealer should be able to tell you about this. Whatever you do, always look very hard at the piece. If in doubt, get a professional conservator to have a look. I've seen drawings that have been ripped into shreds and then stitched back together so skilfully that even dealers have not noticed until it's too late. Always get a quote for restoration work before buying.

Finally, check what comparable works have sold for through galleries and at auction. If it seems a fair price, buy it. With luck you will have bought something of enduring interest to you and others, perhaps so much so that you'll never want to sell it, but if one day you do put it back on the market you will at least have covered your costs, if not increased them.

One addendum, if you think auctions are the cheapest option you'll be surprised. In 2006, a Camille Claudel sculpture sold in a New York auction room for US$1,500,000 – that same day in the same city you could have bought an almost identical work from one of London's best-known commercial galleries for a couple of hundred thousand pounds. That sort of thing happens when people don't know anything about the market but know what they like. Remember too that you can wait for ever for something to come to auction that is readily available through a dealer, and that the good dealers tend to have work of a far higher calibre than that which tends to come to auction.

If you haven't got time to do all of the above then you might be best advised to get hold of people who are independent of the dealers and who know the business. They're called Seymour's. Good luck!

# Change in the structure of the contemporary art market

## A new phenomenon

More artists are now beginning to be taken on by art galleries in their first year of an MA course at art school. This means that instead of having this time to research and develop their technique they are being forced to enter art school with something nearing a fully mature style. In the past you could watch an artist's work changing and developing in the early years after leaving art school and, as a buyer, could follow that artist's progress and decide if you would buy the work, but now you no longer have the luxury of time. Other artists, graduating without galleries, but then shortly afterwards signed up by a reputable gallery, can see their prices quadruple a year later. If an artist's work becomes sought after, in the early years of their careers, it is not uncommon to see prices, already in their thousands, doubling over a six-month period. Everything has speeded up.

## Overheated market?

The New York auction sales in May 2006 and the London auction sales in June 2006 saw many artists' work selling for record amounts. Jeff Koons's bronze *Aqualung* (1985) sold for $4.6 million, and Peter Doig's *Olin Mk IV* (1995) sold for $1.1 million. Marlene Dumas's *Feathered Stola* (2000) sold for $1.2 million. It was reported as having been purchased in 2003 for $300,000.

Many of the works that come up for auction are works by an artist that are impossible to buy on the primary market, ie straight from the artist's representative gallery. These galleries have waiting lists for work, and if you are put on one of these lists you are unlikely to receive a work. Many artists work very slowly, so buying at auction is the only way of acquiring certain works. Sellers now make agreements with auction houses that their property will reach a guaranteed price before agreeing to consign it.

## What is sustaining this boom?

In the last 10 years the number of collectors in London buying contemporary work has increased considerably. Previously there were only five or six really big contemporary collectors but now there are many. People's growing interest in this area, coupled with large increases in salaries, has created a strong market for collecting contemporary art, as Figure 6.2.1 indicates.

## Art as an investment

Serious interest in art as an investment began around 2000 with the decline in the world's leading stock markets, when investors were reminded once again that stock markets can be alarmingly volatile. While long-term economic prospects remain

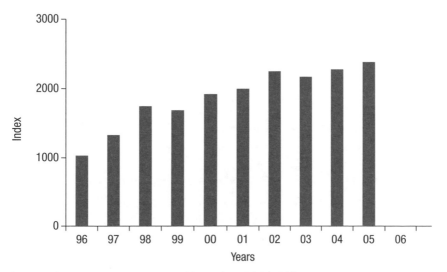

**Figure 6.2.1**   Contemporary Art 100 Index, 1996–2005

uncertain, the allure of fine art as an alternative hard-asset class remains strong for both private and institutional investors.

The investment potential of art remained largely unquantified until the experience of the British Rail Pension Fund provided hard empirical evidence. The Fund bought widely between 1974 and 1980, and by the time it had completely disposed of its collection in the mid-1990s it had achieved an overall rate of return of 11.3 per cent per annum, well in excess of that needed to beat inflation. Certain individual collections yielded significantly better returns (up to 21.3 per cent per annum for Impressionist art).

Independent art market performance statistics are now available, principally the Mei Moses Index (from New York University's Stern Business School) and from Art Market Research. Together they (and others) provide reliable benchmark indicators of art market performance.

The statistics have also effectively refuted the widely held belief that art prices are too volatile to allow art to be treated as a serious investment. Taking the Mei Moses data as a starting point, in 2003 a leading US financial institution used standard risk/return techniques to demonstrate that adding fine art to a diversified portfolio produces a slightly greater return for each unit of risk, and a significantly better return with less volatility than most asset classes on their own.

The Mei Moses Index showed that art outperformed the US S&P 500 Index by a wide margin over the period 1999 to 2004; its authors estimated that investing in both art and stocks can reduce the volatility of a portfolio by up to 20 per cent without sacrificing returns. The Mei Moses data were re-analysed in February 2006 by Barclays Capital in its 50th Annual Equity Gilt Study. It concluded that art does best when the economy is growing, and provides a better hedge against inflation than most asset classes. It advocates a 10 per cent weighting in art in certain situations. Further, unlike an investor in conventional stock markets at the present time, a well-advised investor in art can expect to achieve returns significantly in excess of those achieved by randomly traded works as represented by the Mei Moses and other fine art indices.

So the present time represents a unique confluence of factors; fundamentals point to fine art being a sound alternative hard-asset class, especially against the background of continuing uncertainty in the world's leading stock markets; there is more reliable information than ever before by which to monitor such investments objectively, with a range of increasingly sophisticated analytic tools; and independent research points to the fact that the market's volatility actually works in favour of such diversification. Figures 6.2.2 and 6.2.3 illustrate the point.

# Conclusion

Collecting any possessions should be a passionate pastime. It requires serious contemplation, a great deal of research and a trusted associate in the trade. Any collector wants to know that value is achieved with any acquisition and that long-term capital gains are available, and with the right partners all of this is realistic.

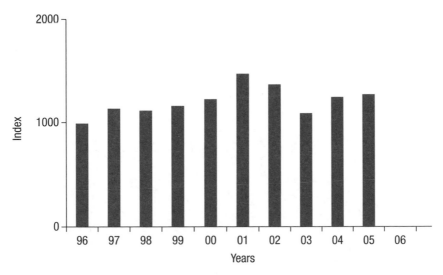

**Figure 6.2.2**  English 20th-century painting, 1996–2005

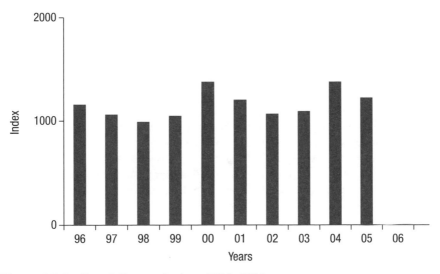

**Figure 6.2.3**  French Impressionists, 1996–2005

# Art and antiques

*James Goodwin*

## Introduction

'Nearly all the steps upward in civilisation have been during periods of internationalism', wrote the celebrated art historian Kenneth (later Lord) Clark. Never has this been truer than today, thanks to the free movement of international capital, with the possible exception of the 19th century, which importantly saw the birth of today's art market.

The link between art and money is intimate and long-standing, with auctions known in Ancient Rome. The first documented art markets developed in Italy and Flanders (modern Belgium) during the 15th century.

Despite its long history, the art market remains one of the last examples of almost unregulated laissez-faire capitalism, one where supply tends to stimulate demand and objects tend to become more highly valued as their original purpose (or even beauty) is lost.

As Western investors experience slim returns on cash, record stock markets and high-priced property, art might be considered a safe haven for a diversified portfolio or another source of speculation, but now on a global scale.

Still, works of art remain what the viewers, the buyers, the sellers and the users think they are. The often-repeated advice is to buy an item because it touches your heart and you enjoy looking at it – an aesthetic or emotional investment. Consequently, the majority of art owners consider themselves collectors rather than investors, believing that higher returns are seldom achieved without a genuine love of art. *The Economist* suggested recently that one in three people will remain collectors even in adulthood.

Whatever the motivation, information and advice are available, often via the internet, to indulge in this unique and potentially lucrative pleasure.

# The art market

Today's art market grew out of the 19th-century industrial revolution and accelerated in the period up to the First World War, owing to changes in British property law and the awakening of industrial America. Like today, this was a period when collectors traded works by living artists, notably Impressionists after the 1880s.

As investments, the best-regarded paintings have delivered rising real returns since the 1830s, according to Peter Watson. This appreciation culminated in the exceptional price increases of 1985–90, resulting in an art market bust, from which it has now mostly recovered. According to artprice.com, global art prices have risen 87 per cent in 10 years. Today, headline-catching record sales, especially in modern and contemporary art, continue to attract attention, though in inflation-adjusted (real) terms the top 2 per cent of the art market could rise by up to 20 per cent before reaching its 1990 peak, according to Art Market Research. Using this measure, the rise would need to be greatest for Impressionists and contemporary and modern art, though old masters may have already exceeded their peaks (see Figure 6.3.1).

Globally, it is estimated there are over 1.5 million art transactions annually of fine and decorative art changes of ownership. It is further estimated that about a quarter of all sales are within the trade, though an increasing number are directly to private buyers. Official figures from the UN Statistics Division in 2005 indicate trade of $27 billion, with the UK the biggest exporter and the United States the net beneficiary of world trade. Based on sales by the auction houses, according to artprice.com, the UK art market has a world market share of 35 per cent, second to the United States' 41 per cent.

The UK, in 2005, imported £1.7 billion and exported £2.86 billion 'works of art, collectors' pieces and antiques' from outside the EU and £125 million and

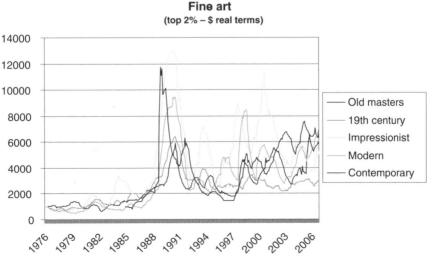

Fine art
(top 2% – $ real terms)

*Source:* Art Market Research, 2006

**Figure 6.3.1**  Fine art returns, 1976–2006

£129 million within the EU, according to HM Customs and Excise. By value, the trade was mostly with the United States, Switzerland, Norway and the Netherlands, though measured by volume Dubai and Japan should be added. Supporting this trade, Britain employs about 37,000 staff in 10,217 art and antique businesses, which includes 9,463 dealers and 754 auctioneers. Moreover, London remains the preferred location for several international art categories owing to historical expertise, its position as a world financial centre and a favourable tax regime. UK company performance in the last five years has been best at dealers and better at auction houses in the last two years, according to Keynote.

Worldwide, in 2004/05, 216 paintings from 113 artists (14 living) sold worldwide for more than £1 million, according to the Art Sales Index. This outnumbered all years since 1989/90, when an astonishing 367 were sold, and for the first time included a living Chinese artist. For the 2005/06 season, nearly half of the world record prices were recorded in the UK, totalling over $200 million. In November 2006, a new record of $140 million for an art work was paid for a Jackson Pollock painting.

Today the market for fine and decorative art trade in 40 countries includes paintings and drawings (British, Scottish, Irish, European, American, Australian, Canadian, German, Austrian, Greek, Scandinavian, Spanish, Swiss, Israeli, Latin American, Orientalist, Indian, Chinese, Russian, South-East Asian), prints, sculpture, furniture (English, French, European, American), rugs and carpets, tapestries, ceramics, glass, silver and vertu (English, European, American, Russian), clocks, watches and barometers, jewellery, diamonds, icons, works of art (antiquities, Chinese, Judaica, Islamic, Indian, Aboriginal, African and Oceanic, pre-Columbian, American Indian, Japanese, Korean) and garden statuary.

The smaller market for collectables loosely refers to old cars, postage stamps, numismatic coins, banknotes, stock certificates, scripts, medals, musical instruments, fashion, vintage wines and spirits, playing cards, objets de vertu, bric-a-brac, scientific instruments, books and manuscripts (English, Continental, American), photographs, sporting memorabilia, arms and armour, dolls and toys, luggage and other memorabilia.

# Formulating an art investment strategy – the pros and cons

Challengingly, the art market remains more visual than intellectual and therefore hard to standardize and difficult to quantify. It is impossible to predict with complete accuracy the price of any given object at auction, hence the convention of estimating the lower and upper range of prices based on similar objects sold previously. In essence, therefore, all art is valued by insurers at basic cost of manufacture, compounded of time and materials.

Intrinsic factors weighing upon art's value include quality, artistic merit, condition, subject matter and size. Secondary factors include authenticity, attribution, artist's reputation, historical importance, familiarity, provenance, fashion, sale location and sale inducements. Today, the growing importance of the internet, online auctioneering and technology for scientific art analysis is adding an extra dimension to art's valuation or re-evaluation.

An article in the *Art Newspaper* indicated that certain subject matter could make a difference to the price of a work of art: beautiful young women and children, higher social status, sexiness, horses and figures in landscapes, sunny scenes, flowers, calm water, attractive dogs and game birds, as well as bright, bold and pale colours.

Nevertheless, the laws of supply and demand continue to play the dominant role in the value of art on the market. Recent studies by Victor Ginsburgh and Sheila Weyers (2005) have shown that the number of best-quality works is usually in the same proportion to the total number, with the market tending towards long-term upward price equilibrium.

A key factor is therefore freshness on the art market. An item that has appeared comparatively recently on the market will lead to a lower price than one that has been in a particular collection for a number of years. During the last hundred years, the average holding period for a painting was 20–30 years, but it is now shortening. However, studies have also shown that prices that rise during an artist's lifetime, often round the time of death, fall subsequently.

Simultaneously, the market's rises and falls are to some extent exacerbated by a consensus of opinion, in the form of the art trade, museums, academia and the media. Orley Ashenfelter and Kathryn Graddy (2002) suggest that art experts provide an accurate prediction of art prices, while Jianping Mei and Mike Moses (2005) argue that the price estimates for expensive paintings have a consistent upward bias over 30 years. They suggest that high estimates at the time of purchase are associated with adverse subsequent abnormal returns and that the error tends to persist over time.

Moreover, studies have shown a correlation between exhibitions and art prices. In 2005, according to the *Art Newspaper*, the three most popular exhibitions were held in Japan, though New York records the highest numbers of overall attendances. Among the most popular were those for 19th-century art, decorative art and Impressionism.

Historically, supply to the art market benefits from debt, divorce and death. Today, sales to meet tax bills provide auction houses with the greatest flow of works. During the 1980s boom, high prices made art less accessible, with many of the great works disappearing semi-permanently into museums. To a large extent the supply gap may have been filled by inferior works reflected in changing tastes. After all, what one generation finds ugly and nonsensical, the next may find beautiful. Today, older works are often sold at a discount to new market taste, adding to the view that people buy contemporary art when they are confident about their future and reminders of the past when they are not.

Naturally enough, demand is driven by new money, and major auctions are often an irresistible spectacle of celebrities and millionaires. In the past, higher art price rises were typified by economic booms in Holland in the 17th century, Britain in the 18th and 19th centuries, the United States in the late 19th and 20th centuries, and Japan in the 1980s. In the 21st century, there is evidence of faster price rises in developing countries, particularly China and India. In Hong Kong, average art sale prices have been higher in the last two years than in the United States and the UK, albeit from a much lower turnover.

Figure 6.3.2 plots the relative levels of activity in the secondary art markets in 2005.

According to the Cap Gemini/Merrill Lynch World Wealth Report, in the 10 years to 2006 the number of high net worth individuals with more than $1 million in financial wealth rose 7.6 per cent annually to 8.7 million. The highest number are in the United States (2,669,000, rising by 6.8 per cent between 2004 and 2005), Germany (767,000, +0.9 per cent), the UK (448,000, +7.3 per cent) and China (320,000, +6.8 per cent). The fastest-rising are in India (83,000, +19.3 per cent), Russia (103,000, +17.4 per cent) and Brazil (109,000, +11.3 per cent). Worldwide, the amount invested in alternative investments including art has doubled between 2002 and 2005. An alternative report by the Boston Consulting Group indicates that the highest millionaire populations per household are in the UAE, Switzerland, Singapore and the United States.

Reflecting this, in the UK in the last two years, a dealer selling ancient and Islamic art recorded some of the highest returns. Sotheby's London reported Asians buying 11 per cent of the mostly Western contemporary works on sale in March 2006. In May, also in London, the highest recorded sales of Russian art were made by the three main auction houses. In Dubai, UAE, at its inaugural sale, Christie's sold art far above estimate, including 45 new price highs for Arab artists.

Battling against the private sector, UK public sector spending on acquisitions for its five major museums has fallen by 90 per cent over the past decade. In 2005, the Heritage Lottery Fund spent less than 1 per cent of its budget on art acquisitions, while the National Heritage Memorial Fund's spending has fallen by over 40 per cent in the past 10 years. By comparison, the Art Fund, which is an independent art charity with 80,000 members, can generate £3–4 million each year.

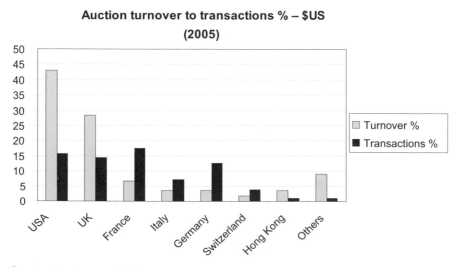

*Source:* Artprice.com.2006

**Figure 6.3.2** Levels of activity in the primary art markets, 2005

In future, ageing and shrinking populations in many countries will have an even more dramatic effect on supply and demand in the art market. Art works bought by previous generations may reappear on the market in greater number, while the art tastes of the newly wealthy, mostly of a younger generation, particularly in emerging economies, may after the perception of western art value.

Figure 6.3.3 illustrates the 2005 pattern of art collectors' purchases.

## Art as investment

There are two main schools of thought on collecting purely for investment purposes: specialization in a particular area or by artist/craftsperson, or in one that has remained unfashionable for years.

Unlike most investments, art is based only on the capital gain when the investment is realized, since there is little or no interest, dividend or rent on the capital invested. The profit on sale must be greater, therefore, than other capital gains, including these dividends, all less inflation. The theory is that, as the number of buyers in the market goes up, supply stays static or declines, so promising a long-term upward movement in prices.

The capital appreciation has to be substantial to make up for the initial cost of acquisition and disposal, valuation and provenance research fees as well as insurance, conservation and storage. A recent study by Zurich Financial Services demonstrated that, even without these costs, a painting bought at auction for £1,000 net in 1997 would need to fetch a sum of £2,159 in 2007 to produce an 8 per cent compound annual return including an inflation rate of 3 per cent.

Added to this, place of purchase has a substantial influence on price. From 1998 to 2001, according to a TEFAF survey, the average price of a painting sold in the UK advanced 54 per cent to $22,039, and 75 per cent to $69,736 in the United States, while declining by 39 per cent to $6,761 in the EU. Moreover, the *Art Newspaper* found that a typical contemporary work sold from the United States

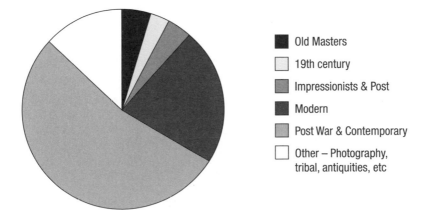

- ■ Old Masters
- □ 19th century
- ▨ Impressionists & Post
- ▦ Modern
- ▨ Post War & Contemporary
- □ Other – Photography, tribal, antiquities, etc

*Source:* ArtNews, 2006

**Figure 6.3.3**   Top 200 collectors by art categories

would have no added taxation in that country and Canada, 5 per cent in the UK and Dubai, and between 5.5 per cent and 10 per cent in Europe, rising to 28 per cent and 29 per cent in Russia and China respectively. In a recent survey in the UK, 90 per cent (up from 6 per cent in 2002) of the Society of London Art Dealers' (SLAD) members claim to be 'seriously or slightly affected' by EU-imposed import VAT and 65 per cent (up from 51 per cent) by its Droit de Suite tax. Moreover, a recent ruling by the European Court of Justice now imposes a VAT rate of 17.5 per cent, rising from 5 per cent, on auctioneers' commissions. The British Art Market Federation argues that the Droit de Suite tax will put off those buying art in the £50,000–£100,000 range.

To benefit the investor, the art market has price data going back hundreds of years. Collection of these data has helped swell the number of economic studies measuring art market returns in the last 30 years.

One of the earliest by John Stein (1977) found that paintings were no more or less attractive than other assets, yielding the going rate for their systematic risk. He also found art prices susceptible to stock market performance. A longer-term study by William Baumol (1986) compared returns from art and government bonds that were sold two or more times at auction from 1952 to 1961. He concluded that they brought a mean return of 0.85 per cent: far less than the 2.5 per cent UK government securities would have produced. With others he demonstrated that returns on pictures fluctuated more widely the shorter the period between sales. In a similar study, William Goetzmann noted that investing in art is 10 times more risky than investing in shares.

Today, the best known study is by Jianping Mei and Mike Moses (2002), using data from 5,000–8,000 repeat art sales since 1875. They calculated that, from 1954 to 2003, art returned an annualized 12.6 per cent, which was slightly ahead of the S&P 500's 11.7 per cent and well above Treasury bonds. They also demonstrated that the art market never really crashes. Art prices have experienced only moderate declines during the 27 recessions since 1875. Moreover, in the last four major wars, art outperformed the S&P 500, growing by 108 per cent during the Korean War compared to 67 per cent for shares.

Further study by Mei and Moses showed that, as with other investments, the more you pay the lower the return, particularly up to $50,000. This is contrary to traditional advice in the art market suggesting you should buy the best you can afford and buy fewer pieces. Their research has been similarly borne out by study of the sculpture market. They also found that holding objects for over 20 years increased return and reduced risk by 75 per cent. The Mei and Moses findings are illustrated graphically in Figure 6.3.4.

Research into diversification by Rachel Campbell (2006) showed that art has a low correlation with equities and other financial asset classes. Adding fine art to a diversified portfolio is likely to produce a slightly greater return for each unit of risk and a significantly better return with less volatility than stocks and bonds on their own. Based on data from 1980 to 2006, she found that contemporary art offered the highest returns and old masters the lowest, though it was the least volatile. She recommended an optimal asset allocation of 4.19 per cent including transaction costs and 2.82 per cent when hedge funds are part of the portfolio.

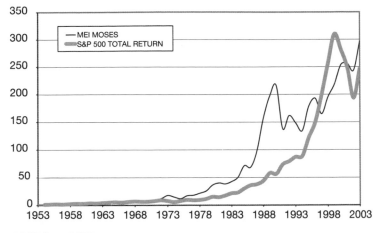

*Source:* Mei/Moses 2002

**Figure 6.3.4** Mei Moses annual All Art Index vs S&P 500

Another study by Clare McAndrew and Rex Thompson (2005), based on a study of Impressionists sold between 1985 and 2001, concluded that by ignoring unsold (bought-in) art the downside risk was understated by as much as 50 per cent. In the fine art market, buy-in rates have averaged just over 30 per cent since 1998.

Among the few emerging art market studies, Henry Mok *et al* (1993) found that modern Chinese paintings resold between 1980 and 1990 had an average holding period of less than four years, concluding that they were an unattractive investment alternative. Sebastian Edwards (2004) found that Latin American artists followed different patterns to US artists, offering a very high rate of return and a very low correlation to international equities.

Other research demonstrates that art is more closely correlated with the real estate market than other assets, as Guido Candela and Antonello Scorcu (1997) first found in their study of Italian modern and contemporary art and property and stock prices. Takato Hiraki *et al* (2003) made similar findings in a study of Japanese land prices, art and Japanese stocks during the late 1980s. Today, many of the world's property markets are overvalued based on prices to rents, notably by up to 50 per cent in Australia and Britain, according to *The Economist*.

Added to this, there is an obvious but often neglected caveat. Art is a lagging indicator, which responds slowly to recession and recovery. When assets fall, people feel less rich and eventually stop buying art, which is usually after about two years. In a study of the UK art market, Rachel Campbell *et al* (2005) found that art price returns tend to be higher during the upward phase of a business cycle.

In response to the growing interest in art investment, a recent Barclays equity/gilt study, for the first time since 1956, included art as a medium to long-term investment based on the Mei and Moses research. Their research demonstrated that, since the Second World War and 1970, art performed best relative to other investments under conditions of above-trend inflation and growth, and worst under conditions of above-trend inflation and below-trend growth. They suggested a portfolio weighting over 10–20 years of 10 per cent in art, 17.4 to 18.0 per cent in equities, 0 to 16.8 per cent in gilts, 5 per cent in cash, 3.1 to 25 per cent in commodities, and 24.9 to 25 per cent in property.

ABN Amro Bank Private Wealth Management have also suggested expanding the range of alternative assets to include art. Their analysis supports an allocation of 4 to 6 per cent in art investment into a medium- to high-risk portfolio, believing art funds could capture 10 per cent of a $300 billion alternative investment market in the next 10 years.

Assisting this in the UK, pension funds are generally free from tax on their gains in art and antiques, while watches, clocks and old scientific instruments are normally exempt from capital gains tax. About 85,000 objects qualify for so-called heritage tax relief under inheritance tax rules, usually levied at 40 per cent, if you choose to give items of national interest to the state on your death. These include certain types of books, manuscripts, and scientific collections of national, scientific, historical or artistic interest. The performance of the decorative art and collectables market over the period 1976 to 2006 is charted in Figure 6.3.5.

The resurgence in art collecting for investment purposes is a phenomenon last experienced in the 1970s. In 1974 the British Rail Pension Fund invested £40 million or 5 per cent of the fund in art. This was the first time a collection had been formed specifically for that purpose. At the end of 1974 economic conditions in the UK were less than favourable: inflation and tax were high, stock and property markets had fallen heavily, the pound was weak, exchange controls were in operation and index-linked gilts were unavailable. Advised by Sotheby's, the fund made 2,525 purchases across a wide range of art sectors. However, political pressure,

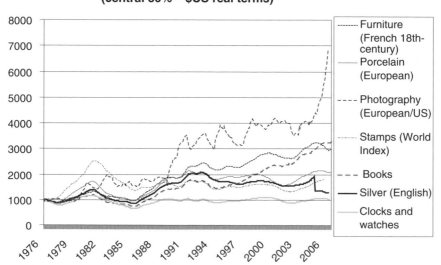

*Source:* Art Market Research, 2006

**Figure 6.3.5** Performance of the decorative art and collectables market, 1976–2006

along with 1980s financial deregulation, a booming stock market, high costs and no accurate measure for art, precipitated the fund's gradual art sales after 1987.

In 1989 a quarter of the art was sold, indicating a better return than property and a worse performance than equities. By 1997 the fund had yielded a real annual return of 4.3 per cent, including 11.9 per cent for Impressionist and modern art and 7.7 to 8.5 per cent for Chinese works of art. It was concluded that the fund had met the primary objective of at least safeguarding pensions by matching inflation over time. Today, the BR Pension Fund invests the same 4 per cent proportion in alternative assets, by increasing exposure to hedge funds.

Following this example, several attempts have been made since the late 1980s to establish art funds that resemble private equity closed-end funds. The reputation of art funds has often been marred by financial scams and in many cases failure. Nevertheless, some economists have likened the growth of art funds today to US real estate investment trusts (REITs), first started 30 years ago, which allow small investors to invest in large buildings.

Until now no funds have been successful except the UK's Fine Art Fund. Advised by a 'Who's Who' of the art and financial world, the fund has attracted $30–40 million from 50 mostly foreign investors, especially in Europe, to invest in old masters, Impressionist, modern and contemporary art. The aim is to achieve returns of 10 to 15 per cent a year over 10–13 years. The fund charges a 2 per cent annual management charge and takes 20 per cent of the profits over a 6 per cent hurdle rate. Other costs include legal costs and capital-raising fees. Costs are kept to a minimum mostly by buying and selling privately, often from distressed sellers, and by cutting out the auctioneers. The appeal of the fund is that it can act quickly, knows the inner workings of the market and can take a long-term view of the market.

Since its foundation in April 2004, the fund has made 80 per cent of its purchases, in old masters (25 per cent), Impressionists (15 per cent), modern (15 per cent) and contemporary (25 per cent), with the rest held in cash. Most buying has been over the $1 million level, ranging from $20,000 to $3 million. To enhance the works' value they have been exhibited worldwide. So far the fund has sold 20 per cent of the portfolio. To date no picture has sold for a loss, and the 12 realized deals have produced an average annualized return of 61.5 per cent. Other active art funds are in Russian, Chinese and Indian art.

Added to this, an increasing number of companies are accepting art works as collateral against loans. At the very least art tends to hold its value against inflation. Loan rates range from 3 per cent over the prime interest rate to 15 per cent for 40 to 50 per cent of the estimated art value because of the risk involved. Because of this high interest, art loans suit less liquid and high, long-term borrowers or those requiring bridging loans. At Sotheby's the minimum loan is $1 million, rising to a total of $3 billion, and is mostly used by estates to pay inheritance taxes. Loans at Citibank, which have been offered since 1979, have doubled in value in the last five years. Art loans are also a practice long offered by Christie's and at Bank of America. Contemporary art accounts for much of the current interest in this field, owing to greater liquidity, frequent trades and a growing belief in its long-term value. Evolving these activities, in a recent paper Max Rutten proposes an art exchange as a mechanism for the issuing of securities with art or collections as the underlying asset.

A related development has been the growth in rental income from art. Paul Graeser (1978) first suggested that total returns of rent plus capital gain from American antique furniture easily stood comparison with yields on financial instruments. In the UK public sector, Southampton City Art Gallery earns more than £40,000 a year by renting some of its 300 paintings to local institutions, while in the commercial sector the world-renowned collector Charles Saatchi recently published a catalogue of 600 works that might bring in £150,000 a year to defray the costs of running his gallery.

# How to invest in art and antiques

*James Goodwin*

## Art and antiques journals, guides and price indexes

Linking the finance and art worlds is a new breed of specialist advisers that have experience in either or both. They have access to leading experts, valuation, investment research, marketing and other operating procedures. However, for those wishing to go it alone, there is no shortage of information on art and the art market. Britain is blessed with a large number of auctioneers, dealers, galleries, art libraries, museums and trade organizations.

Information on the UK and international art markets are available from the weekly *Antiques Trade Gazette*, and the monthly journals *Art Newspaper*, *Antique Collecting*, *Art and Auction*, *Art Review*, *Art Monthly* and *Art News*, as well as some of the daily newspapers, periodicals and guides.

Among the best-known price guides published since 1985 are *Miller's* antique guides, which cover 60 subjects and 10,000 items from 20 auctioneers. Prices include buyer's premium and VAT. Their other buyer's guides cover the individual collecting areas in more detail and are available in pocket size.

Based on similar data, art indexes are the closest thing to an objective, statistical analysis of the art market and an invaluable tool, now mostly available online. Still, it should be noted that most exclude transaction costs and dealer prices, which are generally double hammer prices and represent the remaining 70 per cent of the market.

One of the oldest is John Andrews's ACC Index, which is based on the average prices for 35 types of 1,200 typically good-quality pieces of British furniture from seven periods dating from 1650 to 1860. These are illustrated in a book and discussed in a monthly magazine. The index has been published annually in

January since 1968, and is compared to the FTSE 250, house prices in the South-East excluding London, and UK inflation. According to the broader ACC Index, not shown, English furniture follows a 10- to 12-year cycle (see Figure 6.4.1).

Also dating from 1968 but measuring the fine art auction market is LTB Gordonsart Art Sales Index, which is published every August in three languages and updated continuously on the internet. Last year the index included 2.7 million pieces of data on 210,000 artists, covered by 2,400 auctions. Bought-in (unsold) items are excluded, and the figures are net of auction premium and tax.

Offering the broadest range of art prices are Robin Duthy's Art Market Research indexes. The 500 indexes, which are internet-based and include most fine and decorative art categories sold at auction, have been compiled annually since 1976 with the help of Christie's. Data on stock markets, UK property markets and other forms of investment are also available. Each graph can be calculated in five different currencies, adjusted for inflation, segmented into five parts, eg top 10 per cent, and measured by compound interest. Their clients include the US and UK revenue services, banks, insurers, galleries and newspapers.

Located abroad but written in the English language are a number of fine art websites used by the art auction market, journalists and academics.

From Italy, Gabrius, founded in 1997, provides 470,000 colour images and prices at auction subdivided into old master paintings, 19th-century, modern and contemporary art. It also publishes a confidence and liquidity index adjusted for inflation. Gabrius's intention is to bridge the gap between fine art and finance via a quarterly magazine and distribution on the Bloomberg media network. Gabrius has been one of the pioneers in measuring emerging art markets.

From France, artprice.com, created in 1997, provides 4 million data entries on works, including bought-in works, sold at 2,900 auction houses in 40 countries. Its website provides analysis of art works, artists and their works, market segments

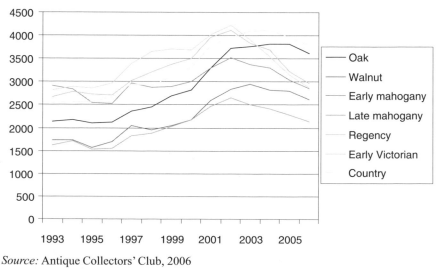

*Source:* Antique Collectors' Club, 2006

**Figure 6.4.1**  ACC Index – English furniture

and market overviews. In 2005, it added a database for the decorative arts and in 2006 launched an art valuation service.

Similarly, artnet.com, founded in the United States in 1989, links works sold by each artist in order of ascending value. Its website and magazine provide general market information including dealer locations and events. It is favoured by a large number of SLAD members and Sotheby's in London.

Also from the United States, ArtFact, founded in 1989, contains 5.5 million public auction sale results and is one of the few archives that include decorative art as well as fine art. It is referred to by a number of leading auction houses and museums.

## Buying and selling art: auctioneers, the internet, dealers, fairs and artists

There are several routes to buying and selling art: auctioneers, online auctioneers, dealers and artists. The primary market is where original works are sold for the first time – artists' studios, most art fairs and galleries. The secondary market is for the exchange of better known works, where participants are likely to have good information, helped by many journals, magazines, the internet, etc.

Olav Velthuis (2003) believes that dealers in the primary market take a longer-term view of contemporary artists and establish a firm market for their work, while Orley Ashenfelter and Kathryn Graddy (2002) believe the auction system is a key determinant of the cost of creating and distributing works of art, and of understanding what is good and bad. A key consideration is that auction prices often rise above 'true value' when two or more people are determined to bid for a work.

Though auction houses are increasingly regarded by some retailers, there remains an interdependence between both parties, with at least a third of sales made to dealers. Consequently, major sales and promotions are often coordinated between all parties. The main selling months in the art calendar are May/June/July and October/November/December, and to a lesser extent January/February/March/April.

In the UK the auction market is represented by the big three of Sotheby's, Christie's and Bonhams, and a large number of provincial auctioneers.

Both Sotheby's and Christie's were founded in the 18th century, and are the world's oldest and most prestigious art auction houses. They have salerooms throughout the globe and hold over 700 auctions every year. Bonhams, from its base in Knightsbridge, London, has 600 international sales annually in most continents, especially the US West Coast and Australia. The UK's largest regional auctioneer is Drewett Neate with 12 salerooms offering 150 sales in southern England.

The Society of Fine Art Auctioneers and Valuers (SOFAA) is the UK's only professional body that exclusively covers the valuation and sale by auction of fine art and antiques. Probity and ethics along with the improvement of knowledge are the central aims of the Society's 48 UK members. It is also advisable to buy from auctioneers or valuers who carry the Royal Institution of Chartered Surveyors (RICS) mark, since they will be governed by the Institution's codes of conduct, such as holding clients' money in a designated bank account separate from their own business.

Today the presence of high-end works in provincial salerooms is also becoming more commonplace. This is partly thanks to online catalogues, which project works worldwide at 'competitive' premiums, thereby avoiding higher charges in London and New York. An increasing number of provincial auctioneers regularly auction over £1 million per sale and often sell internationally prestigious works.

At Christie's, the maximum commission for selling an item in the UK up to £2,500 is 15 per cent and 10 per cent thereafter. Similarly, Bonhams charges vendors 15 per cent for the first £2,000, while Tennant's charges 15 per cent up to £500, 12.5 per cent for £500–£1,000 and 10 per cent thereafter.

Buyer's fees at Christie's and Bonhams are 20 per cent up to a £70,000 hammer price and from 12 per cent thereafter. The threshold for the same charges at Sotheby's is £100,000. At Drewett Neate charges are 17.5 per cent on the first £25,000 and 12.5 per cent thereafter. At Tennant's it is 15 per cent for the first £30,000.

The advent of online auctions in August 1999 has made sought-after items even more accessible and is transforming the traditional art market. It is estimated that it is five times more expensive to sell a £750,000 painting at a traditional auction house than online. Until recently, the internet has been generally considered less suitable for the sale and auction of larger and more costly art because of the lack of specialist assistance to verify quality and authenticity. Improved technology has changed this. In July 2006, Christie's launched its live auction website in New York and London, selling £1.5 million online in 42 sales with over 6,700 bids accepted. Twenty-five per cent of the internet bidders were new to Christie's. Items sold include prints, jewellery, silver, clocks, sporting guns, arms and armour, old master pictures, sculpture and furniture.

Many dealers consult the online auctioneer eBay for price information for buying ceramics, silver and jewellery. eBay registers 135.5 million users, 56.1 million of which are active. It costs between 15p and £2 to list on eBay and between 1.75 per cent and 5.25 per cent of the price attained. For qualified listings, buyers are protected for purchases of up to $1,000, which includes the launch prices of most items. Buying tends to be concentrated at the end of an auction, and in the United States prices of stamps sold by eBay tended to be 10 to 15 per cent lower than for a traditional auctioneer.

Buying and selling through a dealer can represent a more straightforward transaction than at auction since purchases can mostly be made on sight. In fact, the top dealers' collective turnover is still greater than the UK sales from the two main auction houses.

The most reputable dealers are typically those belonging to the Society of London Art Dealers (SLAD), British Antique Dealers' Association (BADA) and Association of Art and Antique Dealers (LAPADA). As well as organizing fairs and exhibitions, these trade organizations offer a wide range of services including restoration, valuation and consumer information, such as lists of packers and shippers.

In the UK, antique shops and collectors' fairs are still the preferred trading place for collectors, thanks to increased dealer specialization. In any given week you could expect to find no fewer than 25 British general fairs listed in the *Antiques Trade Gazette*. For SLAD members the most popular fairs are: 20/21 British Art

Fair, Grosvenor House and TEFAF, New York International Fine Art Fair, Art Islington, and Palm Beach Art and Antiques, with Art Basel the most highly rated. According to the most recent survey, their members' trading conditions have much improved since 2002, with 70 per cent of output sold to private buyers. The majority of SLAD dealers trade in post-War contemporary art, Impressionists and 19th-century European pictures. Most sales are made in the UK, but are down since 2002, while increasing into the EU. According to a recent LAPADA survey, the majority of their dealers specialize in 19th-century art, 59 per cent of turnover is from their shops or galleries, 68 per cent trade on the internet, mostly sold to a growing 40–50 age range.

More collectors are also buying directly from artists. In the contemporary market, art fairs provide the opportunity to see the work of hundreds of different artists under one roof and are good for judging what's on the market. For the more adventurous, the MA degree shows, often in June, are worth considering, following the successful promotion of young British artists like Hirst and the Chapman brothers by collectors such as Charles Saatchi.

According to a recent article in *Independent*, 3,700 graduates leave art school every year, adding to the 60,000 or more practising artists. The best UK colleges are the Royal College of Art, Goldsmith's College, Central Saint Martins College, Slade School, Camberwell College, Chelsea College of Art, Glasgow School of Art and the Ruskin School of Drawing. As a result of these activities, sales in the contemporary art market exceeded £500 million in 2005. Revealingly, future trends according to a recent survey in the *Art Newspaper*, students at these colleges elected the following artists as the most influential: Marcel Duchamp, Pablo Picasso, Francis Bacon, Henri Matisse and Lucian Freud.

## Conclusion

Investing in art has been likened to investing in a small start-up company where both risk and returns can be very high. Similarly reflecting the upward trend in private equity transactions, during the last five years fine art has outperformed the USA's S&P 500 Share Index, according to the Mei and Moses Index of 6,000 repeat sales since 1875. Moreover, according to their latest results art is now above its all-time high levels of 1990, albeit representing a small fraction of the market. On average in the last 125 years only two artists have emerged whose work has increased in value over time.

The challenge for the uninitiated collector is choosing from the bewildering range of art now available, as more familiar art, once used as a benchmark, becomes scarcer.

Nevertheless, their striking conclusion that the more you pay for art above a certain level the lower the return would indicate greater opportunities in 'under-valued' markets selling art of increasingly recognizable style and pedigree or that rejected in the past. In future, art investment seems likely to mirror emerging economies, which today account for the bulk of world production, as they did until the late 19th century. To a lesser extent it will also benefit art from developed

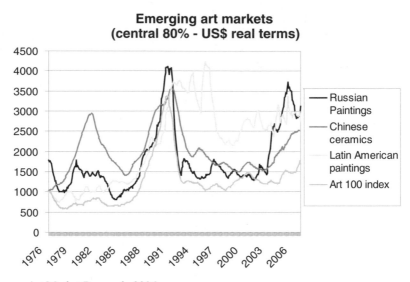

*Source:* Art Market Research, 2006

**Figure 6.4.2**  Fluctuations in the emerging art markets, 1976–2006

economies that have invested there. In both cases it is worth remembering that art buying appears to have a home bias, like equity investment.

Figure 6.4.2 illustrates fluctuations in the emerging art markets over the period 1976 to 2006.

Today more than ever, the best advice is to buy something because you like it and hope your enthusiasm is shared with buyers of the future.

# Investment in fine wines

*Nick Stephens, Interest in Wine Ltd*

This chapter is based on years of experience acquired in wine investment and in the practical running of www.interestinwine.com and www.bordeaux-undiscovered. co.uk. Bordeaux-Undiscovered has brought selected wines of the finest quality and limited production to the UK for the first time. We deal directly with the Bordeaux *négociants* (châteaux' sales agents) who offer us wines that are predominately for the French market and until recently were undiscovered within the UK market. Our sister company – Interest in Wine Ltd – offers grand cru classes wines for investment. Thanks to these companies I have gained exclusive access to some great wines.

## Why invest in wine?

Fine wine is a finite product. Demand is outstripping supply. A Château can only produce a finite quantity each year, which then diminishes over time as the wine is consumed. This in turn leads to limitations on availability, and prices can subsequently rise. The fine wine market is growing. It's worth around £500 million a year globally, and a sizeable part of that goes straight into the cellar.

HM Revenue and Customs considers fine wines to be a 'wasting asset', as they are perishable. A wasting asset is an asset whose useful life is not likely to exceed 50 years. As most quality wines reach their peak of maturity around 25 years it is difficult to argue that they have a useful life over 50 years. Of course this varies from vintage to vintage. The winemaker from Château Palmer told me a story of when he met a wealthy American whose passion was Château Palmer. In his cellar he had some 3,000 bottles of varying vintages. After asking the winemaker to taste

a 1945 Palmer he presented him with a blind tasting of another vintage, asking him to guess the year. The winemaker suggested it was younger than the 1945 and put a date of 1948 to the sample. In actual fact it was 1928!

The wine must be held by a private individual who is not a wine dealer or trader. Fine wines benefit from an exemption from tax, both capital gains and income tax. However, rules apply. As John Stimpfig has pointed out in 'A cautionary tale' (*Decanter*), HMRC may require evidence that your wine was bought to drink rather than sell. You need to clarify any concerns with your independent financial adviser. Fortunately inheritance tax is only paid on the value of the original purchase price, provided you have proof of the original cost.

# What sort of wines should I invest in?

Try to buy the best wines from the greatest vintages – the demand is high. Historically the best performers for wine investments are the top 30 châteaux in Bordeaux. Most vintages have a 'hot' wine that far outperforms the crop. An example of this is La Fleur Morange. In recent spring tastings in Bordeaux I came across this right-bank garage wine (ie made by a small producer). The 2003, 2004 and 2005 were all excellent quality but are relatively unknown. I am convinced that wines such as these will be highly praised when revisited by critics like US-based Robert Parker. Another prize is the second wine of Valandraud, Virginie de Valandraud 2005. You need to make an informed choice when selecting wines for investment and take advice, not simply going for the branded names.

The wines of Burgundy have also accrued good value in the past. I steer clear of cult Australian and Californian wines, as they are highly speculative and have no proven track record. The fact remains that the French still produce the best wines in the world, as is acknowledged by many wine gurus – including Parker.

Prices may fluctuate suddenly, usually because of the effect of a complimentary write-up from a wine critic such as Parker. His 100-point system of scoring wines has a huge influence on the fine wine market. It is a sore point that one critic's opinion has such sway over the market, but as it is a fact it must be taken into account. Parker enjoys big, bold, heavy wines, and his UK counterpart Jancis Robinson prefers the more elegant style. This is shown in a comparison of their ratings; for example, in the 2005 vintage Parker rated Château Pavie 2005 as 98–100 (the same as Latour!) and Robinson rated it 14.5 out of 20!

# Why invest in Bordeaux?

Bordeaux produces some of the best wine in the world and still remains the only wine in the world with a wine classification system. Its experience in winemaking goes back many centuries, with the traditional methods of winemaking being handed down from generation to generation. Its wines can be more complex than most, and we have been enjoying them since Henry II married Eleanor of Aquitaine, bringing claret with her as her dowry.

There is tremendous interest and speculation in the Bordeaux 2005 vintage. The *Financial Times* Investment Special on 10 June 2006 ran an article by John Stimpfig entitled 'There's gold in those Bordeaux fields'. He says:

> Huge demand, short supplies; fine wine investors – and suppliers – have never had it so good... Certainly, collectors, investors and drinkers are bracing themselves for the most expensive en primeur prices in history on the back of what has been touted as potentially the greatest ever Bordeaux vintage.
>
> Of course quality and 'Parker Points' are only part of the equation when the first growth proprietors come to price their wines. What is arguably more important is the state of the market. In 2006 the fine wine business finds itself in the midst of a rampant bull run as world wide demand is at its strongest for 5 years.

Jancis Robinson writes in her website www.jancisrobinson.com with David Lester of Manchester University that 'rising global prosperity and economic liberalisation especially in China and Russia are leading to a world wide increase in demand for fine wines'.

John Stimpfig agrees:

> This vintage couldn't have come at a better time for the Bordelaise. By the beginning of May Berry Bros & Rudd has already received more than 5000 en primeur enquiries. Other UK suppliers such as Lay & Wheeler, Armits, Bibendum and Montrachet Fine Wine Merchants have also reported unprecedented interest in Bordeaux's latest crop.
>
> Moreover the Americans will be buying with a vengeance this year irrespective of the state of the dollar or the state of the US stock market. Meanwhile massive orders for cru classe wines are pouring in from new super-rich buyers in Asia and India.

Simon Staples of Berry Bros & Rudd is quoted as saying: 'We have had huge orders from Taiwan of people wanting 100 cases of first or second growths. We'll be lucky to get them a case.'

The demand is obvious. However, as supplies are down, Bordeaux wine prices can only escalate. Stimpfig continues: 'As if this wasn't enough to push prices through the roof, supply in 2005 is also down by around 25%. Chateau Margaux for instance has only produced about 13,000 cases – about 3,000 shy of its usual output.'

David Lester points out that sometimes supply can be deliberately slowed up: 'be aware that some producers, most famously the previous owner of Chateau d'Yquem, may reduce supply by holding back some of their production for later sale'.

Choosing Bordeaux's 2005 vintage as an investment is a sound move. Liv-ex's (a wine exchange) most recent 12-month figures show that its 100 Index is up by 30 per cent, which means that it has easily outperformed the FTSE 100, UK gilts, the US Stock Market and the FT House Price Index.

www.wine-searcher.com also notes that the global demand for fine wine, which is produced in very small quantities, has increased enormously over the last two decades. Wine can outperform, and often has outperformed, the FTSE 100 and the Dow Jones, offering significant returns without the volatility of the stock market.

For those wishing to invest in Bordeaux's 2005 and other vintages there are some important points to consider. The real problem is getting hold of enough of it at the lowest price. Producers sell globally to insure against any weakness in individual markets.

# A–Z of buying wine for investment

I have put together a guide to buying Bordeaux as an investment. For further information check out these sites: www.decanter.com, www.wine-searcher.com, Jim Budd's www.investdrinks.org, www.jancisrobinson.com and www.wine&spirits.com.

■ Buy *en primeur* and focus on the top wines for the best vintages. *En primeur* refers to buying wine after it is made, but before it is bottled. Cask samples of wines are made available for tasting to wine journalists and large wholesale buyers in the spring following the vintage. Brokers and merchants sell on the wine to their customers. Wine is generally bottled and shipped around two years later. In good vintages wine futures can offer the investor the greatest return; the initial release prices are usually the lowest at which the wines will ever be sold. However, when buying wine futures it is strongly recommended that you deal only with reputable and established retailers and importers. No storage charges have to be paid for a couple of years, until the wines are shipped to your cellar.

■ However, buying *en primeur* wines poses its own risks. Such wines are unfinished and there is the risk they can go wrong as they mature or during bottling, storage or shipment.

■ Buy your wine in unmixed, sealed wooden cases. An important part of your wine's provenance is its original wooden case.

■ Make sure that you know the provenance of your wine. A wine that can be traced holds a completely different value to one that cannot.

■ Check the wine scores and rating systems to make sure you are buying wines that will sell on. The following are useful scoring systems:

– Robert Parker's www.thewineadvocate.com;

– *Wine Spectator* magazine;

– Michael Broadbent from *The Great Vintage Book*;

– www.decanter.com;

– Allen Meadows at www.burghand.com;

– Jancis Robinson's Purple Pages at www.jancisrobinson.com;

– Stephen Tazer at www.internationalwinecellar.com;

– James Halliday at www.winepros.com.

■ When it comes to choosing a merchant, remember you are going to be paying for wines two years before they are delivered. So go for established, reputable companies with a proven track record. Drinks investments are often not covered by the financial regulators. In the UK, for example, anyone can set up a drinks investment business without having to satisfy the financial authorities that they are operating a legitimate business and are competent to offer drinks investment advice. Do not respond to cold calls or unsolicited approaches, and check the accounts that have been filed with Companies House at www.companies-house.gov.uk. Check that the company is not one of the suspect drinks investment companies listed on Jim Budd's www.investdrinks.org website.

■ If purchasing in Europe, buy and store wines 'under bond' so that duty and taxes do not become payable.

■ Pay by credit card, as you have a better chance of getting your money back in the event of things going wrong.

■ Store wines correctly in a professionally temperature-controlled cellar. It's best to store your wine with an independent company or with your merchant – the charge is normally around £8 to £20 per case, per year. In this way your wine is stored under bond, delaying the payment of duty and VAT. If you store it yourself there is a risk it could be harder to sell as there is no guarantee that it has been stored correctly. Storage companies such as Octavian or LCB have proper systems for labelling customers' cases with full traceability and code numbers, but always ask what the policy is for labelling customers' cases and ask if you could visit the warehouse to see your wine. If you put your wine in the garage after purchase you will do more harm to the wine than anything else, owing to the fluctuating temperatures. Proper storage is a must.

■ Check that the wine is insured at the current market value, not the purchase price. Insurers usually cover only the actual damage, not diminution in value. If your house burns down and all the bottles are destroyed then you will be paid in full. But if your cellar floods and the labels are ruined but the bottles are intact, you will get next to nothing on a normal household policy. Most people are blissfully unaware that a standard policy won't cover that sort of damage. It's important to know that you can insure for loss of value due to something like water damage.

■ Costs. Take into account the 10–20 per cent fee that most merchants take for selling on the wine. Moving a single case of wine typically costs £10 per case, and there is a discount for multiple cases. You might be expected to pay this when it is delivered and when it is sold. Professional wine valuations and the premium for insurance purposes are also a cost you need to include. www.wine-searcher.com offers a valuation service at $750.

■ When it comes to selling your wine remember that most experts agree that wine investment is viable for 10 years or longer. Unless the wine that you bought is spectacularly rare there is no point trying to sell it on until it is ready to drink. And the longer you wait the more likely it is that other stocks of the same wine will have been exhausted, making yours even more valuable. Always sell through a wine broker or auction house. Auction houses charge a seller's commission of up to 18 per cent of the value of the hammer price, and wine brokers operate on similar or higher margins. Obviously a worldwide economic slowdown or anxiety about the future will affect the market for fine wine, just as it will the market for other investments.

■ Be aware of counterfeit wines. It is estimated that counterfeits make up 5 per cent of all wine on the market. Recent scandals include Sassicaia and Penfolds

Grange. Check your wine's provenance – wines that have been traded many times or where there is vagueness about the ownership trail are clearly more open to fraud. At the other end of the market there are wines that have been cellared at the château since bottling and rightly command a premium.

■ Look out for fraud and dubious practices – a wine investment company might offer wine at an inflated price, so use www.winesearcher.com to check prices. Sometimes companies sell wine they don't own. Typically this is an *en primeur* sale, giving the perpetrator 18–24 months before the fraud is uncovered. There is a dubious practice of borrowing from customer reserves, eg brokers receive an urgent request for a case of Mouton Rothschild, are unable to supply it immediately but know they have a case in customer reserves and know they can get a replacement. The provenance of the two cases is unlikely to be the same. If the original was purchased *en primeur* and has never moved and the second has travelled round the world, the second case will be worth considerably less.

I have drawn your attention to possible pitfalls, but the reality is that buying through the right company can be very rewarding. Remember, do not buy a wine unless you would love to drink it!

# Fine Wine – Investing In A Cellar

Starting a wine cellar is an exciting challenge for those struck by the wine bug but it can be daunting knowing where to begin. Whether you have £500 or £5,000 to spend, the advice is basically the same: identify your tastes and which of the collectible regions and styles you are likely to relish opening in years to come; get to know the important names from top regions – Bordeaux, but also from Burgundy, the Rhone Valley, Champagne, Australia and Italy, and ask questions about drinking windows and vintage variations.

Some people buy just for the enjoyment of having a well-stocked cellar to hand, others for pure speculation. An increasing number buy for the combined rewards of drinking and funding future consumption. There can also be tax advantages such as any exemption from capital gains tax in most circumstances. If you are hoping that your vinous choices will increase in value, the golden rule is to buy wines that have a proven market.

Bordeaux is the single most important fine wine region due to the volume of top quality wine produced, with a track record of delicious results. Historically interest is concentrated on the best: properties from the Left Bank that were ranked in 1855. The established hierarchy persists to this day with notable exceptions, such as Lynch Bages that out-performs its Fifth Growth status. The five First Growths are always in highest demand, along with 'Super-Seconds' such as Cos d'Estournel and Pichon Lalande.

The Right Bank of Bordeaux rose to prominence in the latter half of this century with stellar wines such as Saint Emilion's Cheval Blanc and, Bordeaux's most expensive wines, Pomerol's Petrus and Le Pin. The 1990s gave rise to the "garage" wine phenomenon – limited production micro-cuvées such as Valandraud and La Mondotte traded at eye-watering prices – kickstarting a drive towards even higher quality across the entire region.

Top names from other regions are also important in the trading market – Burgundy's Domaine de la Romanée Conti, super-cuvées from Chateauneuf du Pape and Italy's Sassicaia and Masseto.

It pays to seek advice from a reliable merchant who can advise on market trends and pricing. Albany Vintners is a specialist in Bordeaux, the Rhone, Champagne & Italy, and offers informed, friendly advice and genuinely competitive prices. Our services provided include valuations and storage: a crucial consideration as fine wine needs to be kept in temperature and humidity-controlled surroundings to ensure that it stays in peak condition. Storage costs are the same whether you buy wines worth £100 or £1,000 per case, and serious collectors buy and store wine "under bond' so that sales taxes do not become payable.

Those who want an independent review of a wine's credentials past and future can look to the wine critic Robert Parker. Wines are scored out of 100 with the results published in his bi-monthly "The Wine Advocate" journal. Parker is the single most important influence on prices, having built his reputation on his predictions for the legendary 1982 Bordeaux vintage. In more recent times, he has enthused over the consistency of the 2000 vintage, which has rewarded drinkers and investors alike with marvellous wines and spiralling prices. Parker points are important but merchants watch these too and can give advice on the importance of these ratings.

2006 is the current "en primeur" vintage – the fine wine futures market where wines are offered for sale in the April-June following the harvest, to be bottled and shipped in 2009. Customers are offered the chance to buy wines at the lowest possible prices while the wines are still in barrel, theoretically before prices rise and rare wines become even harder to find.

In the past, careful wine choices have brought higher returns than the stock market. But prices can go up as well as down as any good merchant will tell you. A cautionary tale is of the 1997 vintage where wines were over-priced on release and have since dropped significantly.

At the other extreme, Le Pin 1982 was released at £185 per case in 1983 and is now worth £30,000. More recently, Lafite 2003 was released at £1850 and is now worth £4,000 since it was awarded the ultimate 100 points by Robert Parker in April 2006. Clearly investing in wines can still be an attractive proposition if you do your research. The mantra is to concentrate on the best names, take advice and be prepared to hold on to favoured wines for a few years.

**For further information please contact Albany Vintners on 0845 330 8858 or visit www.albanyvintners.com**

Investing in wine is not for everyone, but should it interest anyone at all? Shouldn't wine be bought to be enjoyed? Should we buy wine solely with the intention of drinking it one day? If it rises dramatically in value well, then we'll cross that bridge when we come to it, won't we?

I would sympathise with this view. Being a wine merchant and obsessed (I assure myself, in an entirely healthy way) with the subject, the viewing of fine wine simply as an investment vehicle is demeaning to the passion that keeps me at my desk.

And yet there's no denying that collectors have made fantastic, tax-free returns in the past, either taking profits or funding further cellar expansion on the back of their returns. (N.B. As a "wasting chattel", returns on wine are tax free if the transaction is less than £6,000 and relates to a collection of wines that are either identical, or could be considered sufficiently similar as to form a set.) As a result, some time ago I started building a separate investment account of my own. Now having had a running-in period – giving me time to observe the market and learn more about what I am doing – I have garnered some understanding of where the potential lies. My thoughts follow:

## Who Should Invest

Speculating in wine should be viewed as a fun addendum to an existing portfolio of investments. If you are clasping a cheque for £1,000 and considering where to make your first ever investment, I would urge you to look elsewhere.

Of course, the value of your investment may go down as well as up, as they say, but the beauty of wine is that, should a particular purchase not provide the returns one was hoping for, one can get busy with a corkscrew and have one's revenge by drinking it. So here's the first rule of thumb: the investor should have sufficient disposable income that he or she is happy to open and consume the bottles in which one invests, the core of which will, on the table, be in the range £30 to somewhere approaching the stratosphere.

## Characterising the Targets

First and foremost, target wines have to fulfil a couple of basic requisites. Firstly, they should be age-worthy, preferably coming to maturity slowly over a period of a decade or more and then, ideally, remaining on a drinkable plateau of perfection for some years. "Why?" I hear you ask. "Does age-worthiness necessarily make a wine finer?" To which the answer is, of course, no. However, the world's greatest wines are those that not only carry the stamp of the vineyards from which they come, but are also capable of carrying that stamp with them as they transmogrify, over time, into something far removed from the fruit from which they came; an ultimate stage referred to in wine circles, rather confusingly, as both secondary and tertiary, that is so much above and beyond simple fermented grape juice as to be another beast altogether. In terms of both the investment and the wine, this stage represents maturity.

The second requisite of the target wine is that it is relatively well understood by the collecting public. By far the greater part of the wine held in the cellars of the world is in private hands, self-selected by collectors who are sensible enough to buy what they like; what they could see themselves drinking one day should a) all their horses come in, or b) the investment not prove as beneficial as one had hoped.

### Principal Targets

So, what to buy? Well, neatly fulfilling both the requirements listed above are the red wines of Bordeaux and it is in these wines that one finds by far the most activity in the secondary markets.

Driving the market is both claret's ability (in strong vintages) to age into the long term with reasonably predictable maturation profiles and the confidence with which collectors buy these wines, most finding its understanding within grasp. Many of the châteaux of the region cover vast areas and make, each vintage, a considerable amount of wine. Château Gruaud-Larose, for example, is capable of producing 40,000 cases of wine and every bottle contains exactly the same fluid, be it bought in New York, London or Hong Kong. This is because, prior to bottling, the entire vintage's production is blended together and then bottled at the same time. Clear branding is key to defining suitable investments.

### Secondary Targets

For the time being, this is of such limited importance as to require the bare minimum of space. There is a small number of Burgundy domaines that could be considered, two major – the Domaine de la Romanée-Conti and Domaine Leroy – and a smattering of minor, including Armand Rousseau and the newcomers Claude Dugat and Dugat-Py.

Most articles on wine investment will mention a couple of Australian wines – Grange, certainly; Hill of Grace, probably – perhaps an Italian or two. I would suggest that we're into niche territory here. Secondary markets for these wines lack the liquidity Bordeaux offers. Decent returns are the exception, rather than the rule.

## The Future

That the market for fine Bordeaux is growing is not in doubt. The emerging economies in China, Russia, India and South America are creating private wealth and with it is coming demand. Those in the UK that used to buy First Growth claret for drinking at £750 or even £1,000 a case are being priced out of the market and are having to trade down. This cascade is only serving to firm up prices of wines further down the Bordeaux hierarchy. In effect, everything is steadily moving up in price.

Is it possible that we will see the collector turning to other regions; appellations producing wine that offers similar age-worthiness and the predictable ageing process of claret? The most obvious alternative to Bordeaux is, in my view, the Rhône Valley, where the red wines, both from the north and south, are capable of lasting quite as long as the greatest clarets.

In addition, the wines of the Rhône are more about brand than appellation. Two of the greatest wines from the appellations of the northern Rhône – the Hermitages of Chave and Jaboulet (under the La Chapelle label) – are more commonly identified by producer name and brand name respectively than by their physical origins. However, I would certainly regard investment in the wine of the Rhône Valley as higher risk.

## Vintages

At the time of writing, we are still caught up in the throes of the French 2005 vintage. Consumer excitement at the release of the Bordeaux vintage has been unprecedented, as have been the prices paid; all fair enough, since this is quite possibly the greatest ever vintage for the reds of the region. Vintages that are transparently of great quality – 1982, 1990, 2000, 2005 for example – offer the collector the opportunity to purchase a broad range of châteaux. Wines produced in years like these will always be in demand. But what about those in-between vintages? Should they be written off altogether by the investor?

The answer to this question is now different to that one would have had to give 20 years ago. One would have had to point at a harvest like 1984 – the last truly pedestrian vintage for Bordeaux – and suggest that the symptoms of bubonic plague would be more welcome than the presence of these wines in one's portfolio. Whether or not one would proffer global warming as part of the reason for this change, or simply greater levels of sophistication in viticulture (vineyard management) and viniculture (wine making), vintages wholly lacking in merit are a thing of the past.

This phenomenon, when combined with the fact that the Bordelais are now more inclined to price their wines according to quality (more than simply by what they think the global market will support), means that, in every vintage, there are target wines for the investor. It's just that one's target range of châteaux in the "lesser" vintages is narrower i.e. stick to the Blue Chip producers: the First Growths and their Libournais equivalents.

## Robert Parker

One cannot discuss wine investment without the mention of the US critic Robert M Parker Jnr: the world's most powerful wine journalist. Although his influence appears to be waning – his torch being picked up by The Wine Spectator (a US publication) amongst others – it would be irresponsible not to recommend that a serious investor follow his musings. A positive note from Sir Bob can be the making of a wine in both primary and secondary markets. Ignore him at your peril!

## When to Sell

Wine is unique amongst commodities in that it attains a stage when it will start to disappear from the market. The reason for this is that it has become mature and its owners start to consume it. Global supply shrinks whilst (as we have discussed) demand is increasing; provided that the global economy is experiencing an upswing, the maturity of one's investment has arrived. It is now down to the individual investor to decide whether he or she can bear to be parted with such celestial fluid for which one has been caring for so long!

## Conclusion

Investing one's capital is part of life, but rarely a part that fires one's enthusiasm. The addition of wine to one's portfolio can add a degree of colour and a real sense of excitement; here, after all, is where hobby and the rather clinical world of investment collide. To those considering wine as an investment, I would add these final points:

- Buy what you like; you may want to drink your investment someday
- Be prepared to invest one's money for the medium to long term. The best clarets take a minimum of a decade to attain maturity
- Keep your wine in a reputable cellar
- Keep your wine under bond (the value of the duty and VAT is much better off in your pocket than the chancellor's, plus bonded and duty paid wines command much the same prices in the secondary markets)
- Don't take it too seriously…and anticipate some excellent drinking in the years to come!

# Racehorse ownership and investing in bloodstock

*Harriet Rochester, British Horseracing Board*

## Bloodstock investment is worthy of thorough exploration

There's an old saying that the quickest way to get a small fortune from horse racing is to start with a large one, and although racehorse ownership is not generally a route to prosperity there are certainly ways of making significant money from investing in thoroughbreds.

There are just under 15,000 racehorses in training in Britain and all of them are products of a global horse-breeding or bloodstock industry worth billions. The breeding and sale of prospective racehorses is a big business in which many invest – and from which huge fortunes can be made and lost.

## A history of horse racing

Horse racing was recorded in ancient Greece in 100 BC and by the late 16th century the sport was a favourite among the aristocracy in Britain, with King Charles II taking steps towards more formalization of the sport in the late 1660s. Three Arabian stallions – Byerly Turk, Darley Arabian and Godolphin Arabian – imported into Britain between 1688 and 1730 were the founding fathers of modern horse racing, with nearly every racehorse able to be traced back to them through breeding records that have been kept meticulously through to the present day.

There are five Classic races in Britain, of which the Derby, first run in 1780, is the most famous. The four other Classics – all for three-year-old horses – are the 1,000 Guineas, the 2,000 Guineas, the Oaks and the St Leger.

Racing in Britain was only on the flat until the mid-19th century when races over obstacles (known as chases and hurdles), such as the Grand National, were introduced.

## A few facts and figures

From early 2007, there are 60 racecourses in Britain, of which 17 stage only flat racing, 24 stage only jump racing, and 19 stage both. Five courses stage all-weather flat racing (on an artificial non-grass surface), two of them under floodlights. Around 6 million people went racing in 2006, compared to 5.8 million in 2005; this slight decrease in 2005 is attributed largely to the closure of Ascot racecourse for redevelopment.

Prize money reached a total of just over £100 million in 2006. In 2007, 1,415 fixtures have been programmed, providing over 9,000 races. Racing and breeding support some 60,000 jobs, including the equivalent of one in eight agricultural workers, and 40,000 are employed in the betting industry, which relies on horse racing for over half of its profits.

## Racehorse ownership

There are presently over 9,000 active racehorse owners in Britain and overall some 40,000 people are involved through various types of co-ownership. There are around 14,800 horses in training, and between them they race around 80,000 times a year. Many people derive enormous pleasure from owning part or all of a racehorse but, although there are occasions when large profits can be made, these are rare and ownership should be viewed more as a hobby than an investment.

The annual cost of having a horse in training is approximately £17,000, not including the horse's purchase price, which is usually in five figures. Some horses do recover their costs in prize money, although the principal way to make money from a horse in training is to sell the animal on at a profit, either to race in Britain or abroad for another owner or to sell it as a stallion or broodmare prospect.

Every year there are owners who have not spent a fortune who end up hitting the jackpot and perhaps none more so in 2006 than retired solicitor Anthony Pakenham and his wife Victoria, whose colours were carried to victory in the Vodafone Derby at Epsom by Sir Percy.

The Pakenhams spent a modest £16,800 on Sir Percy – only their second racehorse – as a yearling at Tattersalls sales in Newmarket and he has earned them over £1 million in prize money. Sir Percy will carry on racing next year and is also now worth a seven-figure sum as a stallion prospect.

Fenland trainer Pam Sly purchased Speciosa from the Doncaster Bloodstock Breeze-Up Sale for £31,500 in the spring of 2005. After Speciosa won the Group 2 Owen Brown Rockfel Stakes as a two-year-old, her owners (Sly herself, her son

Michael and Dr Tom Davies) were approached and offered a reputed $1.1 million for their filly, which they refused, preferring to take their chance to live out their racing dreams (despite Pam Sly admitting that she had advised them to accept!). Patience paid off when the filly landed the 2006 Stan James 1,000 Guineas at Newmarket, providing Sly with her first Classic winner and making her the first woman trainer based in Britain to taste victory in the historic race.

# Racehorse breeding

From the late 1700s a meticulous record of every thoroughbred horse has been kept in what is known as the General Stud Book. Weatherbys, a company based in Northamptonshire, has maintained that record. Using the General Stud Book, the pedigrees of every racehorse in Britain can be traced back to the three mentioned Arabian stallions imported into the country 300 years ago. The modern-day thoroughbred breeding industry is of course a vastly different affair from horse breeding in those days, turning over billions of pounds each year and utilizing the very best vets and consultants from around the world.

The thoroughbred breeding world has its own peculiar language, which can be confusing at first but is mostly based on common sense:

- Female horses, called fillies up to the age of four, become known as mares at the age of five onwards and are often referred to as broodmares when retired to be bred from.
- A male horse is a colt until he reaches five, when he is known as an entire horse when racing and a stallion if he retires to stand at stud. If a horse is castrated, he becomes a gelding.
- A colt from a successful family with some top racecourse performances to his name can become a very valuable stallion. Some major owners stand stallions at their own studs while other owners sell their colts to become stallion prospects.
- When a stallion has his sexual liaison with a broodmare it is known as a cover, and the covering season takes place from early February until July or August. Many stallions are now flown out to either Australia or New Zealand, where the covering season runs from August onwards, to maximize their earning potential.
- The gestation period for a broodmare is 11 months, and all thoroughbreds have an official birthday, for the sake of their racing age, of 1 January of the year they were born.
- A foal is a young horse in its first year, which becomes a yearling as a one-year-old. Most yearlings are put into training from September onwards and are educated to be ready for racing as two-year-olds.

The key breeders standing stallions in Britain are headed by the Maktoum family of Dubai, the country's biggest racehorse owners. Sheikh Mohammed, Dubai's ruler, runs Darley, a global breeding programme based in Newmarket. There are currently 18 stallions under the Darley banner in Britain. The cost of a cover, also known as a nomination, to those stallions ranges from £5,000 for Tobougg, whose first foals raced in 2006, to £40,000 for Green Desert and £35,000 for Singspiel, both world-renowned sires.

Green Desert is now 23 and covering a limited book of mares, but the 15-year-old Singspiel can be expected to be visited by around 140 mares, producing an annual income of £7 million. He could carry on covering for up to 10 years, and his fee – and popularity – will go up and down as his results vary on the racecourse.

Traditionally a covering fee would be paid in October when the mare was scanned in foal, but competition is high in the stallion business and studs such as Darley now offer deals where the fee is paid only once the resultant foal has been sold, giving those investing in bloodstock an extra edge.

Sheikh Mohammed's brother Hamdan also stands stallions at Shadwell Stud, while Prince Khalid Abdullah, a member of the Saudi royal family who breeds as Juddmonte, also bases a hugely successful breeding operation in Britain. Other major stallion farms are Cheveley Park Stud, owned by Hillsdown Holdings founder David Thompson and his wife Patricia, Lanwades Stud, the property of Swedish heiress Kirsten Rausing, the National Stud, formerly run by a government subsidiary and now owned by a charitable trust, and Whitsbury Manor Stud in Hampshire, established by the late bookmaker William Hill. There are other studs across the country that stand stallions and where owners can keep their mares; the cost is usually between £15 and £20 per day.

# The bloodstock sales

There are two main thoroughbred auction companies in Britain, Tattersalls in Newmarket and South Yorkshire-based Doncaster Bloodstock Sales.

Tattersalls – founded in Knightsbridge in 1776 – is the oldest and most famous equine auction company in the world. The privately owned firm operates on a 50-acre site at Newmarket in Suffolk, racing's 'headquarters'. Chaired by Irishman Edmond Mahony, Tattersalls employs a full-time staff of 45, drafting in a large number of part-timers for its six annual sales.

Bloodstock sales in Britain still sell in guineas (£1.05), and the sales company takes an entry fee for each auction and charges a vendor 5 per cent of the sale price for every horse sold. In 2006, Tattersalls turned over £245 million.

Doncaster Bloodstock Sales, founded just over 40 years ago, is another privately owned company, which actually operates from offices at Hawick in the Scottish Borders. It turned over nearly £78 million in 2006.

Horses begin racing at two, and in April both Doncaster and Tattersalls stage sales of ready-to-race two-year-olds, which do a workout before coming up for sale. These sales are known as the breeze-up sales. For the first time in 2006, Tattersalls staged an additional sale in May.

But most flat horses are sold as yearlings, and Doncaster stages the first British yearling sale at the end of August, with Tattersalls major yearling sales following on a month later. The price of a yearling varies massively, anywhere from £840, the minimum bid at the cheaper sales, to £4.83 million, the record price at Tattersalls.

In November and December both venues stage auctions of foals (animals born that year), which are often bought by investors to sell on the following year. The companies both sell fillies and breeding stock, and the December sale at Tattersalls attracts buyers from every corner of the world looking to enhance their bloodstock portfolios.

There are also opportunities to buy older, tested horses throughout the year, as detailed in Table 6.6.1. There are several other mixed sales throughout the year, and details can be found at www.tattersalls.com or www.dbsauctions.com.

## Investing in bloodstock

While only the very lucky can hope to profit from racehorse ownership, there are many people who can and do make money by trading in bloodstock.

Jimmy George, Marketing Director at Tattersalls, explains:

> There are a number of different ways of investing in bloodstock but – except at the top level – buying a horse to race has to be viewed in sporting terms. There are a lot of investment opportunities within the bloodstock business, though. And if you're looking at it as an investment opportunity, then your best bet is to get into pinhooking.

'Pinhooking' is another term peculiar to the racing world and describes buying a horse, be it a foal, yearling or mare, to resell at a future date.

'Contact a bloodstock agent and discuss plans with them, think of your budget, what you want to pinhook – foals to yearlings, yearlings to two-year-olds in training, fillies to broodmares or buying a mare and selling the foals from her', adds George.

Bloodstock agents will advise you at the sales and usually charge a commission of 5 per cent of the purchase price for their services. Most novice investors continue to use the advice of an agent, stud owner or similar expert to advise on the best course of action with the purchase, whether of a foal, yearling or mare. If possible, the best

**Table 6.6.1**  Major bloodstock sales in Britain

| Sale | Category | Time |
|---|---|---|
| Doncaster Breeze-Up | Ready-to-race two-year-olds | April |
| Tattersalls Craven Breeze-Up | Ready-to-race two-year-olds | April |
| Tattersalls Guineas Breeze-Up | Ready-to-race two-year-olds | May |
| Doncaster Spring | Jumpers | May |
| Doncaster St Leger Sale 1 | Yearlings | Late August |
| Doncaster St Leger Sale 2 | Yearlings | September |
| Tattersalls October | Yearlings | October |
| Doncaster October | Yearlings | October |
| Tattersalls Horses in Training | Tested racehorses | October |
| Doncaster November | Mixed | November |
| Tattersalls December | Mares, foals and yearlings | November/December |

way to select an agent or adviser is through personal recommendation, although the sales companies and British Horseracing Board can provide some guidance.

For those looking to invest in foals, one of the safer ways is to be involved in a syndicate that has several animals.

According to bloodstock agent David Redvers, who has run a successful pinhooking syndicate from his Gloucestershire-based Tweenhills Stud for the past four years:

> The biggest problem with investing in bloodstock is that you can buy a foal for £100,000 who's worth £1,000 the next day. But if you've got a share in 20 the chances are you'll make a profit overall if you've done your job right. Even if one goes wrong, another will go dramatically right to make up for it. You're effectively spreading the risk through your portfolio.

Redvers's latest syndicate, like several others, takes advantage of the Enterprise Investment Scheme, offering investors tax breaks if they keep their money in for three years. The new partnership purchased nearly 30 foals in 2006 to resell this year, and there are 50 shares costing £10,000 each. Redvers adds:

> We made a 30 per cent net profit on the horses we had to sell in 2006, which was our best year yet, and despite having no huge hits several made 200 per cent profits. We've made between 15 and 25 per cent in the five years we've been doing it. We haven't lost money yet, but bloodstock is a high-risk investment; I make no bones about that. But equally it can be very rewarding and fun. People can actually see their stock walking around the paddock, and you can watch the stallion's progeny race and know it will affect your investment.
>
> Our biggest shareholder has seven shares, and a lot are City people keen to dip their toe into the water and have a taste of the bloodstock business in a relatively safe environment. We can't guarantee it but so far it's been a far better return than you'd get in the bank.

Redvers calculates that £6,000 in costs is incurred from the time a foal is purchased to its resale date, and he charges 2.5 per cent commission on purchase price, largely to cover expenses, and 15 per cent of the net profit.

Another form of investment is to buy a broodmare either to breed from commercially or, as with a foal or yearling, to resell. There are many instances of buying a mare in foal and the purchaser reselling the foal to more than cover the initial purchase price.

At the top end of the market, few have fared better than Lord Lloyd Webber, who with his wife Madeleine established Watership Down Stud at their Berkshire home in the early 1990s. Several of the select band of mare purchases have proved real cash cows for the stud. The first foals sold by the Lloyd Webbers out of Darara, who was bought for around £460,000 in 1994, each made £525,000 as yearlings, while the next one to be offered at Tattersalls hit the jackpot when making £3.57 million. Silver Lane, a mare who cost around £500,000, has produced youngsters that realized £2.31 million, £410,000, £420,000, £190,000 and £160,000 when selling.

Meanwhile, City headhunter Jim Furlong, who has a small inexpensive band of broodmares, is another to have landed a notable coup with a mare purchase. In 1997 at the Tattersalls December Sale, Furlong paid £6,825 for a mare named Sumoto. In 1999, a colt she produced – Compton Admiral – won the Group 1 Coral-Eclipse, one of the summer's top races, and she was resold at the December Sale in 2000, when she realized a cool £966,000.

At the 2005 December Sale breeder Paul Thorman purchased a mare named Halland Park Lass for a partnership for just £12,600. Her son Dutch Art was subsequently one of the best two-year-olds to race in 2006, enhancing the family's value massively. The foal Halland Park Lass was carrying was sold for £294,000 in November 2006, and the mare herself realized £745,500, providing a healthy profit for the breeding partnership in less than a year.

'It was a fluke set of circumstances that led us to buy the mare. We had a budget and she was a correct mare from a speedy family with an attractive cover, but to claim we said "Wow, we've got to have her" would be a lie', admitted Thorman. 'It's a once-in-a-lifetime thing really.'

These are just a few of the examples that show that, with good advice and plenty of luck, investing in bloodstock – while certainly not without risk – can yield bumper returns.

## Essential websites for anyone interested in racehorse ownership and breeding

■ www.welcometoracehorseownership.co.uk
■ Owning and Breeding section of www.britishhorseracing.com

# Engaged philanthropy

*Stefan Velvick, Charities Aid Foundation*

The UK is a generous nation. Almost 70 per cent of people in the UK give to charity on a regular basis and a growing number ensure their gifts are tax-efficient too. Higher-rate taxpayers gave a colossal £1 billion tax-efficiently to charity in 2004/05. And that included tax reliefs worth a staggering £210 million.

The landscape of charitable giving in the UK has changed dramatically. Since the government introduced a raft of new tax incentives in 2000, the UK has enjoyed one of the most liberal tax environments for charitable giving in the world.

But now there's evidence to suggest that, as well as giving tax-efficiently, people want to feel more engaged with the charities and causes they support. They want to develop a long-term relationship with the charities and see for themselves the difference their support is making. This emerging trend even has a name: engaged philanthropy.

The desire for engaged philanthropy is particularly marked among those who can commit significant cash or resources to the causes that matter to them. Billionaires like Bill Gates and Warren Buffett are taking extraordinary care over how they spend their charitable dollars. Equally, many affluent people appear no longer satisfied with making one-off donations to household-name charities. They too want to engage with charities and measure the impact of their giving.

We at the Charities Aid Foundation (CAF) have the skills and expertise to help you get actively involved with the charities that matter to you. Our advice and specialist financial services have been designed with one aim in mind – to put you in control of your giving. And experience has shown us that the best place to start is to encourage you to be clear about what it is you want your support to achieve.

# Business head. Charitable heart.

Deciding to give money to good causes is a decision that comes from the heart. But to really make a difference you need to engage your business head too.

That's where we come in. Our specialist services have been designed with one aim in mind – to put you in control of your giving. And we know that your charitable goals are best achieved through informed decisions.

It pays to consult your head before you follow your heart.

Call us today on **01732 520 028** to learn more or visit **www.cafonline.org/iod**

Charities Aid Foundation
*Registered charity number 268369*

0429A/0207

■■■committed to effective giving

# Developing your giving strategy

## Defining aims and objectives

What are the causes that matter to you? Who do you want to help? What do you hope to achieve? By talking to you about your charitable interests, we can help you clarify your aims and objectives and suggest a strategy to help you achieve them.

## Designing your portfolio

Do you want to support a range of causes or focus on a single project? We can create a giving portfolio for you that suits your needs and can be regularly reviewed to ensure it is still making a difference to the causes that matter to you.

## Refining your strategy

Philanthropy works best when you have a clear and costed strategy for achieving your goals. This means applying business thinking to your philanthropy. We can work with you to design a personal giving plan to help you to be strategic in your choice of causes.

## Measuring your impact

It's natural to be concerned about how much of your gift will ultimately reach the people and projects that you wish to support. Using benchmarks, we can assess the impact of each donation you make and report on what your support has achieved.

## Supporting your community

If you want to support people or projects close to home, we can help you identify local charities working in your local area. Whether that's by finding a local project that matches your interests or by identifying an organization with a track record of delivering results, we can design the right solution for you.

## Providing international solutions

If you want to support international projects, you may want to consider donating to organizations based overseas. But how can you discover which overseas charities are making a real difference?

As an international organization, CAF is ideally placed to advise you on the impact of your international giving. With offices in seven countries and projects in six continents, we can provide you with quality information and research on charities' work across the world.

## Making a lasting impact

If you want to ensure your philanthropy makes a real difference, you may want to commit to supporting your portfolio of charities for a set number of years. We can help you to structure and manage your giving over an agreed period to ensure your philanthropy has a lasting impact.

## Taking advantage of the tax breaks

To help you adopt a planned and informed approach to your giving, you need to be aware of the available tax incentives for charitable gifts.

### Gift Aid

Make sure every gift you make to charity is a Gift Aid donation. Using Gift Aid means the charity will receive an extra 28 per cent.

When you make a Gift Aid donation to charity, it is treated as net, ie as though tax has been deducted. For example, if you give £100, tax can be reclaimed and added to your donation, making it worth £128 to the charity. Tables 6.7.1 and 6.7.2 show how the tax breaks work out in the case of basic-rate and higher-rate taxpayers.

### Who can use Gift Aid?

Anyone who has paid enough income tax or capital gains tax in the current financial year to cover the amount reclaimed by the charity can use Gift Aid. So if you give £100 you need to have paid at least £28 in income tax or capital gains tax.

### How does it work?

You need to complete a simple declaration for the charity. This can be done in writing, over the phone or online. The declaration can apply to all past donations you have made (since April 2000) and to all future donations you make.

**Table 6.7.1**  Basic-rate taxpayer

| | |
|---|---|
| Your donation to charity | £1,000 |
| Amount reclaimed by charity from HM Revenue and Customs | £280 |
| Total amount received by charity | £1,280 |
| Cost to you to give £1,280 | £1,000 |

**Table 6.7.2**  Higher-rate taxpayer

| | |
|---|---|
| Your donation to charity | £1,000 |
| Amount reclaimed by charity from HM Revenue and Customs | £280 |
| Total amount reclaimed by donor in tax return | £230 |
| Cost to you to give £1,280 | £770 |

# Where's the best place to invest £2,187?

## In a future for Orbert

**£2,187 could buy all the bricks needed for one classroom in the Democratic Republic of Congo. This will help build the hopes and dreams of a child like Orbert.**

Away from the financial markets you might normally consider, in countries like the Democratic Republic of Congo, investing £2,187 into building materials could generate outstanding returns.

This great opportunity is brought to you by ActionAid – one of the UK's largest development charities dedicated to empowering poor people around the world to build better lives for themselves. And while investing won't benefit you financially, it will benefit children like Orbert whose lives have been devastated by war, violence and disaster.

Fighting in their hometown forced Orbert's family to flee to Goma. But a volcano erupted, destroying virtually everything in its path. Today, surviving under wood and tattered plastic, Orbert has little hope for the future.

**Just one additional year of schooling can raise a child's future income by as much as 20%.**

We believe an education is the best chance children have to find employment and work their way out of poverty. And in areas so badly hit by disaster an exceptional response is required. That is why we have drawn up plans for new classrooms throughout the region.

But children won't be the only beneficiaries. Poor people will be employed to construct classrooms. Parents will be involved in their management. And school gardens will be used to grow food to help feed everyone.

This is how highly rewarding your £2,187 could be for poor children and communities – if you choose to invest it. Please do.

**To make a donation or to find out how you could help change lives, please call Dawn Wyatt on 01460 23 8000 or email changinglives@actionaid.org.uk Alternatively, visit www.actionaid.org.uk for more details on where and how we work.**

This is just one of ActionAid's vital projects. Your investment will go where the need is greatest and from time to time we will send you details on the huge difference you are making.
Photo: Emma Scullion/ActionAid

ActionAid is a registered charity no. 274467

# All you need to know about lifetime investments

**As one of the UK's largest development charities, with 35 years of experience in changing lives, ActionAid is in a position to offer you a unique investment opportunity.**

Although we guarantee you a significant return on your money, not one penny will find its way to you. Instead, your investment will help us tackle the causes of poverty and shape the long-term future of some of the world's poorest people.

From 1972 to the present day, ActionAid has been responsible for thousands of life-saving and life-changing projects worldwide. The success of each and every one of these is based on empowering poor communities to access their basic rights and change their own lives for the better.

**Your reward for investing with us today is the knowledge that you are funding projects that will help communities like Orbert's to forge a brighter tomorrow.**

Orbert is desperate for an education. Even at his young age, he knows it could change his life for the better. However, he lives in Goma, in the Democratic Republic of Congo, a country with a troubled history. War, violence and disasters have all played a part in destroying lives there. The country may now be at peace but people are still struggling to survive.

Orbert and his family fled to Goma to escape fierce fighting in their hometown. Here, in relative safety, they planned to begin their lives again. However, they had been settled just a few months when a nearby volcano erupted without warning, pouring lava into the town, destroying virtually everything in its path – shops, schools and their home.

*Poor children stand on hardened lava in front of a building severely damaged by the eruption in Goma.*

**In order to rebuild communities and give them the chance of a bright, independent future, we need to offer the people of Goma long-term support.**

We believe an education is the best chance children have to find employment and work their way out of poverty. And in areas so badly hit by disaster an exceptional response is required. That is why we have drawn up plans for new classrooms throughout the region.

**£2,187 could provide all the bricks needed for one classroom in the Democratic Republic of Congo.**

An investment in building materials will do more than create the next generation of teachers, doctors and entrepreneurs, who can play a positive role in helping their communities break out of the cycle of poverty. It will also help transform a whole community. People in poor villages will be employed to construct the classroom. Parents will be involved in its management. Even the school gardens will be used to grow food to help feed the families of the children who attend.

**Just one additional year of schooling can raise a child's future income by as much as 20%.**

Once established, these simple classrooms will be filled with children sitting happily at their desks listening attentively to every word their teacher utters. They will not want to miss a moment of the education that will change their lives for the better.

**ActionAid do more than just tackle the effects of poverty.**

This year we are celebrating 35 years of fighting poverty. We are currently working in over 40 countries and last year helped over 13 million people. Our aim is to empower poor people to access their basic rights. For example, clean water, healthcare and an education. We also help tackle the causes of poverty by challenging unfair policies that keep people poor and by putting pressure on governments to keep their promise of free education to all children.

The school building project in the Democratic Republic of Congo is just one of the many projects that ActionAid need help to fund.

**Are you interested in an investment of a lifetime?**

ActionAid is looking for people to invest in poor children's futures. This commitment may never make it into your portfolio or leave you with outstanding financial returns. However, funding projects in the world's poorest countries and changing lives can be the most fulfilling reward of all.

Your investment will go where the need is greatest and from time to time we will send you details on the huge difference you are making.

*If you think you can make a difference with an investment and would like to find out more about ActionAid's work, please call Dawn Wyatt on 01460 238000, email changinglives@actionaid.org or visit www.actionaid.org.uk*

*Photo:* Emma Sculliion/ActionAid.

## What can I receive in return for a Gift Aid donation?

You cannot use Gift Aid to pay for goods or services, eg school fees. However, Gift Aid can be used to pay certain charitable subscriptions and membership fees, eg for heritage charities.

If you are a higher-rate taxpayer you can claim the difference between the basic rate and higher rate as a personal benefit or give it to charity on your annual tax return.

## How can I plan my giving more effectively?

There are several ways CAF can help you plan your giving. We offer a number of financial services that help you tailor your giving to your circumstances.

### CAF Charity Account

The CAF Charity Account is a brilliantly simple way to plan your giving throughout the year. It works like a current account, but it's exclusively for your charitable giving. By ensuring that you always have a pool of funds to draw from, your Charity Account enables you to respond to emergency appeals as well as provide regular support to a portfolio of your favourite charities.

For every pound you pay into your Charity Account, we will reclaim the tax and add it to your balance. Charities don't always find it cost-effective to reclaim Gift Aid on every donation, but with the Charity Account you can rest assured that every penny you give is tax-efficient.

Other benefits of using a CAF Charity Account include:

■ You can make anonymous donations.
■ You can give to charities based overseas.
■ You only need to make one Gift Aid declaration.

### Payroll giving

If your employer offers payroll giving, this is one of the simplest ways to make regular tax-efficient donations. Money is simply taken from your gross salary (before tax is deducted) and passed on to your chosen charities. This makes it especially attractive for higher-rate taxpayers, as Table 6.7.3 demonstrates.

If you like to have the option to change the charities you support and respond to emergency appeals, you can fund a CAF Charity Account exclusively from your pay through Give As You Earn, giving you the flexibility to give as much as you wish to any charity you choose. (Please note that you can only give to UK based charities.)

**Table 6.7.3** Payroll giving

| | |
|---|---|
| Your monthly pledge | £1,000 |
| Cost to basic-rate taxpayer (22%) | £780 |
| Cost to higher-rate taxpayer (40%) | £600 |

## Charitable trust

A charitable trust or foundation is a legal organization that can be set up by anyone who has decided that they want to set aside some of their assets or income for charitable causes. Setting up your own trust provides a framework for planning your charitable giving in a systematic and thoughtful way.

Normally you would need to appoint your own trustees and pay up to £1,500 plus VAT in legal fees and yearly accountant fees of up to £1,000 plus VAT.[1] However, if you set up a CAF Charitable Trust you will not need to appoint your own trustees or employ the services of a solicitor or accountant. A CAF Trust allows you to donate a sum upwards of £10,000, which will form an invested fund. You will then be free to give away the income (and the capital if you choose) to any charity of your choice. You can also share the grant-making decisions with your partner or family members.

---

David Pitt-Watson, Chief Executive of Hermes Focus Asset Management, is an enthusiastic advocate of the CAF Trust. He uses his trust to support a wide range of charities. David said:

I wanted the flexibility to give to a range of charities in an enduring way. The advantage of a CAF Trust is that it's so easy. You can do something with it now, or you can park it during a busy time – you don't have to worry about it. The CAF Trust was recommended to me, and I would absolutely recommend it to others. It's a great system.

---

## Giving shares

When people think about supporting charity they usually think of giving cash. But a gift of stocks and shares can be an even more effective way of benefiting the causes you care about.

A gift of shares has the advantage of a double tax benefit. All are exempt from capital gains tax, and you can reduce your income tax bill too providing the shares are quoted on a recognized stock exchange. For example, a higher-rate taxpayer giving shares valued at £1,000 could claim up to £400 income tax relief whilst also making a potential capital gains tax saving of up to £400 (if the holding is showing a loss, by gifting them to charity you will not be able to offset the loss against other gains).

Giving shares isn't the only way your shares could benefit your favourite charities. Selling shares to charity at less than their market value allows the charity to receive shares at a discount. You can then claim relief against your taxable income of the discount.

---

1. 'A guide to giving', www.PhilanthropyUK.org.

If you sell the shares at their original cost or less, the sales to charity will be free of capital gains tax. However, a liability may arise if the sale results in a profit to you.

Table 6.7.4 shows the tax savings related to a donor who has a taxable income of £100,000; the first option shows the position if the donor gives CAF some quoted shares (currently worth £50,000), and the second shows the position if the donor sells them to CAF for what they cost him or her – £10,000.

If you donate shares to CAF we will sell them and place the proceeds in your CAF Charity Account or CAF Charitable Trust. You may prefer to sell shares to CAF at less than their market value and claim relief against your taxable income on the discount.

**Table 6.7.4** Giving and selling shares to CAF

| | Giving Shares | Selling Shares |
|---|---|---|
| Proceeds | 0 | £10,000 |
| Capital gains tax | 0 | 0 |
| Income tax relief at 40% | £20,000 | £16,000 |
| Cash flow | £20,000 | £26,000 |
| CAF received | £50,000 | £40,000 |

## Gifts of land or art work

If you wish to give land, property or works of art, CAF can sell them and place the proceeds in your CAF Charity Account or CAF Trust. This may allow you to avoid capital gains tax and to obtain relief from income tax (the latter is only available on gifts of land and not art).

## Leaving money to charity in your will

You can leave money or property to charity by making provision for this in your will. This is known as a legacy or bequest. You may leave a specified sum of money to charity or leave the residue of your estate – that is the amount that is left once the executors have paid all the necessary outgoings and other legacies or bequests.

Normally, once you have written your will you can't change the charities you wish to leave money to without contacting your solicitor to make a deed of amendment. But with a CAF Legacy Account you can change the charities you wish to support at any time during your lifetime, without changing your will.

## Social investment

As well as giving money away, you may be interested in becoming a social investor. Venturesome, our social investment initiative, provides smaller charities with loans and investments when they can't access mainstream funding. In contrast to a one-off gift, when you make a gift through Venturesome we aim to recycle it three to four times. This offers you a unique opportunity to make your money work harder to achieve a social impact.

## Balancing your commitments

As well as cash, you may want to give your time and share your skills with your favourite charities too. We can source volunteering and mentoring opportunities that match your skill set. That way, not only will your financial support achieve the maximum impact, but your time will be used to best effect too.

## Conclusion

So how do you become an engaged philanthropist? How do you go from making the occasional one-off donation to adopting a more committed and engaged approach?

■ *Commit to a timetable.* Plan your giving over a longer timescale. At CAF we offer a range of giving solutions specially designed to help you to start seeing giving as a permanent fixture in your life.
■ *Structure your gift.* How do you want to give? Do you want to provide regular support or donate a capital sum? Would you prefer to release your donations in phases? Do you want to include a loan as part of your gift? Or offer your skills and expertise to the project?
■ *Make your giving tax-efficient.* Plan your giving tax-efficiently to increase its value. At CAF we offer a range of solutions to help you take advantage of the available tax incentives for charitable giving.
■ *Choose carefully.* Before jumping in with both feet, think carefully about what you want your giving to achieve. Create criteria of things that matter to you. Then develop a strategy that can help you make a difference to the people and projects you wish to support.
■ *Know your impact.* Once you know what your charitable goals are and have developed a strategy to achieve them, you can measure the impact of your giving. We at CAF can use benchmarks that produce tangible evidence of what your giving has achieved.

For further information on how to plan your giving, call Stefan Velvick on 01732 520338 or visit www.cafonline.org/giving.

The following organizations are all potential beneficiaries of philanthropy and charitable giving. As a special sub-section to the *Engaged Philanthropy* chapter, we are including a series of messages from these organizations, and hope that readers of *The Handbook of Personal Wealth Management* will find this information resource to be invaluable when planning their own philanthropic activity. Contributors include:

■ African Children's Educational Trust
■ Age Care
■ Age Concern England

- Amnesty International
- Battersea Dogs & Cats Home
- Cats Protection
- Diabetes Research & Wellness Foundation
- Global Fund for Children
- Greater London Forum for Older People
- Habitat for Humanity
- Harris HospisCare
- Marie Curie Cancer Care
- Meningitis Research Foundation
- NSPCC
- People's Trust for Endangered Species
- Retraining of Racehorses
- Royal Mencap Society
- The Samaritans
- Save the Children
- SSAFA
- The British Library
- UNICEF UK
- YMCA

# AFRICAN CHILDREN'S EDUCATIONAL TRUST

supporting vulnerable children through education

## THE SMALL CHARITY WITH THE BIG IMPACT

"A-CET has change my life and encouraged me that I'll have a bright future. I understand that if I make the effort, nothing is impossible"

– Ethiopian Grande 9 Mahider Aweke

## Contact: David Stables at dgs@a-cet.org
## ☎: 0800-652-9475 or visit www.a-cet.org

Registered Charity 1066869 (England and Wales)

---

## African Children's Educational Trust (A-CET)

- A-CET is changing lives through educational support to needy young Africans. Our aim is to alleviate the poverty of vulnerable African children, generally orphans and/or disabled – through long-term self sustaining educational initiatives.

- A-CET is run by dedicated, experienced professional volunteers in UK. We have few overheads, no fund raising or professional consultancy fees. 92% of your donations going directly to our children or rural elementary school projects.

- Our overseas work is coordinated and selected through well-established local protocols. Projects are community-led and managed through our Ethiopian partner NGO (EYES) – staffed by ex A-CET students.

- Our decades of knowledge and practical working experience in Africa has given us a total belief in and dedication to what we are doing and drives our work forward.

- Direct targeted support at community-level has terrific impact. Our programmes, principally in Ethiopia, are now giving thousands of youngsters hope through improved access to better education.

- From kindergarten to our current research student at Cambridge is proof that we, with your help can make a difference. A CET is effective, efficient and transparent.

## Be different

For every 100 people, only four put a charity in their Will. Even fewer remember the needs of older people. Remember the most forgotten.

**Put Age Concern in your Will.**

For more information on putting Age Concern in your Will, please ask your solicitor for a FREE copy of our magazine *Will to Change*, or call Joel Dunster on: 020 8765 7527

**Age Concern England**
The National Council on Ageing
Room PWM07, Astral House,
1268 London Road,
London SW16 4ER

Email: legacyteam@ace.org.uk
Web: www.ageconcern.org.uk

Age Concern England

Registered Charity No. 261794

---

## Age Concern England

Age Concern is the UK's largest organisation working for and with older people, our aim is to help all older people to get more out of later life.

Locally, Age Concerns provide vital services such as lunch clubs, day centres and home visiting that daily help thousands of older people, many in desperate need, across the country.

Nationally, we strive to influence public opinion and government policy on important issues such as pensions and age discrimination. We also provide specialist information and advice.

Donations in Wills are vitally important to Age Concern. In recent times over a third of the money Age Concern has received from supporters has come from legacies. We urgently need this money to help older people who turn to us – now and well into the future.

For more information about putting Age Concern in your Will please ask your solicitor for a FREE copy of our magazine *Will to Change* or contact us using the details below.

**Age Concern England**, The National Council on Ageing
Room PWM07, Astral House,
1268 London Road, London SW16 4ER
Tel: **020 8765 7527**
Fax: **020 8765 7619**
Email: **legacyteam@ace.org.uk**
Web: **www.ageconcern.org.uk**
Registered Charity No. 261794

**IN 1961 PETER BENENSON CHANGED THE WORLD**

NOW IT'S YOUR TURN

# By investing in the
# **Peter Benenson Memorial Fund,**
## you can change the world

In 1961 a British lawyer by the name of Peter Benenson published an article in The Observer newspaper. It was entitled 'The Forgotten Prisoners' and its publication led to the birth of the world's most influential human rights organisation: Amnesty International.

Peter had been outraged by the case of two Portuguese students who had been imprisoned for drinking a toast to liberty. In his article he wrote about six more individuals in different countries, all of whom had been imprisoned and persecuted

purely because of their peacefully held beliefs. Coining a new phrase, he described them as 'prisoners of conscience' and invited ordinary members of the public to join him in campaigning for the release of these and all other such prisoners.

The response was overwhelming. It was as if people worldwide were waiting for just such a signal. Newspapers in over a dozen countries picked up on Peter's appeal and over a thousand responses poured in.

**In one moment, Peter Benenson had opened a whole new chapter in the history of human rights.**

Following the article's publication, all six of the featured men regained their freedom. Since then Amnesty International has become the world's largest independent human rights organisation with more then 1.8 million members and supporters in 150 countries and territories around the world.

Today Amnesty International continues to campaign on behalf of prisoners of conscience. But now its influence goes even further. It has played a major part, for example, in establishing the International Criminal Court where those accused of genocide, crimes against humanity and war crimes can be brought to justice. Amnesty's campaign for better arms control has helped to persuade the UN to begin work on an International Arms Trade Treaty which could save millions of lives by preventing irresponsible arms transfers. And its work to Stop Violence Against Women, which has included targeting sex trafficking, has recently seen the UK government agree to sign the European Convention Against Trafficking.

**The Peter Benenson Memorial Fund has been set up to honour Peter, and to help keep his vision alive.**

Peter Benenson died in February 2005. To commemorate its founder, and to ensure that the work he began continues long into the future, Amnesty International has recently launched The Peter Benenson Memorial Fund.

The purpose of the Fund, not surprisingly, is to raise money – money that can be used to keep Peter's vision of a fairer world alive. As with all charitable giving, there are a number of ways in which you can support the Fund from a one off donation to making a gift of bonds, stocks or shares. That means that supporting the Fund offers the tax relief benefits that are outlined in the 'Engaged Philanthropy' chapter in this book.

**But the real return you get with this Fund isn't about money. It's about something more valuable than that.**
By supporting the Fund, you are investing in truth, fairness and justice – the basic principles that underpin all of our human rights. And in so doing, you are helping to protect real individual people. They are people you may never meet, in countries you may never visit. But your support could help to save them from the most hideous suffering and abuse.

Peter Benenson's original idea – the idea that by working together, one group of people can protect another group of people from abuse – has been proven to work. In just the last few months a number of cases of prisoners have been freed including Helen Berhane in Eritrea and Jennifer Latheef in the Maldives. Amnesty International does not claim credit when a prisoner is released, when death sentences are commuted or when a government changes its laws and practices. However, former prisoners often say that international pressure secured their freedom and saved their lives. Jennifer, whose only crime was to take part in a peaceful demonstration, has said:
'I am in no doubt that I am only free today thanks to the persistence of Amnesty in bringing my case to the attention of the Maldivian government…I am living proof of what your support can achieve.'

If you'd like more information about the Peter Benenson Memorial Fund, you can contact Robert McCarthy of the Major Donor Team at **Robert.McCarthy@amnesty.org.uk** or on **020 7033 1656**.

The Peter Benenson Memorial Fund
Amnesty International UK Section Charitable Trust
17-25 New Inn Yard
London EC2A 3EA
Registered charity no. 1051681
**www.amnesty.org.uk**

# INVEST IN AMNESTY INTERNATIONAL
# PROTECT THE HUMAN

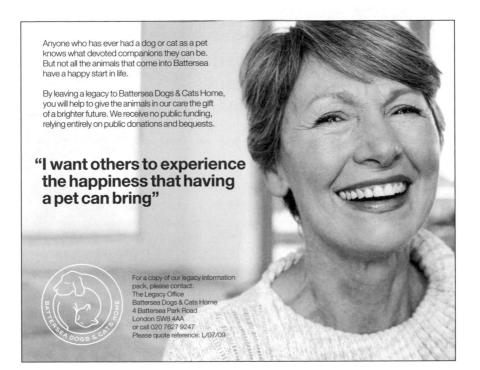

Anyone who has ever had a dog or cat as a pet knows what devoted companions they can be. But not all the animals that come into Battersea have a happy start in life.

By leaving a legacy to Battersea Dogs & Cats Home, you will help to give the animals in our care the gift of a brighter future. We receive no public funding, relying entirely on public donations and bequests.

## "I want others to experience the happiness that having a pet can bring"

For a copy of our legacy information pack, please contact:
The Legacy Office
Battersea Dogs & Cats Home
4 Battersea Park Road
London SW8 4AA
or call 020 7627 9247
Please quote reference: L/07/09

Battersea Dogs & Cats Home was founded in 1860, and since then we've cared for over three million canine and feline waifs and strays. Our aims are to rescue lost and abandoned dogs and cats, reunite them with their owners through the Lost Dogs and Cats Line in London, rehabilitate any that need extra help and rehome the ones that are left behind into loving and permanent new homes.

Last year we cared for over 12,000 dogs and cats, brought in as strays from London's streets or given to us by owners unable – or unwilling – to care for them any more. There is no time limit on how long a dog or cat can stay with us, but it costs over £900 for each animal's stay, no matter how long or short it is. We depend totally on the financial generosity of our supporters. Find out more at **www.dogshome.org**

## THE GLOBAL FUND FOR
# Children
## UK TRUST

Our strategic investments in innovative grassroots organisations, books, films, and photography improve the lives of young people all over the world. More than 1 million children and youth in 64 countries have benefited from our unique model of venture philanthropy.

- Awarded four stars, the highest rank, by Charity Navigator

- Registered as a charity in the United Kingdom and in the United States

**For more information, contact:**

The Global Fund for Children UK Trust
c/o Bates Wells & Braithwaite
2-6 Cannon Street, London EC4M 6YH

E: uktrust@globalfundforchildren.org
T: 001-202-331-9003

www.globalfundforchildren.eu *or* www.globalfundforchildren.org

---

S ince 1997, more than 1 million children and youth in 64 countries have benefited from our unique model of venture philanthropy. We improve young people's lives by strategically investing in innovative grassroots organisations working in four portfolios: learning, enterprise, safety, and healthy minds and bodies. We also invest in books, films, and photography to advance the dignity of young people worldwide.

## THE GLOBAL FUND FOR
# Children
## UK TRUST

www.globalfundforchildren.eu
E: uktrust@globalfundforchildren.org
T: 001-202-331-9003

# Habitat for Humanity – Investing in the future

A gift to Habitat for Humanity could be the most important investment you ever make.

One in three people around the world today are living in severe need of decent housing.

Poverty housing is dangerous and demeaning. It keeps the poor, poor and denies them the opportunity of working themselves towards a better life.

Since 1976 Habitat for Humanity has been building homes in partnership with people in need in 92 countries around the world. In that time we have built over 230,000 homes and helped one and a half million people to change the way they live forever.

The average cost of a Habitat for Humanity home in the developing world is £1,235 – a small investment considering the impact it will have on a family suffering appalling poverty.

Please, add Habitat for Humanity to your investment portfolio today by making a gift to our worldwide building programme – the return will be immense for another family in need of a simple, decent home.

"The Day Hospice is my lifeline...everybody is so kind and caring and there is always somebody to talk to if I need advice"

Harris HospisCare provides clinical home care, day care, outpatient, lymphoedema and hospital services to those people requiring palliative care across the London Borough of Bromley, 24 hours a day, 7 days a week, 365 days a year

**More information from the website www.harrishospiscare.org.uk**

# Harris HospisCare

**caring across Bromley**

Caritas House Tregony Road
Orpington Kent BR6 9XA
Tel: 01689 825755 Fax: 01689 892999
email: fundraising@harrishospiscare.org.uk

Registered Charity No. 1003903

# Harris HospisCare
## caring across Bromley

### Expertise, caring and support

Harris HospisCare is an independent charity which provides care, free of charge, for people living with life threatening illness in the London Borough of Bromley.

We provide clinical home care, day care, outpatient, lymphoedema and hospital services to those requiring palliative care across the London Borough of Bromley, 24 hours a day, 7 days a week, 365 days a year.

Our specialist team of doctors, nurses, social workers, counsellors, complementary therapists and physiotherapists provide a holistic service, offering physical, social and spiritual support to those facing life-threatening illness.

We work hard particularly to support patients in their own home which, for the majority, is where they wish to be cared for.

The care we offer encompasses not just the care of the patient, but extends to their family and friends, giving support and understanding to all those affected.

### Harris Day Hospice

One of the ways in which we support patients and carers is through the work of our Day Hospice. This unit aims to improve quality of life in a secure, comfortable and controlled environment. The Harris Day Hospice provides the opportunity for both social and therapeutic activity, medical treatment and complementary therapies. Through our creative work we help patients to manage their anxiety as well as providing opportunities to explore their thoughts and feelings. This facility can also offer carers a welcome respite from the demanding responsibility of looking after their loved one.

### Home Care

Harris HospisCare provides a 24 hour, 7 day a week on-call service for our patients and their carers, working with local GP's and District Nurses to help families care for their loved ones in familiar surroundings where they will feel most comfortable.

### Hospital Palliative Care

During the course of treatment some patients will be admitted to hospital. Harris HospisCare provides a professional palliative care service to the Princess Royal University Hospital advising, educating and supporting hospital staff regarding symptom control, palliative care and dealing with bereavement.

## Lymphoedema Service

Lymphoedema is a chronic swelling caused by a build up of lymphatic fluid under the skin. This is often a result of infection, trauma, cancer, surgery or radiation. Although it is incurable, our specialist lymphoedema staff can do a lot to help manage and alleviate this unpleasant condition.

## Patient and Family Support

The onset of a serious illness often causes significant difficulties in a patient's life as they, their family and their friends struggle to come to terms with suddenly changed horizons. At Harris HospisCare we have a team of highly trained and experienced counsellors and social workers who support our patients and their families from first diagnosis and through the illness, and continuing afterwards to help with issues of bereavement when required.

## Bereavement Service

Even when you are well prepared, losing a loved one can turn your life upside down. Our Bereavement Services Co-ordinator, who is a qualified social worker and trained counsellor, together with his highly trained team of practitioners are on hand to provide sympathetic and timely assistance.

## The facts

Research suggests that the care we give will be needed more than ever in the future, as the number of families being affected by cancer rises to 1 in 2 (at present this figure is 1 in 3). Medical developments and research identify new treatments all the time, enabling people to live for longer, but ultimately we are likely to need more care.

## How can I help?

All our services are provided to patients free of charge – but the services still have to be paid for, largely through donations and fundraising activities. We need over £2.1 million each year to carry on caring across Bromley. Approximately £1.3 million of this is generated by voluntary contributions from individuals and organisations.

If you are an individual or an organisation you can help us by taking part in a fundraising event or by sending a donation.

Please contact fundraising@harrishospiscare.org.uk or call the fundraising team on: 01689 825755 to discuss how you can help.

If you would like to know about how leaving a gift to Harris HospisCare will help and what your money may be spent on, then please contact our Donor Development Fundraiser on: **01689 825755** or email **fundraising@harrishospiscare.org.uk**

More information is available from our website: **www.harrishospiscare.org.uk**

# Marie Curie Cancer Care

**What we do**

For more than 50 years, across the UK, Marie Curie Cancer Care has been caring for people affected by cancer and their families.

Cancer is the UK's biggest killer, claiming 423 lives every day.

Research has shown that most people dying of cancer would like to be cared for in he comfortable and familiar surroundings of their own home. However the majority of cancer deaths still occur in NHS hospitals.

At Marie Curie Cancer Care, we think people with cancer should be able to decide where they spend the last few weeks of their life. We think that where you die should be your choice.

So for those patients who would like to be cared for at home, the Marie Curie Nursing Service plays a vital role. Our nurses work through the day or night, usually for eight or nine hours at a time, to care for the patient and allow the family to get some well-earned rest.

As well as providing high-valued nursing care for the patient – free of charge – Marie Curie Nurses are also there to give emotional support and advice to the family.

Of course not everyone can or wants to be cared for at home, and that's why Marie Curie Cancer Care provides hospices in England, Scotland, Wales and Northern Ireland. All care in our hospices is totally free. Our hospices also offer day care facilities and home care visits so patients can continue living at home, with their families, for as long as they are able.

In addition to caring for cancer patients and their families, the charity is also researching the disease. Scientists at the world-renowned Marie Curie Research Institute are looking at the causes and treatments of cancer.

**Supporting Marie Curie Cancer Care**

Are you at a stage in your life where you are looking to the future?

Writing or making adjustments to your Will offers you peace of mind and ensures that the family, friends and organisations that you wish to benefit are remembered by you after you die, but have you ever considered including a charitable donation? The gifts that Marie Curie Cancer Care receives in Wills help ensure that we can carry out their vital work for many years to come, meeting the challenges of caring for terminally ill people with cancer.

Leaving a gift in your Will is simple, and your solicitor can advise you on the best ways to leave a gift that best suits your circumstances. Individuals can personally visit their solicitor and arrange for a gift to be written into their Will, or alternatively, a codicil can be requested from the charity and once completed attached to your current Will.

There are also tax advantages in writing a Will, as current Inheritance Tax legislation means that if you don't prepare properly, more of your estate than necessary may go to the taxman. A way that you can limit your estate's liability to Inheritance Tax is by including a donation to charity – this will be totally free of tax.

Now Marie Curie Cancer Care also offers individuals the choice of restricting their gift so that the particular area that they wish to support benefits from the gift. For instance; they could choose to restrict their gift to benefit home nursing in their local area or to the fantastic work their scientists carry out in the Marie Curie Research Institute.

All essential information on leaving a legacy and the benefits of donating can be found by visiting **www.mariecurie.org.uk/legacies** or by contacting a member of staff on freephone **0800 716 146**. Booklets can be requested or downloaded off the website.

Marie Curie Cancer Care greatly depends on legacies, as over a third of our voluntary income comes from this special way of giving. Gifts like yours ensure that our Nurses can continue to help hundreds of patients, families and carers today and long in to the future, providing more hours of practical nursing care to over half of all cancer patients in the UK who choose to die at home each year. Will you help us ensure that even more patients experience the best possible care with the choice to die at home?

# What will your legacy be?

Have you ever wondered what people will remember you for? Will it be your collection of novelty garden gnomes or the fact that you helped give terminally ill cancer patients the choice to die at home? Leaving a gift in your Will ensures our Marie Curie Nurses can provide high quality care, totally free, to patients and their families at home.

For your **FREE 'Gift for the future' booklet, please fill in your details below and send to the Legacy Team, Marie Curie Cancer Care, FREEPOST LON 15438, LONDON, SE1 7YY**
By entering your details you are giving Marie Curie Cancer Care consent to contact you.

Title_____ Initials_____ Surname_____

Address_____

_____

Postcode_____

Email_____

Charity Reg. No. 207994   K82

For more information call **0800 716 146** or visit **www.mariecurie.org.uk/legacies**

Marie Curie Cancer Care provides high quality nursing, totally free, to give terminally ill people the choice of dying at home supported by their families.

Marie Curie
Cancer Care

*Devoted to Life*

**Meningitis Research Foundation** is working towards a world free from meningitis and septicaemia – the blood poisoning form of the disease.

These devastating diseases claim the lives of more young children in the UK than any other infectious disease, and can kill in hours.

With your help, the Foundation can continue its vital work to defeat meningitis and septicaemia.

The charity has funded over £11 million of research into the prevention, detection, and treatment of these diseases. But there is still no vaccine to protect against Group B, the most common form in the UK.

The Foundation also works to raise awareness – distributing life saving information to GP surgeries, hospitals, schools and universities.

Sadly, there are many whose lives have already been affected by meningitis and septicaemia. People who are now living with after effects as devastating as brain damage, deafness and amputations. Others who have lost loved ones to the diseases. Through its **Free**fone 24 hour helpline – **080 8800 3344** – and befriending network, help and support is provided to anyone who needs it.

The Foundation relies on voluntary donations – particularly legacies – to continue our work. For more information call **01454 281814** or email **fundraising@meningitis.org**

# Caring for their future

**A will which includes a legacy to the NSPCC could save a child's life.**

It is no exaggeration to say that the gifts left to us by testators in their wills help to fund services that protect children from cruelty. It is only through the generosity of our supporters that we can help to make sure that all children are able to enjoy safe and happy childhoods.

**For further information, call the NSPCC legacy manager on: 020 7825 2505 or write to: NSPCC, Legacy manager, Weston House, 42 Curtain Road, London EC2A 3NH or email: legacies@nspcc.org.uk**
**www.nspcc.org.uk/legacies**

**Anyone who has concerns about a child at risk should call the NSPCC's free 24-hour Child Protection Helpline on** 0808 800 5000.

**NSPCC** ●
Cruelty to children must stop. FULL STOP.

One choice... One reason... One challenge... One goal... One charity... One thought... One need... One child... One life...

1976/07. Registered charity number 216401

---

## Caring for their future
### A will which includes a legacy to the NSPCC could save a child's life.

The National Society for the Prevention of Cruelty to Children (NSPCC) is still as important for children in the UK as ever.

The facts speak for themselves:
- Between 80-100 children are killed in the UK each year. This figure has remained constant for almost 30 years.
- Babies under one year old are the most likely members of UK society to die a violent death.
- Over a quarter (27 per cent) of all recorded rapes are committed against children.

Through its 180 projects and services, the NSPCC is able to offer help, support and protection to vulnerable children, young people and their families where abuse is a factor.

The NSPCC's services provide a vital lifeline to children, offering them the comfort and support they need to overcome their experiences. Sadly, for every child the NSPCC is able to help, there are many more who continue to suffer in silence.

The NSPCC relies on voluntary donations to fund 85 per cent of the work it does protecting vulnerable children. Of the income it receives, 17 per cent comes through legacies. It is no exaggeration to say that the gifts left to us by testators in their wills help to fund services that genuinely save lives.

It is only through the generosity of our supporters that we can help to make sure that all children are able to enjoy safe and happy childhoods.

For further information, call the NSPCC legacy manager on: 020 7825 2505 or write to: NSPCC, Legacy manager, Weston House, 42 Curtain Road, London EC2A 3NH or email: legacies@nspcc.org.uk
**www.nspcc.org.uk/legacies** Anyone who has concerns about a child at risk should call the NSPCC's free 24-hour Child Protection Helpline on **0808 800 5000.**

The **People's Trust for Endangered Species**
protecting the world's endangered animals and their habitats.
**People's Trust**
a great deal to conserve endangered species. By funding research,
conserving habitats and buying nature reserves we will continue
to help ensure the word's amazing wildlife is cared for so

**People's Trust**, you will help to ensure that
animals and their habitats are protected for years to come.

**Thank you.**

For more information about the work of PTES please write to:
PTES 15 Cloisters House, 8 Battersea Park Road, London SW8 4BG
Call us on 020 7498 4533 or visit us online at www.ptes.org
Registered Charity number: 274206

**PEOPLE'S TRUST**
FOR ENDANGERED SPECIES

Picture credits: Hedgehog on a log by Stephen Oliver, water vole by Steve Lobley, dormouse

# PEOPLE'S TRUST FOR ENDANGERED SPECIES

Our altering climate certainly poses big challenges to those interested in the future of our animals and plants but there are many things that we can do to protect and conserve for the future.

Take, for example, some well known home grown species that perhaps symbolise the British countryside. Over the last ten years or so, Britain has lost over 20% of its hedgehogs in some areas, 75% of its dormice and 90% of its water voles. Such a drastic decline might seem hopeless but already we have been able to start fighting back. It is, after all, depressing to imagine that our grandchildren will inherit a countryside radically depleted of these and other animals just because no-one noticed until it was too late.

There are species under threat all over the world as well as those on our own doorsteps. We adopt the same basic approach. Research the problem, identify and administer the cure.

The People's Trust for Endangered Species, a charity created in 1977, offers funding worldwide for expert conservationists providing practical conservation solutions when animals are threatened, we monitor numbers of native animals remaining in the UK annually, and where species are in serious trouble – such as dormice and water voles – we assist with reintroductions to former haunts. Thousands of people are involved with us giving generously of their time and their financial support.

Your support will make a real difference.

# RETRAINING OF RACEHORSES
*Trained to run, retrained for fun*

*Whether you enjoy competing or simply hacking, former racehorses can offer it all.*

To find out how you can play a part in their future visit
**www.ror.org.uk**

**Retraining of Racehorses, 151 Shaftesbury Avenue, London WC2H 8AL Tel: 07836 293191**
Registered Charity No. 1084787

**Member of the National Equine Welfare Council**

# RETRAINING OF RACEHORSES

*Trained to run, retrained for fun*

## Retraining of Racehorses was founded in 2000 as British Horseracing's official charity for the welfare of horses who have retired from Racing.

Retraining of Racehorses (RoR) aims are:

- to raise funds from within the horseracing community to provide and maintain facilities for the care, retraining and rehoming of former racehorses
- to showcase the adaptability of former racehorses for second careers.

Around 4,000 horses leave Racing each year. While every horse is different, in general thoroughbreds have fantastic temperaments and the capacity to shine in a wide variety of alternative activities such as eventing, polo, dressage, long distance riding, showing, as companions and as hacks. In 2006 the Badminton three-day-event winner was an ex-racehorse! Not all can reach these heights, but RoR's job is to highlight this potential to attract increased interest amongst riders with the appropriate skills.

*Andrew Hoy with his former racehorse Moonfleet, winner of the Badminton three-day-event in 2006.*

Retraining of Racehorses has a well-established growing programme of local and national competition sponsorship. It also stages seminars to show what can be done. These events are advertised on the website – **www.ror.org.uk**, along with success stories and articles covering aspects of looking after an ex-racehorse.

RoR also helps to support four charitable rehabilitation centres dedicated to the retraining and rehoming of racehorses:

Greatwood, Wiltshire **www.racehorsesgreatwood.org**

Heros, Oxfordshire **www.heroscharity.org**

Moorcroft Racehorse Welfare Centre, West Sussex **www.mrwc.org.uk**

Thoroughbred Rehabilitation Centre, Lancashire
**www.thoroughbredrehabilitationcentre.co.uk**

The charitable centres specialise in working with horses that, for whatever reason, need a longer than average period of recuperation before they can be rehomed and, in some cases, with horses that have suffered at the hands of less knowledgeable owners. They provide an invaluable safety net.

Retraining of Racehorses also has a venture in collaboration with the Suffolk Punch Trust at HMP Hollesley Bay. Up to 20 horses just out of racing are rested at the stud located by the prison before moving on to formal retraining. As well as benefiting the horses, the project will provide positive work experience for prison inmates and the opportunity to follow a NVQ training programme.

Contributors to Retraining of Racehorses include racehorse owners, racecourses, trainers and jockeys, breeders, other industry associations, the Horserace Betting Levy Board, the Tote, bookmakers and racing fans. Administration expenses are kept to a minimum, with just one full time employee supported by a team of voluntary Trustees.

In 2007 the RoR amalgamated with Emergency Relief for Thoroughbreds. The Racehorse Owners Association's charity set up to relieve the suffering of racehorses by providing funds to organisations and individuals working towards this objective.

### You too can play a part in their future

- To rehome a former racehorse contact one of the charitable centres or visit our website at **www.ror.org.uk** for more information
- If you would like to make a donation please contact Retraining of Racehorses or one of the charitable centres

Retraining of Racehorses (RoR),
151 Shaftesbury Avenue, London WC2H 8AL
Contact: Di Arbuthnot, Director of Operations
Mob: **07836 293191**
Email: **info@ror.org.uk**
**www.ror.org.uk**
Registered Charity No. 1084787

*"To me there is nothing better than a quality thoroughbred." Pippa Funnell, winner of the Windsor Horse Trials on Blue Horizon, a former racehorse under the name of Crossapol Bay.*

*Member of the National Equine Welfare Council*

"I just want people to understand what I'm capable of. Sometimes people see the disability first, and not me, Sarah — the person and what I'm like."
**Sarah Newman**

At Mencap, we are driven by our passionate belief that every person with a learning disability should have an equal right to choice, opportunity and respect. That's why we campaign for equal rights and challenge attitudes and prejudice. And through our housing, education, employment, leisure and advocacy services, we support people with a learning disability to live their lives the way *they* want.

Registered charity number 222377   2007.035  02.07

**For further information:**
Tel: 020 7454 0454
www.mencap.org.uk

MENCAP
*Understanding learning disability*

Mencap is the UK's leading charity for people with a learning disability, their families and carers. Most learning disabilities are caused by the way the brain develops before, during or soon after birth. A learning disability affects someone's intellectual and social development throughout their life.

There are 1.5 million people with a learning disability in the UK. Mencap exists because children and adults with a learning disability and more profound and multiple disabilities are disadvantaged in society. We campaign for equal rights and chances for all people with a learning disability, and fight for the changes that will transform their lives.

Mencap leads the way in providing high-quality, practical support services that are a real lifeline to thousands of people with a learning disability, and their families and carers. These include:

- **education services** – Mencap's National College enables young people with a learning disability to develop personal, social, and practical skills essential for a successful transition to an independent adult life

- *employment initiatives* – 90% of people with a learning disability are unemployed. Our WorkRight scheme gives people with a learning disability the opportunity to reach their potential, come off benefits and contribute to society, while supporting employers to recruit, retain and develop staff with a learning disability

- *community support services* – access to leisure, arts and sports activities, as well as advocacy projects to ensure that the voices of people with a learning disability are heard.

We need your help to support people with a learning disability to live their lives the way they want. By investing in Mencap you will make a real difference to the lives of thousands of people. We ensure that 94p in every £1 we receive is used to support and empower people with a learning disability, and their families and carers.

*For further information visit
www.mencap.org.uk
or call us on* **020 7454 0454**.

# MENCAP
*Understanding learning disability*

WE DON'T KNOW WHEN YOU MIGHT NEED US, THAT'S WHY (WE'RE) OPEN 24 HRS A DAY

**08457 90 90 90**
www.samaritans.org
**SAMARITANS**

---

**By the year 2020 depression will be the second leading cause of disability world wide**

The World Health Organisation

Samaritans is a multi-award wining charity, which offers 24-hour confidential emotional support to anyone in emotional distress by phone, email, face to face and letter. The service is offered by 17,000 trained volunteers and we are virtually entirely dependent on voluntary support.

It is the aim of Samaritans to make emotional health a mainstream issue and remove the stigma associated with depression. Samaritans believes that offering people the opportunity to be listened to in confidence, and accepted without prejudice, can alleviate despair and suicidal feelings.

All calls are confidential and we do not keep detailed records about why people call. However, anecdotal evidence shows that the most common causes for their feelings of despair are:
- Relationship and family problems;
- loss, including loss of a job, a friend or a family member through bereavement;
- financial worries;
- job related stress or overwork;
- college or study related stress;
- Isolation.

In 2006 Samaritans received 5 million contacts which was an increase of 200,000 over the previous year.

Your support enables us to keep the phone lines operational and to ensure that our volunteers are trained to the highest standard possible.

If you would like more information about Samaritans or how your support can help us, please do not hesitate to contact:
Kirti Shah
Manager, Major Gifts
020 8394 8300

# The answer
# is you

**Your investment can transform children's lives.**

**Find out more by contacting Save the Children on 020 7012 6586 or at leadershipgiving@savethechildren.org.uk**

www.savethechildren.org.uk

 **Save the Children**

## Save the Children

Childhood only happens once. For some it doesn't happen at all.

Save the Children works with children who suffer from poverty, disease, injustice and violence. Because children around the world are suffering what is effectively an emergency every day, 365 days of the year.

Every day, 30,000 children under five die from diseases that could be easily prevented or treated. Around half of them are malnourished.

Education is one of the best routes out of poverty. Yet more than 100 million children aren't in school.

Children can't wait for healthcare, for enough to eat or to go to school.

Save the Children works with the poorest children, and those whose childhoods are destroyed by conflict, natural disasters or their country's economic collapse. We are working to make sure that all children can get an education and good quality healthcare. And that all children have enough food and are safe from harm.

## Bringing lasting solutions

We work with children to find lifelong answers to the problems they face.

When there's an emergency, Save the Children responds quickly to protect children and save lives. Because, whether it's a natural disaster or war, children are most at risk.

We provide food and shelter and make sure that children can come together in a safe place to play and learn. We reunite separated children with their families, and help those forced to fight in wars to get back to ordinary life.

But as well as providing immediate relief, we work with children and their communities to find long-term solutions. Providing basic healthcare for children in the world's poorest countries can save lives tomorrow and in future generations. Educating girls today will mean fewer babies dying in the next decade.

## Yesterday, today, tomorrow

Save the Children has been fighting for children in the UK and around the world since 1919. Our founder, Eglantyne Jebb, campaigned for children in Germany and Austria who were hungry and destitute after the first world war.

Today, our work around the world is based on the same principles – that all children have the right to hope and a secure future.

## Rewrite the Future

Education saves lives. Save the Children knows, as every parent does, that education makes a life-changing difference to children.

Children growing up in countries affected by conflict are more likely to miss out on school than children in other poor countries. Yet education can give them the protection, hope and opportunities they need for a better future.

Today, 40 million children in conflict-affected countries are out of school.

Save the Children has set itself the challenge to get three million out of school children, living in conflict-affected countries, into school by 2010. We pledge to make sure the education they get is good quality, and we will work to improve the quality of education for five million more children who are already in school.

And we are calling on governments and international agencies to put policies and resources in place to provide quality education for all children in conflict-affected countries.

## "School has changed my life"

Mary, 12, from Southern Sudan, is one of the millions of children whose life was torn apart by conflict. Her uncle was killed and her cousins abducted. Mary's mother fell sick and when the family couldn't get medicine for her, she died.

Mary wanted to go to school but couldn't because of fear of attack. It wasn't even safe for her to go out and play. "There was nothing I could hope for", she says.

After more than two decades of conflict, the war ended in 2005. Mary has started going to a school set up by Save the Children, where she has learned to read and write.

"Since I have gone to school my life has changed", she says. "I know how to keep clean and have learned about children's rights. I have friends who play with me. Children who are educated will help by being doctors or teachers. For them, life will be good."

Save the Children is building schools in Southern Sudan, providing equipment, and training teachers.

Education can rewrite the future for Mary and millions of others like her.

For more information please contact Save the Children on **020 7012 6586** or **leadershipgiving@savethechildren.org.uk**

# SSAFA FORCES HELP
## *'One Day's Service, A Lifetime of Support'*

Serving in Britain's Armed Forces is more demanding today than it has been at any time since the Second World War. Our servicemen and women regularly risk their lives for their country, but for some, there are battles that continue long after they have returned from military operations.

Many have witnessed extremes of violence, the distress of civilians, both young and old, the loss of friends and sustained hostility from the very people they thought they could help. These are intense experiences that challenge even well trained troops.

Most never think that they might end up feeling very alone and very adrift after the conflicts are over. Whilst the majority will return to everyday life at home, some will take longer to adjust and others will simply find it too much to cope with. Not only they, but their families too are affected, both during and after their years of service.

That is where the **Soldiers, Sailors, Airmen and Families' Association (SSAFA) Forces Help** can help.

Established in 1885 to look after the families of British soldiers serving in North Africa, SSAFA has been helping service people and their families get back on their feet for more than a century. The charity is committed to supporting those who serve in our Armed Forces, those who used to serve, and the families of both. And SSAFA is continually adapting to meet their changing needs.

Each year, SSAFA provides a reliable, caring and trusted service to more than 50,000 people, delivering both financial assistance and practical and emotional support through a network of professionally trained staff and more than 7,000 volunteers.

 Many of those receiving support will have served in conflicts that are now passing into history but current operations in Iraq and Afghanistan have led to a change in workload. The new generation of ex-servicemen and women often experience different problems to their predecessors, ranging from homelessness and social isolation to debt and alcohol abuse. SSAFA provides the support that they need.

"The care that SSAFA provides is as significant and relevant today as at any time in the past," Air Chief Marshall Sir Jock Stirrup, Chief of Defence Staff recently said.

The scope and scale of SSAFA's work is enormous; from the D-Day veteran in ill health to the isolated young mother in Germany; from the disabled child in need of a holiday to the lonely young widow trying to bring up her children; from the family of a badly wounded soldier to those coping with the stress and worry of separation.

The qualifying period for assistance from the charity is just one day's service in any of our Armed Forces. This includes reservists and members of the Territorial Army, who now play such a key role on all military operations. As such, SSAFA Forces Help is uniquely placed to help servicemen and women from the day they join until the day they die.

*If you would like more information on how you can help SSAFA Forces Help or how we can help you or someone you know, please contact:*
The Soldiers, Sailors, Airmen and Families' Association (SSAFA) Forces Help
19 Queen Elizabeth Street
London SE1 2LP
Tel: **020 7463 9248**
Email: **info@ssafa.org.uk**
**www.ssafa.org.uk**

# ONE DAY'S SERVICE
# A LIFETIME OF SUPPORT

**SSAFA Forces Help** is committed to support members of our Armed Forces and their families from the day they join until the day they die.

For the rest of their life

# THE WORLD'S GREATEST LIBRARY

The British Library is the world's greatest library, holding more than 150 million items from every age and every culture. The collections include such treasures as Magna Carta, the world's oldest Bible, Da Vinci's notebook, Handel's Messiah and Shakespeare's First Folio.

The British Library is an exempt charity and donations from UK taxpayers are eligible for Gift Aid. Should you wish to leave a gift in your Will, please make it payable to 'The British Library, 96 Euston Road, London NW1 2DB'.
For more information please visit

**British Library Development Office
96 Euston Road London NW1 2DB
T 020 7412 7237
legacies@bl.uk
www.bl.uk/legacies**

# The World's Greatest Library

The British Library is the world's greatest library, holding more than 150 million items from every age and every culture. The collections include such treasures as *Magna Carta*, the world's oldest Bible, Leonardo da Vinci's notebook, Handel's *Messiah*, Shakespeare's first folio and the *Lindisfarne Gospels*, as well as unique sound recordings such as Florence Nightingale's voice. More recent items include the original work's of such icons as Austen, Joyce and even the Beatles – as well as the latest information for business right through to today's papers.

Our role is to advance knowledge to enrich people's lives, by helping them unlock the knowledge contained within our collections. Gifts to the Library can help us conserve the unique record we hold of the works of the world's greatest minds throughout the centuries. They can also enable us to acquire new material on behalf of the nation, ensuring they are cared for in the best possible conditions and kept permanently accessible to researchers and the wider public. Furthermore, your gift can support the development of new educational programmes and innovative technologies to further enhance access to the collections.

The British Library is an exempt charity which means that, like any charitable bequest, the gift is deducted from the value of the estate when it is assessed for inheritance tax.

Should you wish to make a gift, please make it payable to "The British Library, 96 Euston Road, London NW1 2DB." Alternatively, please contact us for a copy of our free legacy brochure, or to discuss your plans in confidence:

Development Office
The British Library
96 Euston Road
London NW1 2DB
T: 020 7412 7237
F: 020 7412 7168
legacies@bl.uk
www.bl.uk/legacies

For all the world's children
Health, Education, Equality, Protection

**unicef**

www.unicef.org.uk/legacy1

UNICEF is the world's leading organisation working for children and their rights.

Working closely with families, local communities, partners and governments in more than 150 countries, UNICEF helps to save and improve the lives of millions of children through its emergency and humanitarian programmes. We support children by providing health care, nutrition and education. We protect children affected by crises including war, natural disasters and HIV/AIDS.

Legacies are a vital source of income for UNICEF. Each gift is an investment in a future where every child is given the means and opportunities to reach their full potential.

**UNICEF receives no funds from the United Nations, and relies entirely on voluntary contributions.**

For further information on UNICEF's work or including a gift to UNICEF in your Will, please contact:

Jane Orford                    ✆ janeo@unicef.org.uk
UNICEF UK, Africa House, 64–78 Kingsway, London WC2B 6NB
☎ 020 7405 5592
www.unicef.org.uk/legacy1

Registered Charity No. 1072612

# Part 7

# Taxation issues and estate planning

**Howard Kennedy** is a full service law firm advising clients on all aspects of private client, family law, banking, corporate, employment, leisure, litigation, media, property, and tax. Our clients gain from our experience across a diverse range of industry sectors and the ability of partners and associates from different disciplines to work together easily and effectively.

We are ranked among the top 100 UK law firms and are constantly expanding our areas of service expertise and specialist lawyers.

Jo Summers is the Head of the Private Client department at Howard Kennedy and is recognised as a leader in her field in both Legal 500 and Chambers. The department acts for an extensive variety of clients, specialising in international tax planning, personal taxation, complex asset structuring for high net worth individuals and advising on estate planning.

## How to save inheritance tax

Inheritance tax is becoming an increasingly important issue. With rising house prices, particularly in the South of England, more families than ever before are faced with a possible inheritance tax liability.

Inheritance tax (or "IHT" for short) is currently charged on death at a flat rate of 40% after allowance for a tax-free, or nil-rate, band. This band increases slightly each year. From 6 April 2007 it rose to £300,000. IHT can also be chargeable during your lifetime. Further details are set out below. The lifetime rate of IHT is 20%, with a further 20% being due if you are unfortunate enough to die within 7 years from the date of the lifetime charge arising.

### Exemptions

There are some exemptions, fortunately. Gifts to registered UK charities are entirely free of IHT. It may also be possible to make gifts to overseas charities, either through a UK registered "Friends of" organisation or via charities that have been set up to receive donations intended for overseas. The Charity Commission's web-site **www.charity.commission.gov.uk** contains some helpful guidance. See also the Charities Aid Foundation for advice on charity giving **www.cafonline.org**.

Gifts to political parties are exempt, as are gifts of certain "heritage" property. Two of the most important exemptions are agricultural and business property relief. There are detailed rules governing these exemptions and in some cases only 50% of the value is exempt whereas in other cases there is 100% relief. Shares in an unquoted trading company, for example, qualify for the 100% business property relief.

There are limits, as always, as to when the exemption applies. Shares in property investment companies or companies that hold stocks/shares as investments do not qualify for the exemption. Shares in listed companies will only gain the exemption if you have control of the company. The relief can also be restricted if the company's activities are not wholly of a trading nature. Professional advice should be sought on these issues.

## The spouse exemption

Perhaps the most important exemption applies for gifts (either during lifetime or on death) between spouses. If you and your spouse are both UK-domiciled (or both non-domiciled) there is an unlimited exemption for assets passing between you. If, however, you are UK domiciled and your spouse is not, you can only give £55,000 free of IHT to your spouse. If you are unsure of your domicile status, you should seek advice to avoid an unexpected IHT charge arising. In particular, if you came to the UK from overseas but have been living here for at least 15 years, you need urgent advice on whether you will be deemed to be domiciled for IHT purposes. You may be able to take action to avoid the effects of being deemed domiciled.

This spouse exemption now also applies to registered (same sex) civil partners but is not available to couples who are living together. Unfortunately, the concept of "common law spouse" is not yet recognised by the UK tax authorities. Two sisters, who were living together for years, recently tried to get a court to allow them to rely on the spouse exemption but sadly failed.

The spouse exemption can be helpful in your Wills. If you leave the whole of your estate to your spouse (and vice versa), there would be no IHT on the death of the first to die. However, assuming that your assets remain the same and the rates of IHT remain the same, there could be a significant liability on the death of the survivor of you.

## Tax efficient Wills

A better approach is to make use of both your and your spouse's nil-rate bands. This would produce a potential inheritance tax saving of up to £120,000 currently (i.e. 40% of £300,000). Your Wills would need to include either a legacy (outright gift) or a discretionary trust of anything up to the full nil-rate band. It is better not to state an exact figure, if possible, because the available nil-rate band will change depending on the tax laws at the time and whether substantial gifts have been made in the last 7 years before death. Instead, the amount would be defined as the maximum possible tax-free amount.

The choice of legacy/trust will depend primarily on two factors – whether the surviving spouse will need access to the funds and whether there will be sufficient liquid assets to fund it. The legacy goes to non-exempt beneficiaries, e.g. children, so the surviving spouse will not be able to access these funds. The trust alternative sets aside the maximum tax-free amount and puts it into a discretionary trust. The surviving spouse, children and anyone else you list are allowed to benefit from the trust. The trustees have wide powers to benefit any of the beneficiaries in any way they think fit and can pay the income and capital to them or for their benefit.

If you have insufficient liquid assets to fund the discretionary trust to its top limit, you may be able to use your share in the family home instead. In order to do this you and your spouse will need to own the property as tenants in common rather than joint tenants. If you own the property as joint tenants then this will need to be severed to create a tenancy in common. You should ask for further advice on this option but it should be possible to allow the surviving spouse to continue living in the property, rent-free, whilst still obtaining the tax advantages of using both nil-rate bands to reduce IHT.

**Lifetime gifts**

The best way to save IHT is to spend all your money before you die! You can also choose to make gifts during your lifetime to reduce the final IHT bill. Certain gifts are exempt (e.g. to charities & political parties, small gifts (max. £250 to any number of people) and limited gifts to the "happy couple" on getting married). You can also make gifts of up to £3,000 in one tax year. If you haven't used last year's annual gift allowance, you can roll it forward to make exempt gifts of up to £6,000 this year. There is also an exemption for regular gifts from your surplus income, which currently has no maximum. This could be used to pay the premium on a life assurance policy, where the funds will be paid direct to your named beneficiaries free of IHT.

If you make a gift to another individual outright, there will be no IHT to pay unless you die within 7 years of making the gift. If you survive at least 3 years, a taper relief reduces the amount of IHT payable. There is no monetary maximum to the amount you can give: once you have survived 7 years the whole amount is free of IHT. Clearly making gifts as early as possible would be sensible (as long as you can afford it!).

You need to be careful that you do not make a gift with a "reservation of benefit". Basically, if you give something away, you cannot continue to use it without paying for the privilege. This means you cannot put the house in your children's names but live in it rent-free afterwards. This type of planning has been very difficult since the gift with reservation rules were introduced in 1986 and has become even harder since the "pre-owned assets" income tax charge came into force in 2005. Specialist advice is most definitely needed here.

## Gifts to trusts

Since March 2006, any gift to a trust (whether it is a new trust or an existing trust) will give rise to an immediate IHT charge of 20% unless covered by your nil-rate band or any exemption. Before March 2006, gifts to certain trusts (life interest and accumulation & maintenance trusts for children), were treated in the same way as gifts to individuals. Effectively, all trusts are now treated for IHT as if they are discretionary trusts.

There are transitional provisions to allow certain existing trusts to be altered, before they are caught by the tax charges that apply to discretionary trusts. If you have created a trust, or you are a beneficiary of one, you need advice before the end of the transition period on 6 April 2008. You may need to take immediate action to avoid the charges that apply on every 10th anniversary of the trust's creation and whenever capital comes out of the trust (the exit charge).

## Conclusion

With IHT becoming more relevant, and the rules becoming yet more complicated, specialist advice should be sought. Hopefully these notes will give you an idea of the issues involved, but they should not be seen as a substitute for proper legal advice on your IHT planning options.

**Howard Kennedy ©**
**March 2007**

# Safeguard the future for you and yours

Dealing with your retirement and your own mortality, providing for your heirs and loved ones, and securing your legacy is as complex and complicated as it is emotional and sensitive. But ensuring the peace of mind that comes with knowing your family, property and assets are protected has never been more important.

**Jo Summers** and **the Private Client team** at Howard Kennedy recognise this and can deal with all your personal needs in a sensitive and understanding manner. Services we can provide:

- **Wills and Estate Planning**
- **Administration of estates/probate**
- **Personal Tax Advice Planning**
- **Trusts and Trust Management**
- **Charities**

For thorough advice and guidance though all your personal needs contact Jo Summers on +44 (0) 20 7663 8630 or e-mail j.summers@howardkennedy.com

---

Howard Kennedy is a leading a full service firm with an enviable reputation for delivering high quality, practical advice. Our specialist lawyers are committed to assisting our clients in achieving their personal and business goals by providing quality, proactive and cost-effective legal services without compromising on personal service.

For more information on Howard Kennedy's services, please contact Iain Beresford on +44 (0) 20 7546 8979 or e-mail i.beresford@howardkennedy.com

---

19 Cavendish Square
London W1A 2AW
T +44 (0)20 7636 1616
F +44 (0)20 7491 2899

**HOWARD KENNEDY**

# Tax-efficient investments

*Paul Willans, Mazars*

When you're considering an investment, its tax treatment should always be a factor, as income tax and capital gains tax reduce the effective return from investments. With income tax rates at up to 40 per cent and capital gains tax rates being anything between 10 per cent and 40 per cent, this can materially affect your real return. In this chapter, we will consider some of the opportunities available to investors when constructing investment strategies.

However, it is important not to lose sight of the wood for the trees. Tax is a material factor, but not the only one. Investors must always bear in mind the fact that the investment fundamentals are more important, as tax is only a problem if you make a profit. Although the ability to utilize losses can be important, you have to generate the profit first.

Many investors will already have taken advantage of the ability to generate tax-free returns through Tessas, PEPs and more recently ISAs, as well as the tax-free opportunities available through vehicles like National Savings. Therefore, this chapter takes a very broad overview of the wider opportunities available, and looks at three distinct categories of investment: tax shelters, investments with estate planning potential, and structures designed to provide gross roll-up. In view of the sheer number of options available, this chapter does not consider all the possible alternatives within each field, but focuses on those that are used most frequently.

## Tax shelters

The principal advantage of tax shelters is an immediate tax saving, generated by the investment itself. This can take a number of forms, and offers either outright savings or simply a deferral of the tax until some later time. The market in such vehicles has narrowed considerably over recent years, with the repeal of legislation that created shelters, such as film partnerships. However, there are still a number of opportunities available.

The most widely used shelter is often overlooked in this context – pensions. On the one hand, the introduction of pensions simplification on 6 April 2006 (known as 'A Day') has opened up the possibility of bigger contributions for those with significant earned incomes. But it also imposes a much more rigid ceiling on the maximum pension fund that can benefit from tax relief. Nevertheless, the tax advantages remain the best of any investment vehicle available. Contributions within H M Revenue and Customs (HMRC) limits offer tax relief at your highest marginal rate and, through careful planning using bonus or salary sacrifice, it may also be possible to mitigate National Insurance.

Investment income and gains within a pension fund will not normally be subject to tax, although Gordon Brown's raid on pension funds in 1997 should not be forgotten, as the loss of tax credits on dividends has hit many pension funds hard. When benefits are taken, at least some of the fund may come out in a tax-free form.

The restriction on residential property investment made the headlines after the Chancellor's pre-Budget statement in December 2005. However, pension scheme investments can still be made in a wide range of investments. In fact, strictly speaking, a pension fund can invest in any asset but, if the investment constitutes an 'unauthorized payment', the tax privileges of the fund will be lost in relation to that particular investment.

The hype over the now frustrated possibility of investment in residential property did, however, firmly focus the spotlight on the use of self-invested personal pensions (SIPPs). As a consequence, it is widely predicted that SIPPs will become the pension wrapper of choice for those seeking greater investment flexibility.

The wide-ranging investment scope and ability to manage actively the underlying funds make pensions unique within the tax shelter category. Indeed, the other options all have one major characteristic in common: they severely limit the investment scope, by generally restricting the investment to a specific opportunity and not allowing changes or switches.

They also share another common factor – risk. In general, tax privileges are not given away lightly or without reason. In the case of pensions, the relief is a reflection of the government's desire that people should be encouraged to save for retirement. In the case of other tax shelters, tax privileges are generally an inducement to attract investors into an area that many would not otherwise wish to contemplate, because of either risk or liquidity issues.

The two main tax shelters that fall into this category are venture capital trusts (VCTs) and the Enterprise Investment Scheme (EIS). Both VCTs and the EIS focus on small, unquoted companies (or, for VCTs, AIM-listed companies), the primary difference being that VCTs allow managed investment in a portfolio of companies, while the EIS involves a direct investment in a single company.

Until the start of the 2006 financial year, VCTs had benefited from 40 per cent income tax relief, although this has now been reduced to 30 per cent. The maximum annual investment remains at £200,000, but the size of eligible investee companies has been reduced from £15 million to £7 million at the outset. In addition, the minimum holding period required, in order to avoid clawback of the income tax relief, has been extended from three to five years. There are three main classes of investment area (generalist, AIM and specialist), which enables investors to diversify their holdings and invest in assets as diverse as wind farms and the music industry.

The maximum investment in the EIS has doubled to £400,000 and still offers an income tax relief of 20 per cent, although this can be clawed back if various conditions are breached within a three-year period. It also potentially offers capital gains tax-free growth on the investment, or the ability to offset realized losses against income. Following the 2006 Finance Act, inheritance tax (IHT) planning through the use of trusts became more difficult. EIS investments potentially play a greater role in estate planning, as they become free from IHT after a period of two trading years. EIS shares also offer an opportunity to defer capital gains tax through a form of rollover relief into the investment.

However, both VCTs and the EIS are investments where the investment fundamentals should take precedence over the tax advantages. Both invest in potentially illiquid shares, and the private equity sector is notoriously volatile. However, as a structured part of a larger investment portfolio, these investments can offer valuable diversification from other asset classes and the potential for tax-efficient dividends over the longer term. Indeed, for investors with a higher-risk profile whose pension planning is constrained by A Day, VCTs offer a comparable alternative to approved pension arrangements. This is because the longer-term dividend stream may provide a similar yield to annuities and perhaps more importantly the capital value does not disappear on death.

## Estate planning

One of the traditional forms of investment to attract inheritance tax relief is woodlands. This exploits the availability of relief up to 100 per cent on the value of commercial woodlands, under the business property relief regime. In general, woodlands will not generate significant income until clear-felling takes place – which would defeat the purpose of the investment as an estate tax shelter and will, in fact, generally yield a negative cash flow. However, as the management of the woodland would be contracted out, there is little regular activity required, and possible amenity issues. Unsurprisingly, woodlands do suffer from liquidity issues, and there can also be timing problems. If you have bought woodlands as an estate tax shelter and live too long, the woodlands may need to be felled for commercial reasons. If that were to happen, you could find your tax planning carted away with the timber.

Business property relief has also given rise to a number of products aimed at providing a managed portfolio service for holding shares in AIM-listed companies. Such shares are treated as unquoted for most tax purposes and, consequently, attract both business property relief, for inheritance tax, and business asset taper relief, for capital gains tax. This means that, after the shares have been held for a minimum of two years, there is the possibility of a capital gains tax rate as low as 10 per cent and no liability to inheritance tax. Such investments offer a more liquid opportunity than forestry, though AIM shares do carry a greater degree of risk than investments listed on the main Stock Exchange.

Agricultural property attracts similar reliefs, and has recently begun to attract sufficient interest to warrant promoters offering a packaged product. However, the choice at the moment is very limited.

## Investment wrappers

At its simplest level, an ISA is effectively an investment wrapper, a structure that provides a framework within which investments can be held and managed. However, for most wealthy individuals, an ISA only forms a negligible part of their overall portfolio, because of the limitations placed on the amount invested. For investors looking to invest larger sums and looking at the ability to roll up capital profits within a tax-free framework, there are alternatives.

At the most basic level, this is something that a single-premium life assurance bond can offer, with your premium being invested in the life company's own range of managed funds. However, there is an ever-widening range of funds to choose from, as more life companies adopt the approach of offering external fund links.

It is not possible to get tax-free roll-up if you invest in a UK life policy, as the life company will pay corporation tax on the gains realized within its funds. However, offshore life policies do offer a gross roll-up on capital gains and income, although at the loss of the ability to utilize the annual capital gains tax exemption or to offset any realized losses against other gains, and of tax credits available on the underlying income. The latter can be of little relevance where deposits or fixed interest investments are being used, where there is often no with-holding tax or tax credit.

These products do not, however, offer the perfect solution in every case. In addition to the above, investors also lose out on taper relief, because the profits on such policies are subject to income tax and not capital gains tax. However, for inter-nationally mobile investors, an income tax profit can be more valuable, as there is a greater scope to use periods of non-residence to escape the tax charge. Fundamentally, from an investment perspective, such products are restricted to investments in collective funds rather than direct securities, owing to the penal private portfolio bond legislation introduced in 1999.

For those investors who want taper relief while investing directly, one alter-native is to invest in a personalized open-ended collective investment company (OEIC) or unit trust. While the minimum entry level is in excess of £5 million, this kind of vehicle does offer the option of investment in equities and fixed interest, a gross roll-up of any underlying capital gains and taper relief when capital is required. They do not allow income to be rolled up, but do offer the possibility of management charges being deducted from the income – both reducing the income and obtaining a tax relief that would not otherwise be available.

However, such entities are not without their own problems. There are limits on the percentage that can be held in any individual investment, and they cannot invest in unquoted companies. However, for larger sums, they do offer significant investment opportunities.

## Conclusion

Irrespective of your personal risk and liquidity profile and the amount you have available to invest, there are advantages to be gained from the careful choice of investment products and structures. As with most investment decisions, your choices become wider and more attractive the more you have to invest, although with choice come complexity and the need for professional advice. It is also worth repeating that you should never make any investment on tax grounds alone and should never keep all your eggs in one basket.

# Legal advice today you can trust for the future

At KSB Law we provide clear cut solutions for your personal wealth management needs including:

- capital tax planning; inheritance tax and capital gains tax
- creation, management and administration of private and charitable trusts
- applications for probate and the administration of estates
- applications for and administration of non-UK estates
- preparation of powers of attorney
- preparation of Wills
- charities advice, creation and registration

As our chapter in this book identifies, recent major changes in trust taxation could seriously affect you and your children. If you are concerned about an existing trust or wish to form a new one - KSB Law can help.

For an informal discussion about our tax, trust & probate services contact:
Ian Lane
+44 (0)20 7822 7602
ilane@ksblaw.co.uk

KSB Law LLP
Elan House • 5-11 Fetter Lane • London EC4A 1QD
60 Victoria Street • St Albans • Hertfordshire AL1 3XH

www.ksblaw.co.uk

# Tax planning for high net worth individuals

*Ian Lane, KSB Law LLP*

This is a fairly brief review of the taxation issues faced by individuals having significant capital or income living within the United Kingdom tax net. This chapter does not deal with non-domiciled and non-resident individuals whose situation is beyond the scope of this chapter.

The taxes with which I am concerned in this chapter are principally inheritance tax and capital gains tax but income tax also features in a limited way. For greater clarity I've divided the various issues into separate headings throughout the text. But I think it is first worth briefly outlining the nature of the three taxes we are going to look at.

## Inheritance tax

Inheritance tax came into existence 20 years ago. It is a modified form of capital transfer tax, which was introduced by the Labour Government in 1975. Inheritance tax is a tax on gifts made during lifetime and on the estate of individuals when they die. It is levied at a rate of 20 per cent on lifetime gifts and 40 per cent on death. In both cases the tax charge begins above the so-called 'nil rate band', which is the first part of the amount chargeable to inheritance tax at a zero rate. The nil rate band increases on an annual basis and for the year ended 5 April 2007 it is £285,000. Thus a gift during lifetime of, say, £1,000,000 will be subject to inheritance tax at 20 per cent on the value of the gift in excess of £285,000 (£715,000) and thus £143,000 during the year ended 5 April 2007.

On death, if a person has made lifetime gifts some or all of those gifts may be added back to the person's estate and charged with inheritance tax at that time. In general terms, gifts made during lifetime where the donor of the gift has survived for seven years will be ignored on death.

In the Finance Act 2006 the rules in relation to gifting were changed so that, although gifts between individuals remain exempt (strictly they are potentially exempt) when they are made and therefore only become subject to inheritance tax if the donor does not survive seven years, gifts into almost all kinds of trust (the exceptions are charitable trusts and disabled trusts) are now chargeable when they are made and thus subject to the lifetime rate of charge at 20 per cent above the nil rate band. This has led to a wholesale rethink of tax planning using trusts and wills. For those with wills made prior to the coming into force of the Finance Act 2006 (22 July 2006), where there are provisions in favour of persons who do not take a share from the estate absolutely there may be implications, which should be investigated further. There may be an inheritance tax charge inherent in a will drawn up prior to the Finance Act 2006 of which people are not yet aware.

# Capital gains tax

Capital gains tax is charged on 'chargeable disposals' made during lifetime on specific kinds of assets. There is no capital gains tax charge on assets on death. In fact, the value of assets acquired during lifetime are 'uplifted' to the value at the date of death and charged to inheritance tax. Most of the assets that you would expect to be subject to a capital gains tax are indeed so subject. So, for example, shares, securities and real property among other things are all subject to a capital gains tax charge either on sale or on disposal by way of gift. Capital gains tax is charged on the gain between the cost of the asset and its sale price. However, there are a number of ways to reduce the amount of tax.

For chargeable items owned prior to 31 March 1982, an indexation allowance is available, which increases the base cost of the item by a factor based on the retail price index covering the period from 31 March 1982 to 19 March 1998. At that point indexation allowance was phased out, but it is still effective to provide a relief for assets owned during the relevant period. From 1998 a new relief was introduced called taper relief, which comes in two forms. The basic form for non-business assets does not begin to give any relief at all until the third year of ownership, and the maximum taper available after 10 years of ownership reduces the percentage of the gain chargeable by 40 per cent. Business assets taper relief is much more advantageous – a 50 per cent relief is available after one year, and after two years the relief is 75 per cent and therefore only 25 per cent of the gain is actually chargeable to tax.

In addition to these reliefs, the costs of acquisition and disposal and various other expenditures can be set against the gain. Finally, of course, every individual has an annual allowance for capital gains tax purposes, which can also be used to offset the gain. For the current year that is £8,800. Therefore it is often our advice that it is better to dispose of an item now (perhaps by way of gift) and possibly pay a small amount of capital gains tax than hold on to it and suffer a 40 per cent inheritance tax charge on the value of the asset on death.

# Income tax

There have been numerous schemes to reduce or mitigate the effect of income tax liabilities but they are beyond the scope of this chapter. I am confining this chapter to a brief discussion of the income tax charge that was introduced in the Finance Act 2004 and is known as pre-owned assets tax. This was a measure introduced by the government to combat what it saw as unacceptable tax avoidance mostly using private residences in order to shelter those residences (often the greater value of a person's estate) from an inheritance tax charge while at the same time avoiding a capital gains tax charge. There were a number of different schemes involving houses, one known as the Loan and Trust Scheme and the other the Eversden Scheme (named after the relevant case). All of these were brought to a halt by the Finance Act 2004 legislation, although in most cases the schemes could not be pursued without great cost following the introduction of stamp duty land tax to replace stamp duty on the disposal of real property from December 2003. Nevertheless, there is now an income tax charge in certain circumstances where an asset that you formerly owned is no longer in your ownership but you can still use it.

You might, for example, have transferred a property of which you were the owner and occupier to a trust. You were paid for the sale by some form of IOU, which you then also gave away. At the same time you retained the right to remain in the property. In those circumstances this legislation creates an income tax liability based on a notional rent that you should otherwise have paid to continue to occupy the property while taking into account any actual rent that you might be paying (if any). This is a further aspect of taxation that must be borne in mind in relation to tax planning for high net worth individuals.

Having now looked at the taxes involved, let's consider the possibilities for an individual who wishes to reduce the burden of all this taxation.

# Lifetime giving – individuals

There are a number of small exemptions available for inheritance tax purposes that are wholly out of account for inheritance tax purposes during lifetime and that are not added back to an individual's estate when he or she dies. I will deal with these only briefly but they are important because over a lifetime they can produce significant savings. There is the small gifts exemption of £250 to any number of people at any time, and there is the annual £3,000 allowance, which if not used for one tax year can be carried over for one further tax year. There are also gifts in relation to marriage available to parents and grandparents, which are useful tools in passing sums of money on to children and grandchildren. The gifts for parents are limited to £5,000 each and for grandparents to £2,500 each.

The main annual exemption that is of considerable use to those individuals with substantial incomes is that for gifts out of normal expenditure of income. For individuals who are not spending their net income on an annual basis it is possible to make gifts out of the surplus income on an annual basis, all of which will be out of account in the estate on death. The exemption is very useful, but its terms are not entirely clear in the legislation. Her Majesty's Revenue and Customs (HMRC) has produced guidelines in relation to this exemption that are useful, and indeed it has recently produced a form that must be completed when someone dies, setting out the details of the surplus income gifts. Although this seems a chore, it is extremely useful because it makes it very difficult for HMRC to deny the surplus income gifts if the information fits the criteria of its own form. Again, for an individual with significant income over a period of a number of years very significant sums of money can be given away tax-free.

The next major exemption is the exemption as between spouses and following the Civil Partnerships Act 2005 as between civil partners. A gift of any sum of money between spouses or civil partners is free of inheritance tax whenever it is made during lifetime or on death. This is a major exemption and is of considerable use in tax mitigation.

Gifts made to other individuals during lifetime are tax-free when made but become taxable if the person who makes the gift dies within seven years from the date it was made. It is the value of the gift at the date it was made that is brought back into account, not the value of the gift at the date of death. So, for example, if shares in a private company valued at £1,000,000 are given away in year one and the donor of the gift dies in year five when the shares are worth £2,000,000 the amount added back to the estate for tax purposes is still only £1,000,000 and therefore the increase in value has been saved from taxation even if the original sum has not. Gifts in excess of the nil rate band are also subject to taper relief, which applies to reduce the tax payable on death where a gift is brought back into account if the donor has survived at least three years from the making of a gift. It should, however, be noted that, if the gift made is below the nil rate band because the gift is added back to the estate and 'soaks up' the nil rate band first, taper relief will not apply as there is no tax to taper.

## Lifetime giving – trusts

Gifts into trusts, as mentioned above, are now all chargeable transfers, with the exception of gifts to charities or to disabled trusts. Gifts to charities are discussed further on in this chapter. A disabled trust is a very limited form of trust for a person suffering under a disability, and specialist advice should be sought where such a trust is to be established.

All other trust transfers are now chargeable following the Finance Act 2006. This means that, to the extent that the gift into the trust exceeds the nil rate band, there is a charge of 20 per cent on the value of the trust fund above the nil rate band on entry. In addition to that, all trusts are now in the so-called 'relevant property' regime, which used to apply only to discretionary trusts. This means that in addition to the charge on entry there is a charge every 10 years of 6 per cent of the value of the trust fund above the nil rate band and there is also a charge on any exit (withdrawal) of monies from the trust between 10-year anniversaries subject to the nil rate band at a proportion of the 10-yearly charge. Finally there is a charge if the trust is terminated on the whole of the value of the fund above the nil rate band based on a proportion of the percentage of the 10-year anniversary charge depending on when the termination occurs. Thus the taxation of trusts with values in excess of the nil rate band has become more complex.

If, for example, spouses or civil partners were prepared to do so they could place assets totalling £570,000 (they each have a nil rate band) this year and then wait seven years plus one day and do the same thing again at the then nil rate band (then in excess of £600,000) and similarly every seven years or so. It is therefore possible over a period of 21 years to remove about £2 million from the estate, which is a significant saving (approximately £800,000) over time. These gifts would all be free of inheritance tax when they are made and depending on the nature of the investment in the new trust could also be free of inheritance tax long-term. Therefore the idea of using trusts to save tax is not dead but the way in which it is achieved has changed and the way in which trusts are drafted to achieve a tax-planning purpose has also changed to take account of the new rules.

## Charities

It is often the case that individuals would like to consider charitable giving, both during their lifetime but also for posterity. One of the ways to achieve this on a tax-free basis is for them to establish a charitable trust or company registered with the Charity Commission. This can be done during lifetime and can also be dealt with by will. In both cases the gift into the charity is free of inheritance tax provided the gift is for wholly charitable purposes. This is often helpful for those who have considerable assets but who have no immediate family whom they wish to benefit or alternatively who simply wish to set up a charity for entirely altruistic purposes. In any event it is a tax-free zone!

## Wills

No discussion of taxation issues in this context would be complete without mentioning wills.

Wills remain the most efficient and important means of tax planning in the UK. They are convenient in that they only have effect from death and therefore do not affect the lifestyle of the individual owning the assets and thus have considerable attraction as a result. The structure of the will is vital when it comes to maximizing the tax-saving potential following someone's death, and expert advice should always be sought in relation to the making of a will in this context. It is always better to get it right in the will rather than depend on matters outside your control after death.

## Investment products

We all know of the existence of individual savings accounts and, although the thresholds are relatively low at £7,000 for a Maxi ISA, those who started setting up PEPs on an annual basis now have significant PEP and ISA portfolios. Many hundreds of thousands of pounds are free of income tax and capital gains tax within their individual plans. Many investment management firms are set up to manage these schemes and if you are not setting up an ISA every year with your investment manager you should consider it.

# Businesses/agriculture/forestry

There are considerable reliefs available for business property and agricultural property under the inheritance tax system. Business property relief and agricultural property relief are in certain circumstances available at 100 per cent of the value of the property passing on death and during lifetime and so assets in private companies are often considered as part of the tax-planning strategy both during lifetime and in a will. It should also be noted that securities quoted on the Alternative Investment Market (AIM) are presently also available for business property relief and as a result many investment managers have specialist teams who will create an AIM portfolio for you, all of which will be free of inheritance tax in your hands and on your death, under current legislation, provided you have owned the shares for two years prior to the point when the tax becomes payable. There are inherent risks in purchasing shares on the AIM market but of course that is the reason why the relief has been given.

There is a separate relief for inheritance tax for commercial forestry. Although only a minority of people are involved in forestry it can be a significant relief in certain circumstances.

# Insurance-based products

Following the Finance Act 2006 it was thought that a number of the products offered by insurance companies for tax-saving purposes would be rendered, if not valueless, certainly pointless. However, the full rigours of the legislation have not proved to be so damaging and therefore there are still a number of insurance products such as discounted gift trusts and loans and insurance bonds that can be valuable tools in the tax-planning armoury. As I am not qualified to comment on the detail of these plans I will say no more here but would certainly suggest that anyone interested in insurance-based products should take advice from a reputable independent financial adviser.

# Wine, bloodstock and similar assets

I do not intend to discuss these in any detail since they will be discussed in far greater length in this book. Nevertheless they can also form part of a tax-planning strategy for some individuals.

Hopefully, this short review of some of the issues facing high net worth individuals has been of interest.

# The offshore tax angle

*Ian Abrey, Mazars*

More and more often today, UK individuals are facing overseas tax issues. This is partly a consequence of increasing levels of wealth: most well-diversified investment portfolios will include investments in overseas markets. In addition, an increasing number of people are investing in property abroad and spending time there. Some are going further and emigrating, either temporarily or as a permanent change in lifestyle.

In this chapter, we will be looking at issues that may arise either from investment abroad or through spending time there. We will also briefly cover the basis and advantages non-domiciliaries enjoy here for tax purposes and why the UK can be a 'tax haven' to some. Because every country's tax system is unique, it will not be possible to give more than a brief overview of the issues involved. Before making a major investment or lifestyle decision, you should always check out both the UK and the local tax implications.

## Investment abroad

First, let us clear up one apparently common misconception. For most UK-resident individuals, investing offshore will not affect the amount or timing of UK taxation. Most UK-resident taxpayers are, and will remain, taxable on worldwide income and gains, and should declare offshore income and gains accordingly. Any failure to do so constitutes tax evasion. As a spur to people's conscience in this regard, the European Savings Directive – which came into force in July 2005 – will now provide HM Revenue and Customs (HMRC) with ammunition to pursue individuals who have invested abroad but forgotten to declare it.

The European Savings Directive was introduced to counter cross-border tax evasion, perceived by European governments to be a widespread problem. Taxpayers seeking to evade high personal tax rates at home deposited monies in countries that had no local withholding tax, and failed to declare the interest at home. Under the directive, all EU countries and connected jurisdictions (such as the Channel Islands) must either collect a withholding tax on interest – starting at 15 per cent, rising ultimately to 35 per cent, and which is shared out among EU governments – or, alternatively, disclose the existence of the account and the amount of interest on it to the tax authorities in the country in which the taxpayer resides. The first notifications from offshore locations such as Guernsey were sent to HMRC in the summer of 2006. These are being cross-checked to the individual taxpayer's returns by a specialist tax team at HMRC to ensure that everything is properly declared.

Investing overseas can also generate tax issues in other jurisdictions. Investing in tax havens such as the Channel Islands may have few local tax implications. However, most countries will levy withholding tax – particularly on dividends, but sometimes also on interest. In general, UK investors will get a tax credit against their UK tax liability for the withholding tax, so why is it a problem? The UK has a wide network of double tax agreements, which often provide for a lower level of withholding tax than would normally be the case. However, getting this lower rate in practice can sometimes be time-consuming and difficult for direct investments abroad, and will normally need to be claimed in advance. Merely accepting the higher rate of withholding tax and claiming it as a credit against UK tax may not work, as HMRC would be within its rights merely to allow credit at the correct rate. This adds to the advantages of collective vehicles for overseas investment, as the fund manager will normally make arrangements to reclaim excess tax, or arrange for the correct withholding rate to be used.

# Buying property abroad

For those individuals who want to own property in a foreign country, tax and legal issues are much more significant. Purchasing property in another jurisdiction exposes an investor to a range of legal issues:

■ Real property will normally be subject to the laws of the country in which it is situated. Leaving tax aside, these can include rights of access across land, public liability and, more particularly, inheritance law. The inheritance regime in many European countries is fundamentally different to the UK system. In particular, it often provides compulsory rules for the devolution of your estate. In France, *la réserve légale* (sometimes known as *la réserve héréditaire*) will often provide a very different result to what you might wish, in that the estate is divided in fixed portions between the spouse and children.

■ Such property will also be liable to capital taxes in the local jurisdiction. As well as capital gains tax, there is inheritance tax and wealth tax (again, an alien concept to the UK tax system). The level of tax varies between countries, but can be better or worse than the equivalent UK tax. For example, the normal rate of French capital gains tax is 27 per cent (it can be lower for non-residents), but for residential property the gain is reduced by 10 per cent for each year above five years that a property is held. So after 15 years, the gain is exempt in France. The fact that a gain is taxable in the local jurisdiction does not necessarily prevent it being taxable in the UK as well, as this will depend upon the terms of the relevant double tax agreement. At the very least, you should obtain a credit for any overseas tax paid in working out your UK tax liability.

■ The foreign legal system will also have an impact on inheritance tax. Because property devolves under fixed rules, it may generate a UK inheritance tax on the first death. This might not arise until the second death if left according to your own wishes. Also, you may not be able to get full credit for any tax paid abroad in calculating your UK liability. Transfers between spouses and civil partners in the UK are free from inheritance tax, whereas in other European countries (again, France is an example) such transfers are taxable. The tax paid in France under such circumstances is not available as a credit, as there is no UK tax payable.

■ If the property is a holiday home, and is rented out for some of the summer, you could again face tax in both countries. Furthermore, the rules for calculating the rental profit are likely to be different in each country. Even if you are making a loss, it can be a time-consuming and expensive process to comply with both sets of rules.

■ Most importantly, a great deal of thought should go into how to structure the purchase of the property. Every country has its own property laws and legal structures for owning property, so it is not possible to give generic advice. Furthermore, local property taxes will often vary depending on how the property is to be held. Detailed legal advice should be taken not only in the local jurisdiction, but also back in the UK, to ensure that the recommended structure works in both countries. Two general warnings can be given where you are contemplating buying a property through a legal vehicle such as a company or trust. First, if the property is in Europe, a purchase by a trust is almost certain to give rise to problems and should be avoided. This is because most European countries either do not recognize the existence of trusts or have great difficulties applying local laws to them. Second, if a property is to be acquired through a company and occupied rent-free, HMRC is likely to charge income tax on the notional benefit of using your 'own' property.

# Tax residence

For those taking the plunge and buying a property as a second (or even first) home, there is also the question of residence. Most countries, like the UK, have an objective test of residence, based on the number of days that you spend in the country. Many also have a subjective test, depending on where your permanent home or centre of vital interests lies. It is quite possible to be resident in more than one country. It is also possible to be resident in none, but this is much more difficult to achieve. A further complication is that few countries have the same tax year as the UK. Most use the calendar year basis, so resident and non-resident periods are very likely to overlap.

There is very little statute law governing residence in the UK – taxpayers often have to base decisions on HMRC guidance and practice. More worryingly, HMRC has recently taken a case to court where it appeared to argue against its own guidance – and won! Taxpayers who are aiming to become non-resident while spending significant amounts of time in the UK now need to take great care in what is currently an uncertain world.

# International agreements

As mentioned earlier, the UK has a wide network of double tax agreements, designed to ensure you are not taxed twice or, if you are, that appropriate credit is given for tax paid in the other country. The agreements also determine which country can tax what source of income or gain. Each treaty has a 'tie-breaker' clause, designed to ensure that, if you are resident in both countries, there is a mechanism for identifying which is your principal country of residence for applying the treaty. Typically, such a tie-breaker will firstly look at whether you have a permanent home in either or both of the countries. Should you have a home in both, it will then go on to look at your centre of vital interests. This is the country with which your economic, social and personal ties are the strongest. While the question of whether you have a permanent home available is clearly ascertainable, the centre-of-vital-interest test is harder to judge. For those who wish to spend time in more than one country, it is likely that your centre of vital interests will not shift from the UK to another country overnight. You are, therefore, going to remain treaty-resident in the UK for some time. If it is not possible to determine residence for treaty purposes on the basis of centre of vital interests, the test then looks at where you are habitually resident, and finally looks at your nationality.

As well as national legislation and double tax agreements, there is another layer of complication that should be considered – namely, EU law. Many readers will have heard of the Marks & Spencer case, which challenged aspects of the UK corporation tax regime, and which Marks & Spencer won. However, the principles involved can apply equally to individuals, and a number of cases have been heard by the European Court of Justice in recent years.

The EC treaty guarantees certain freedoms, including the freedom of movement of persons or capital, and the freedom of establishment. These freedoms apply equally to individuals and companies, although the amounts involved for companies make a challenge through the European Court of Justice more financially worthwhile.

A number of European countries (including the UK) have measures designed to prevent taxpayers reducing their liability to tax by changing residence. Typically, this involves capital gains tax. Some measures provide for a deemed disposal, and consequent liability to tax, as the taxpayer leaves the country. Others extend the period for which the taxpayer is liable after departure, so that gains realized shortly after departure are taxed. In recent cases, the European Court of Justice has held that measures of the former type introduced by France were incompatible with the treaty, and required these to be reviewed and revised. There has been no test under the freedom of movement of persons on measures of the second type, which the UK uses. There has been an unsuccessful attempt regarding measures of a similar type for Dutch estate tax under the freedom of capital provisions. Because the person involved was not an EU citizen, freedom of movement was not considered but might have formed a stronger case. The European Court of Justice can, therefore, be the friend of the taxpayer in this context, in that, although it will not support tax avoidance, it may support the rights of the taxpayer to choose the most favourable tax regime under which to live and pay tax.

# Domicile

While all developed countries have the concept of residence (and some have ordinary residence) for tax purposes, the UK and a number of other Anglo-Saxon countries also have the concept of domicile. This is the country that is your permanent home. As well as a fundamental part of the legal system, it is a concept that carries over into the tax system. Individuals who may be resident in the UK, but who have retained a domicile elsewhere, have a number of advantages for UK tax purposes.

For UK tax purposes, everyone throughout the world has a domicile of origin. This is the country in which your parents were domiciled when you were born. Although it is possible to change this domicile by your actions, it is also quite possible that this domicile will remain even if you are resident in another country for lengthy periods of time. A domicile of origin is very tenacious in this respect.

If you enjoy a domicile outside the UK then, even as a UK resident for tax purposes, you enjoy a number of advantages in relation to assets held abroad. First, such assets are outside the scope of inheritance tax, as may be trusts set up to hold such assets. If you have come to the UK but retained the bulk of your wealth in your country of origin, this can be a valuable benefit – particularly if your country of origin levies inheritance tax on the basis of residence.

More importantly, on an ongoing basis, income and gains that arise abroad will only be taxable in the UK to the extent they are remitted to the UK. This offers a valuable means of deferring the tax charge on such income and gains, and allows you to manage your tax liability according to your need for funds rather than the level of your income and gains. With careful planning, it may also be possible to enjoy the benefit of such profits in the UK without a tax charge, but professional advice should be obtained and carefully implemented to ensure this.

Non-domiciled taxpayers may also escape the worst effects of the changes introduced to the inheritance tax treatment of trusts. For such individuals, trusts remain a valuable tax planning tool.

## Conclusion

As noted at the outset, it is not possible in a chapter as brief as this to give any detailed guidance. Hopefully, it has been possible to outline where pitfalls and opportunities lie. Unfortunately, for many readers of this chapter the biggest opportunity – that of non-domiciled status – is not available. If you were born with a domicile of origin in the UK, it will rarely be possible to be resident here and domiciled somewhere else.

# Capital gains tax and inheritance tax planning for the high net wealth individual

*Allan Holmes, Dickinson Dees*

## Introduction

Capital gains tax (CGT) and inheritance tax (IHT) are generally called the 'capital taxes' for the obvious reason that they are the two main direct taxes on capital. Whilst, very broadly, CGT is a tax on disposing of assets during lifetime and IHT is a tax on passing assets on to another person, the two taxes overlap in many instances. Neither CGT nor IHT raises huge revenues for the government but they are significant taxes for the high net wealth individual and substantial savings can be made with appropriate planning.

I will first set out some basic points to think about in relation to CGT and IHT and will then outline some planning ideas ranging from the simple to the complex.

## Capital gains tax

- Capital gains tax is mainly a tax on the disposal of assets. It applies to sales and gifts of assets made during lifetime but not to transfers on death.
- The calculation is based on the rise in value of the asset, with adjustments for inflation (to April 1998) and taper relief (from April 1998). There are other

reliefs that are not considered here. An annual exemption (currently £8,800) is also available.

∎ For the high net wealth individual, the highest effective rate is typically 40 per cent and the lowest 10 per cent, depending upon the rate of taper relief that applies. The maximum rate of taper is 75 per cent and is currently available for assets that qualify as business assets and that have been held for at least two years. Non-business assets only qualify for a maximum taper relief of 40 per cent and it is necessary to own the asset for 10 years. The taper relief rules have changed most years since the legislation was introduced and there are a number of anomalies, so extreme caution is needed.

∎ Transfers between spouses or civil partners do not trigger a capital gains tax charge, regardless of the price paid by the spouse or civil partner receiving the asset. Instead, the transfer is treated as taking place at a price that creates neither a gain nor a loss. However, this does not necessarily mean that the donee spouse or civil partner simply acquires the donor's tax history; the taper relief position can be completely changed.

∎ Capital gains tax is payable on gifts, and the donor is deemed to sell the asset at its open market value. However, certain gifts can be made with no immediate charge to capital gains tax by making a hold-over election. Instead the donee inherits the donor's tax cost and the taper relief clock is reset to zero. The gain arising on gifts of certain business assets can be held over, as can the gain on gifts to trusts, excluding gifts to settlor-interested trusts. A settlor-interested trust is a trust where the settlor, his or her spouse or civil partner, or his or her minor children can benefit.

# Inheritance tax

## Death

∎ Inheritance tax is mainly a tax on an individual's estate on death and on transfers made within seven years of death. In short, the value of the deceased's net estate is established and transfers made in the previous seven years are added to it. An amount is taxed at 0 per cent (called the nil rate band – currently £285,000) and the balance is taxed at 40 per cent.

∎ The tax is reduced on a sliding scale for transfers made within seven years of death, depending upon how much time has elapsed between the transfer and death. Credit is also given for any tax paid on lifetime transfers (see below).

## Lifetime transfers

∎ A number of lifetime transfers are exempt provided the donor survives the gift by seven years. If the donor dies within seven years then there is an IHT liability (see above). These transfers are called potentially exempt transfers (PETs).

∎ However, IHT is charged on certain lifetime transfers at half the death rates, ie the excess over the available nil rate band is taxed at 20 per cent. The available nil rate band is the nil rate band for the year less chargeable transfers made in the previous seven years. Finance Act 2006 means that almost all transfers into trusts will be chargeable lifetime transfers.

■ There is a major exemption for amounts transferred to spouses or civil partners, usually referred to as the 'spouse exemption'. Assets can be gifted to a spouse or civil partner IHT-free. There is a trap if the donee spouse or civil partner is not domiciled in the UK as the exemption is limited to a meagre £55,000.

■ There are a number of small exemptions: a £3,000 annual exemption; gifts of £250; gifts in consideration of marriage of £5,000. There is also an underused and very important exemption for normal expenditure out of income (see page 363).

## Asset disposals – capital gains tax

In this section I will set out some CGT mitigation ideas.

### Using tax-efficient investments

■ *ISAs.* Gains on assets in ISAs are CGT-free so it is worth making the maximum investment each year.

■ *Pension funds.* Pension funds are highly tax-efficient vehicles and there is no CGT on gains arising in these funds.

■ *Open-ended investment companies (OEICs).* These are highly regulated investment vehicles, aimed at providing a pooled investment fund for a number of investors. These companies are subject to a favourable tax regime; in particular, they are not liable to capital gains tax on disposal of investments. It is possible to create a private OEIC for an individual or a family either in the UK or offshore.

■ *Insurance bonds.* These are also tax-efficient investment vehicles as they enable low or no tax growth, with tax-free asset switches within the bond. There are quite complex income tax rules, which provide that amounts received on surrender or partial surrender of the bond are liable to income tax. It is possible to surrender up to 5 per cent of the premium paid on the bond with no immediate charge to tax.

■ *Other vehicles.* There is a range of other funds available both onshore and offshore that provide for at least tax deferral on gains arising on investments.

### Pre-disposal planning

■ *Make sure you maximize your business asset taper relief (BATR).* Many owner-managers of companies automatically assume that their shares qualify for the generous BATR. In most instances they are right, but we come across a number of established family companies that have a valuable ongoing trade but that have also invested surplus cash into property or other investments. These investment activities can cause the loss of BATR, and the problem needs to be spotted early so that remedial action can be considered, such as a demerger.

There are other instances where there has been a transfer of shares between spouses that has resulted in a loss of BATR. The usual circumstance is where a spouse transfers shares in the quoted company in which he or she works to a non-working spouse to enable that spouse to have an income. The position can be rectified pre-sale, but extreme care is needed.

■ *Transfer to your spouse or civil partner.* The no-gain no-loss provisions apply regardless of the actual amount paid for the shares and regardless of the tax-residence status of the spouse. This opens up a number of opportunities. It can sometimes be beneficial to transfer shares from one spouse to another just before the sale of shares. Here are three possible reasons:
  - the use of the spouse's or civil partner's annual exemption;
  - the use of the spouse's or civil partner's losses;
  - to improve the taper relief position.

■ *Use the principal private residence (PPR) exemption.* Gains on an individual's main residence are exempt from tax. In most cases the position is simple, but there arc additional rules to cover a variety of situations. One helpful provision that applies in all cases is that, once a property has been an individual's PPR at any time, it is treated as being his or her PPR for the last three years of ownership. There is also a lettings exemption, of up to £40,000, for gains on a let property that at some time has been the individual's PPR. For individuals buying a second property that they will use as a residence, it will usually be worthwhile making an election to treat the second property as the PPR for tax purposes. The election need only be made for one week, but it will enable the last three years of ownership to qualify for PPR and the lettings exemption will become available.

■ *Emigrate.* The UK, unlike a number of other countries, neither taxes individuals on emigration nor taxes gains made by individuals who are not resident or ordinarily resident in the UK. A point to watch is that some gains that havc been held over or deferred are brought into charge on emigration. There is a restriction for people who leave the UK and return within five complete tax years. A common planning idea is simply to emigrate from the UK in one tax year, make a disposal the next and remain out of the UK for at least five complete tax years. Of course the tax position in the country you move to needs to be considered but, depending on the precise circumstances, it is possible to a move to a number of countries, including Canada, Australia, Spain, Belgium, France, Ireland and most of the tax havens, and not suffer a significant amount of tax on the disposal.

■ *Realize losses.* It is often possiblc to realize losses on assets in the same tax year or an earlier tax year to the disposal of the asset at a gain. An interest in the asset standing at a loss can be retained by transferring the asset into trust. The asset standing at a gain also needs to be transferred to the trust to be able to utilize the loss. There are also ideas that result in capital losses. These are sophisticated tax planning ideas and are most suitable for individuals who are willing to have a degree of uncertainty in their planning if the potential reward is high enough.

## Planning on disposal

■ *Use of loan notes and/or shares.* Often an individual selling a company will be offered shares in the buying company or loan notes. It is generally possible to ensure that there is no gain on the disposal of the old shares and the new shares or loan notes pick up the original capital gains tax cost. There are two types of loan notes: one effectively is an asset on which taper relief accrues and the other does not accrue taper relief at all. The taking of shares and/or loan notes can be used to extend the qualifying period for BATR purposes. The deferral can also be useful, as the individual may decide to emigrate and then dispose of the shares.

■ *Enterprise Investment Scheme (EIS) deferral relief.* Payment of CGT can be deferred by subscribing for shares, in cash, in an EIS qualifying company. There is no space to go into further detail here, but this will usually enable the tax to be deferred until the disposal of the EIS company shares, unless the disposal arises on death.

■ *Tax deferral ideas.* Whilst only really appropriate where the tax rate is close to the maximum 40 per cent, it is possible to defer tax on a gain by participating in a trading partnership that triggers losses in early years, followed by profits in later years. Fundamentally, these schemes are effectively a low-rate loan from the government. The most common of these types of partnership are film partnerships, but there are other ideas around. The tax rules for film partnerships have changed and, whilst there are still a few 'old style' partnerships around, there are new structures available.

## Passing wealth on – inheritance tax

■ *Give early.* As gifts to other individuals are exempt from IHT if the donor survives the gift by seven years, it is worth making gifts early. It is possible to insure against death within the seven years. It is also possible to make more complex gifts where either a part of the existing growth or future growth is given away. A major potential issue is that the gifts may be subject to CGT. In many cases the use of a trust will enable the CGT charge to be held over at the cost of a potential IHT exposure. If the gift is worth less than the IHT nil rate band then the gift can be made with no immediate charge to tax. It is not possible to hold over into settlor-interested trusts.

■ *Use nil rate bands.* Typically, spouses establish similar wills that provide that the estate of the first to die passes to the survivor. There is no IHT to pay on the first death and the whole of the estate is passed to the survivor. Basic planning for high net wealth individuals is to include a nil rate band discretionary trust in their will. This provision ensures that, to the extent the nil rate band is available, assets are transferred into a discretionary trust for the surviving spouse and others. This planning ensures that the nil rate band of the first to die is not wasted, and it can save £114,000 at current rates. It is also possible to include assets that qualify for 100 per cent BPR or APR in this will planning.

■ *Use the 'normal expenditure out of income' exemption.* This is simple and relatively painless – just give away surplus income on a regular basis. Of course it is necessary to be able to prove that the payments are 'normal expenditure' out of income, and it is essential to keep good records.

■ *Use the spouse exemption.* The spouse exemption can be used to ensure that there is no tax on the estate of the first spouse to die. If the surviving spouse immediately makes gifts then they will be PETs and there will be no tax if he or she survives for seven years. As there is a revaluation to market value for CGT purposes, assets can be transferred tax-free. It is possible to include a trust for the surviving spouse, which will give a measure of control over the assets. This can be useful in second marriages.

■ *Maximize IHT business property relief (BPR).* It is still possible to obtain 100 per cent IHT relief on a range of business assets after two years of ownership. BPR often arises on family companies, but there is also a range of ideas on the market including AIM companies, trading partnerships and furnished holiday lets. Some of the ideas are linked to EIS (see above) so CGT and IHT can be mitigated at the same time.

■ *Obtain IHT agricultural property relief (APR).* Some people still advocate buying an interest in farmland to obtain 100 per cent APR after two years of ownership. There are, as always, conditions attached to the relief; in particular, farmhouses are an increasing source of difficulty.

■ *Insurance products.* There is a range of insurance-related products that can be used in IHT mitigation. These range from simple insurance written in trust to complex products that enable individuals to move assets out of their estates yet still have access to the capital over a period of years. There are a number of variants on a theme, the most common being the discounted gift trust.

■ *Pensions.* These can be very IHT-efficient, but a drawback has always been the need to purchase an annuity. Now that this requirement has been removed there is scope for long-term effective planning.

## Non-domiciliaries

The UK is one of the finest tax havens in the world for individuals who are not UK-domiciled. The tax breaks are significant in that, even if UK resident, non-domiciliaries will only be liable to UK CGT on gains arising in the UK and non-UK gains remitted to the UK. The IHT position is similar in that they are only liable to tax on assets located in the UK. Relatively simple planning can improve the position even further.

For IHT only, individuals who have been resident in the UK for 17 out of the last 20 tax years are deemed to be UK-domiciled.

## Final comments

CGT and IHT planning for a high net wealth individual is a complex process, and the government keeps changing the goal posts. Many wealthy individuals neglect their personal finances, which is not surprising if all of their focus and energy are devoted to their businesses and their families. I believe that most high net wealth individuals would benefit from an integrated wealth management approach, covering legal, tax and financial planning. The equivalent of a business plan can be drawn up, including regular financial statements and forecasts, and these can be considered at 'board meetings' between the individuals and their advisers.

# The use of trusts

*Neil Morris and Amanda Nelson, Dawsons Solicitors*

## Types of trust

A trust can be a formal, or informal, structure for the ownership of assets by trustees for the benefit of beneficiaries, following a gift or transfer to the trustees by an individual (known as the 'settlor'). A trust is a flexible way for individuals to protect and control their estate either during their lifetime or after their death. There are three main types of trust. (There used to be a fourth, known as an accumulation and maintenance trust, for minor beneficiaries, and whilst there will still be many of these types of trust in existence they can no longer be established, following recent legislative changes.) The three main types of trust are as follows:

- *Discretionary trust.* The trustees of a discretionary trust hold the trust assets on behalf of a class of beneficiaries. None of the beneficiaries named in the trust document has a right to receive any benefit from the trust; instead the trustees are able to use their absolute discretion to provide capital and/or income to, or for the benefit of, any of those beneficiaries. Under English law, income can be retained within the trust fund for a maximum of 21 years, but after this time it must be paid out to the beneficiaries or used for their benefit.

    A settlor of a discretionary trust should always consider completing a letter of wishes. This is an informal document that sets out the settlor's wishes for the administration of the trust and the distribution of the assets. It is not legally binding on the trustees, and the trustees do not have to follow the wishes. However, it is a useful tool for the trustees, as it will often indicate the settlor's intention in establishing the trust.
- *Interest in possession trust.* A beneficiary of an interest in possession trust is entitled, as of right, to receive the income from the trust or to use the property held by the trust. After the beneficiary's death (or other specified event) the capital will pass to another beneficiary or group of beneficiaries.

■ *Bare trust.* The assets subject to a bare trust belong absolutely to the beneficiary but are held in the legal name of another. The trustee (sometimes referred to as a nominee) will hold the assets in his or her name but the beneficiary can direct the trustee to deal with the assets as the beneficiary requires.

## Trust applications

Trusts can be used in many different areas, such as in employee benefit schemes, pension schemes, and trusts for charity. However, the most common use of a trust is that which is established by a settlor, often for the benefit of his or her family. Offshore trusts remain a useful tool in certain circumstances, eg where the settlor is not domiciled in the UK, but this is outside the scope of this chapter.

The main purposes of establishing such trusts are as follows:

■ *Estate planning.* Settlors may wish to provide for successive generations whilst they are still alive (and therefore transfer assets out of their estate, without a tax charge, during their lifetime) or on their death, but may, for various reasons, wish to avoid the beneficiaries becoming absolutely entitled to those assets.
■ *Control.* Rather than a settlor giving assets to such beneficiaries outright, they may instead put the assets into a trust where, during their lifetime, they may retain some control over the funds (they may be a trustee, or they may provide the trustees with a letter of wishes as to the distribution of funds that the trustees may be minded to follow – although as discussed above the trustees do not have to follow such wishes). After their death they may want to give someone else control, eg the surviving spouse, or a professional (solicitor or accountant).
■ *Protection for vulnerable beneficiaries.* Settlors could gift assets to their children (or grandchildren) outright, but they may wish to avoid such beneficiaries having an absolute right to what could be substantial sums – a child's age may mean that he or she cannot be responsible for money, or he or she may be an adult but be financially immature or physically or mentally disabled. In the latter case the beneficiary may be in receipt of state benefits. A right to income from a trust could jeopardize such benefits, potentially causing the beneficiary hardship.

As well as a settlor's children, there may be other beneficiaries who require protection. A surviving spouse may encounter difficulties when managing money. Other family members may need funds but may not be in a position to control those funds themselves.

A trust, whether set up during a settlor's lifetime or on his or her death, may go some way to protecting the settlor's assets from depletion by such beneficiaries, or by the inadvertent actions of such a beneficiary, eg if the beneficiary became bankrupt.
■ *Protection from potential claimants.* As mentioned above, a potential beneficiary may be vulnerable to bankruptcy and so a settlor will not want to give that beneficiary an absolute entitlement to any assets that might then be claimed by his or her creditors.

Such trusts are often used by settlors to attempt to protect their assets from potential divorce proceedings by a spouse of a child. Although no trust is immune to the potential scrutiny of the courts in such proceedings, if a child is merely a beneficiary of a discretionary trust, with no right to receive any assets from the trust, then the assets may be less vulnerable to attack by the child's spouse than if the assets had been gifted to the child outright.

■ *Restricting entitlement and preserving capital.* Where a settlor wishes to provide for beneficiaries, but does not want them to have an absolute interest, he or she can reduce their entitlement immediately, or at least restrict it for a period of time. For example, a settlor could provide the children with an income only (by way of an interest in possession trust) or may include the children in a class of beneficiaries but give the trustees absolute discretion as to whom they benefit, when they benefit them and in what proportions.

■ *Preparing for future uncertainties.* Settlors may not wish to document precisely their beneficiaries' entitlement – they may be unsure as to how one or more of their children will develop, or they may anticipate their estate growing substantially in the future. In these circumstances they may prefer to leave their estate on purely discretionary trusts with a full letter of wishes to the trustees, guiding the trustees on how they would like them to deal with the estate if a number of eventualities occur.

■ *Privacy.* A particularly wealthy, or well-known, settlor (or one who is simply a very private individual) may wish to preserve an element of privacy over the estate. An individual's will becomes a public document once he or she has died and a grant of probate to the estate has been taken out by the executors. Trusts do not become public documents and so, by providing that assets are transferred to an existing trust on death, rather than including the trust within the will, a settlor can keep the details of the beneficiaries of the estate a secret from prying eyes.

■ *Tax mitigation.* Trusts are often used by settlors to mitigate their tax liability. As mentioned above, a trust can be a useful tool to decrease the size of a settlor's estate during his or her lifetime, thereby resulting in a smaller estate on which inheritance tax will be charged on death. Trusts are often used for capital gains tax planning and, to a lesser degree, income tax planning. Following the Finance Act 2006, tax mitigation by use of trusts has been limited but, if they are structured properly, there remains a good deal of scope for such planning.

It used to be the case that settlors could gift any amount to an interest in possession trust without an inheritance tax charge if they survived for seven years after the date of the gift. Under the Finance Act 2006 this is no longer the case, and gifts to interest in possession trusts are now treated, for inheritance tax purposes, in the same way as gifts to a discretionary trust, ie the value of a gift in excess of the settlor's available tax-free threshold (£300,000 as of April 2007) will be taxed at (currently) 20 per cent. Whilst this is quite a serious restriction on the use of such trusts, it does not preclude careful tax planning. Each individual settlor's tax-free threshold is renewed after seven years, so the individual can make a gift into trust on 1 January 2008 of £300,000 and a further gift of the then available tax-free threshold in January 2015. The available tax-free threshold in 2015 will be reduced by any gifts that the individual has made within the seven years between 2008 and 2015. In addition to the tax-free threshold, settlors can make tax-free gifts each year up to the value of £3,000 (£6,000 if they have not used the previous year's exemption, but this carry-forward provision is only permitted for one year). Also, if settlors have surplus income that is not required to maintain their normal standard of living they could establish a pattern of gifts to a trust, which will also be exempt from inheritance tax and will not be taken into account when calculating the tax-free threshold.

Another consequence of the Finance Act 2006 is that settlors must be careful to review the inheritance tax implications when providing for their children in their wills. Whilst there may be a charge to inheritance tax on a settlor's estate following death, a bequest in the will to a child absolutely at the age of 18 will not be subject to any ongoing inheritance tax charges. A bequest to a child absolutely at an age over 18 but before the age of 25 will be subject to a limited inheritance tax charge when the child reaches the specified age. A bequest to a child over the age of 25 will cause that child's fund to be treated as a discretionary trust (for the purposes of inheritance tax only) from the date of the settlor's death, resulting in a potentially higher tax charge when the beneficiary attains the specified age.

# Wills

## *Why make a will?*

Many people in the United Kingdom do not have wills, and one common reason is because they believe that, under the law of intestacy, if they die without a will the persons they wish to benefit will inherit. It is commonly assumed that a person's spouse or civil partner will inherit the whole of the estate. This, however, is not necessarily the case.

The law of intestacy sets up a regime that is meant to apply to a plethora of situations where somebody dies without a will. It therefore often fails to cover the specific situation that applies to a person's estate.

In the common situation where a person dies leaving a spouse or civil partner and children, under the law of intestacy the spouse receives personal chattels, the first £125,000 of the estate and interest on that sum until it is paid, and the income from one-half of the remainder of the estate for his or her life. The remainder of the estate passes to the children of the deceased in equal shares at age 18.

In some situations jointly owned property passes to the joint owner automatically and independently or a will or the law of intestacy.

There are a number of problems with the law of intestacy, including the following:

- Often people inherit the estate other than those intended by the deceased. Only close relatives receive any benefit.
- To the extent that children inherit, they receive their benefit at age 18, which in the case of substantial assets will often be considered as far too young.

■ It is not possible to cut beneficiaries out from inheriting, so if, for example, the deceased was not on speaking terms with one of his or her children, the child could not be disinherited.
■ Stepchildren and persons with whom the deceased lived but to whom the deceased was not married do not inherit.

## Matters to be covered by a will

■ Funeral wishes.
■ The appointment of executors and trustees. It is sensible to appoint persons who know the intended beneficiaries personally and understand the financial implications of the estate. These are often close family, close friends or professional advisers (solicitors, accountants or a bank trustee company).
■ A guardian can be appointed to take legal decisions for a child of the deceased aged under 18.
■ Cash legacies or legacies of specified chattels can be left to family members, friends or charity.
■ Residuary estate usually passes to close family members, friends or charity.

## Trusts in wills

It is often necessary to include trusts in wills, either for tax planning purposes or to protect intended beneficiaries. For tax planning purposes, a discretionary trust of the inheritance tax nil rate band (currently £285,000) for the benefit of the surviving spouse and children is often used to preserve the inheritance tax exemption of the first spouse to die as otherwise, if all the estate passes to the surviving spouse, the exemption of the first to die will be lost.

Trusts are often used in wills to provide for a surviving spouse in a second-marriage situation where capital is eventually to pass to the children of the first marriage. The surviving spouse will receive income during his or her lifetime, with power to give him or her capital or to make provision for children. A trust is often necessary because children are too young to inherit at the time the will is made. An age is generally specified when they receive capital and income, although the age is not necessarily the same.

In cases of vulnerable beneficiaries, wills can include a trust for disabled persons, with the assets being protected and managed for them, and in cases of impecunious beneficiaries a protective mechanism can be added so that income is received until such time as an event to trigger the protective mechanism takes place, such as bankruptcy.

## Finance Act 2006

Following the changes to the inheritance tax treatment of trusts, it is necessary to review existing wills to see whether any changes are needed to the provisions made.

## Deeds of variation

Although when people make wills they endeavour to ensure that the will takes care of the beneficiaries for whom they wish to provide at the time the will is made, circumstances may change before a testator dies. For tax purposes, it is possible for a beneficiary named in a will to redirect benefit to third parties, provided it is done within two years of death and there is no consideration for the variation.

# TOTALLY
# FIRST CLASS

At Forsters, we pride ourselves in handling our private clients' affairs with the utmost integrity, discretion and professionalism. Our Mayfair-based team, recognised as one of the top advisers in the UK, also offers superlative off-shore trust and international jurisdictional expertise.

Our advice on wills, tax and trust planning, estate administration and family and matrimonial issues is second to none. We help UK and international clients structure and protect family wealth, business assets and private property.

Our lawyers passionately believe in working with their clients to create tailored solutions to maximise their interests and achieve the best possible outcomes.

All of which places us, we believe, in a class of our own.

For further information, please call Carole Cook on:

## 020 7863 8333
www.forsters.co.uk

FORSTERS

Forsters LLP • Solicitors • 31 Hill Street • Mayfair • London • W1J 5LS

# Inheritance tax, wills and estate planning for high net worth individuals

*Carole Cook and Clare McCulloch, Forsters*

Death is the only certainty in life. Most individuals have a natural aversion to planning for this event, but forward planning will help to protect your family's financial security as well as maximizing the amount you can pass on to them.

## What is inheritance tax and when is it payable?

Inheritance tax (IHT) is a tax on 'chargeable transfers' made by individuals during their lifetime and on the value of their assets on death. A number of exemptions and reliefs help to reduce the impact of IHT, the most important of which is the spouse exemption: transfers between married couples or civil partners are completely free of inheritance tax. In addition, transfers of certain types of agricultural and business property qualify for reliefs at the rate of 100 per cent and 50 per cent.

Individuals domiciled in the UK are potentially liable to IHT on their worldwide assets. Individuals domiciled outside the UK are only liable to IHT on their UK assets.

Every individual must have a domicile at any given time. Domicile is different from residence, which merely denotes physical presence. At birth, a child acquires a domicile of origin, which is generally the father's domicile at that date. This is not necessarily the country in which the child is born or one in which the child ever resides. Domicile can change when an individual voluntarily acquires a new domicile. To acquire a new 'domicile of choice', an individual must move to a new country (or state) with the intention of making it his or her permanent home.

An individual domiciled outside the UK can nonetheless be deemed to be domiciled in the UK for IHT purposes. This happens in two circumstances: 1) when a non-UK domiciliary has been resident in the UK for income tax purposes for 17 out of the last 20 tax years; and 2) for the first three years following the emigration of an individual previously domiciled in the UK.

There are a number of IHT planning opportunities for non-domiciled individuals; these are outside the scope of this chapter, and we recommend that specific advice is obtained.

## Rates of tax

IHT is payable on death at the rate of 40 per cent, after allowance for a tax-exempt (or nil rate) band. The nil rate band is currently £300,000, but is set to rise to £312,000 in 2008/09 and £325,000 in 2009/10. IHT on lifetime chargeable transfers is payable at half the death rate, ie 20 per cent. Chargeable transfers are aggregated over a seven-year period. Therefore, the rate of tax on a chargeable transfer depends on the total value of any chargeable transfers made in the last seven years. Chargeable transfers cease to be aggregated after seven years.

# How can an individual reduce the burden of IHT on death?

This can best be achieved by a combination of lifetime gifts, a sensible tax-efficient will (that is kept up to date) and insurance.

Lifetime gifts can be made either to individuals absolutely or in trust for their benefit. Changes in the 2006 Finance Act have significantly reduced the potential for IHT planning by way of lifetime gifts to trusts.

When contemplating making significant lifetime gifts, individuals must ensure that they retain sufficient for their own needs and should consider the effect of possible future changes to their personal circumstances and the fiscal climate.

## Lifetime gifts

The current tax regime favours outright lifetime gifts to individuals.

In order to be effective for IHT, all gifts must be absolute and unconditional. If the donor retains any benefit in the subject matter of the gift, it will be a 'gift with reservation' and will still be included in the donor's estate. There is another trap for the unwary in the form of the income tax charge on 'pre-owned assets'. Where a gift is not caught by the reservation-of-benefit rules, but the donor continues to benefit in some way after the gift has been made, the donor may be subject to an income tax charge on the annual value of the benefit received.

The well-advised individual should take full advantage of the various IHT exemptions available for lifetime gifts:

- *The annual IHT exemption.* Everyone can make gifts up to a total of £3,000 in every tax year without attracting IHT. This exemption can be carried over for one year only.
- *Gifts on the occasion of a marriage or registration of a civil partnership.* Gifts in consideration of a marriage or registration of a civil partnership are also exempt (up to a limit of £5,000 for a parent, £2,500 for a grandparent and £1,000 for others).
- *Small gifts.* Gifts not exceeding £250 to any one person in any one year are exempt. This exemption cannot be combined with another exemption.
- *Gifts that qualify as normal expenditure out of income.* This is a particularly useful exemption for individuals with high incomes. The exemption can be claimed where the gifts in question:
  - are made out of income;
  - are part of the normal expenditure of the donor; and
  - leave the donor with sufficient income to maintain his or her usual standard of living.

Anyone intending to rely upon this relief should keep detailed annual records of salary and investment and other income, together with details of all gifts made, bills paid, nursing home fees and other expenditure. It is important to establish a regular pattern of giving; a letter of intent addressed to the donee can provide helpful evidence in relation to the first in a series of gifts. Provided all the conditions are satisfied there is no upper limit to the amount of income that can be given away free of IHT under this exemption.

## Gifts up to the nil rate band

In addition to gifts that qualify for one of the above exemptions, an individual can give away assets up to the value of the nil rate band every seven years without incurring IHT. This could be one large gift or a series of smaller gifts.

## Potentially exempt transfers

Outright gifts to individuals that are in excess of the nil rate band (or that, when aggregated with gifts made in the preceding seven years, come to a total in excess of the nil rate band) are potentially exempt transfers (PETs). No IHT is payable at the time of the gift, and the gift is completely exempt if the donor survives for seven years after the gift is made. If the donor does not survive seven years, but survives for at least three years, the rate of IHT is reduced in accordance with a sliding scale. It is important to remember that this 'taper relief' only operates to reduce the tax bill where the value of the PETs exceeds the nil rate band.

## Which assets should be given away?

Ideally an individual should make gifts of assets that are expected to increase in value, for example private company shares, or art by a living artist. Not only will the individual have removed the future growth in value from his or her estate, but the relevant value for IHT purposes will be the value as at the date of the gift.

Careful thought should also be given to capital gains tax. Gifts are disposals for capital gains tax purposes; therefore gifts of assets standing at a gain may result in a charge to capital gains tax.

## *Lifetime gifts to trusts*

Outright gifts to minors or young adults of significant sums of money or assets may not always be appropriate. Therefore, historically, trusts have been a useful tool to pass assets on to the next generation, without necessarily giving them control of the relevant assets. However, the rules relating to gifts to trusts were radically changed in the 2006 Finance Act. All lifetime settlements (with the exception of trusts for the disabled) are now taxed under 'the relevant property regime'. This means that they are subject to an IHT entry charge (at 20 per cent of the value in excess of the nil rate band) and periodic charges (every 10 years) and exit charges (whenever capital leaves the trust) to IHT. Under current rules, the periodic and exit charges cannot exceed 6 per cent.

'Nil rate band' trusts can still be established every seven years without incurring an immediate IHT charge. Therefore a married couple could, between them, gift £600,000 to a trust for their children or grandchildren, without incurring an immediate charge. The exercise could be repeated after seven years.

One alternative where the contemplated gift is to a minor may be to use a 'bare trust'. A bare trust is where the single beneficiary has an immediate and absolute right to both income and capital. It is merely the legal title to the property, which is held by the trustees. A transfer to a bare trust will be treated as an outright gift for IHT purposes, but it should be noted that the minor will be able to call for the assets at the age of 18.

## *Tax-efficient wills*

The importance of making a will cannot be overstated. Not only will it avoid the application of intestacy rules (which can sometimes have surprising and unintended results), but individuals can select executors and trustees to carry out their wishes and ensure that their assets are dealt with as tax-efficiently as possible.

If a married couple leave all of their assets to each other, there will be no IHT on the first death because of the spouse exemption, but they may have wasted the nil rate band of the first to die and a potential tax saving of £120,000 (40 per cent of £300,000).

Taking a married couple with children, a typical tax-efficient will for the first to die might provide:

■ Property to the value of the nil rate band is directed to a discretionary trust for a class of beneficiaries including the spouse and children. This enables the surviving spouse to benefit from these assets if necessary, but ensures they are not part of his or her estate for IHT purposes.

- Agricultural and/or business property qualifying for 100 per cent relief is left to the children.
- The remainder of the estate goes absolutely to the spouse or civil partner or into a life interest trust for his or her benefit. The latter enables the first to die to control the ultimate destination of the assets.

This structure will ensure that no IHT is payable on the first death.

As a result of changes in the Finance Act 2006, where individuals wish to leave assets in trust for their children under their will, unless the trust is one of three favoured types the trust will be subject to the relevant property regime, ie to periodic and exit charges to IHT. The three favoured types of trust are:

- *Bereaved minors' trusts.* The only minors who can benefit are children or stepchildren (not grandchildren) of the individual making the will. In addition, there must be equality between each of the beneficiaries (the trustees cannot have flexibility to pick and choose) and the beneficiaries must become entitled to the income and capital at the age of 18.
- *Age 18–25 trusts.* These are a possibility only if the children are under the age of 25. Age 18–25 trusts are more flexible than bereaved minors' trusts in that capital does not have to pass to the children until they reach the age of 25. Such flexibility does, however, come at a price: there is a special IHT charge (on a sliding scale of up to 4.2 per cent, depending on the age of the recipient) to pay if the trust remains in being after the children reach the age of 18.
- *An immediate post-death interest.* This is an immediate life interest trust created by will. The assets in the trust are then taxed for IHT purposes as if the beneficiary owned them personally.

# The family home

The family home deserves a separate mention as it raises a common dilemma – it is of significant value, and yet the wish to give away part, or all, of it to save IHT is incompatible with the owner's need to keep a roof over his or her head. Mitigating the IHT that would otherwise fall due on the death of the owner is a difficult task, owing to the various anti-avoidance provisions in the IHT legislation. However, there are some simple steps that should always be considered.

Where the home is owned solely by one party to a marriage or civil partnership, the sole owner should consider transferring it into joint names as tenants in common. This means that the share of the first to die can pass according to the terms of that person's will and would enable the person to leave his or her share to the children. Alternatively a share up to the value of the nil rate band could be given to a discretionary trust for the benefit of the surviving spouse and the children. This would ensure that the share is outside the survivor's estate for IHT purposes, without affecting the survivor's ability to remain in occupation, or the main residence exemption for capital gains tax purposes.

Equity release schemes are a popular way of releasing part of the value of the family home whilst the owners continue to occupy it. The cash raised can be given away subject to the normal IHT rules. However, the equity release scheme itself must be entered into with an independent provider – if entered into with family members the pre-owned assets income tax charge will apply.

Giving part of the house to other family members is another alternative. However, unless all co-owners occupy the house this may fall foul of the reservation-of-benefit provisions.

## Other planning points

### Equalization of assets

It is advisable for the assets of a married couple or civil partners to be divided equally between them to give the greatest scope for tax planning. Transfers between spouses or civil partners are not only exempt from IHT, but are also on a no-gain no-loss basis for capital gains tax, ie no capital gains tax is payable. Individuals should ensure that, at the very least, their spouse or civil partner has sufficient assets to use up his or her nil rate band.

### Insurance

It may be appropriate to make arrangements to cover all or part of the anticipated IHT bill on death with life assurance. The life assurance should be written into trust to ensure it is outside the individual's estate for IHT purposes.

### Other insurance products

These are outside the scope of this chapter, but may be useful planning tools for some individuals.

### Assets that qualify for relief

If individuals own business or agricultural property at the date of their death, the property may attract relief at either 100 per cent or 50 per cent (depending on the exact nature of the property in question and the period of ownership). As business property includes AIM investments, it is possible for a well-managed AIM portfolio to be a satisfactory investment in itself, whilst also attracting IHT relief at 100 per cent.

### Gifts to charities

It is worth noting that gifts to charity qualify for 100 per cent relief from IHT.

## Conclusion

This is a very complex subject, and this chapter can do no more than set out general guidelines and limits. It is no substitute for professional advice.

# Tax issues: evasion, avoidance and mitigation

*Trevor James, Mazars*

It was Denis Healey who once famously said that the difference between evasion and avoidance was the thickness of a prison wall! This chapter looks at the distinctions between evasion and avoidance and asks whether there is a blurring of the two. It also considers where mitigation fits in. Finally, the article looks at how Her Majesty's Revenue and Customs (HMRC) detects evasion and avoidance and how its Special Civil Investigations office deals with these.

## Avoidance and mitigation

'Tax avoidance' is the legal utilization of the tax regime to one's own advantage, in order to reduce the amount of tax that is payable by means that are within the law. Examples of tax avoidance involve using tax deductions, changing one's tax status through incorporation or changing one's tax residence (or domicile) and establishing a company, trust or foundation in an offshore tax haven.

In the UK, despite consultations going back many years, there is no general anti-avoidance rule. This in itself is unusual amongst developed countries in that the UK has neither statute nor a legal principle to counter tax avoidance in general. There are, however, certain provisions within the tax legislation (known as 'anti-avoidance provisions') that apply to prevent tax avoidance in specific circumstances where the main object (or purpose), or one of the main objects (or purposes), of a transaction is to enable tax advantages to be obtained. Judicial doctrines, relying on a purposive construction of tax legislation, are continually being evolved to prevent tax avoidance involving circular, self-cancelling transactions (*WT Ramsay Limited* v *CIR* 54 TC 101), or where steps with no commercial purpose other than the avoidance of tax are inserted into a transaction (*Furniss* v *Dawson* (1984) 2 WLR 226). A purposive interpretation of legislation seeks to look at what Parliament intended rather than the exact words used.

Controversially, in the 2004 Budget, it was announced that 'promoters' and users of certain tax avoidance schemes would be required to disclose details of the schemes to HMRC. It is widely agreed that these rules have allowed HMRC to identify and close down avoidance loopholes more quickly than previously.

The UK authorities use the term 'tax mitigation' to refer to acceptable tax planning, minimizing tax liabilities in ways expressly endorsed by Parliament. For example, the provision of a company van to an employee would cost the employee a significant amount less tax (and the employer less Class 1A National Insurance) than a company car. Or perhaps loss relief or pension relief could be carried back to a year where there was a higher-rate liability. It has been suggested that tax mitigation is within what Parliament intended, but that it is tax avoidance if it is outside those intentions. Clearly the issue of just what Parliament intended when it enacted the legislation is key, but far too often unclear.

As set out above, on this view tax avoidance flouts the spirit of the law while following the letter and is therefore thought by some to be unacceptable, albeit not criminal in the way that evasion is. This is certainly the view of HMRC. Upholding a difference between mitigation and avoidance relies on a purposive reading of legislation, and commentators disagree as to the extent to which this is permissible.

## Avoidance and evasion

By contrast, 'tax evasion' or 'tax fraud' is the general term for efforts by individuals, firms, trusts and other entities to evade the payment of taxes by illegal means. Tax evasion involves intentional behaviour or a degree of knowledge and normally includes taxpayers deliberately misrepresenting or concealing the true state of their affairs to the tax authorities in order to reduce their tax liability. It includes dishonest tax reporting (such as the understating of income, profits or gains, or the overclaiming of expenses and deductions).

Tax avoidance may be considered to be the amoral flouting of one's duties to society or, in the eyes of the tax adviser, the right of everyone (individuals and companies) to structure one's affairs in a manner allowed by law, to pay no more tax than is required. In the words of Lord Tomlin, in the House of Lords in *IRC* v *Duke of Westminster* (1936) 19 TC 490, [1936] AC 1:

> Every man is entitled if he can to order his affairs so as that the tax attaching under the appropriate Acts is less than it otherwise would be. If he succeeds in ordering them so as to secure this result, then, however unappreciative the Commissioners of Inland Revenue or his fellow taxpayers may be of his ingenuity, he cannot be compelled to pay an increased tax.

Whilst this held good 70 years ago, the Ramsay case back in 1981 was evidence that the courts would no longer see tax avoidance as acceptable where schemes were wholly artificial and preordained in their outcome.

Tax evasion, however, is a specific application of the doctrine of evasion and, as such, it is a crime in almost all countries and subjects the guilty party not only to fiscal penalties but potentially to imprisonment.

# The detection of evasion

HMRC bases its investigation work around information and risk. All tax returns, be they corporate or personal, are risk-assessed. Individual entries are analysed by computer and comparisons made with other entries on the return and with previous years. For example, HMRC would be concerned with a director's remuneration that failed to keep pace with inflation, or that fell year on year. Clearly the risk analysis would look at other income available, eg dividends or rents, but not necessarily a partner's income.

More recently, HMRC's attention has been moving towards personal tax compliance and it has set up a number of personal tax units specifically to bring together the affairs of high-earning or high net worth individuals so that their returns can be monitored more closely by inspectors who specialize in subjects such as capital gains tax, enterprise management incentives, share schemes, termination payments, etc.

Another target is UK-resident non-domiciliaries who declare little in the way of income – on the basis that there must be capital and/or income available offshore that will have been remitted to finance the lifestyle. In the writer's experience, remitting income (which would attract a tax liability), usually contrary to the instructions given by the adviser, is a good illustration of where avoidance and evasion run close together. It is sometimes difficult to know what is innocent error and what is deliberate. Whilst any unpaid tax would be seen as culpable, and therefore subject to interest and penalties, the matter would rarely be considered as serious fraud even if the amounts were significant. The writer had one case whilst at the Special Compliance Office that involved a non-domiciliary who had omitted a £2.8 million gain from his 2001 tax return and even this was dealt with under the more relaxed Code of Practice 8, rather than Code 9, which is used where there are suspicions of serious fraud.

Analyses of trading accounts, be they of a company, a partnership or a sole trader, would look at relationships between various entries: purchases to stock and creditors, for example, or sales to debtors. They also routinely make sure (where possible) that expected gross profit rates have been achieved, that drawings are adequate and that capital introduced can be afforded. Where an investigation is contemplated, the local office will put together a package of information, including land registry and district valuer details relating to the trader's or director's house, and notes of a field visit that describe the property, estimate its value and detail what vehicles are present. The pack will also contain third-party information – anonymous letters, details of bank and building society interest received, and investments in ISAs and PEPs, copies of previous tax returns and the results of the analysis work mentioned earlier.

# Serious tax fraud

The largest or most serious cases are dealt with by HMRC's Special Civil Investigations (SCI) (formerly the Special Compliance Office). This chapter will look at those dealt with under Code of Practice 9 – cases in which SCI suspect serious fraud. Until 31 August 2005 the investigation procedure was known simply as 'Hansard'. It had been around for over 80 years, successfully underpinning the Board of Inland Revenue's selective prosecution policy, and involved, in brief, a financial settlement with the taxpayer (as an alternative to a prison sentence) in exchange for a full confession of all tax irregularities.

In late 2003, the procedure was enhanced following the decision in the case of *R v Gill and Gill* (2003) STC 1229,CA. In the Court of Appeal, Clarke LJ rejected the Revenue's argument that the Hansard process was a civil one, instead concluding that tax fraud involved the commission of a criminal offence or offences and, as such, it was held that the investigation should have been conducted under the Police and Criminal Evidence Act 1984 (PACE 1984). This in turn requires a caution along the lines of: 'I must caution you that you do not have to say anything but that anything you do say will be taken down and may be used in evidence against you.' Interviews with the taxpayer would also be recorded.

Following the merger of the Inland Revenue with Customs and Excise on 18 April 2005, a new procedure for dealing with serious fraud was devised that would allow for the recovery of both direct and indirect taxes. This was introduced on 1 September 2005 and is known as CIF – the Civil Investigation of Fraud. As its name suggests, this is a wholly civil procedure and PACE no longer applies. There is now no requirement to caution a taxpayer or to record meetings. The investigation is still dealt with under Code of Practice 9, although this has been substantially rewritten.

Once a case has been registered by SCI for investigation under Code 9, an opening letter is issued to the taxpayer and his or her agent advising them of this and requesting a meeting. During that meeting the taxpayer is advised of the Board of HMRC's policy on tax fraud, which is this:

The practice of HM Revenue and Customs in cases of suspected serious tax fraud is as follows:

1.  The Commissioners reserve complete discretion to pursue a criminal investigation with a view to prosecution where they consider it necessary and appropriate.
2.  Where a criminal investigation is not considered necessary or appropriate the Commissioners may decide to investigate using the Civil Investigation of Fraud procedure.
3.  Where the Commissioners decide to investigate using the Civil Investigation of Fraud procedure they will not seek a prosecution for the

tax fraud which is the subject of that investigation. The taxpayer will be given an opportunity to make a full and complete disclosure of all irregularities in their tax affairs.

4.  However, where materially false statements are made or materially false documents are provided with intent to deceive, in the course of a civil investigation, the Commissioners may conduct a criminal investigation with a view to prosecution of that conduct.

5.  If the Commissioners decide to investigate using the Civil Investigation of Fraud procedure the taxpayer will be given a copy of this statement by an authorized officer.

Upon signifying his or her understanding of this statement, the taxpayer is then asked five questions relating to direct taxes (ie income tax, corporation tax, capital gains tax, inheritance tax, National Insurance contributions and tax credits):

■  *Question 1.* 'Have any transactions been omitted from or incorrectly recorded in the books of any business with which you are or have been concerned whether as a director, partner or sole proprietor to the best of your knowledge and belief?'

■  *Question 2.* 'Are the accounts sent to HM Revenue and Customs for each and every business with which you are or have been concerned whether as a director, partner or sole proprietor, correct and complete to the best of your knowledge and belief?'

■  *Question 3.* 'Are all the tax returns of each and every business with which you are or have been concerned whether as a director, partner or sole proprietor correct and complete to the best of your knowledge and belief?'

■  *Question 4.* 'Are all your personal tax returns correct and complete to the best of your knowledge and belief?'

■  *Question 5.* 'Will you allow an examination of all business books, business and private bank statements and any other business and private records in order that HM Revenue and Customs may be satisfied that your answers to the first four questions are correct?'

Each answer should be either yes or no and must be in writing, signed by the taxpayer. The questions have no time limit and cover the taxpayer's whole taxation lifetime. They also refer to worldwide income and gains, not just those arising in the United Kingdom.

There are a further four (broadly similar) questions asked where there may be irregularities involving indirect taxes.

On the basis that the taxpayer has a disclosure to make, he or she is invited to tell the meeting just what the irregularities are, what amounts are involved, how the irregularities were committed and over what period they occurred. The taxpayer is also invited to make a payment on account in respect of the unpaid duties.

The taxpayer is then invited to commission a report (known as a disclosure report) that tests the original disclosure for accuracy and that examines all other business and private financial affairs in detail to ensure there are no other irregularities. At the end of the day, if a full disclosure is made, there is a guarantee of no prosecution. If the disclosure report is materially incomplete or incorrect or it is supplied with false statements or documents, HMRC will seriously consider prosecuting that action.

The report itself will typically take between 4 and 12 months to complete, depending on the complexities of the case, and should be accompanied by a number of certificates, namely:

■ an adoption certificate, which effectively makes the report that of the taxpayer rather than his or her agent;
■ a certificate of bank and building society accounts operated;
■ a certificate of credit cards operated; and
■ a statement of assets and liabilities and business interests.

Each of these carries the stark warning 'False statements may result in a criminal investigation with a view to prosecution.' It is felt that HMRC will want to test and bolster the new procedure by carrying out its threat just as soon as a suitable case presents itself.

# Contributors' contact list

**Arc Fund Management Ltd**
22 Lovat Lane
London EC3R 8EB
Tel: +44 (0) 20 7623 3345
Fax: +44 (0) 20 7623 3362
Contact: Chris Powell
e-mail: c.powell@arcfundmanagement.com

**Ashcourt Group**
22–24 Ely Place
London EC1N 6TE
Tel: +44 (0) 20 7269 7550
Fax: +44 (0) 20 7404 8816
Contact: Peter Hearn
e-mail: peterhearn@ashcourt.uk.com

**Atkinson Bolton Consulting Ltd**
Cheveley House
Fordham Road
Newmarket
Suffolk CB8 7XN
Tel: +44 (0) 845 458 1223
Fax: +44 (0) 845 458 1224
Contact: Simon Gibson
e-mail: simon@atkinsonbolton.co.uk

**Beringea Ltd**
39 Earlham Street
London WC2H 9LT
Tel: +44 (0) 20 7845 7820
Fax: +44 (0) 20 7845 7821
Contact: Jeff Cornish
e-mail: jcornish@beringea.co.uk

**British Horseracing Board**
151 Shaftesbury Avenue
London WC2H 8AL
Tel: +44 (0) 20 7152 0047
Contact: James Oldring
e-mail: joldring@bhb.co.uk

**Charities Aid Foundation**
25 Kings Hill Avenue
Kings Hill
West Malling
Kent ME19 4TA
Tel: +44 (0) 1732 520338
Contact: Stefan Velvick
e-mail: svelvick@cafonline.org
www.cafonline.org/giving

**Cheviot Asset Management**
90 Long Acre
London WC2E 9RA
Tel: +44 (0) 20 7845 6150
Fax: +44 (0) 20 7845 6155
Contact: Alan McIntosh
e-mail: alan.mcintosh@cheviot.co.uk

**Cunningham Coates Stockbrokers**
19 Donegall Street
Belfast BT1 2HA
Tel: +44 (0) 28 9032 3456
Fax: +44 (0) 28 9023 1479
Contact: Catharine Dixon
e-mail: cathy.dixon@ccstockbrokers.com

**Dawsons Solicitors**
2 New Square
Lincoln's Inn
London WC2A 3RZ
Tel: +44 (0) 20 7421 4838
Fax: +44 (0) 20 7421 4850
Contact: Neil Morris
e-mail: n.morris@dawsons-legal.com

**DiaMine Explorations, Inc.**
5225 Orbitor Drive, #23
Mississuaga
Ontario L4W 4Y8
Canada
Tel: +001 905 625 4391
Fax: +001 905 625 0677
Contact: H John Stollery
e-mail: info@diamineexplorations.com

**Dickinson Dees**
112 Quayside
Newcastle upon Tyne NE99 1SB
Tel: +44 (0) 191 279 9000
Fax: +44 (0) 191 279 9100
Contact: Allan Holmes
e-mail: Allan.Holmes@dickinson-dees.com

**EFG Private Bank Ltd**
12 Hay Hill
London W1J 6DW
Tel: +44 (0) 20 7872 3646
Fax: +44 (0) 20 7872 3706
Contact: Claire Griffiths
e-mail: claire.griffiths@efgl.com

**Forsters LLP**
311 Hill Street
London W1J 5LS
Tel: +44 (0) 20 7863 8333
Fax: +44 (0) 20 7863 8444
Contact: Carole Cook
e-mail: cacook@forsters.co.uk
www.forsters.co.uk

**Fortis Private Investment Management**
63 St Mary Axe
London EC3A 8LT
Tel: +44 (0) 20 7369 4800
Fax: +44 (0) 20 7369 4888
Contact: Tony Munson
e-mail: fpiminformation@fortis.com

**FortunaLand Investments SL**
Edificio Hotel Fuengirola Beach Complex
Avenida de la Encarnacion, No 2
Fuengirola 29640
Malaga
Spain
Tel: +34 (0) 952 922 400; UK local rate: 0871 990 2005
Fax: +34 (0) 952 922 401
Contact: Steve Oakenfull

**fountains plc**
Forestry Division
Blenheim Court
George Street
Banbury
Oxfordshire OX16 5RA
Tel: + 44 (0) 1295 753252
Contact: Alan Guy
e-mail: alan.guy@fountainsplc.com

**James Goodwin**
Street Farm
Newbourne
Woodbridge
Suffolk IP12 4PX
Tel: +44 (0) 794 707 3939
e-mail: jamesdgoodwin@hotmail.com

**Grosvenor International**
51 Welbeck Street
London W1G 9HL
Tel: +44 (0) 20 7586 0088
Contact: Jan Morgan
e-mail: mail@grosvenorinternational.com

**Harlon Overseas Property**
363 West Barnes Lane
New Malden
Surrey KT3 6JH
Tel: +44 (0) 20 8942 9558
Fax: +44 (0) 20 8404 7003
Contact: Anna Farrugia
e-mail: property@harlon.co.uk
www.harlon.co.uk

**Interest in Wine Ltd**
Hillfield House
Eldersfield
Gloucestershire GL19 4NN
Tel: +44 (0) 1452 840116
Contact: Nick Stephens
e-mail: nick.stephens@interestinwine.com

**Katalyst Ventures Ltd**
Sulney Fields
Upper Broughton
Melton Mowbray
Leicestershire LE14 3BD
Tel: +44 (0) 1664 823810
Contact: Anthony Collinson
e-mail: invest@katalystventures.com
katalystventures.com/wealthregister

**KMS Baltics**
Woodland Place
West Street
Belford
Northumberland NE70 7QA
Tel: +44 (0) 1668 213693
Contact: Felix Karthaus
e-mail: felix_karthaus@msn.com

**KSB Law LLP**
Elan House
5–11 Fetter Lane
London EC4A 1QD
Tel: +44 (0) 20 7822 7500
Fax: +44 (0) 20 7822 7600
Contact: Ian Lane
e-mail: ilane@ksblaw.co.uk

**Lincoln Financial Group**
Barnett Way
Barnwood
Gloucester GL4 3RZ
Tel: +44 (0) 1452 374242
Fax: +44 (0) 1452 374042
Contact: Stuart Tyler
e-mail: stuart.tyler@lincolnuk.co.uk

**Mazars**
Sovereign Court
Witan Gate
Milton Keynes MK9 2HP
Tel: +44 (0) 1908 680737
Fax: +44 (0) 1908 690567
Contact: Paula Gurney
e-mail: Paula.Gurney@mazars.co.uk

**Partners Capital Investment Group LLC**
60 Sloane Avenue
London SW3 3DD
Tel: +44 (0) 20 7925 8070
Contact: Stan Miranda
e-mail: Stan.Miranda@partners-cap.com

**Pastor-Genève BVBA**
118 rue du Rhône
Genève, CH-1204
Switzerland
Tel: +41 22 810 3338
Fax: +41 22 810 3339
Contact: Stephen Hershoff
e-mail: info@pastor-geneve.com

**Pointon York SIPP Solutions Limited**
Pointon York House
Welland Valley Business Park
Valley Way
Market Harborough LE16 7PS
Tel: +44 (0) 1858 419300
Fax: +44 (0)1858 419400
Contact: Christine Hallett
e-mail: challett@sippsolutions.com

**Sarasin Chiswell**
Juxon House
100 St Paul's Churchyard
London EC4M 8BU
Tel: +44 (0) 20 7038 7099
Fax: +44 (0) 20 7038 6850
Contact: Nicholas Lambert
e-mail: nicholas.lambert@sarasin.co.uk

**Seymour Management**
22 Grafton Street
London W1S 4EX
Tel: +44 (0) 20 7493 2662
Fax: +44 (0) 20 7493 1661
Contact: Spencer Ewen
e-mail: spencer.ewen@seymourmanagement.co.uk

**Suffolk Life Annuities Limited**
153 Princes Street
Ipswich
Suffolk IP1 1QJ
Tel/fax: +44 (0) 1794 324608
Contact: John Moret
john.moret@suffolklife.co.uk

**Sun Kissed Homes**
80 Thurston House
Lincoln Road
Peterborough
PE1 2SN
Tel: +44 (0) 845 370 8870
Contact: Ian Hunter
e-mail: ian.hunter@sunkissedhomes.co.uk

**Taylor Young Investment Management**
Tower Bridge Court
224–226 Tower Bridge Road
London SE1 2UL
Tel: +44 (0) 20 7378 4500
Fax: +44 (0) 20 7378 4501
Contact: Nick Rundle
e-mail: Nick.Rundle@tyim.co.uk

**World Gold Council**
55 Old Broad Street
London EC2M 1RX
Tel: +44 (0) 7826 4700
Fax: +44 (0) 7826 4799
Contact: Natalie Dempster
e-mail: natalie.dempster@gold.org

# Index

# Index of advertisers

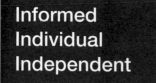

# Informed
# Individual
# Independent

**FORTIS**

"I never thought managing my money would be more difficult than making it; it was more time consuming and complex than I ever imagined. But at Fortis they understand how to balance my demand for performance and interesting ideas with my aspiration for a comfortable lifestyle; it continues to be a great partnership."

To build or lead a successful business takes determination, discipline and reliability, amongst many other attributes.

Whether you are still building your business or have created and sold your company, it is likely that you will be used to making swift decisions and choosing to deal with people who share your principles and understanding of service needs.

Our forte is always to adapt our investment management services to the requirements of our clients – our approach is as individual as each client. However, our investment strategies are devised to react dynamically to market changes and are based on a clearly structured and disciplined framework.

Please contact us:

**Fortis Private Investment Management**

Telephone +44 (0)20 7369 4800, Fax +44 (0)20 7369 4888

Email fpiminformationuk@fortis.com

**www.fpim.fortis.com**

The value of investments and the income from them varies and you may realise less than the sum invested. Fortis Private Investment Management Ltd is authorised and regulated by the Financial Services Authority. Registered office: 63 St Mary's Axe London EC3A 8LT. Registered in England under company no. 2123174.

**Private Investment Management**